AUSTRALIAN Signpost MATHS

4

Alan McSeveny Rachel McSeveny Diane McSeveny-Foster

Pearson Australia
(a division of Pearson Australia Group Pty Ltd)
459–471 Church St, Level 1, Building B, Richmond, Victoria, 3121
PO Box 23360, Melbourne, Victoria 8012
www.pearson.com.au

First published 2024 by Pearson Australia
2028 2027 2026 2025
10 9 8 7 6 5 4 3 2 1

Publishers: Sophie Matta and Kerry Nagle
Project Manager: Michelle Thomas
Production Editor: Laura Rentsch
Development Editor: Rachel Elliott
Designer: Anne Donald
Proofreader: Laura Rentsch
Rights & Permissions Editor: Alice McBroom
Cover Design: Jennifer Johnston
Cover Art: Michael Barter
Illustrator: Michael Barter
Publishing Services: Jit-Pin Chong
Printed in Malaysia by Vivar

ISBN 978 0 6557 0878 0
Pearson Australia Group Pty Ltd ABN 40 004 245 943

Attributions
We would like to thank the following for permission to reproduce copyright material.

Shutterstock: AndyOman, p. 87 (USB); Tatiana Foxy, p. 152 (ruler); Nayoka, p. 24 (toy car); Phovoir, p. 95 (scales); Sandsun, p. 112 (pool); Shane White, p. 150 (coin).

123rf.com: Shootingtheworld, p. 53 (stamps).

Acknowledgement of Country
Pearson respects and honours Aboriginal and Torres Strait Islander Elders past, present and future. We acknowledge the stories, traditions and living cultures of the Traditional Custodians of the lands on which our company is located and where we conduct our business. Pearson is committed to honouring Australian Aboriginal and Torres Strait Islander peoples' unique cultural and spiritual relationships to the land, waters and seas and their rich contribution to society.

Aboriginal and Torres Strait Islander peoples are advised that this text may contain images, voices and names of deceased persons.

What is Australian Signpost Maths?

Australian Signpost Maths is a mathematics program providing direction and support for teaching and learning. The series covers the content and skills presented in the Australian Curriculum (v9) Mathematics F–6.

A Student Book and an online Teacher Resource are provided for Foundation.

For Years 1 to 6, a Student Book, an online Teacher Resource and a Mentals Book are provided for each year level. The online Teacher Resources provide a wealth of support for teachers.

The content has been carefully sequenced within each year level and across the F–6 series to take into account students' expected mathematical development. However, from the rich and varied material provided, teachers can develop individual learning programs to meet the needs of each student.

The Student Books are designed to support explicit teaching methods. Many group activities are provided in Activity, Investigation and Fun spots within the Student Books and the online Teacher Resource.

To maximise the benefits of the program, the Student Book, the online Teacher Resource and the Mentals Book should be used together.

Student Books

Mentals Books

Teacher Resource

Structure of Australian Signpost Maths

In the Year 3 to 6 books, the worksheet pages cover all three elements: Number sense and algebra, Measurement and geometry, and Statistics and probability. These are presented in five chapters:

- Number and algebra
- Operations and algebra
- Measurement
- Space
- Statistics and probability.

This gives teachers flexibility in programming. The contents cross-reference allows teachers to quickly find the pages where each concept has been covered.

Within the program, explicit teaching, critical and creative thinking, language development and identification and treatment of weaknesses are given high priority.

Identification and addressing areas of need

Five progress tests are designed to identify each student's areas of need, and the follow-up program after each of the tests is designed to address these needs. A reference to the relevant worksheet page is given for each test question. A remediation record page is used to track the student's progress.

These testing resources can be found in the online Teacher Resource.

Parallel progress retests are provided for further testing after remediation has taken place.

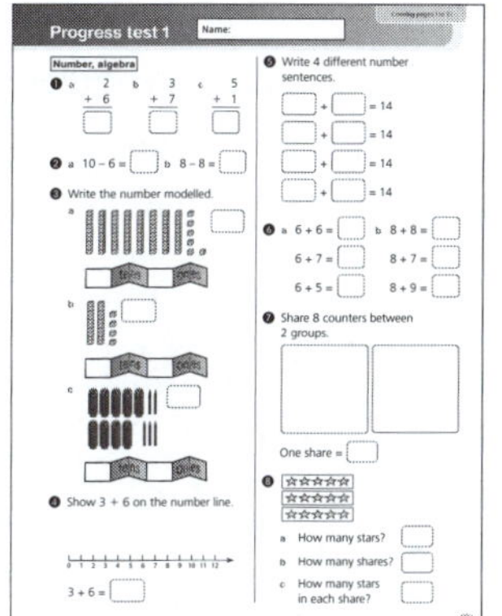

Progress test 1 Name:

Number, algebra

1. a 2 + 6 = ☐ b 3 + 7 = ☐ c 5 + 1 = ☐
2. a 10 − 6 = ☐ b 8 − 8 = ☐
3. Write the number modelled.
   a ☐ tens ☐ ones
   b ☐ tens ☐ ones
   c ☐ tens ☐ ones
4. Show 3 + 6 on the number line.
   0 1 2 3 4 5 6 7 8 9 10 11 12
   3 + 6 = ☐
5. Write 4 different number sentences.
   ☐ + ☐ = 14
   ☐ + ☐ = 14
   ☐ + ☐ = 14
   ☐ + ☐ = 14
6. a 6 + 6 = ☐ 6 + 7 = ☐ 6 + 5 = ☐
   b 8 + 8 = ☐ 8 + 7 = ☐ 8 + 9 = ☐
7. Share 8 counters between 2 groups.
   One share = ☐
8. a How many stars? ☐
   b How many shares? ☐
   c How many stars in each share? ☐

147

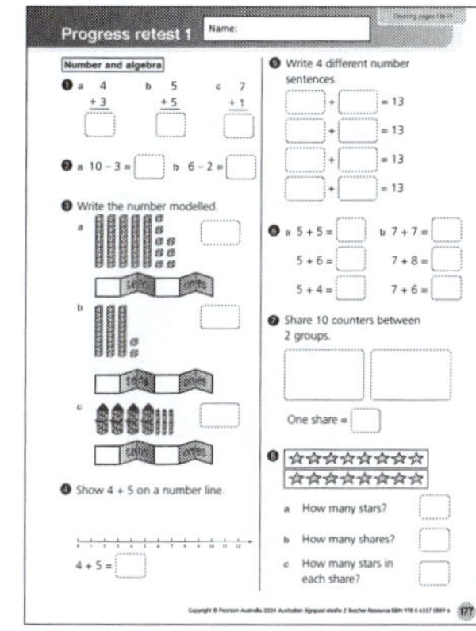

Progress retest 1 Name:

Number and algebra

1. a 4 + 3 = ☐ b 5 + 5 = ☐ c 7 + 1 = ☐
2. a 10 − 3 = ☐ b 6 − 2 = ☐
3. Write the number modelled.
   a ☐ tens ☐ ones
   b ☐ tens ☐ ones
   c ☐ tens ☐ ones
4. Show 4 + 5 on a number line.
   4 + 5 = ☐
5. Write 4 different number sentences.
   ☐ + ☐ = 13
   ☐ + ☐ = 13
   ☐ + ☐ = 13
   ☐ + ☐ = 13
6. a 5 + 5 = ☐ 5 + 6 = ☐ 5 + 4 = ☐
   b 7 + 7 = ☐ 7 + 8 = ☐ 7 + 6 = ☐
7. Share 10 counters between 2 groups.
   One share = ☐
8. a How many stars? ☐
   b How many shares? ☐
   c How many stars in each share? ☐

177

Special features of Australian Signpost Maths

- **The traffic light icons**
  These are found on the top right of each worksheet page in the Student Books. They allow students to assess their own progress and give feedback to the teacher.
  - ☐ **Green:** I found this work easy.
  - ☐ **Orange:** I found some work on the page difficult.
  - ☐ **Red:** I don't understand the work on this page.

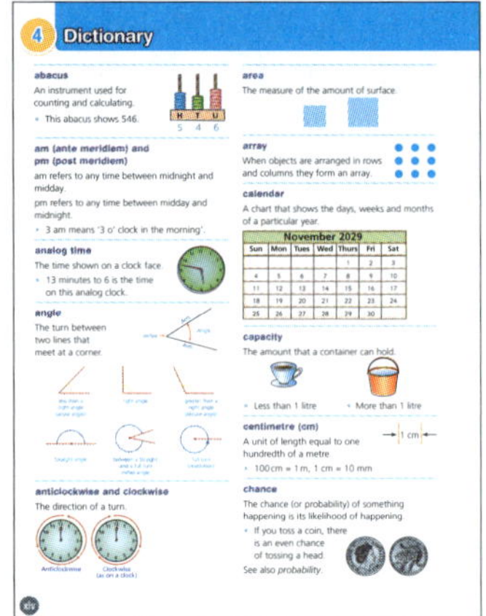

- **Dictionary**
  Terms used in the Student Book and terms that should be understood at this level are recorded here to provide a reference for students and teachers. This is found on pages xiv–xxii of this book.

- **ID cards (Years 1 to 6)**
  These cards review the language of Mathematics by asking students to identify common terms, shapes and symbols. They are designed to be reused and are found in the online Teacher Resource and in the front of the Mentals Books.

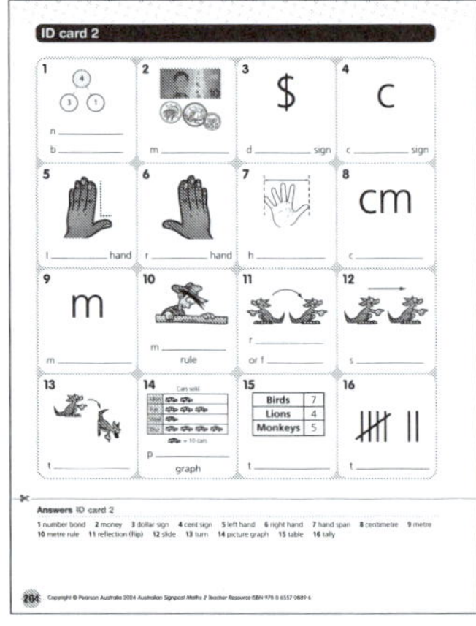

- **Progress tests**
  These allow the teacher to identify each student's strengths and needs. Cross-references for each question direct teachers and students to the pages where that work is introduced. Tables are provided to record any follow up and parallel tests are provided for retesting. These tests are in the online Teacher Resource.

- **Year 4 Consolidation booklet**
  This booklet is found in the online Teacher Resource. It is designed to reinforce work completed in class and provides practice of important skills and addition and subtraction facts. The booklet can be used when there is limited supervision or when a student finishes classwork early.

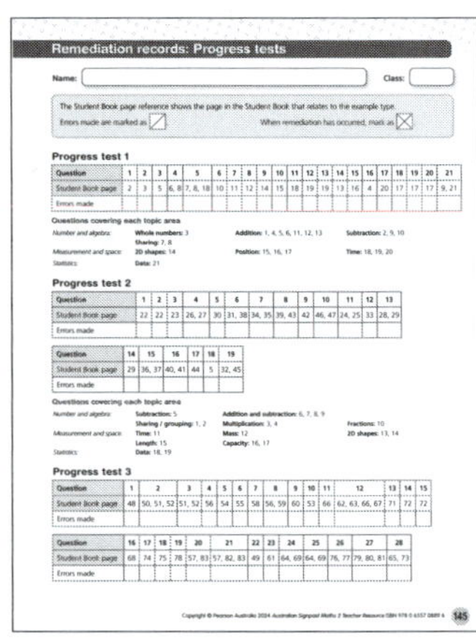

- **Answers**
  These are supplied in the Student Book and the online Teacher Resource.

- **Blackline masters (BLM)**
  References are made to the blackline masters in the online teacher notes provided for each Student Book work page. The BLMs are also accessed online.

- **Differentiation**
  Each Student Book work page has a Teacher Resource page to support it. Cross-references direct the teacher to pages where the concept is introduced and developed. These references may be from the Student Book for the previous year, the current year or the next year.

  The online Teacher Resource support pages provide additional learning activities for students who need remediation or extension activities. The Blackline Masters provide activities to support students of various learning abilities.

- **Cartoons**
  Cartoons are used to motivate and instruct.

- **Extra support pages**
  Addition and subtraction facts are reinforced in Extra support 1. In Years 3 and 4, the algorithm strategy pages extend the fast workers. In Years 5 and 6 there is support for decimals, fractions, multiplication and problem solving.

Australian Signpost Maths icons

Signpost icons are used throughout the book as cues to the essential nature of exercises and activities, and as a guide to ways of engaging with them. These icons often indicate alternative or more concrete approaches to dealing with concepts.

This icon highlights **important rules and concepts** occurring throughout the book. It often appears with worked examples.

Activities provide **applications and enrichment**. These activities usually involve the use of concrete materials and partner or group work.

These enjoyable activities are used to **motivate and involve** students in mathematical pursuits. They usually involve games and puzzles.

Investigations allow students to **explore and discover** maths concepts.

These activities involve the use of computers or other **information and communications** technology.

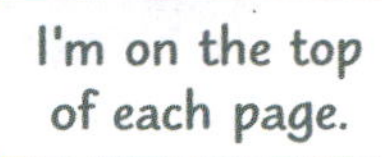

Structure of the Australian Curriculum, F–6 (v9)

Numeracy elements

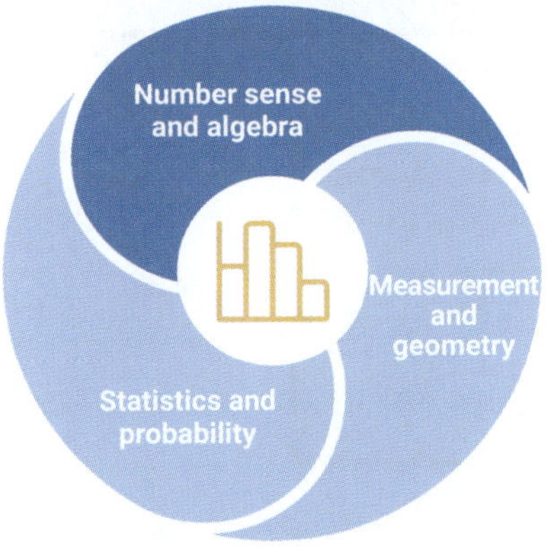

Curriculum content is organised under 6 interrelated strands: Number, Algebra, Measurement, Space, Statistics and Probability.

Sub-elements for Number sense and algebra

- Number and place value
- Counting processes
- Additive strategies
- Multiplicative strategies
- Interpreting fractions
- Number patterns and algebraic thinking
- Understanding money

Sub-elements for Measurement and geometry

- Understanding units of measurement
- Understanding geometric properties
- Positioning and locating
- Measuring time

Sub-elements for Statistics and probability

- Understanding chance
- Interpreting and representing data

The Curriculum strives to develop in students proficiency in Mathematics, highlighting Understanding, Fluency, Reasoning and Problem solving.

Mathematics content of the Australian Curriculum

- It is important that you download the **GENERAL CAPABILITIES** document from 'Downloads' in the top navigation bar of the website homepage. It contains the tables that list the progression level expectations for each Year, F to 10. It also provides the content of all progression levels.
- The LEARNING AREAS download gives a summary of Content descriptions and Elaborations. CROSS-CURRICULUM PRIORITIES can also be found there.

Contents and curriculum overview

Suggested program

This weekly program aligns with the Mentals Book, e.g. Mentals Book, Unit 9 covers work taught in Weeks 7 and 8 of this book.

Number and algebra

Page	Unit	Title	Content	Counting, number	Place value	Rounding	Fractions	Decimals	Patterns, algebra	Suggested program	Term
1	1:01	Numbers to 10 000		●	●					Week 3	Term 1
2	1:02	Numbers to 100 000		●	●						
3	1:03	Rounding off		●	●	●					
4	1:04	Fractions					●			Week 4	
5	1:05	Comparing fractions					●				
6	1:06	Improper fractions					●			Week 6	
7	1:07	Mixed numbers					●				
8	1:08	Large numbers		●	●					Week 8	
9	1:09	Hundreds of thousands		●	●						
10	1:10	Fraction patterns					●		●	Week 9	
11	1:11	Equivalent fractions					●				
12	1:12	Equivalent fractions					●		●		
13	1:13	Numbers using millions		●	●					Week 11	Term 2
14	1:14	Rounding off		●	●	●					
15	1:15	Hundredths					●			Week 12	
16	1:16	Decimals					●	●			
17	1:17	Tenths					●	●	●	Week 13	
18	1:18	Comparing decimals						●			
19	1:19	Place value in decimals								Week 14	
20	1:20	Place value of hundredths			●			●			
21	1:21	Reading and writing decimals			●		●				

The teacher will decide when testing occurs. The Progress Tests are found in the online Teacher Resource.

The first two units of the Mentals Book review the previous year and could be completed in Weeks 1 and 2.

Operations and algebra			Content								Suggested program This weekly program aligns with the Mentals Book, e.g. Mentals Book, Unit 9 covers work taught in Weeks 7 and 8 of this book.	
Page	Unit	Title		Addition	Subtraction	Multiplication	Division	Mental strategies	Number patterns	Money	Problem solving		
22	2:01	Number patterns							●			Week 3	Term 1
23	2:02	Multiplication tables revision				●							
24	2:03	×4 tables				●						Week 5	
25	2:04	Times tables review				●							
26	2:05	Addition, no trading		●						●		Week 7	
27	2:06	Addition and subtraction, no trading		●						●			
28	2:07	Addition to 99 with trading		●						●	●	Week 8	
29	2:08	Addition to 99 with trading		●						●	●		
30	2:09	Jump strategy, +		●				●				Week 11	Term 2
31	2:10	Jump strategy, –			●			●					
32	2:11	×8 tables				●						Week 12	
33	2:12	×8 tables				●							
34	2:13	Addition, trading 2 tens		●								Week 15	
35	2:14	Addition involving hundreds		●							●		
36	2:15	Addition problems to 99		●							●		
37	2:16	×3, ×6 tables				●		●				Week 16	
38	2:17	×3 and ×6 tables				●							
39	2:18	Subtraction with trading			●						●	Week 17	
40	2:19	Subtracting from tens			●					●	●		
41	2:20	Subtracting with trading			●					●			
42	2:21	×9 tables				●		●				Week 18	
43	2:22	×9 tables				●							
44	2:23	Addition to 999		●								Week 19	
45	2:24	Addition to 999		●									
46	2:25	Writing algorithms		●							●		
47	2:26	What's the rule?							●			Week 21	Term 3
48	2:27	Number patterns							●				
49	2:28	×7 tables				●						Week 22	
50	2:29	×7 tables				●							
51	2:30	Multiplication tables review				●							
52	2:31	Subtraction without trading to 999			●							Week 23	
53	2:32	Subtraction with trading to 999			●								
54	2:33	Subtraction with trading to 999			●							Week 24	
55	2:34	Subtraction with 2 trades to 999			●								
56	2:35	Mental strategies, + and –		●	●			●				Week 25	
57	2:36	Mental strategies, + and –		●				●					
58	2:37	Subtraction from hundreds			●						●	Week 26	
59	2:38	Subtraction from hundreds strategy		●	●					●			
60	2:39	Division as repeated subtraction					●				●	Week 27	
61	2:40	Understanding division					●						
62	2:41	Division facts				●	●				●	Week 28	
63	2:42	Division facts					●						
64	2:43	Odd and even numbers		●	●							Week 29	
65	2:44	Odd and even		●	●	●	●						
66	2:45	Division using a grid					●					Week 30	
67	2:46	× and ÷ tables (by 2, 4, 8)					●	●	●				

* The teacher will decide when testing occurs. The Progress Tests and Re-tests are found in the online Teacher Resource.

Operations and algebra

Page	Unit	Title	Content	Addition	Subtraction	Multiplication	Division	Mental strategies	Number patterns	Money	Problem solving	Suggested program: This weekly program aligns with the Mentals Book, e.g. Mentals Book, Unit 9 covers work taught in Weeks 7 and 8 of this book. Term 4
68	2:47	Mental strategies, × and ÷				●	●	●				Week 31
69	2:48	Working with numbers				●	●					
70	2:49	x and ÷ tables (by 3, 6, 9)				●	●					Week 32
71	2:50	Division facts				●	●	●				
72	2:51	Money		●						●		Week 33
73	2:52	Rounding off money		●						●		
74	2:53	Counting change		●						●		
75	2:54	Multiplying by 10, 100, 1000				●		●				Week 34
76	2:55	Dividing by 10, 100, 1000					●	●				
77	2:56	Linking ÷ and ×				●	●	●				Week 35
78	2:57	Missing number strategies		●	●	●	●	●				
79	2:58	Partitioning, + and –		●	●			●				Week 36
80	2:59	Mental strategies, + and –		●	●			●				

Page	Unit	Title	Content	Length	Area	Capacity	Mass / Temperature	Telling the time	Duration	Problem solving	Suggested program	
Measurement											This weekly program aligns with the Mentals Book, e.g. Mentals Book, Unit 9 covers work taught in Weeks 7 and 8 of this book.	
81	3:01	Analog time						●			Week 4	Term 1
82	3:02	Analog and digital time						●				
83	3:03	Analog and digital time						●		●		
84	3:04	Using a ruler		●							Week 5	
85	3:05	Centimetres and millimetres		●								
86	3:06	Using millimetres		●								
87	3:07	Square centimetres			●						Week 6	
88	3:08	The square centimetre			●							
89	3:09	The square centimetre			●							
90	3:10	Temperature					●				Week 10	
91	3:11	Recording temperature					●					
92	3:12	Using millilitres				●					Week 16	Term 2
93	3:13	Using millilitres				●						
94	3:14	Using L and mL				●						
95	3:15	Measuring mass					●				Week 22	Term 3
96	3:16	Using grams					●					
97	3:17	Telling time						●			Week 23	
98	3:18	Time						●	●	●		
99	3:19	am and pm time						●	●			
100	3:20	Recording length		●							Week 24	
101	3:21	Comparing measurements		●								
102	3:22	Using measurement scales		●			●					
103	3:23	Recording length		●							Week 25	
104	3:24	The square metre			●							
105	3:25	The square metre			●							
106	3:26	Timelines							●	●	Week 28	
107	3:27	Timetables							●	●		
108	3:28	The calendar							●		Week 29	
109	3:29	The calendar							●			
110	3:30	The passage of time						●	●	●		
111	3:31	Measuring mass					●			●	Week 31	Term 4
112	3:32	Personal benchmarks		●	●	●	●					
113	3:33	Finding area			●							
114	3:34	Using mm when building		●							Week 35	
115	3:35	Length on a map		●								
116	3:36	Problem solving		●		●	●		●	●	Week 36	
117	3:37	Problem solving		●	●	●	●		●	●	Week 37	

- 'Money' can be found in Chapter 2.
- 'Angles' can be found in Chapter 4.
- The teacher will decide when testing occurs. The Progress Tests are found in the online Teacher Resource.

Space

Page	Unit	Title	Content	2D space	Angles, lines	Symmetry, turning	3D objects	Position, directions	Suggested program This weekly program aligns with the Mentals Book. Mentals Book, Unit 9 covers work taught in the Weeks 7 and 8 of this book.	
118	4:01	Flip, slide and turn				●			Week 7	Term 1
119	4:02	Angles and 2D shapes		●	●					
120	4:03	Comparing angles			●					
121	4:04	3D objects					●		Week 13	Term 2
122	4:05	Prisms and pyramids					●			
123	4:06	Faces of prisms and pyramids		●			●		Week 14	
124	4:07	Prisms and pyramids					●			
125	4:08	Drawing angles			●				Week 17	
126	4:09	Angles as quarter and half turns			●					
127	4:10	Investigating polygons		●					Week 18	
128	4:11	Visualising shapes		●						
129	4:12	Maps						●	Week 19	
130	4:13	Creating a map						●		
131	4:14	Cones, cylinders and spheres					●		Week 21	Term 3
132	4:15	Views of 3D objects					●			
133	4:16	Compass directions						●	Week 26	
134	4:17	Compass directions						●		
135	4:18	Describing position		●	●		●	●	Week 27	
136	4:19	Using position in maps						●		
137	4:20	Visualising shapes		●					Week 32	Term 4
138	4:21	Acute and obtuse angles			●					
139	4:22	Angles of any size			●					
140	4:23	Horizontal and vertical					●		Week 34	
141	4:24	Tessellations		●		●				
142	4:25	Rotational symmetry				●				
143	4:26	Spreadsheets						●	Week 36	

The teacher will decide when testing occurs. The Progress Tests are found in the online Teacher Resource.

Statistics and probability

Suggested program

This weekly program aligns with the Mentals Book, e.g. Mentals Book, Unit 9 covers work taught in Weeks 7 and 8 of this book.

Page	Unit	Title	Collecting data	Surveys	Creating data displays	Analysing data displays	Chance language	Chance experiments	Suggested program	Term
144	5:01	Drawing tables	●						Week 8	Term 1
145	5:02	Chance					●	●	Week 9	
146	5:03	Chance					●			
147	5:04	Using graphs			●	●			Week 15	Term 2
148	5:05	Reading graphs				●				
149	5:06	Ordering events					●		Week 20	
150	5:07	Chance used in games					●			
151	5:08	Tally marks	●			●			Week 26	Term 3
152	5:09	Collecting information	●	●					Week 27	
153	5:10	Constructing spinners					●	●	Week 33	Term 4
154	5:11	Unequal outcomes					●	●		
155	5:12	Surveys		●					Week 35	
156	5:13	Graphing data			●	●			Week 36	
157	5:14	Chance experiments				●		●	Week 37	
158	5:15	Carry out your own survey		●						
159	5:16	Chance experiments					●			

Extra Support pages

160	1 Addition and subtraction facts	2 Building to the next 10	3 Tangrams
163	4 Flip, slide, turn	5 Addition of money	6 Addition to 9999
166	7 Addition to 9999	8 Addition to 999 999	9 Subtraction of money
169	10 Subtraction with trading to 9999	11 Four-digit subtraction from 1000s	12 Subtraction to 999 999
172	13 Comparing decimal measurements		

Suggested Program	Term 1	Term 2	Term 3	Term 4
Number and algebra	1:01 - 1:12	1:13 - 1:21		
Operations and algebra	2:01 - 2:08	2:09 - 2:25	2:26 - 2:46	2:47 - 2:59
Measurement	3:01 - 3:11	3:12 - 3:14	3:15 - 3:30	3:31 - 3:37
Space	4:01 - 4:03	4:04 - 4:13	4:14 - 4:19	4:20 - 4:26
Statistics and probability	5:01 - 5:03	5:04 - 5:07	5:08 - 5:09	5:10 - 5:16
Total number of pages:	37	43	45	34

- See the Teacher Resource for a more detailed suggested program.
- The suggested program aligns with the Mentals book, Progress Tests and Retests.

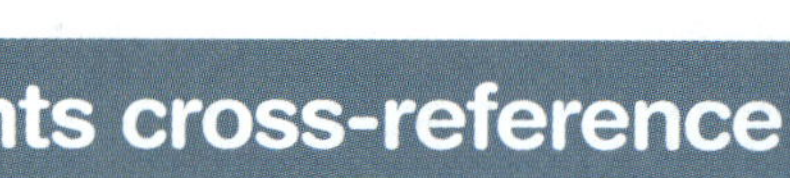

Contents cross-reference

Number and algebra

Measurement and space

1 Measurement	Pages
Length	84, 85, 86, 100, 101, 102, 103, 112, 114, 115
Area	87, 88, 89, 104, 105, 112, 113
Capacity and volume	48, 92, 93, 94, 112
Mass (weight)	95, 96, 102, 111, 112
Temperature	90, 91, 112
Time (duration)	98, 99, 106, 107, 108, 109, 110, 172
Clocks	81, 82, 83, 97, 98, 99, 110
Problem solving with measurement	83, 98, 99, 109, 110, 116, 117
Estimation of measurements	85, 86, 87, 93, 95, 100, 103, 104, 105

2 Space	Pages
2D shapes	xxii, 119, 123, 127, 128, 135, 137, 162
Angles, parallel and perpendicular lines	119, 120, 125, 126, 138, 139, 140
Symmetry, flip, slide, turn, tessellations	118, 126, 127, 141, 142, 162, 163
3D objects	xxii, 121, 122, 123, 124, 131, 132, 134
Position, maps	129, 130, 133, 134, 135, 136, 143

Statistics and probability

1 Data	Pages
Collecting data and recording data	144, 147, 151, 152, 153, 154, 155, 158, 159
Analysing data displays	147, 148, 150, 151, 152, 153, 154, 156
Chance and the language of chance	145, 146, 149, 150, 154, 157, 159
Chance experiments	145, 150, 153, 154, 157, 159

4 Dictionary

abacus

An instrument used for counting and calculating.

- This abacus shows 546.

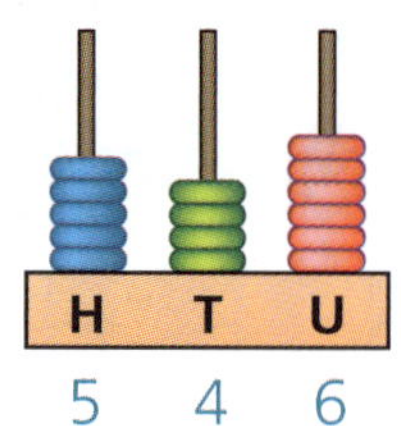

am (ante meridiem) and pm (post meridiem)

am refers to any time between midnight and midday.

pm refers to any time between midday and midnight.

- 3 am means '3 o' clock in the morning'.

analog time

The time shown on a clock face.

- 13 minutes to 6 is the time on this analog clock.

angle

The turn between two lines that meet at a corner.

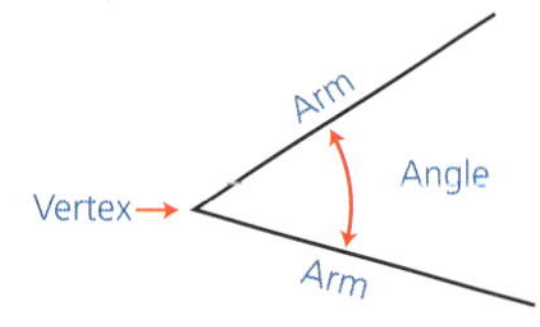

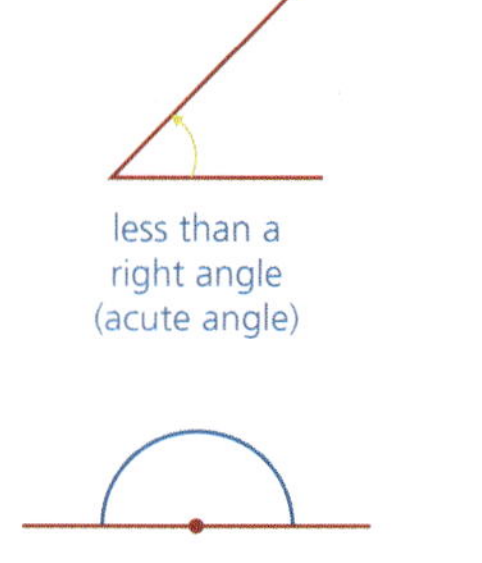

less than a right angle (acute angle)

right angle

greater than a right angle (obtuse angle)

Straight angle

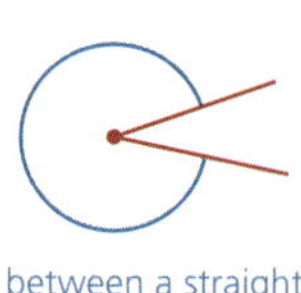

between a straight and a full turn (reflex angle)

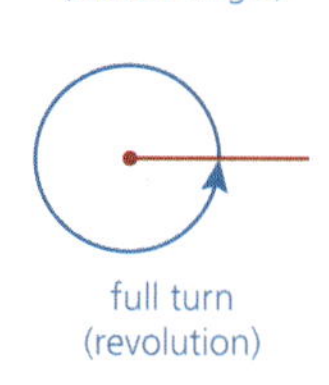

full turn (revolution)

anticlockwise and clockwise

The direction of a turn.

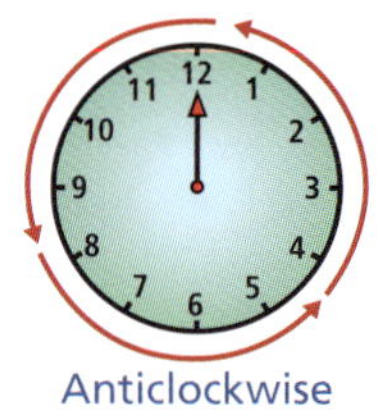

Anticlockwise

Clockwise (as on a clock)

area

The measure of the amount of surface.

array

When objects are arranged in rows and columns they form an array.

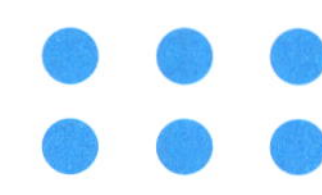

calendar

A chart that shows the days, weeks and months of a particular year.

November 2029						
Sun	**Mon**	**Tues**	**Wed**	**Thurs**	**Fri**	**Sat**
				1	2	3
4	5	6	7	8	9	10
11	12	13	14	15	16	17
18	19	20	21	22	23	24
25	26	27	28	29	30	

capacity

The amount that a container can hold.

- Less than 1 litre

- More than 1 litre

centimetre (cm)

A unit of length equal to one hundredth of a metre.

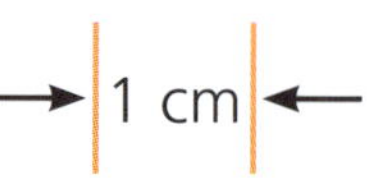

- 100 cm = 1 m, 1 cm = 10 mm

chance

The chance (or probability) of something happening is its likelihood of happening.

- If you toss a coin, there is an even chance of tossing a head.

See also *probability*.

compass directions

A compass needle always points north.

- The points of a compass are north, east, west and south.

cone
cube
cylinder

See *3D shapes*.

cross-section

The shape formed when an object is cut.

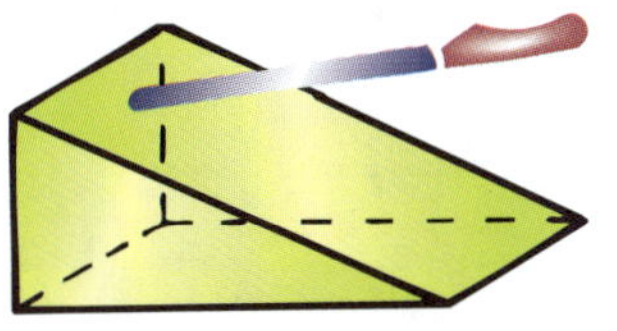

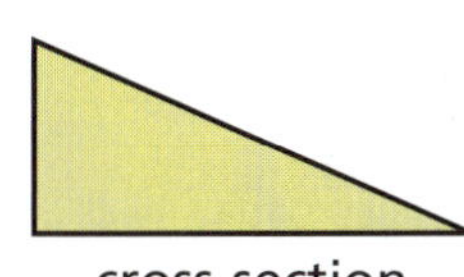

cross-section

curved surface

A curved surface on a 3D object is not flat. It allows an object to roll. A cylinder and cone each have one curved surface.

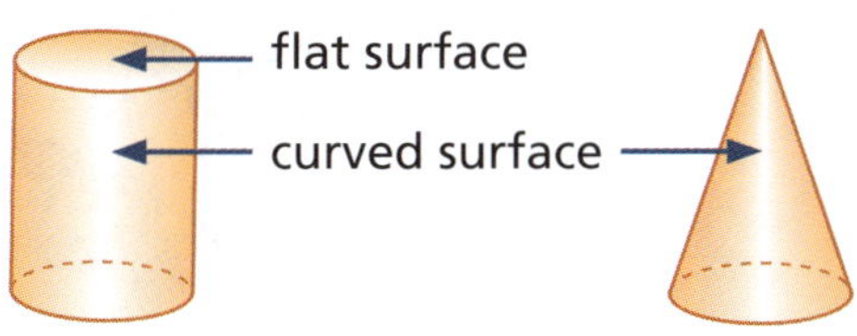

date

The date shows the day, the month and the year. For example, 30.5.23 means the 30th day on the 5th month (May) in the year 2023.

decimal notation

The decimal point separates the whole number from the fraction.

7·5

↑

decimal point

0·7 means 7 tenths.

6·5 means 6 ones and 5 tenths.

diagonal

A line that joins any two non-adjacent corners of a polygon.

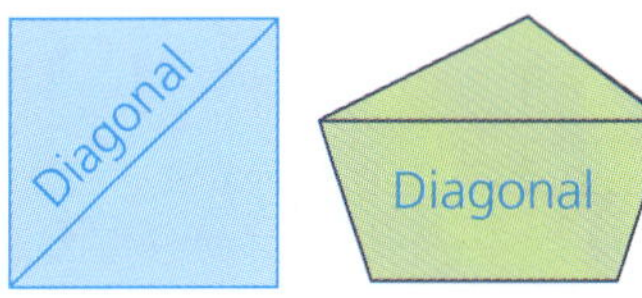

difference

How many more?

The difference between 16 and 13 is 3.

- For smaller numbers, line up each group in a row to find the difference.
- For larger numbers, place the numbers on a number line to find the difference.

digital time

Time expressed using digits.

- This digital clock shows 24 minutes past 10.

digits

Symbols used to write a number.

- 6 Six is a 1-digit number.
- 47 Forty-seven is a 2-digit number.

division (÷)

Breaking up groups into equal parts.

- 6 ÷ 3

a Sharing 2 each

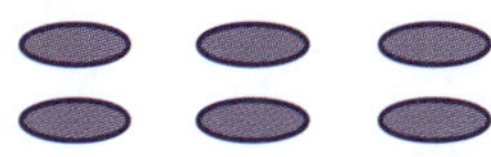

b Grouping 2 groups

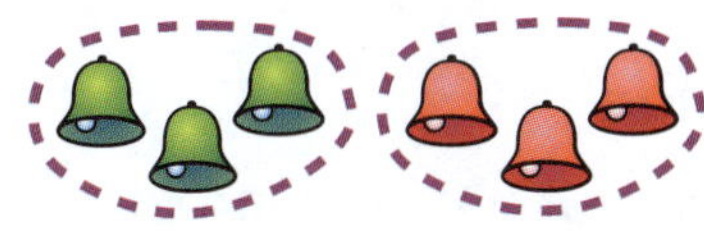

edge

Two faces of a 3D object meet at an edge.

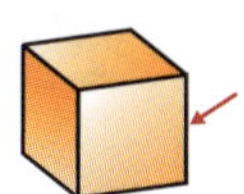

equivalent fractions

These are equal. They refer to the same part of the whole.

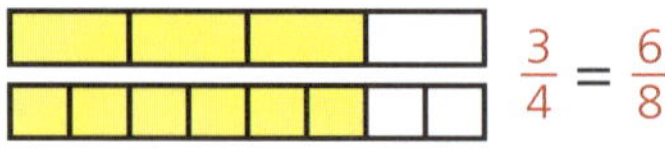

$\frac{3}{4} = \frac{6}{8}$

even number

Any number that is a multiple of two and can be grouped in twos. They end in 0, 2, 4, 6 or 8.

- 16, 300, 4394

The other counting numbers are **odd**.

expanded notation

A way of writing numerals to show the place value of each digit.

- $137 = (1 \times 100) + (3 \times 10) + 7$
  $= 100 + 30 + 7$

face

A flat surface of a three-dimensional object that is bounded by only straight lines.

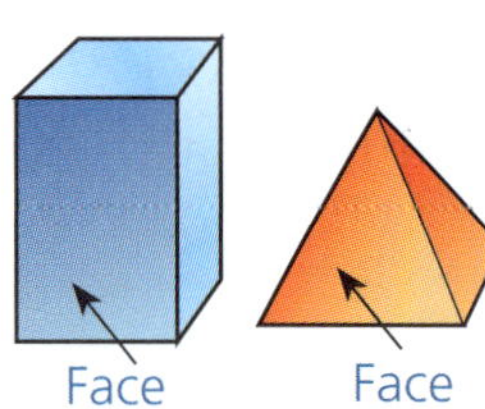

flat surface

A cylinder has 2 flat surfaces, one on both ends, and one curved surface.

A cube has 6 flat surfaces.

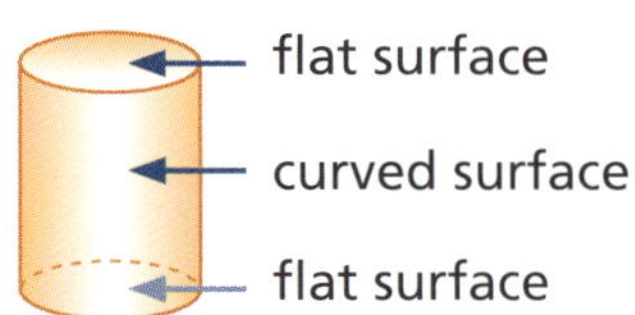

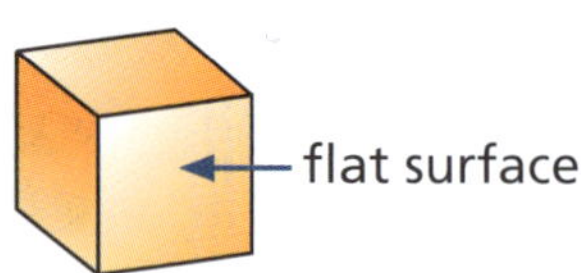

fraction

Any part of a whole, group or object.

- 2 out of 6 shaded
- $\frac{1}{4}$ is shaded

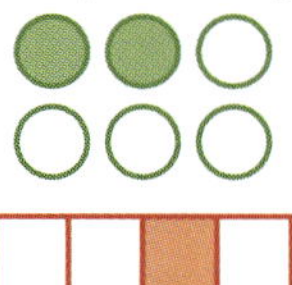

gram (g)

A unit of mass used to measure how heavy something is.

- 1 kilogram = 1 000 grams

graph

A diagram or drawing used to record a collection of data.

- Column graph

  Groups are compared using the lengths of columns or bars. The graph can be vertical or horizontal.

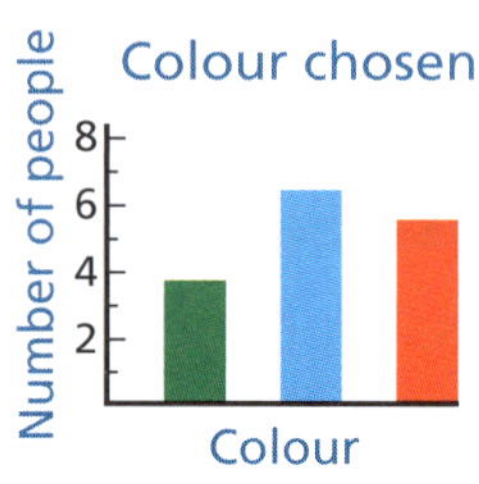

- Picture graph

  A picture is used as a unit to show how many.

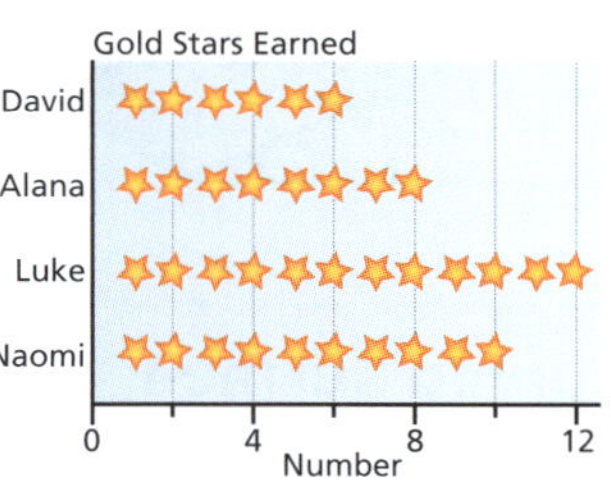

heft

To compare masses by lifting them with your hands.

hexagon

See *2D shapes*.

horizontal

- parallel to the horizon
- going straight across
- makes a right angle with the vertical

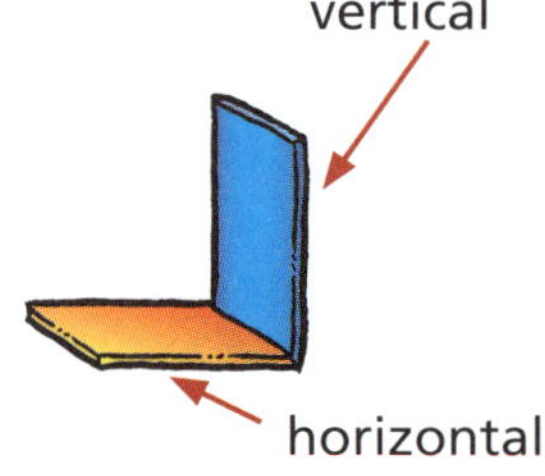

improper fraction

A fraction where the numerator is larger than the denominator.

-   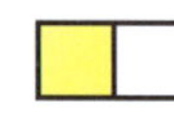 $\frac{5}{2}$

inverse operations

Adding 8 is the opposite (the inverse) of subtracting 8.

- 100 + 8 − 8 = 100

Multiplying by 2 is the opposite (the inverse) of dividing by 2.

- 4 × 2 ÷ 2 = 4

jump strategy

Adding or subtracting numbers, jumping by hundreds, tens and ones.

- 52 − 14 = 38

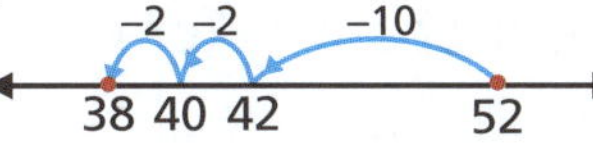

kilogram (kg)

The basic unit of mass, equal to 1000 grams.

- 1 kg = 1 000 g

left and **right**

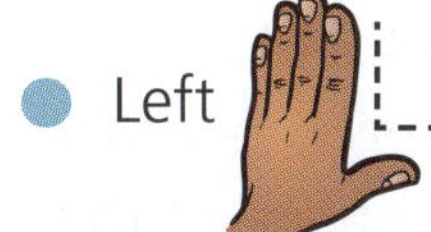

- Left

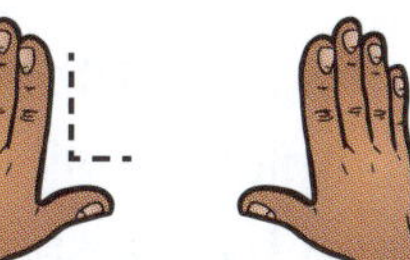

- Right

line of symmetry

A line that divides something in half so that each half is a mirror image of the other part.

Line of symmetry

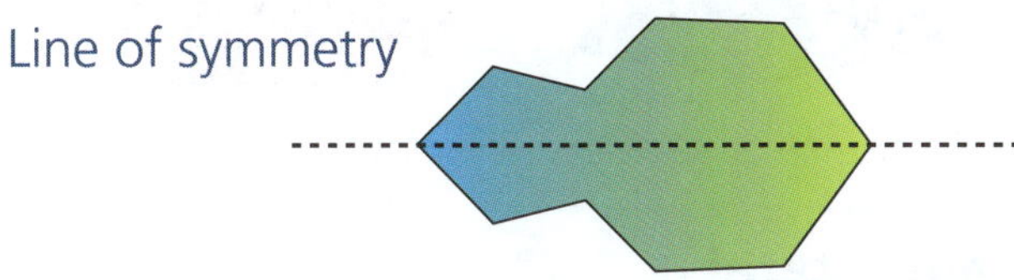

litre (L)

A unit of capacity (or volume) used for the measurement of liquids.

- 1 L = 1 000 mL

map or **plan**

A picture of an area viewed from above.

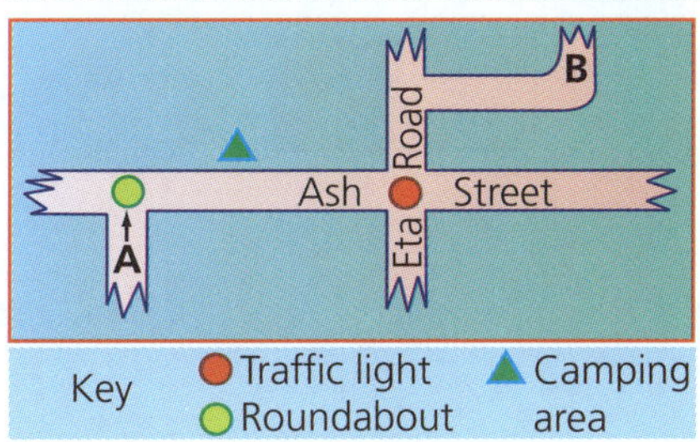

mass

The amount of matter in an object, a measure of how heavy it is.

metre (m)

The basic unit of length, equal to 100 centimetres.

- 1 m = 100 cm

millilitre (mL)

A unit of capacity (or volume) equal to one thousandth of a litre.

- 1 000 mL = 1 L

millimetre (mm)

A unit of length equal to one tenth of a centimetre, or one thousandth of a metre.

- 10 mm = 1 cm
- 1 000 mm = 1 m

1 mm

mixed numbers

Mixed numbers have a whole number part and a fraction part.

- 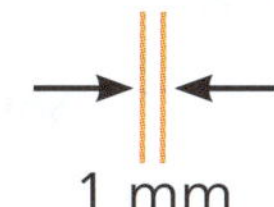 $2\frac{1}{2}$

net

A flat shape that can be folded to make a three-dimensional object.

Net of a cube

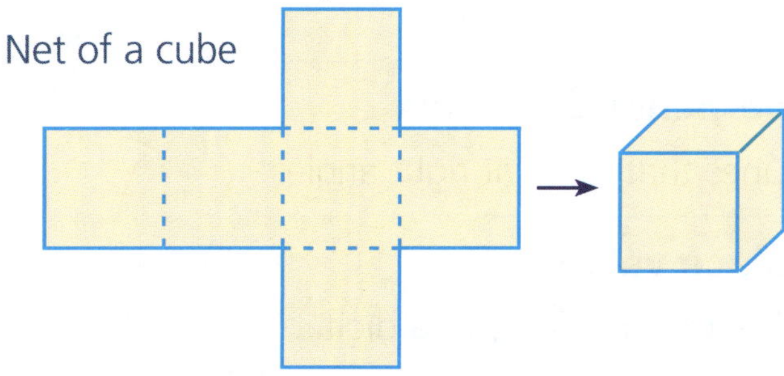

number bonds

These show how a number can be broken up into parts (e.g. the top number, 4, can be broken up into 3 and 1).

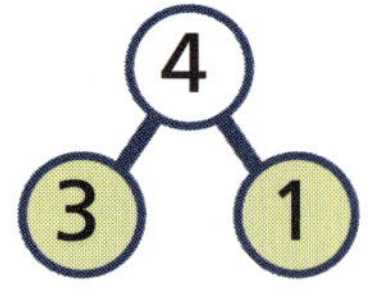

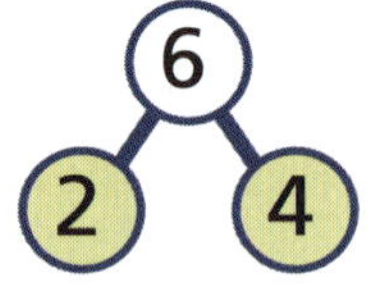

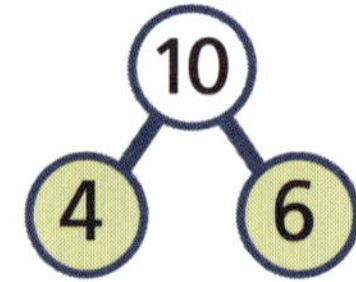

odd and even numbers

Odd numbers end in 1, 3, 5, 7 or 9.

They cannot be arranged in pairs.

- 13, 481, 23 527, 5035

Even numbers end in 0, 2, 4, 6 or 8.

They can be arranged in pairs.

- 8, 252, 9746, 7770

parallel lines

Straight lines on the same flat surface that do not meet.

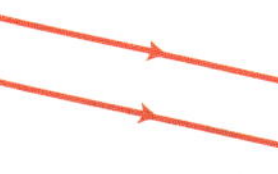

perimeter

The distance around the outside of a shape; the boundary.

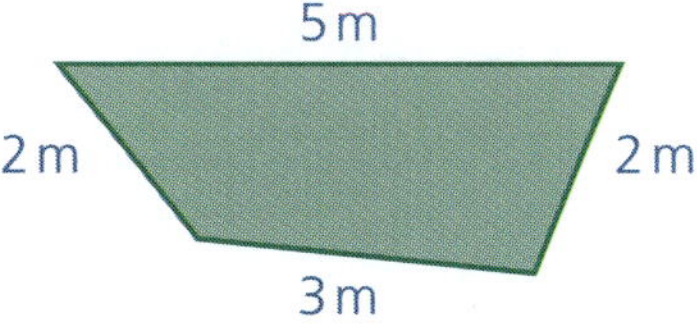

- Perimeter = 2 m + 3 m + 2 m + 5 m
  = 12 m

perpendicular lines

Lines that meet at right angles.

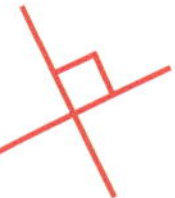

place value

The column value of a digit.

polygon

A polygon is a 2D shape that has only straight sides.

- Examples are: triangle, rectangle, pentagon, hexagon, ...

prism

A three-dimensional object with a uniform cross-section. The ends are identical shapes and all other faces are rectangles. Prisms are named by the shape of their ends.

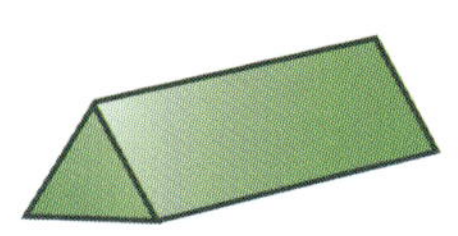

Triangular prism

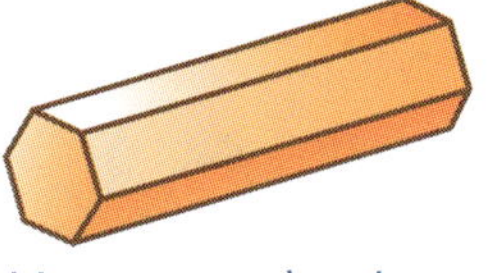

Hexagonal prism

probability

The probability (or chance) of something happening is its likelihood of happening.

- **Chance language**
  possible, impossible, certain, more likely, less likely, least likely, outcome, event

pyramid

A three-dimensional object that has a polygon for a base and triangles for all other faces. Pyramids are named by the shape of their base.

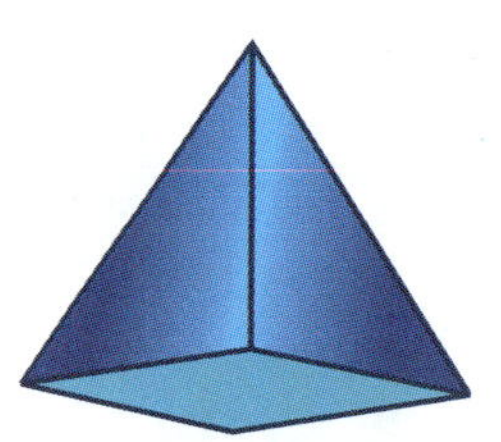

Square pyramid

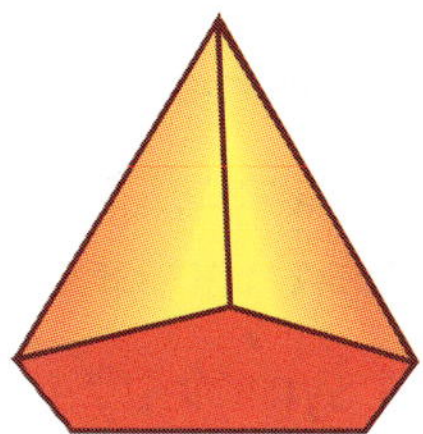

Pentagonal pyramid

quadrilateral

A two-dimensional shape with four straight sides.

quarter of a whole or collection

One of four equal parts.

One quarter of the rectangle is coloured.

One quarter of the collection is coloured.

A quarter of 8 is 2. Another way to say this is 8 divided by 4 is 2. That is $8 \div 4 = 2$.

Three quarters of the rectangle is coloured.

Three quarters of the collection is coloured.

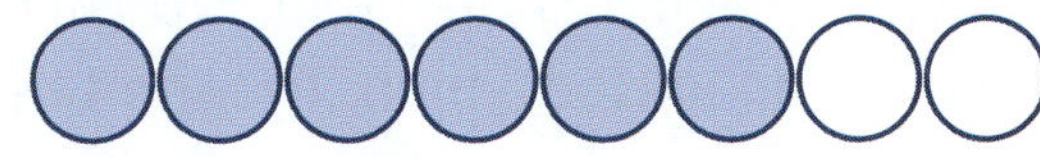

random selection

Choosing without looking.

Each item has an equal chance of being chosen.

rectangle and **rhombus**

See *2D shapes*.

regular and **irregular shapes**

Regular shapes have all sides and all angles equal. Irregular shapes do not.

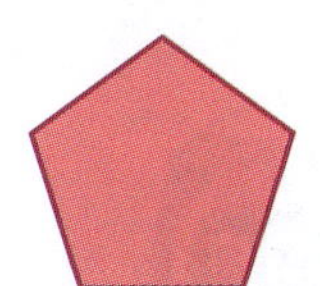

Regular shape

Irregular shape

right and **left**

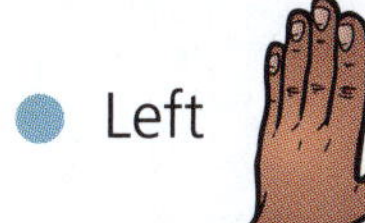

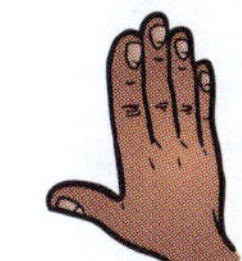

rounding

Writing a number to the nearest 5, 10, 100, 1000.

- 3786 rounded to the nearest 100 is 3800.

skip counting

Counting on, adding the same number each time.

- 5, 10, 15, 20, 25, … is skip counting by 5.

sphere

See *3D objects*.

split strategy

Adding numbers by splitting them into their parts.

- $36 + 52 = 30 + 6 + 50 + 2$
  $= (30 + 50) + (6 + 2)$
  $= 80 + 8$
  $= 88$

spreadsheet

See page 143.

square

See *2D shapes*.

square centimetre (cm²)

A unit for measuring area that is equal to a square with sides of 1 cm.

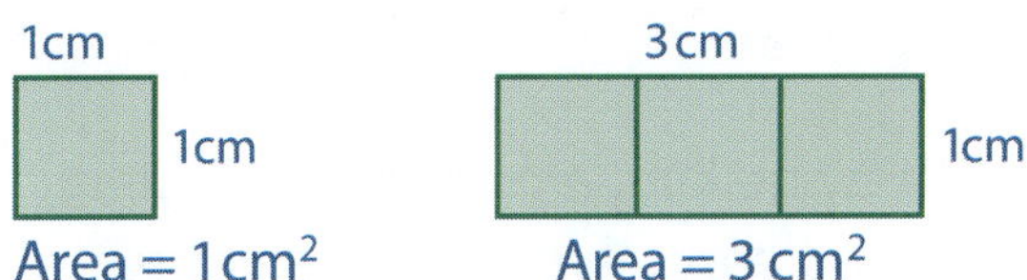

A square metre is written as m^2.

square metre (m²)

A unit for measuring area that is equal to a square with sides of 1 m.

surface

The outside layer of a three-dimensional object. A surface can be flat or curved.

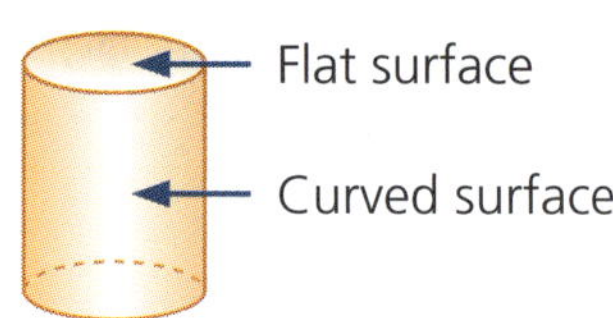

See also *face*.

survey

A list of questions used to discover information.

symmetry

If a figure has a line of symmetry, it can be folded so that the two halves exactly overlap.

Each half is a mirror image of the other.

Line of symmetry

A figure has **rotational symmetry**, if, when spun about its centre it matches itself before one whole turn.

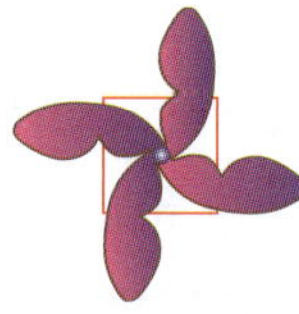

tally

To keep count by making a mark for each item. To make counting easy, the marks are drawn in groups of five, with each fifth mark crossed over the other four marks.

-  = 18

temperature

Temperature is the measure of how hot or cold something is.

- If a day is very hot, it could have a temperature of 40 degrees Celsius (40°C).

time words

Days			
Sunday	Monday	Tuesday	Wednesday
Thursday	Friday	Saturday	

Months			
January	February	March	April
May	June	July	August
September	October	November	December

Seasons			
Summer	Autumn	Winter	Spring

- clocks
- o'clock

When the long hand (minute hand) is pointing to 12, the time is an 'o'clock' time. The short hand (hour hand) points to the hour (e.g. the hour hand above is pointing to the 3 so it is 3 o'clock).

3 o'clock

- half past

When the long hand is pointing to the 6, the time is a 'half past'. The short hand on this clock points halfway between the 3 and the 4 so it is half past 3.

half past 3

- quarter past

When the long hand is pointing to the 3, then the time is 'quarter past'. The short hand on this clock is a quarter of the way from 6 to 7, so it is a quarter past 6.

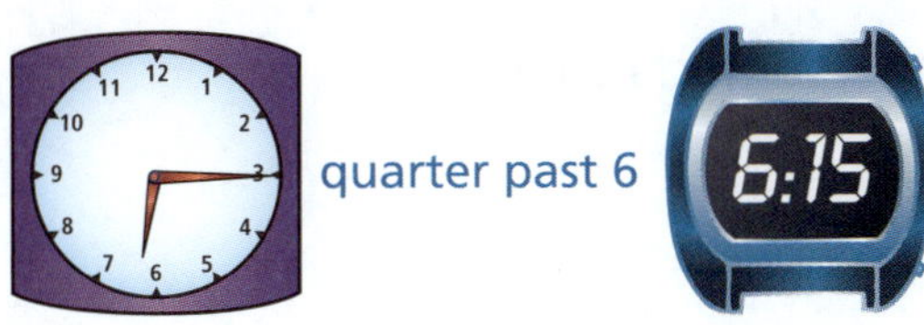

- quarter to

When the long hand is pointing to the 9, then the time is 'quarter to' the next hour. The short hand on this clock is a quarter of the way from the next number 7, so it is a quarter to 7.

- The number of days in each month:

How to know the number of days in each month.

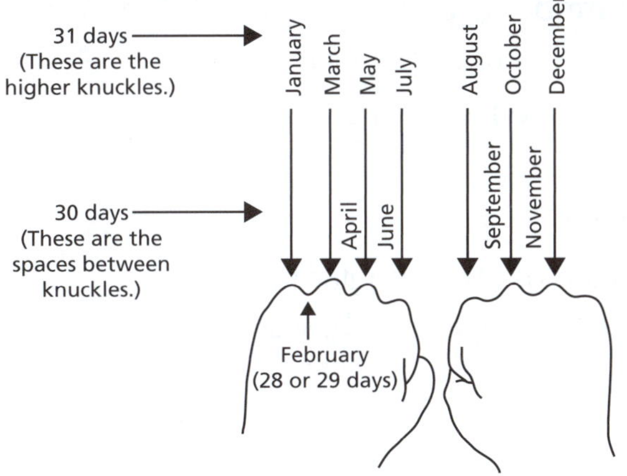

30 days has September, April, June and November. All the rest have 31, except February alone, which has 28 days clear and 29 days each leap year.

timeline

Shows a sequence of events in time.

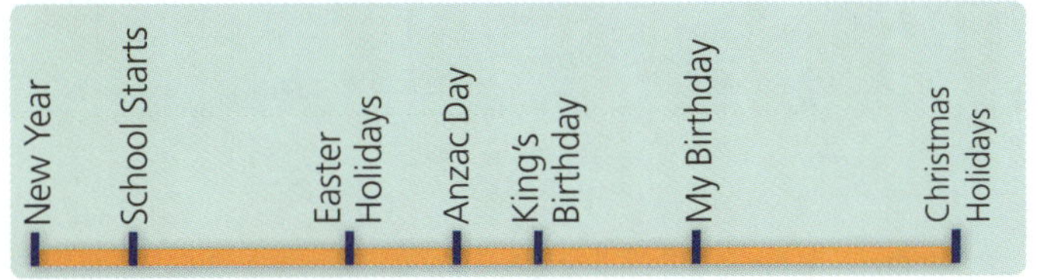

turn

Moving a shape in a clockwise or anticlockwise direction.

- quarter turn
- half turn
- three-quarter turn
- full turn

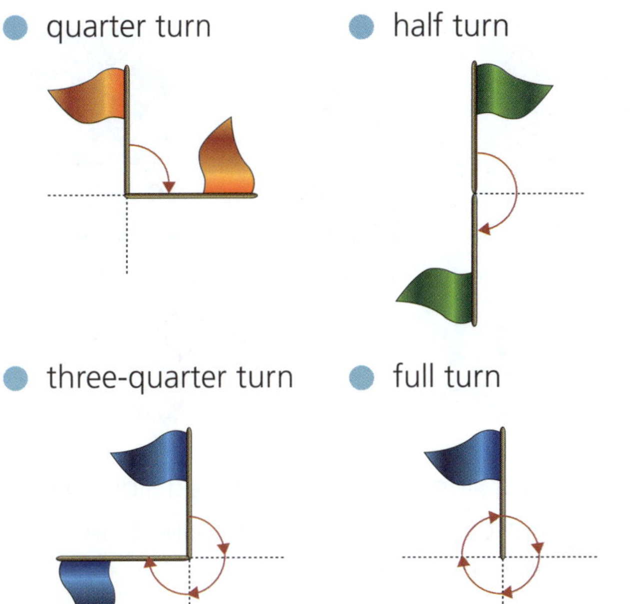

vertex

A point at which two or more lines meet to form a corner on a plane shape or object.

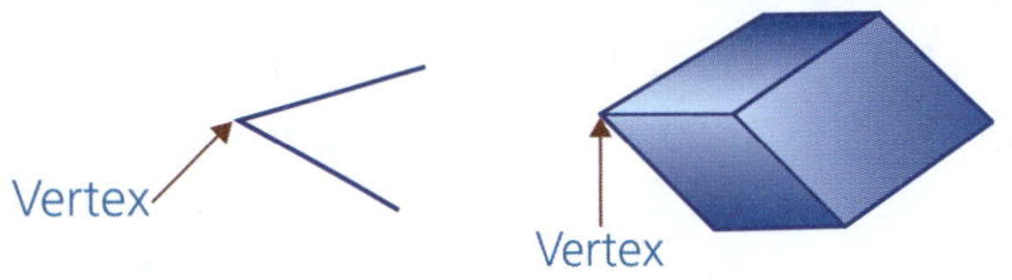

The plural of *vertex* is *vertices*.

vertical

- at right angles to the horizontal.
- straight up and down
- the direction in which an object falls under gravity.

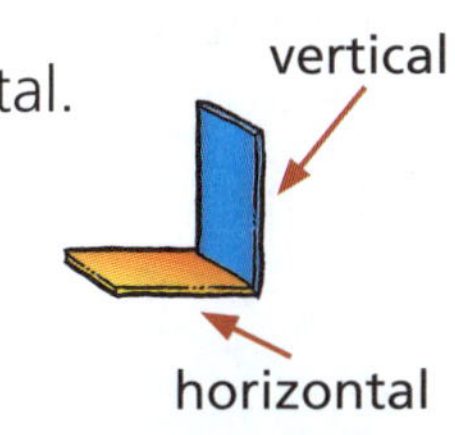

volume

The amount of space an object takes up.

year

There are 365 days in a year and 366 days in a leap year (which is every 4th year). There are 12 months in a year.

2D (two-dimensional) shapes

Flat shapes are two-dimensional.
They have length and width.

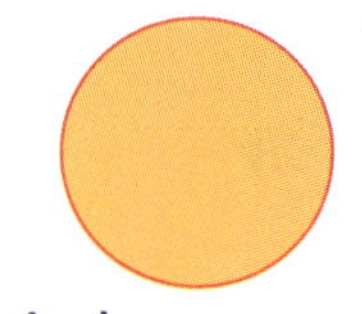

circle
1 curved side

triangle
3 sides
3 corners

square
4 equal sides
4 corners

rectangle
2 equal long sides
2 equal short sides,
like a stretched square

oval
1 curved side, like
a squashed circle

pentagon
5 sides
5 corners

hexagon
6 sides
6 corners

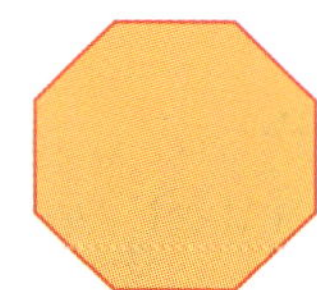

octagon
8 sides
8 corners

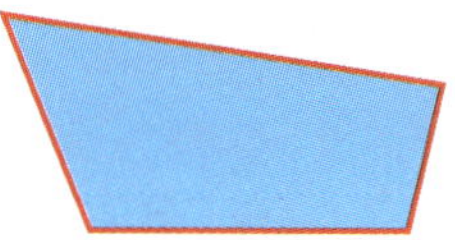

quadrilaterals
4 sides
4 corners

parallelogram
two sets of parallel lines
opposite sides equal

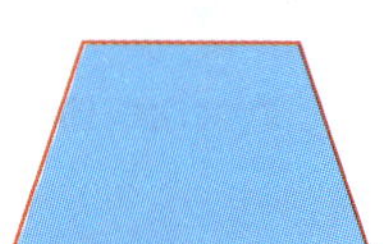

trapezium
one set of
parallel lines

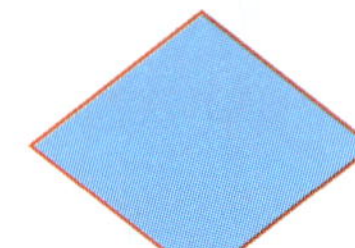

rhombus
all sides equal
(a diamond)

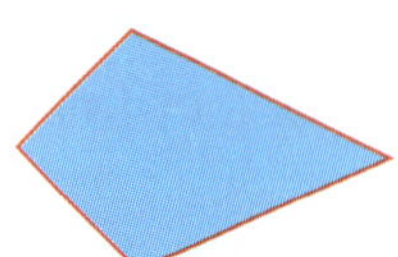

kite
two pairs of
equal sides

All of the blue shapes are quadrilaterals.

3D (three-dimensional) objects

Solid objects are three-dimensional.
They have length, width and height.

sphere

A sphere is curved and round.

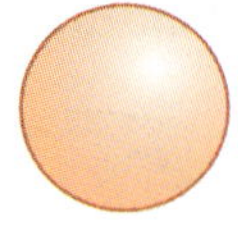

cube

A cube has 6 identical faces,
8 vertices and 12 straight edges.

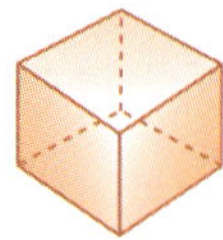

cylinder

A cylinder has 2 circular flat surfaces
and 1 curved surface.

cone

A cone has 1 circular flat surface
and 1 curved surface.

pyramid

A pyramid has triangular
faces joined around a base.

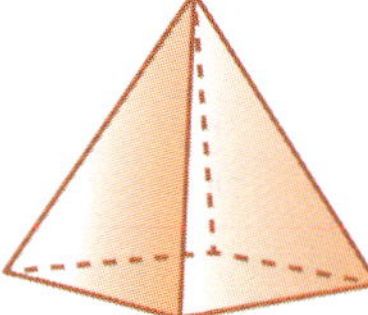

prism

A prism has rectangular faces
joining two identical bases.

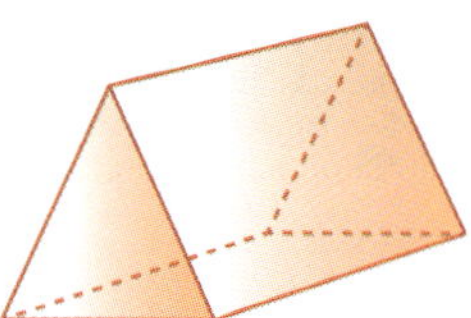

1:01 Numbers to 10 000

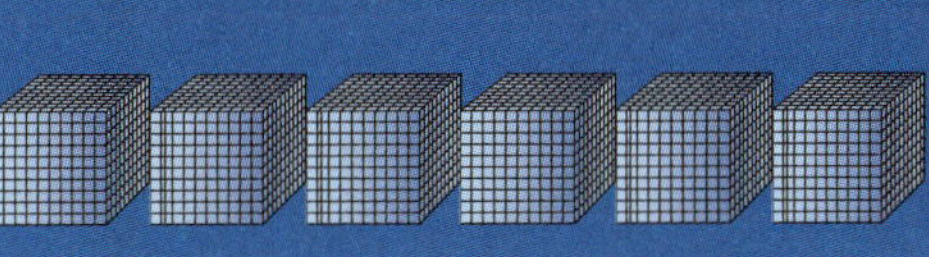

CONCEPT

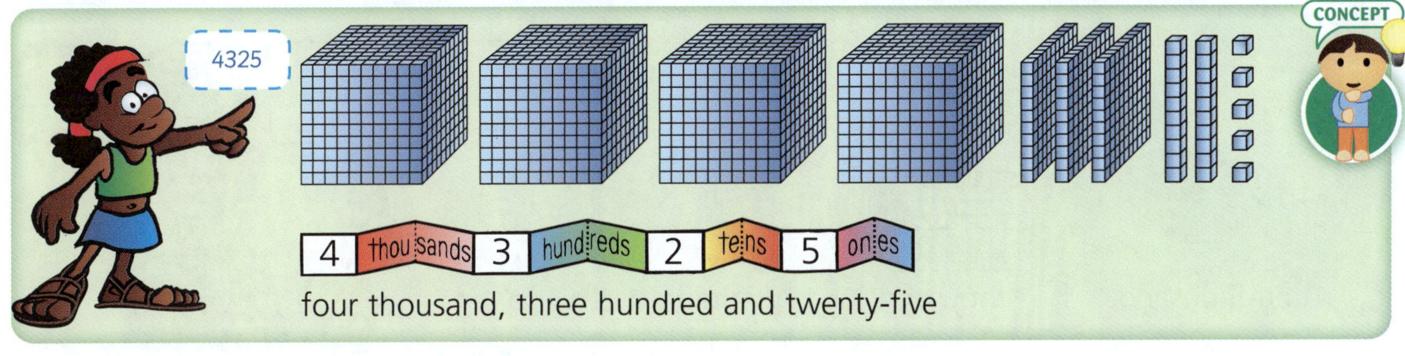

four thousand, three hundred and twenty-five

1 Fill out the numeral expander and write the numeral.

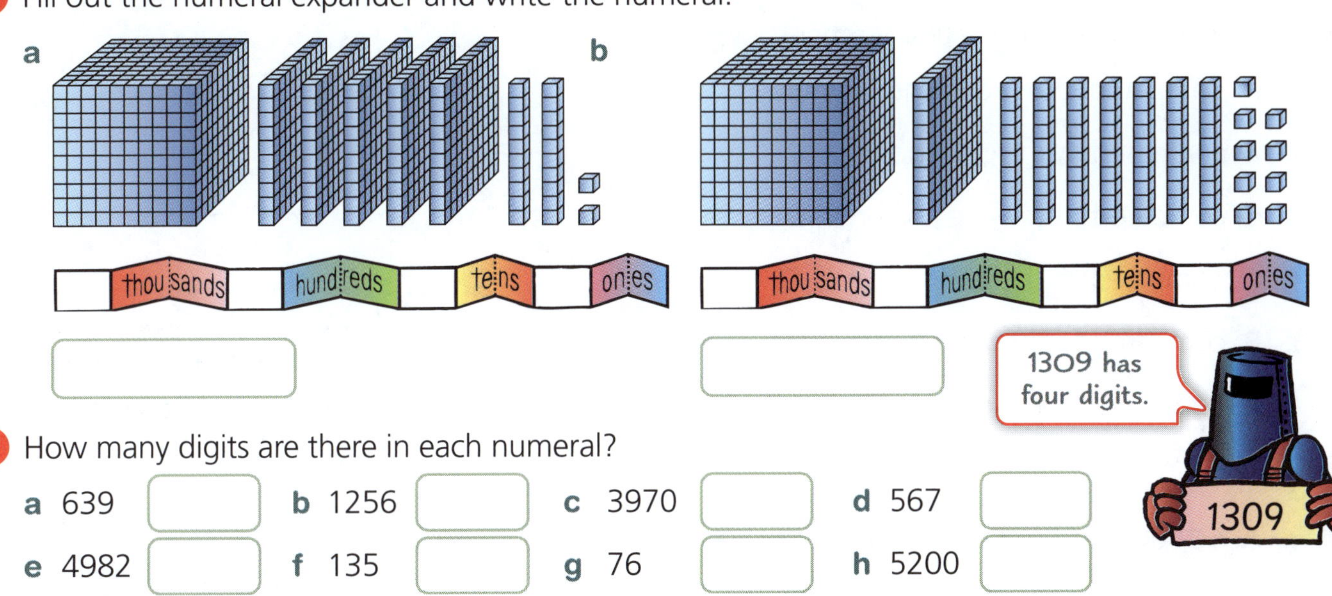

1309 has four digits.

1309

2 How many digits are there in each numeral?

a 639 ☐ **b** 1256 ☐ **c** 3970 ☐ **d** 567 ☐

e 4982 ☐ **f** 135 ☐ **g** 76 ☐ **h** 5200 ☐

3 Write these as numerals.

a one thousand and forty ☐

b seven thousand and eighteen ☐

c five thousand, one hundred and seventy-nine ☐

d nine thousand and seven ☐

e two thousand, six hundred and thirty-four ☐

f two thousand, six hundred ☐

g eight thousand, five hundred and sixty-eight ☐

h four thousand and thirty ☐

4 Write in words:

a 4023 ______

b 9030 ______

c 7500 ______

d 2901 ______

Ten thousand = 10 000 = 10 × 1000 = 100 × 100 = 1000 × 10. There are 4 zeros in each.

 • *AUSTRALIAN SIGNPOST MATHS 4* • ISBN 9780655708780

1:02 Numbers to 100 000

We leave a space after the 1000s column except when there are only four digits.

67 208
14 000
8172

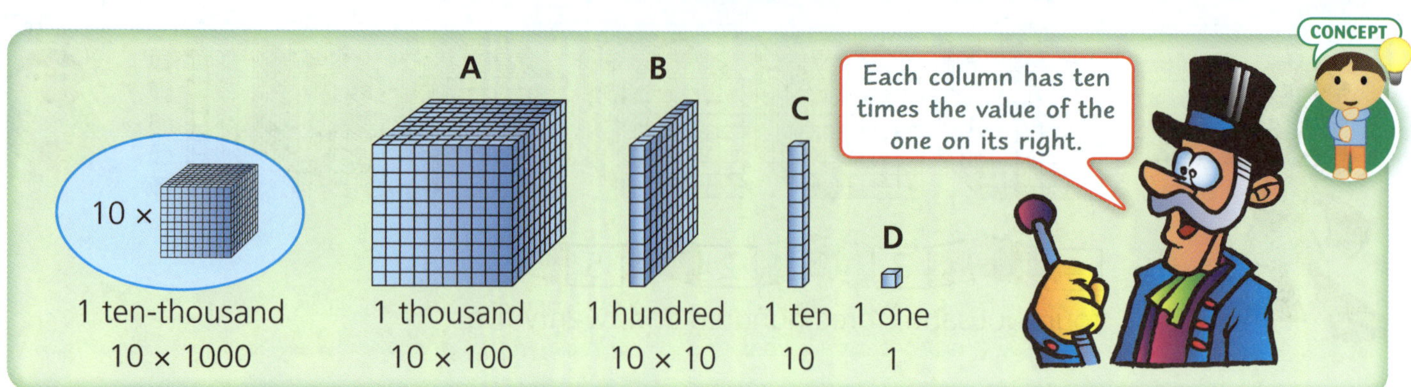

1 How many times as big is the number shown in:

a **A**, compared to the one shown in **B**?

b **B**, compared to the one shown in **C**?

c **C**, compared to the one shown in **D**?

d **A**, compared to the one shown in **C**?

e **B**, compared to the one shown in **D**?

f **A**, compared to the one shown in **D**?

92 thousand			5 hundred and sixty-one		
100 000	10 000	1000	100	10	1
	9	2	5	6	1

When we multiply by 10 we add a zero.

2 Which number is larger:

a **A**: 60 000 + 7000 + 600 + 80 + 1 or **B**: 60 000 + 900 + 90 + 9?

b **C**: 80 000 + 1000 + 200 + 40 + 9 or **D**: 80 000 + 2000 + 100 + 60 + 2?

c **E**: 20 000 + 5000 + 700 + 10 + 8 or **F**: 20 000 + 5000 + 800 + 80 + 1?

d **G**: 50 000 + 3000 + 900 + 90 + 2 or **H**: 50 000 + 9000 + 700 + 90 + 2?

3 **A** 74 186 **B** 79 146 **C** 60 715 **D** 40 207 **E** 97 364 **F** 98 170

a Which number has a 7 that stands for 7000?

b Which numbers contain 6s that have the same value?

c Which numbers contain 9s that have the same value?

d Which numbers contain 7s that have the same value?

e How many times as big is the 7 in **B** compared to the 7 in **E**?

What other questions could you ask?

Wipe out a digit

- A student enters any 5-digit number into a calculator.
- A partner selects any digit to be 'wiped out', i.e. changed to zero.
- Only one operation can be entered into the calculator to wipe out a digit.
- Take turns and score one point for each successful wipe out.

 • *AUSTRALIAN SIGNPOST MATHS 4* • ISBN 9780655708780

1:03 Rounding off

We round 15 off to 20 (to the nearest 10).
We round 15 000 off to 20 000 (to the nearest 10 000).

CONCEPT

3478 rounds off to 3000 (to the nearest 1000).

closer to 3000 | closer to 4000

3000 — 3500 — 4000

3500 rounds up to 4000.

65 432 rounds off to 70 000 (to the nearest 10 000).

closer to 60 000 | closer to 70 000

60 000 — 65 000 — 70 000

65 000 rounds up to 70 000.

When rounding a number to a particular place, look at the next digit.
If it is 5 or more, round up.
If it is less than 5, round down.

This rounds off to 97 000.

96 834

1 Round off these numbers to the nearest hundred.

a 3674 ____ b 4237 ____ c 1396 ____ d 9271 ____
e 6549 ____ f 6704 ____ g 8962 ____ h 5854 ____

2 Round off these numbers to the nearest thousand.

a 31 569 ____ b 82 738 ____ c 10 846 ____ d 57 249 ____
e 23 496 ____ f 52 301 ____ g 46 972 ____ h 69 347 ____

3 Round off these numbers to the nearest ten-thousand.

a 46 867 ____ b 82 999 ____ c 25 000 ____ d 88 235 ____
e 92 675 ____ f 33 951 ____ g 65 007 ____ h 74 000 ____

4 a Circle numbers that round off to 53 000.

53 640	52 967	52 849
52 621	52 076	53 297
53 599	53 346	52 374

b Circle numbers that round off to 80 000.

79 621	87 231	81 119
85 000	74 649	75 000
83 713	71 998	76 014

5 Answer **true** or **false** for each statement.

a 4639 rounds off to 4600. ____
b 1854 rounds off to 1800. ____
c 6341 rounds off to 6400. ____
d 9782 rounds off to 9800. ____
e 35 000 rounds off to 40 000. ____

6

____ thousands ____ hundreds ____ tens ____ ones
____ hundreds ____ tens ____ ones
____ tens ____ ones

1:04 Fractions

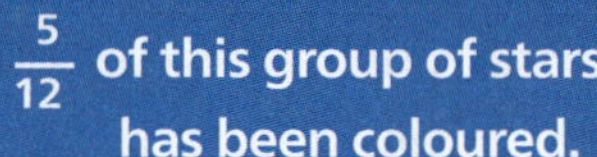

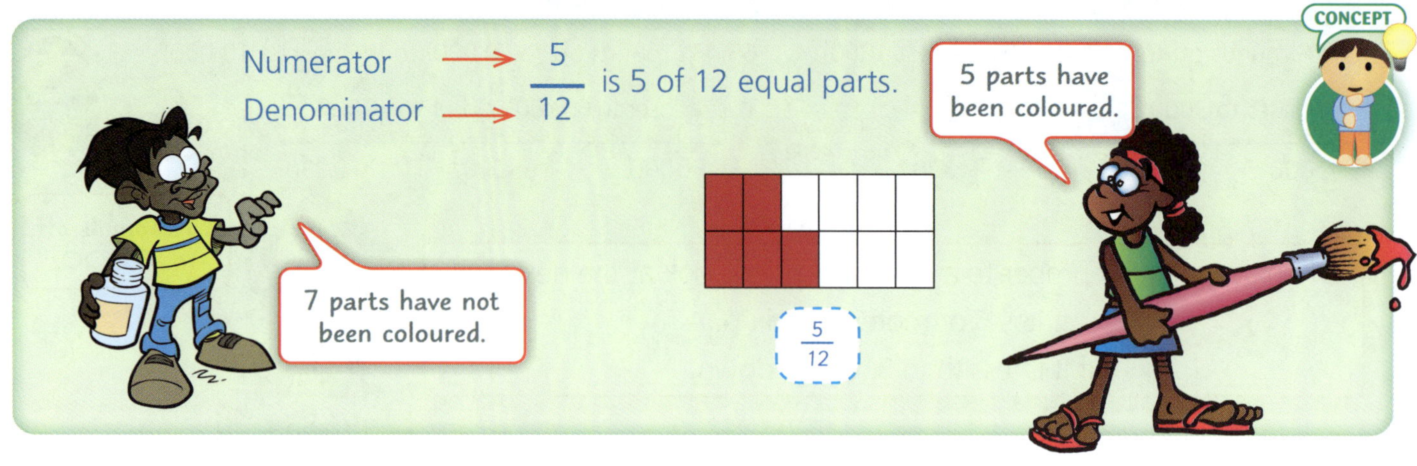

1 What part of each shape has been coloured?

a ☐ b ☐ c ☐ d ☐

e ☐ f ☐ g ☐ h ☐

2 What part of each shape above has not been coloured?

a ☐ b ☐ c ☐ d ☐ e ☐ f ☐ g ☐ h ☐

3 Colour part of each shape to match the given fraction.

a $\frac{4}{12}$ b $\frac{1}{6}$ c $\frac{1}{3}$ d $\frac{4}{6}$

e $\frac{9}{12}$ f $\frac{5}{6}$ g $\frac{6}{12}$ h $\frac{10}{12}$

4 What part of each group has been coloured?

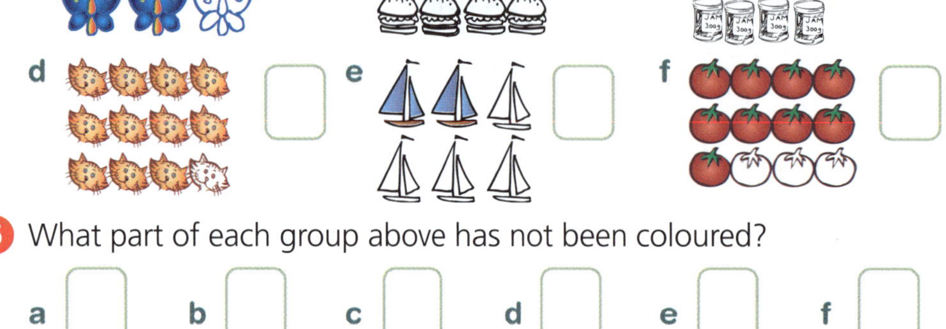

a ☐ b ☐ c ☐

d ☐ e ☐ f ☐

The part coloured is $\frac{7}{12}$.

5 What part of each group above has not been coloured?

a ☐ b ☐ c ☐ d ☐ e ☐ f ☐

 • *AUSTRALIAN SIGNPOST MATHS 4* • ISBN 9780655708780

Comparing fractions

one-fifth, two-fifths, three-fifths, ...
$\frac{1}{5}$ $\frac{2}{5}$ $\frac{3}{5}$

$\frac{1}{2}$ $\frac{1}{5}$

$\frac{1}{2}$ is bigger than $\frac{1}{5}$.

We need to have equal wholes to compare fraction parts.

1 Circle the larger fraction.

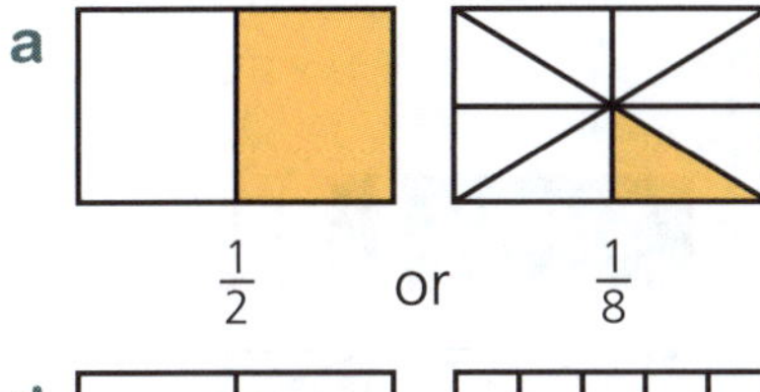
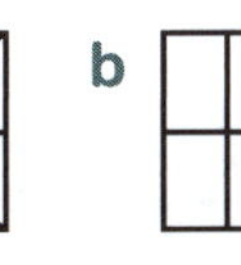
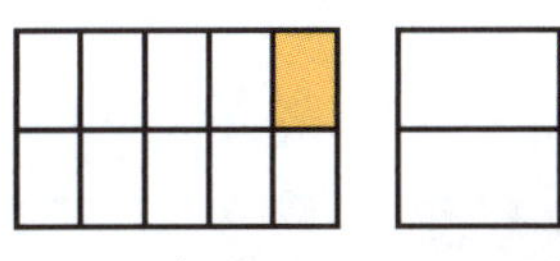
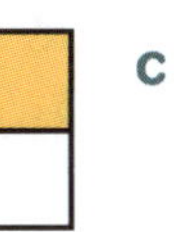
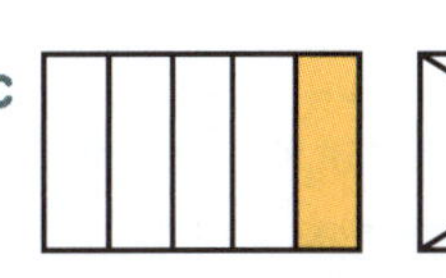
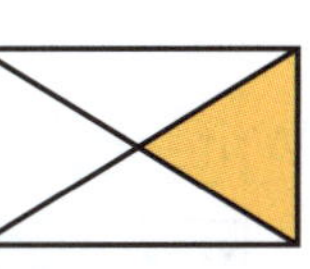

a $\frac{1}{2}$ or $\frac{1}{8}$ b $\frac{1}{10}$ or $\frac{1}{4}$ c $\frac{1}{5}$ or $\frac{1}{4}$

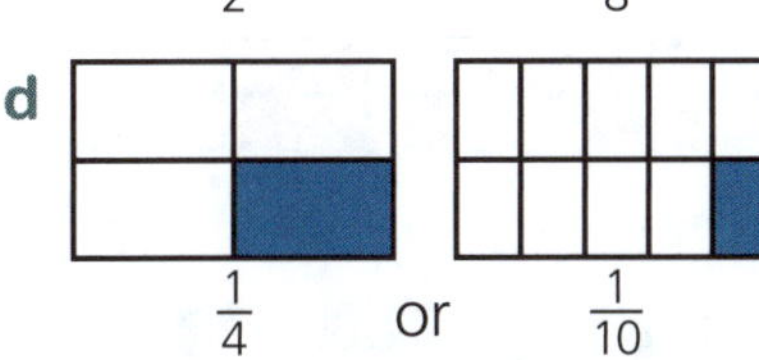
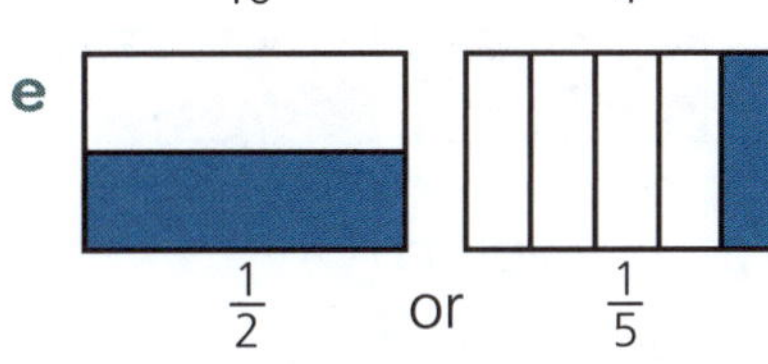
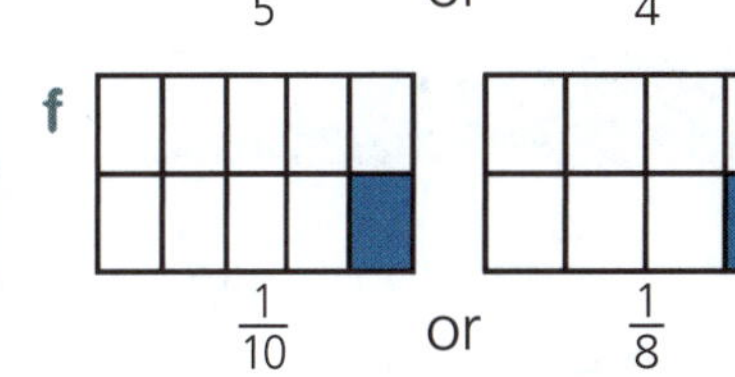

d $\frac{1}{4}$ or $\frac{1}{10}$ e $\frac{1}{2}$ or $\frac{1}{5}$ f $\frac{1}{10}$ or $\frac{1}{8}$

2 Colour part of each shape to match the given fraction.

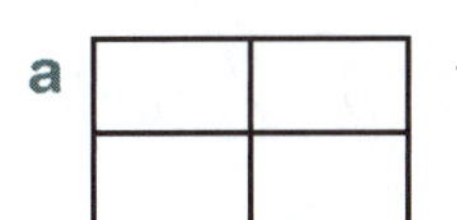

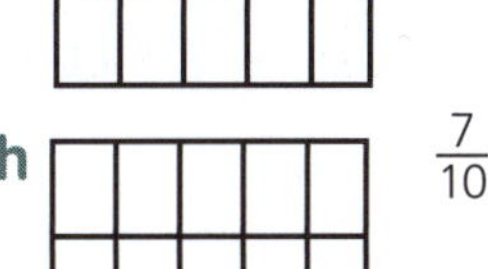
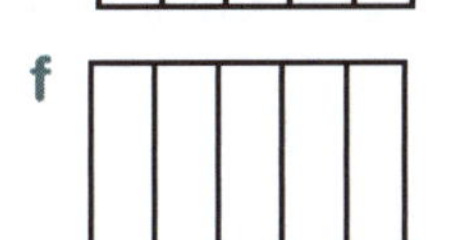

a $\frac{3}{4}$ b $\frac{2}{10}$ c $\frac{2}{5}$ d $\frac{3}{10}$

e $\frac{6}{10}$ f $\frac{4}{5}$ g $\frac{1}{4}$ h $\frac{7}{10}$

3 Write **true** or **false** for each statement.

a $\frac{2}{2} = 1$ ______ b $\frac{4}{5} = 1$ ______ c $\frac{8}{8} = 1$ ______

d $1 = \frac{10}{10}$ ______ e $1 = \frac{3}{8}$ ______ f $1 = \frac{5}{5}$ ______

$\frac{2}{2}$, $\frac{5}{5}$ and $\frac{10}{10}$ are all 1.

4 Find the coloured fraction.

a Fraction coloured = ______

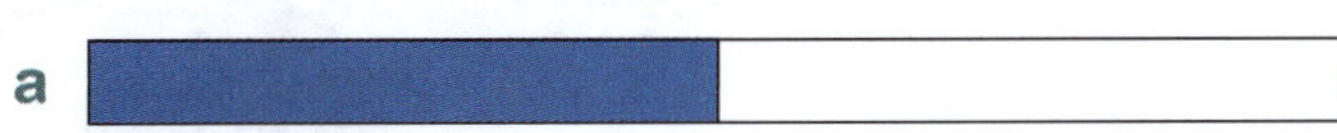

b Fraction coloured = ______

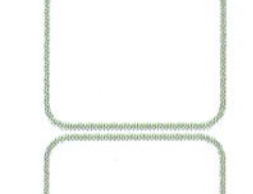
c Fraction coloured = ______

Circle the larger fraction.

d $\frac{1}{10}$ or $\frac{1}{5}$ e $\frac{1}{2}$ or $\frac{1}{5}$ f $\frac{1}{2}$ or $\frac{3}{5}$ g $\frac{7}{10}$ or $\frac{1}{2}$ h $\frac{3}{10}$ or $\frac{1}{5}$

1:06 Improper fractions

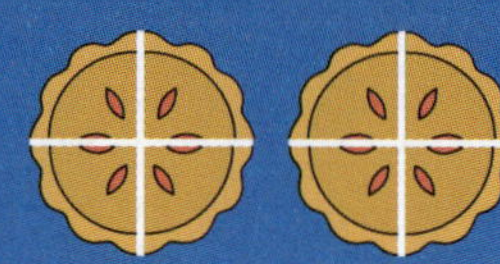

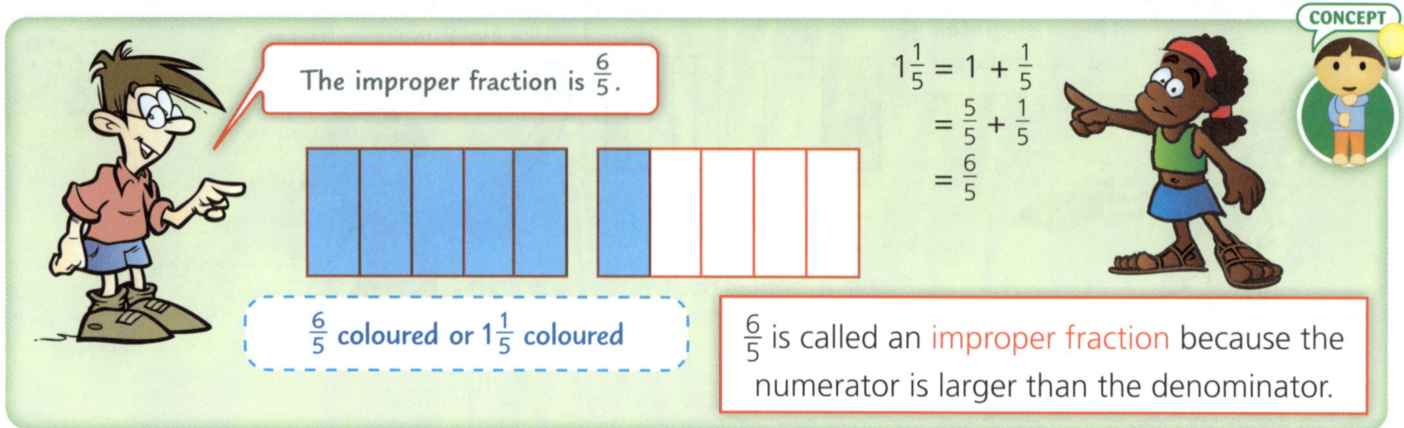

1 Write the improper fraction for the parts coloured.

a ___/4 b c

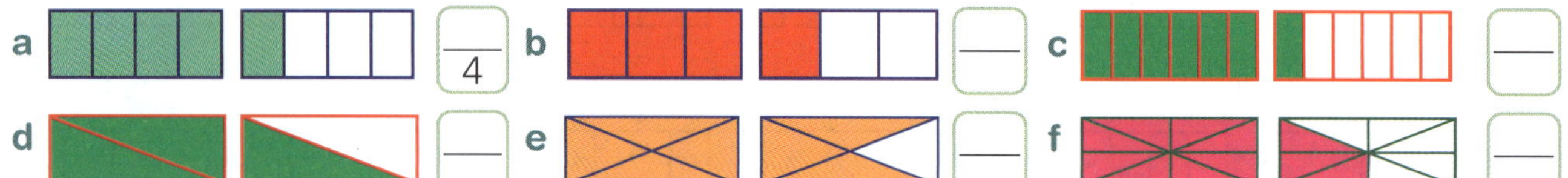

d e f

2 Write the mixed number for the parts coloured.

a b c

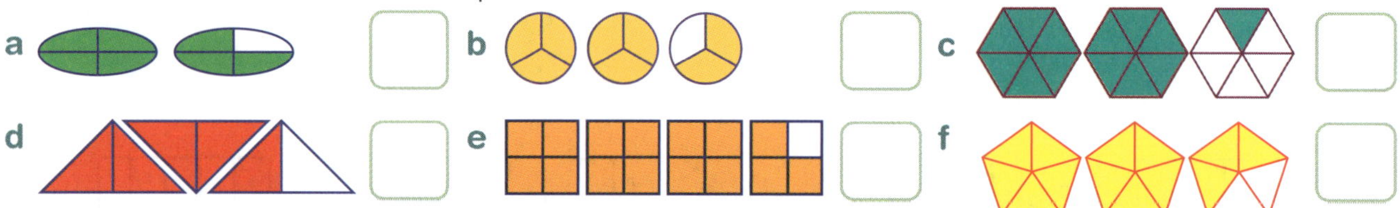

d e f

3 Complete the number line. Practise counting forwards and backwards.

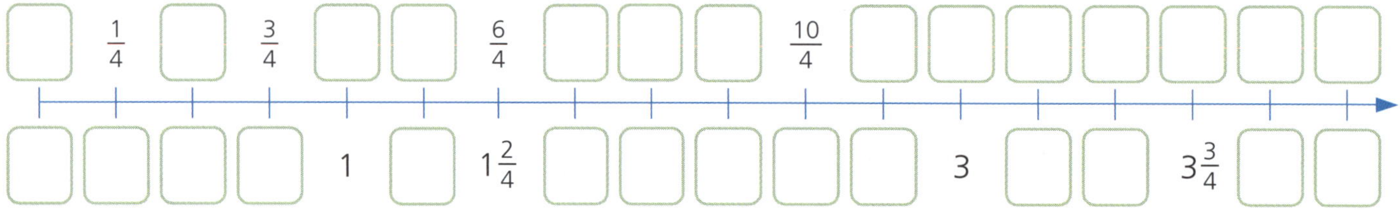

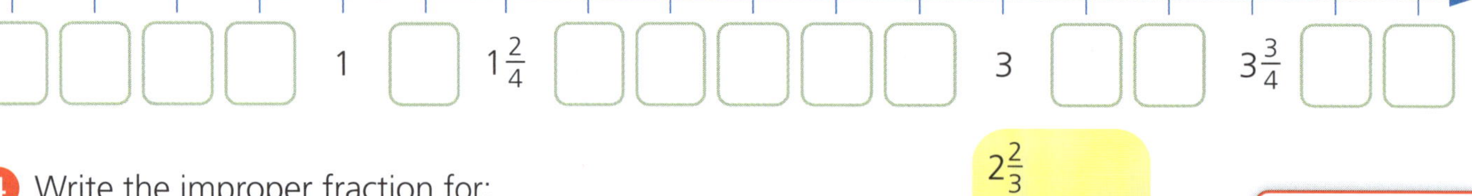

4 Write the improper fraction for:

a $1\frac{1}{2}$ b $2\frac{1}{5}$ c $3\frac{2}{4}$ d $1\frac{4}{5}$

e $2\frac{3}{4}$ f $2\frac{5}{4}$ g $4\frac{2}{3}$ h $2\frac{5}{8}$

$2\frac{2}{3} = \frac{3}{3} + \frac{3}{3} + \frac{2}{3} = \frac{8}{3}$

5 Write the mixed number for:

a $\frac{7}{4}$ b $\frac{9}{5}$ c $\frac{11}{4}$ d $\frac{11}{5}$

e $\frac{8}{5}$ f $\frac{13}{4}$ g $\frac{14}{5}$ h $\frac{17}{4}$

 • *AUSTRALIAN SIGNPOST MATHS 4* • ISBN 9780655708780

Mixed numbers

five-quarters $\frac{5}{4}$  one and one-quarter $1\frac{1}{4}$ 

Scott had 2 halves of a biscuit. Rachel gave him another half. Now he has 3 halves.

$\frac{3}{2} = \frac{2}{2} + \frac{1}{2}$
$= 1 + \frac{1}{2}$
$= 1\frac{1}{2}$

He has $\frac{3}{2}$ or $1\frac{1}{2}$ biscuits.

$\frac{3}{2}$ is called an **improper fraction** because the numerator is larger than the denominator.

$1\frac{1}{2}$ is called a **mixed number**. It has a whole part and a fraction part.

1 Write the mixed number and improper fraction for each.

a 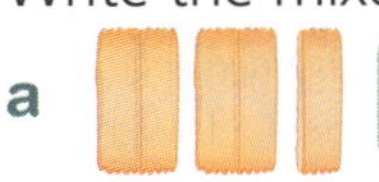 [ ] $\frac{5}{2}$  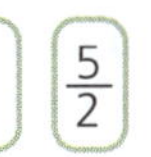
5 halves

b    [ ] [ ]
[ ] halves

c 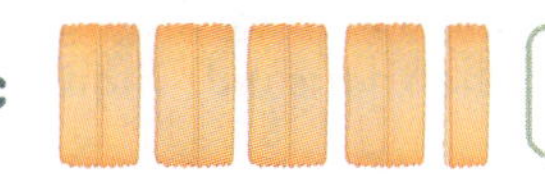 [ ] [ ]
[ ] halves

d  [ ] $\frac{\ }{4}$
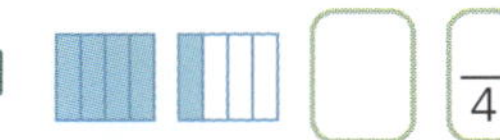
[ ] quarters

e 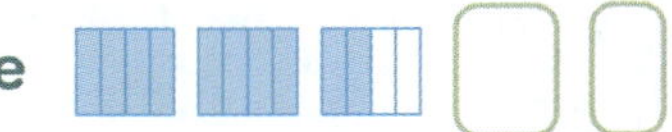 [ ] [ ]
[ ] quarters

f 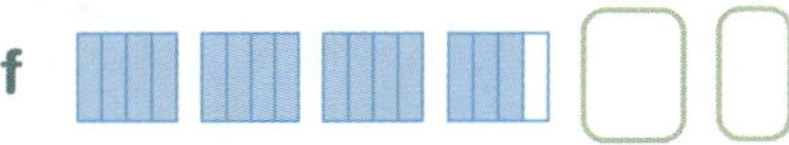 [ ] [ ]
[ ] quarters

g   [ ] [ ]
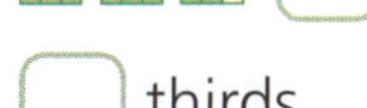
[ ] thirds

h   [ ] [ ]
[ ] sixths

i  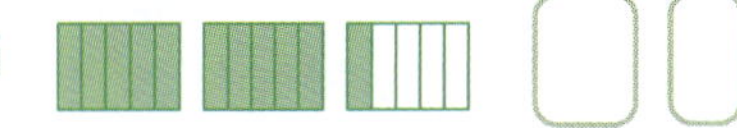 [ ] [ ]
[ ] fifths

2 a $\frac{1}{3}$, $\frac{2}{3}$, 1, $1\frac{1}{3}$, $1\frac{2}{3}$, 2, $2\frac{1}{3}$, $2\frac{2}{3}$, [ ], [ ], [ ]

b one-third, two-thirds, three-thirds (or 1), four-thirds, [ ], [ ]

3 Write an equivalent whole or mixed number.

 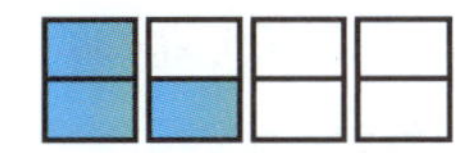 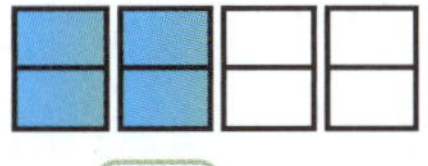 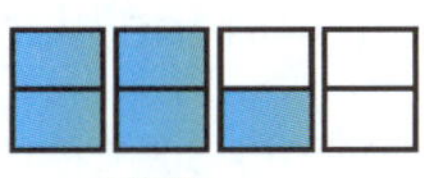

a $\frac{2}{2}$ [ ] b $\frac{3}{2}$ [ ] c $\frac{4}{2}$ [ ] d $\frac{5}{2}$ [ ]

4 Write the mixed number.

a $\frac{7}{5}$ [ ] b $\frac{5}{2}$ [ ] c $\frac{13}{5}$ [ ] d $\frac{9}{4}$ [ ]

e $\frac{13}{8}$ [ ] f $\frac{12}{5}$ [ ] g $\frac{15}{2}$ [ ] h $\frac{17}{5}$ [ ]

$\frac{11}{4} = 11 \div 4$
$= \frac{4}{4} + \frac{4}{4} + \frac{3}{4}$
$= 2\frac{3}{4}$

5 Write the improper fraction.

a $1\frac{1}{5}$ [ ] b $5\frac{1}{2}$ [ ] c $3\frac{2}{5}$ [ ] d $6\frac{1}{3}$ [ ]

e $1\frac{3}{8}$ [ ] f $2\frac{5}{6}$ [ ] g $4\frac{4}{5}$ [ ] h $1\frac{7}{10}$ [ ]

$8\frac{2}{3} = (8 \times 3 + 2)$ thirds
$= \frac{26}{3}$

 • *AUSTRALIAN SIGNPOST MATHS 4* • ISBN 9780655708780

1:08 Large numbers

65 000 has 5 digits.
137 896 has 6 digits.

CONCEPT

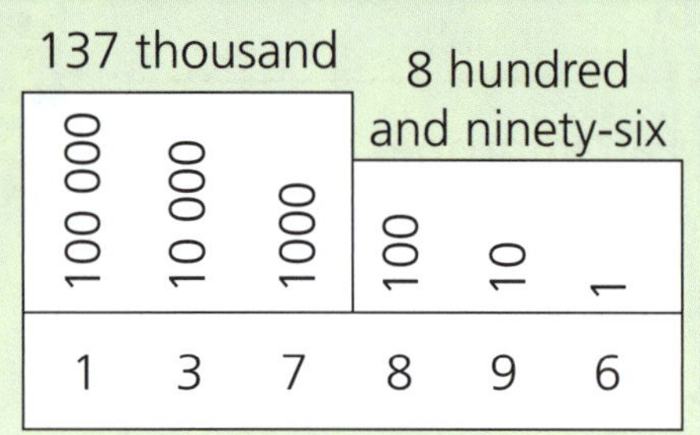

Using numeral expanders allows us to see how many hundreds or tens are in a number.

The expanded form of 137 896 is 100 000 + 30 000 + 7000 + 800 + 90 + 6.

1. Write the numeral for:

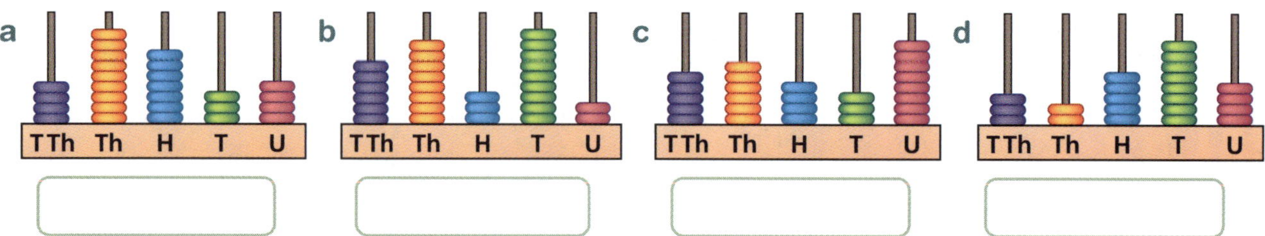

2. Read these numbers and then write them in figures on the place-value chart.
   - a twenty-six thousand, three hundred and twenty-four
   - b thirty-five thousand, one hundred and sixty-two
   - c eighty-two thousand, nine hundred and seventy

T Thous	Thous	Hund	Tens	Ones

3. Write the numeral for:
   - a 30 000 + 4000 + 500 + 20 + 8
   - b 60 000 + 7000 + 900 + 30 + 4
   - c 50 000 + 8000 + 400 + 60 + 2
   - d 90 000 + 2000 + 700 + 40 + 8
   - e 80 000 + 2000 + 300 + 50 + 9
   - f 40 000 + 8000 + 600 + 70 + 3

4. When are large numbers like these used?

Hundreds of thousands

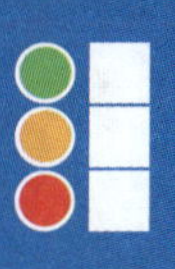

(206)459 (96)789
To compare numbers, start with the digits on the left of the space.

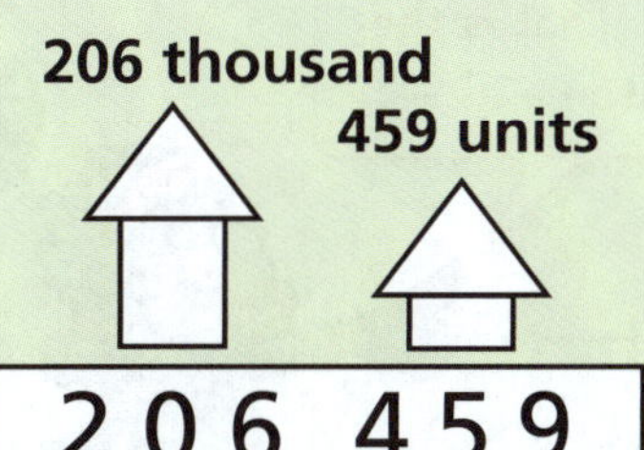

- The value of the 2 is 200 000.
- The value of the 6 is 6000.
- The value of the 4 is 400.
- The value of the 5 is 50.
- The value of the 9 is 9.

two hundred and six thousand, four hundred and fifty-nine

1 Circle the larger number in each pair.

a 49 768 49 713 **b** 37 281 36 281 **c** 84 971 81 302 **d** 345 022 344 997

2 Circle the smallest number in each group.

a 29 642 27 849 26 301 **b** 72 642 69 309 70 624 **c** 718 022 692 997 709 165

3 Write the numeral for:

a twenty-eight thousand, seven hundred and forty-seven ☐

b fifty thousand, three hundred and seventy-eight ☐

c eight hundred and thirty-nine thousand, six hundred and twenty-five ☐

d four hundred and seventeen thousand, seven hundred and thirteen ☐

4 Write the numeral for:

a 500 000 + 20 000 + 6000 + 400 + 90 + 3 ☐

b 800 000 + 90 000 + 5000 + 600 + 50 + 1 ☐

Leave a space to the right of the thousands digit.

5 Write the value for each coloured digit in these numbers.

a 48 603 ☐ **b** 91 738 ☐ **c** 675 132 ☐

d 32 480 ☐ **e** 80 965 ☐ **f** 401 360 ☐

Make the number

- For this game you need a set of playing cards marked with digits 0 to 9.
- The dealer selects a number to be made, e.g. 'Make the number closest to 30 000'.
- Five cards are then dealt to each player. The winner is the player able to arrange the five cards closest to the chosen number.
- Each winner scores one point.

1:10 Fraction patterns

$\frac{6}{4} = 1\frac{1}{2}$

CONCEPT

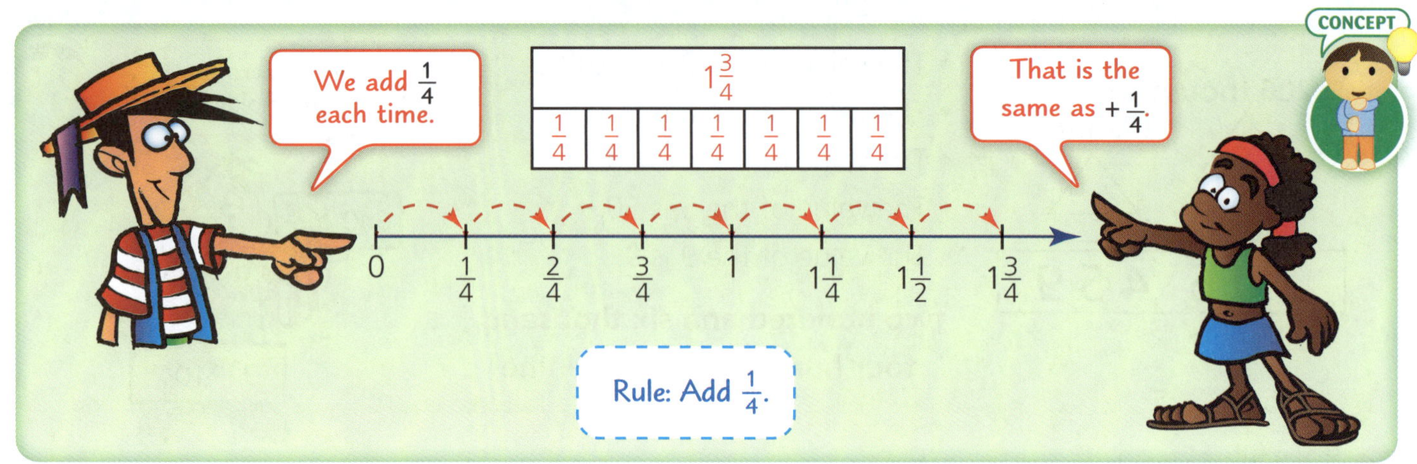

1. Complete each number line and write the rule.

a

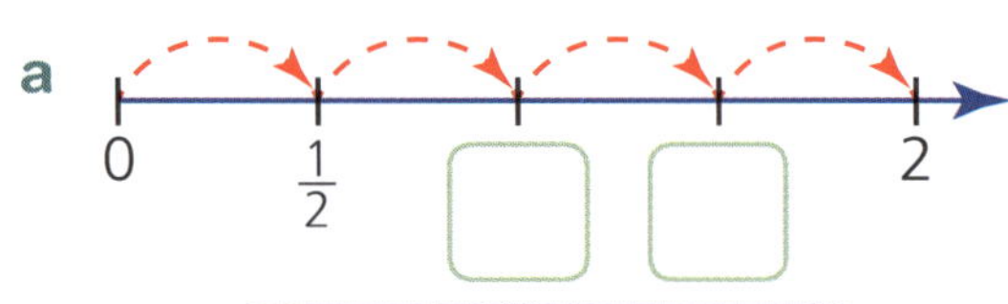

Rule: ☐

b 0 $\frac{1}{4}$ $\frac{1}{2}$ ☐ ☐

Rule: ☐

c

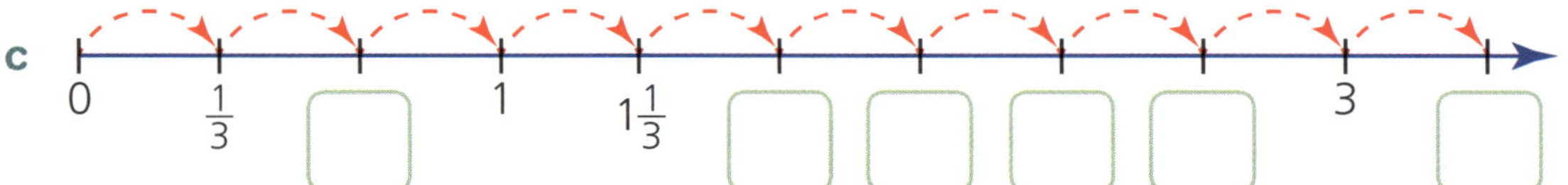

Rule: ☐

d

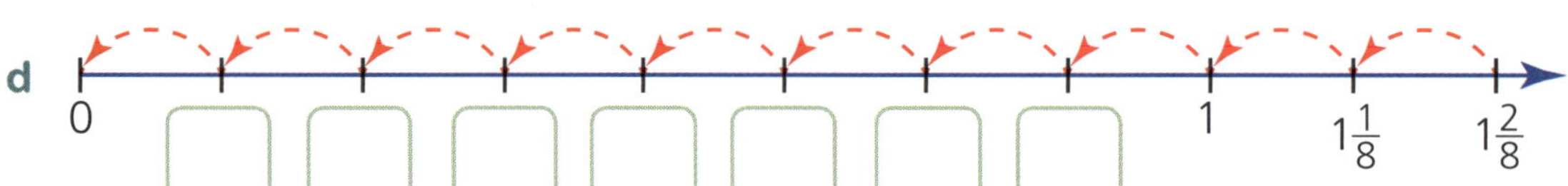

Rule: ☐

e

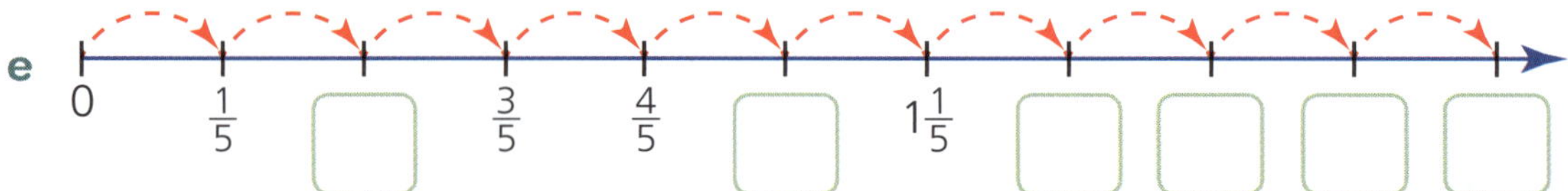

Rule: ☐

f 0 ☐ ☐ ☐ ☐ ☐ ☐ ☐ $1\frac{2}{6}$ $1\frac{3}{6}$ $1\frac{4}{6}$

Rule: ☐

Be careful!

 • *AUSTRALIAN SIGNPOST MATHS 4* • ISBN 9780655708780

Equivalent fractions

Fold the paper, fold again and fold again.

CONCEPT

1 Use the number lines to show an equivalent fraction for:

a $\frac{1}{5}$ = ☐ **b** $\frac{4}{10}$ = ☐ **c** $\frac{4}{5}$ = ☐ **d** $\frac{6}{10}$ = ☐

e $\frac{5}{10}$ = ☐ **f** $\frac{2}{5}$ = ☐ **g** $\frac{1}{2}$ = ☐ **h** $\frac{10}{10}$ = ☐

2 Use the number lines above to compare the two fractions. Circle the smaller fraction.

a $\frac{1}{5}$ $\frac{1}{10}$ **b** $\frac{6}{10}$ $\frac{1}{2}$ **c** $\frac{8}{10}$ $\frac{3}{5}$ **d** $\frac{4}{5}$ $\frac{9}{10}$

3 Complete the number lines. Count forwards and backwards.

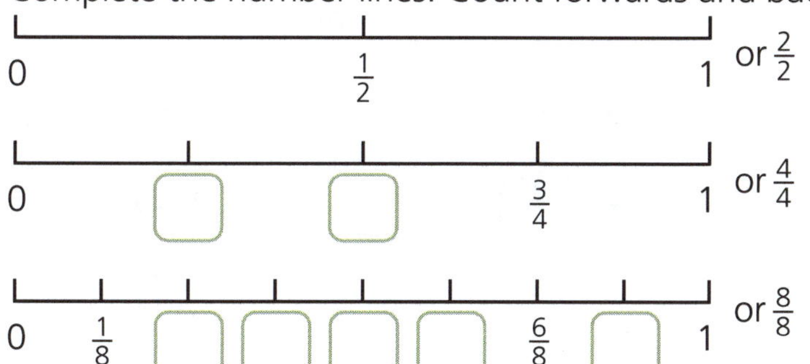

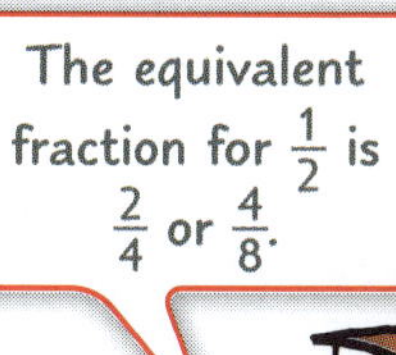

4 Use the number lines above to show an equivalent fraction for:

a $\frac{1}{4}$ = ☐ **b** $\frac{4}{8}$ = ☐ **c** $\frac{2}{4}$ = ☐ **d** $\frac{1}{2}$ = ☐

e $\frac{6}{8}$ = ☐ **f** $\frac{3}{4}$ = ☐ **g** $\frac{2}{8}$ = ☐ **h** $\frac{8}{8}$ = ☐

Equivalent fractions are equal fractions.

5 True or false?

a $\frac{6}{6} = \frac{3}{3}$ ☐

b $\frac{2}{6} = \frac{1}{3}$ ☐

c $\frac{1}{3} = \frac{1}{6}$ ☐

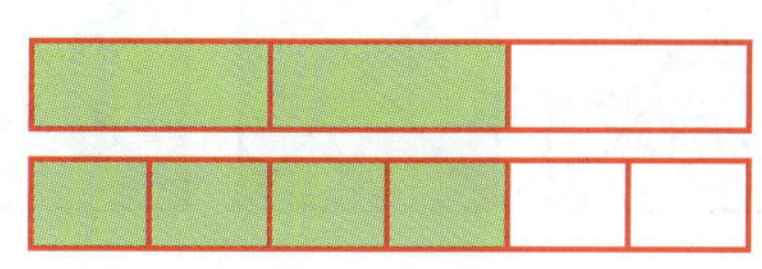

d Is $\frac{1}{6}$ half of $\frac{1}{3}$? ☐

e Is $1\frac{4}{6}$ equal to $1\frac{2}{3}$ ☐

 • *AUSTRALIAN SIGNPOST MATHS 4* • ISBN 9780655708780

1:12 Equivalent fractions

$\frac{3}{4}$ is 3 in each 4, so this would also be 6 in each 8.

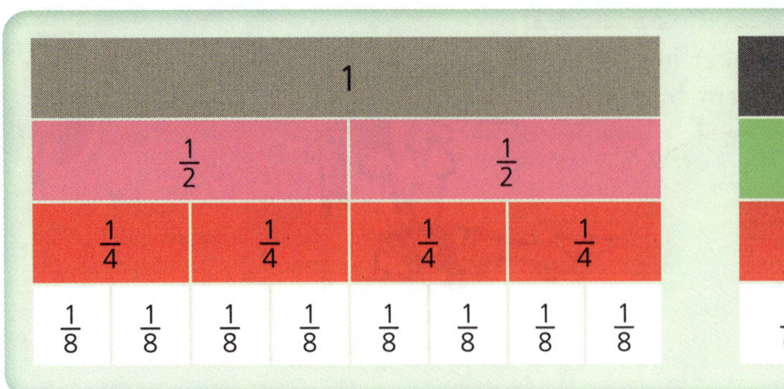

1							
$\frac{1}{2}$				$\frac{1}{2}$			
$\frac{1}{4}$		$\frac{1}{4}$		$\frac{1}{4}$		$\frac{1}{4}$	
$\frac{1}{8}$	$\frac{1}{8}$	$\frac{1}{8}$	$\frac{1}{8}$	$\frac{1}{8}$	$\frac{1}{8}$	$\frac{1}{8}$	$\frac{1}{8}$

1					
$\frac{1}{2}$			$\frac{1}{2}$		
$\frac{1}{3}$		$\frac{1}{3}$		$\frac{1}{3}$	
$\frac{1}{6}$	$\frac{1}{6}$	$\frac{1}{6}$	$\frac{1}{6}$	$\frac{1}{6}$	$\frac{1}{6}$

1 What fraction is equal to:

a $\frac{2}{4}$? ☐ b $\frac{4}{8}$? ☐
c $\frac{6}{8}$? ☐ d $\frac{4}{4}$? ☐
e 1 ? ☐ f $\frac{1}{2}$? ☐

2 What fraction is equal to:

a $\frac{2}{6}$? ☐ b $\frac{4}{6}$? ☐
c $\frac{6}{6}$? ☐ d $\frac{3}{3}$? ☐
e $\frac{1}{3}$? ☐ f $\frac{2}{3}$? ☐

3 **True** (**T**) or **false** (**F**)?

a $\frac{1}{2} = \frac{2}{4}$ ☐ b $\frac{3}{4} = \frac{6}{8}$ ☐
c $\frac{4}{8} = \frac{2}{4}$ ☐ d $\frac{5}{8} = \frac{3}{4}$ ☐
e $\frac{8}{8} = \frac{4}{4}$ ☐ f $\frac{2}{2} = 1$ ☐

4 **True** (**T**) or **false** (**F**)?

a $\frac{2}{3} = \frac{4}{6}$ ☐ b $\frac{1}{3} = \frac{2}{6}$ ☐
c $\frac{3}{3} = \frac{6}{6}$ ☐ d $\frac{1}{6} = \frac{1}{3}$ ☐
e $\frac{3}{6} = \frac{2}{3}$ ☐ f $\frac{6}{6} = 1$ ☐

5 Complete each pattern.

a $\frac{1}{3}, \frac{2}{3}, \frac{3}{3},$ ☐, ☐, ☐, ☐
b $\frac{1}{4}, \frac{2}{4}, \frac{3}{4},$ ☐, ☐, ☐, ☐, ☐
c $\frac{1}{6}, \frac{2}{6}, \frac{3}{6},$ ☐, ☐, ☐, ☐, ☐, ☐
d $\frac{1}{8}, \frac{2}{8}, \frac{3}{8},$ ☐, ☐, ☐, ☐, ☐, ☐, ☐

1 whole is the same as $\frac{2}{2}, \frac{3}{3}, \frac{4}{4}, \frac{6}{6}$ or $\frac{8}{8}$.

6

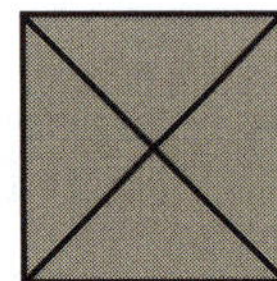

Count by quarters. One-quarter, two-quarters,…

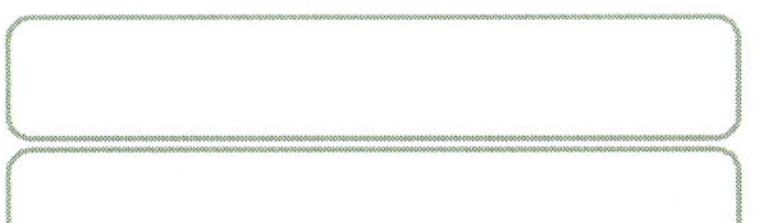

- Cut 5 strips of paper the same length to construct your own fraction wall.
- Use one strip at a time to make separate strips folded into:
  - halves
  - quarters
  - eighths
  - thirds
  - sixths
- Paste these onto a large sheet of paper.

 ISBN 9780655708780

1:13 Numbers using millions

8 204 450

There is also a space after the millions place.

CONCEPT

- The population of Australia on 5 March 2023 was 26 288 482.

26 million			288 thousand			482		
100 000 000	10 000 000	1 000 000	100 000	10 000	1000	100	10	1
	2	6	2	8	8	4	8	2

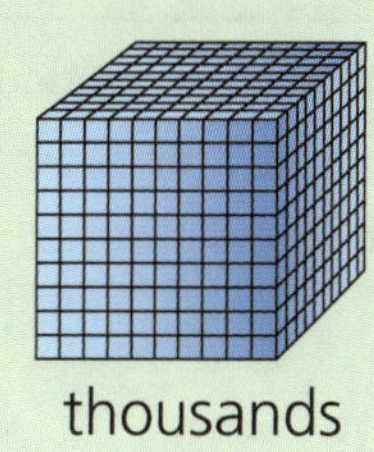

- The population of the United States of America in 2023 was 336 million.

1 a Round off Australia's population to the nearest million. ______

b To the nearest million, how many more people lived in the United States than in Australia in 2023? ______

2 Write the numeral for:

a 80 000 000 + 2 000 000 + 400 000 + 80 000 + 3000 ______

b 10 000 000 + 9 000 000 + 600 000 + 40 000 + 2000 ______

c 6 000 000 + 300 000 + 70 000 + 2000 + 800 + 40 ______

d (8 × 10 000 000) + (5 × 1 000 000) + (9 × 100 000) + (4 × 10 000) + (5 × 1000) ______

Use the zero as a place holder.

3 Read these numbers and then write them in the place-value chart.

a seven million, three hundred and two thousand, four hundred and twenty-four

b seventy-one million, six hundred and fifty thousand, eight hundred and ninety-five

c fifty-five million, six hundred and fifty thousand

d eight hundred and sixty-nine thousand

20 K is sometimes used for 20 000.

	Ten Millions	Millions	Hundred Thousands	Ten Thousands	Thousands	Hundreds	Tens	Ones
a								
b								
c								
d								

- Time how long it takes to count from 20 000 to 20 100.
  Use this to estimate the time it will take to count up to 100 000.

 • *AUSTRALIAN SIGNPOST MATHS 4* • ISBN 9780655708780

1:14 Rounding off

56 853 478 rounds off to 57 000 000 (to the nearest million).

closer to 56 000 000 | closer to 57 000 000

56 000 000 — 56 500 000 — 57 000 000

56 500 000 rounds up to 57 000 000.

When rounding a number to a particular place, look at the next digit.
If it is 5 or more, round up.
If it is less than 5, round down.

CONCEPT

Remember, less than 5 round downwards.

1 Round off each number to the nearest million.

a 5 400 000 ______ b 2 850 000 ______
c 11 400 000 ______ d 21 500 000 ______
e 8 974 807 ______ f 14 282 853 ______

2 Round off each number to the nearest thousand.

Look at the number in the hundreds column.

a 9 263 750 ______ b 12 648 468 ______
c 42 255 903 ______ d 7 888 435 ______
e 13 706 288 ______ f 67 435 700 ______

3 Circle the largest number and underline the smallest.

a 12 563 852, 12 099 762, 12 558 000
b 8 373 964, 8 730 132, 8 542 876
c 36 832 000, 35 932 000, 36 198 000
d 9 476 350, 10 102 533, 9 999 850
e 9 643 850, 12 261 032, 11 899 122
f 23 609 320, 23 618 864, 23 610 000

4 Write the value of each coloured digit.

a 2**3** 009 650 ______ b 8 **0**56 732 ______
c **2**8 350 600 ______ d 19 6**6**4 950 ______
e 8**5** 000 000 ______ f 7 4**5**0 000 ______

ACTIVITY

- List three things that would cost more than $1 000 000.

______

______

1:15 Hundredths

One half is 50 out of 100. $\frac{50}{100}$

One quarter is 25 out of 100. $\frac{25}{100}$

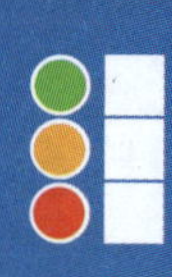

1 What part of each hundred square has been coloured?

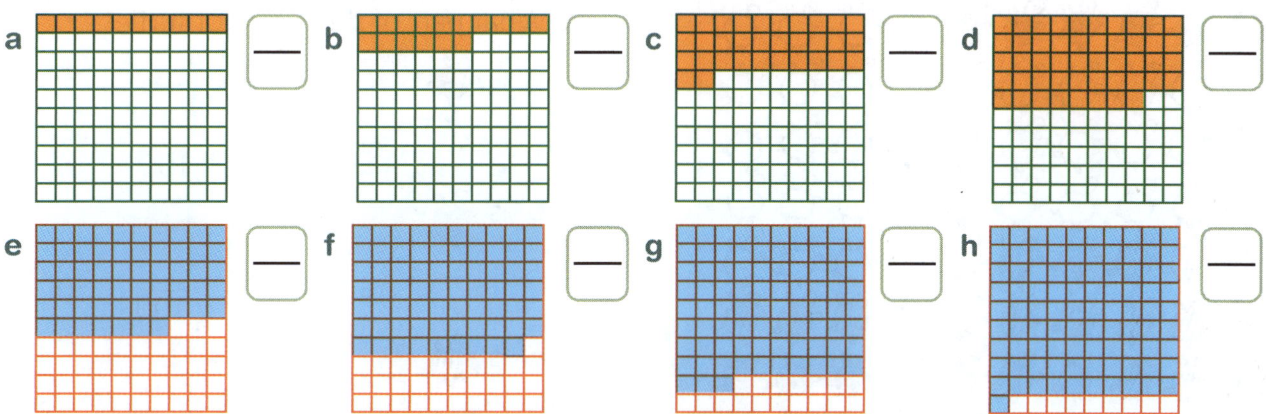

2 Colour part of each hundred square to match the given fraction.

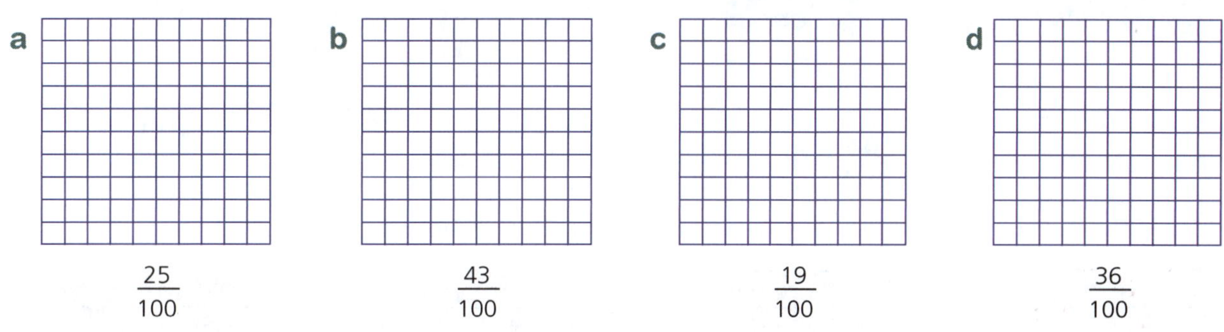

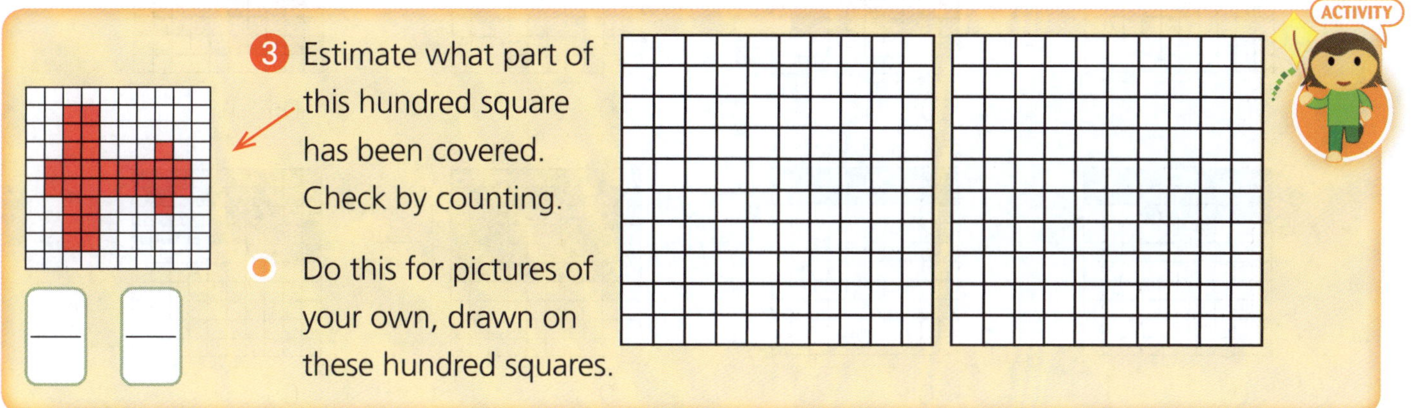

3 Estimate what part of this hundred square has been covered. Check by counting.

- Do this for pictures of your own, drawn on these hundred squares.

1:16 Decimals

$0.05 is $ $\frac{5}{100}$. $0.10 is $ $\frac{10}{100}$.
$0.20 is $ $\frac{20}{100}$. $0.50 is $ $\frac{50}{100}$.

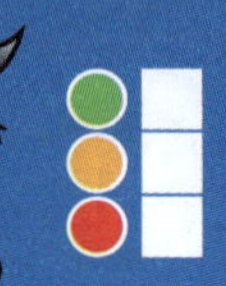

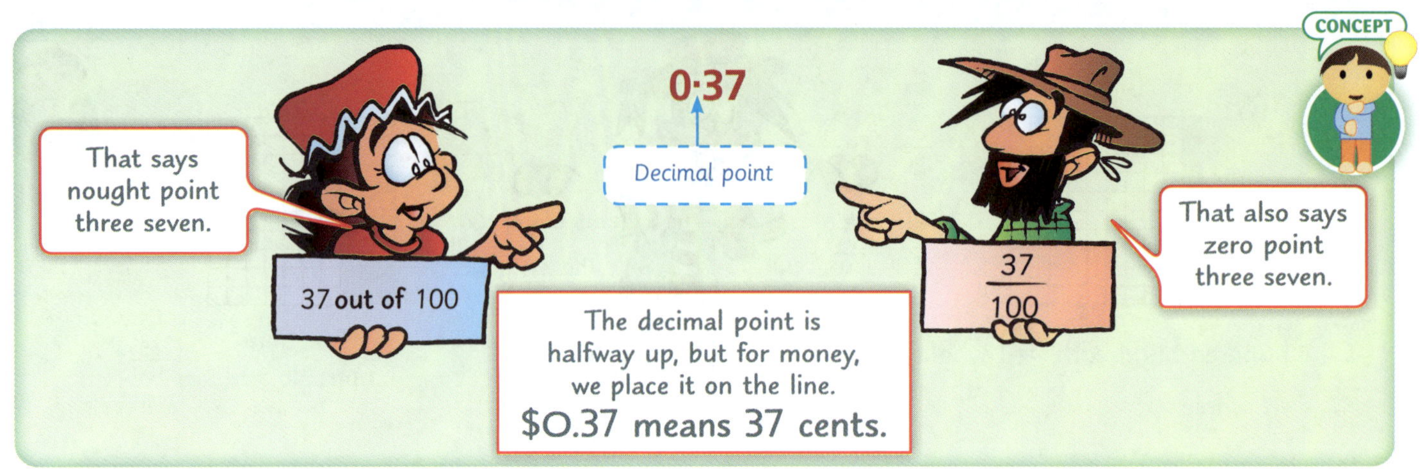

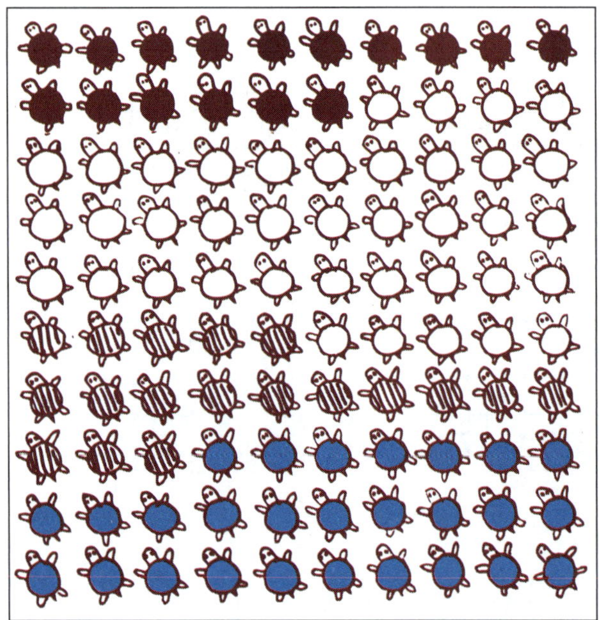

1 How many turtles are inside the box? ☐

2 What part of the group of turtles:

a is ?
☐ out of 100 $\frac{☐}{100}$ 0·☐

b is ?
☐ out of 100 $\frac{☐}{100}$ 0·☐

c is ?
☐ out of 100 $\frac{☐}{100}$ 0·☐

d is and together?
☐ out of 100 $\frac{☐}{100}$ 0·☐

3 What part of the group is ? 0·☐

4 Write the decimal and fraction shown on each hundred square.

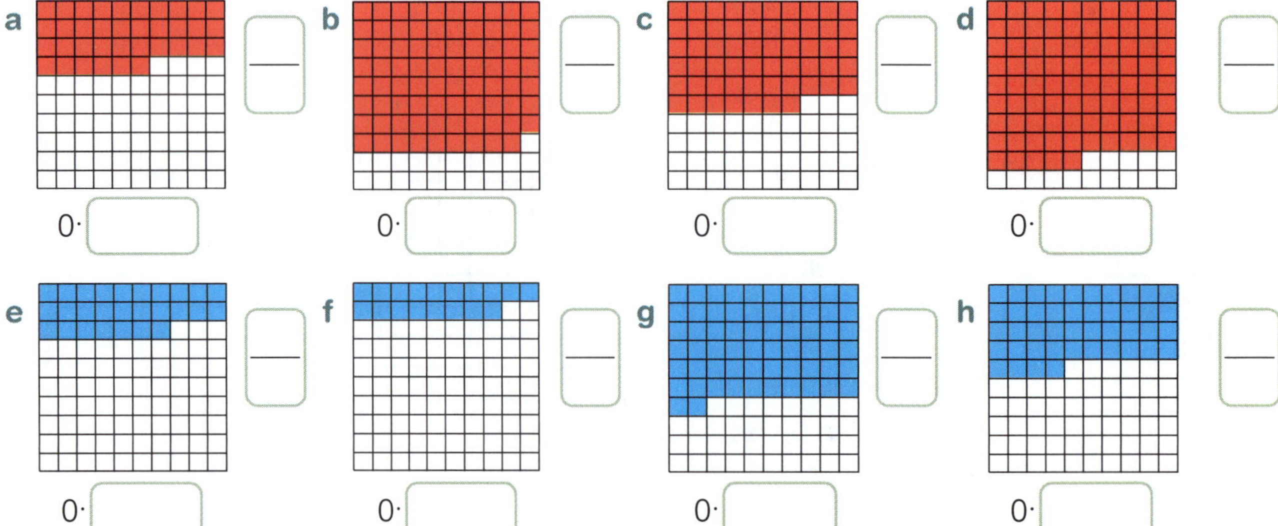

a 0·☐ b 0·☐ c 0·☐ d 0·☐

e 0·☐ f 0·☐ g 0·☐ h 0·☐

 ISBN 9780655708780

Tenths

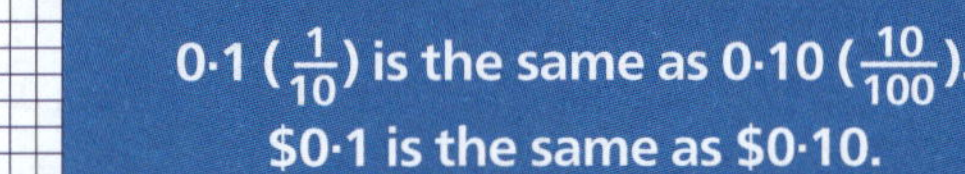

$0{\cdot}1$ ($\frac{1}{10}$) is the same as $0{\cdot}10$ ($\frac{10}{100}$).
$0·1 is the same as $0·10.

CONCEPT

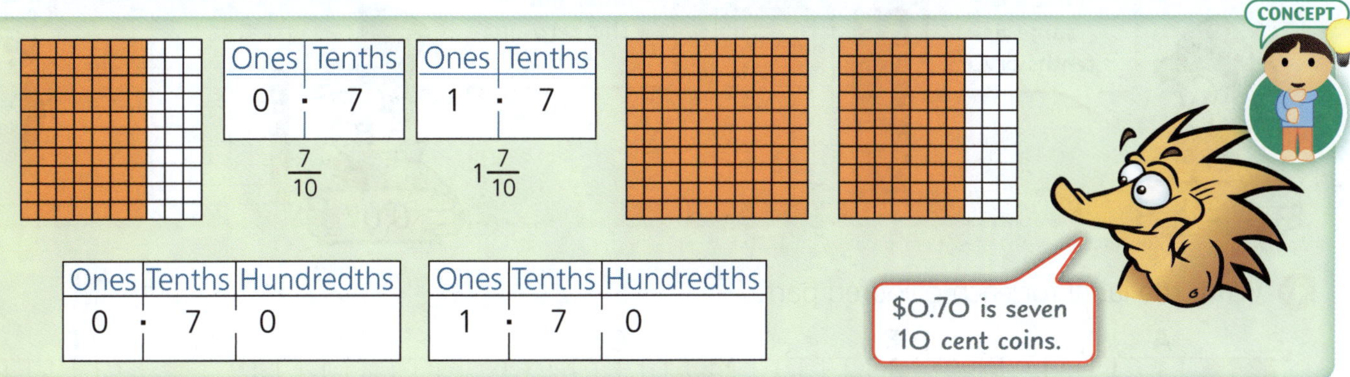

1. Write the decimal for:

a $\frac{7}{10}$ ☐ **b** $\frac{5}{10}$ ☐ **c** $\frac{6}{10}$ ☐ **d** $\frac{1}{10}$ ☐
e $\frac{8}{10}$ ☐ **f** $\frac{9}{10}$ ☐ **g** $\frac{2}{10}$ ☐ **h** $\frac{4}{10}$ ☐
i $1\frac{1}{10}$ ☐ **j** $1\frac{3}{10}$ ☐ **k** $1\frac{9}{10}$ ☐ **l** $1\frac{8}{10}$ ☐

2. Match each fraction with the correct decimal.

a

$\frac{5}{10}$	0·6
$\frac{1}{10}$	0·5
$\frac{6}{10}$	0·1

b

$\frac{8}{10}$	0·9
$\frac{4}{10}$	0·4
$\frac{9}{10}$	0·8

c

$1\frac{2}{10}$	2·3
$2\frac{7}{10}$	2·7
$2\frac{3}{10}$	1·2

3. Use decimals to write:

a 9 tenths ☐ **b** 7 tenths ☐ **c** 6 tenths ☐ **d** 2 tenths ☐
e 8 tenths ☐ **f** 3 tenths ☐ **g** 5 tenths ☐ **h** 10 tenths ☐
i zero point one ☐ **j** zero point eight ☐ **k** zero point five ☐
l one point nine ☐ **m** one point three ☐ **n** one point zero ☐

4. Complete the number lines.

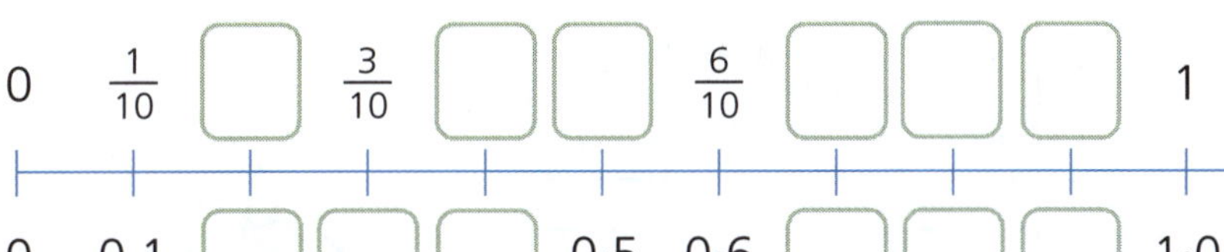

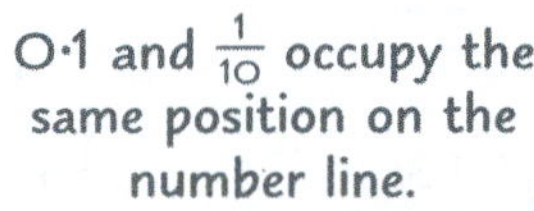

5. Tick the larger decimal.

a

0·2	
0·7	

b

0·23	
0·25	

c

0·5	
0·4	

d

0·15	
0·14	

0·1 = 0·10
0·2 = 0·20
0·3 = 0·30
0·4= 0·40

1:18 Comparing decimals

$\frac{20}{100}$ is 0·20 or 0·2.
$\frac{2}{100}$ is 0·02.
$\frac{35}{100}$ is 0·35.
$\frac{5}{100}$ is 0·05.

1 Write the label for each coloured part.

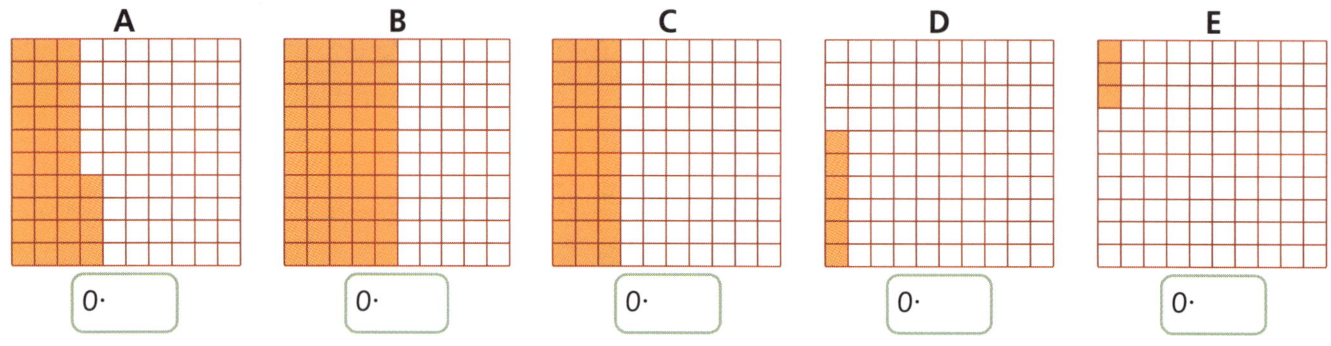

2 Which hundred square shows the bigger coloured fraction:

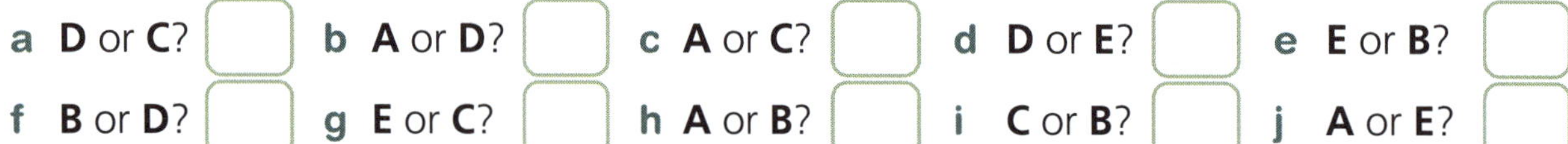

a **D** or **C**? ☐ **b** **A** or **D**? ☐ **c** **A** or **C**? ☐ **d** **D** or **E**? ☐ **e** **E** or **B**? ☐

f **B** or **D**? ☐ **g** **E** or **C**? ☐ **h** **A** or **B**? ☐ **i** **C** or **B**? ☐ **j** **A** or **E**? ☐

3 Which hundred square shows the biggest coloured fraction:

a **C**, **D** or **E**? ☐ **b** **A**, **C** or **E**? ☐ **c** **B**, **C** or **D**? ☐ **d** **A**, **D** or **E**? ☐ **e** **A**, **B** or **E**? ☐

4 Write the decimal fraction that follows:

a 0·26, 0·27, ☐ **b** 0·83, 0·84, ☐ **c** 0·47, 0·48, ☐ **d** 0·35, 0·36, ☐

5 Write the missing decimals under the number line.

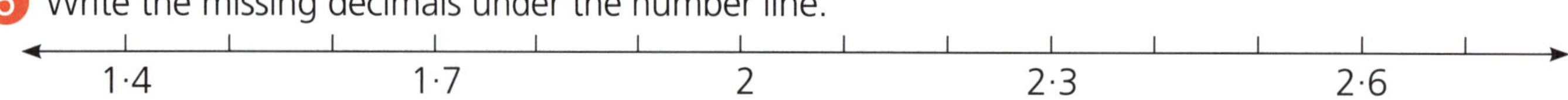

6 Tick the larger decimal.

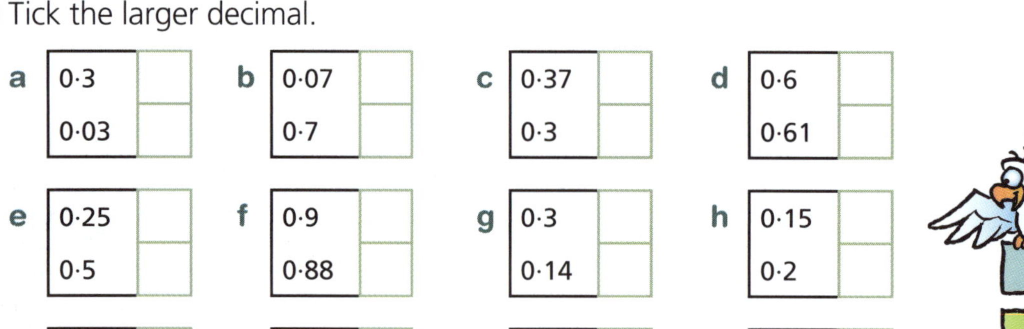

a	0·3 / 0·03	**b**	0·07 / 0·7	**c**	0·37 / 0·3	**d**	0·6 / 0·61
e	0·25 / 0·5	**f**	0·9 / 0·88	**g**	0·3 / 0·14	**h**	0·15 / 0·2
i	1·2 / 1·21	**j**	2·23 / 0·3	**k**	1·5 / 2·4	**l**	2·2 / 2·02

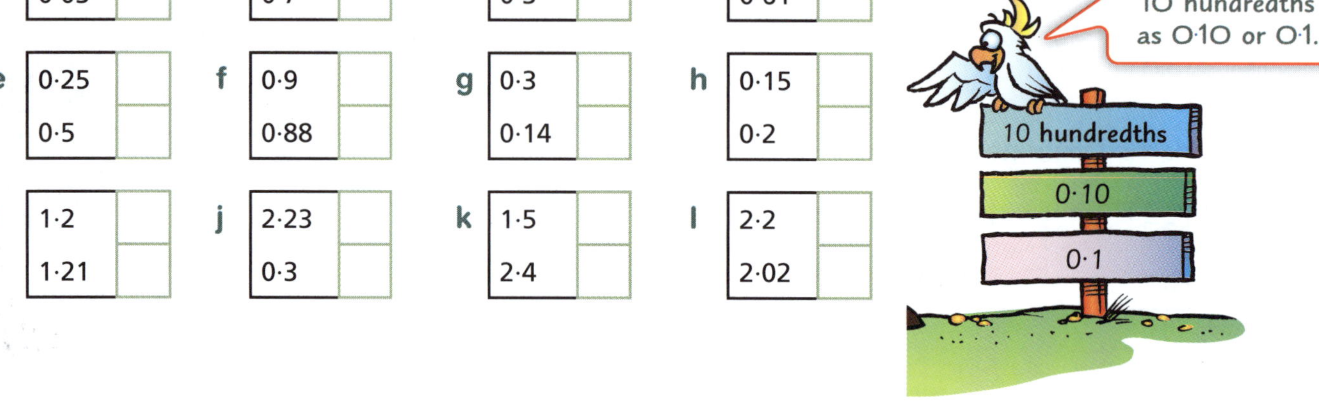

1:19 Place value in decimals

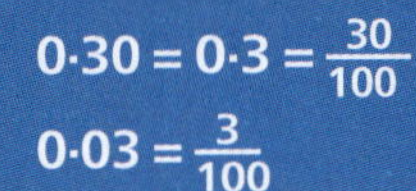

1 Match the part coloured on each hundred square with the correct label.

0·5 0·02 0·1 0·3 0·05 0·06 0·9 0·7 0·4 0·09

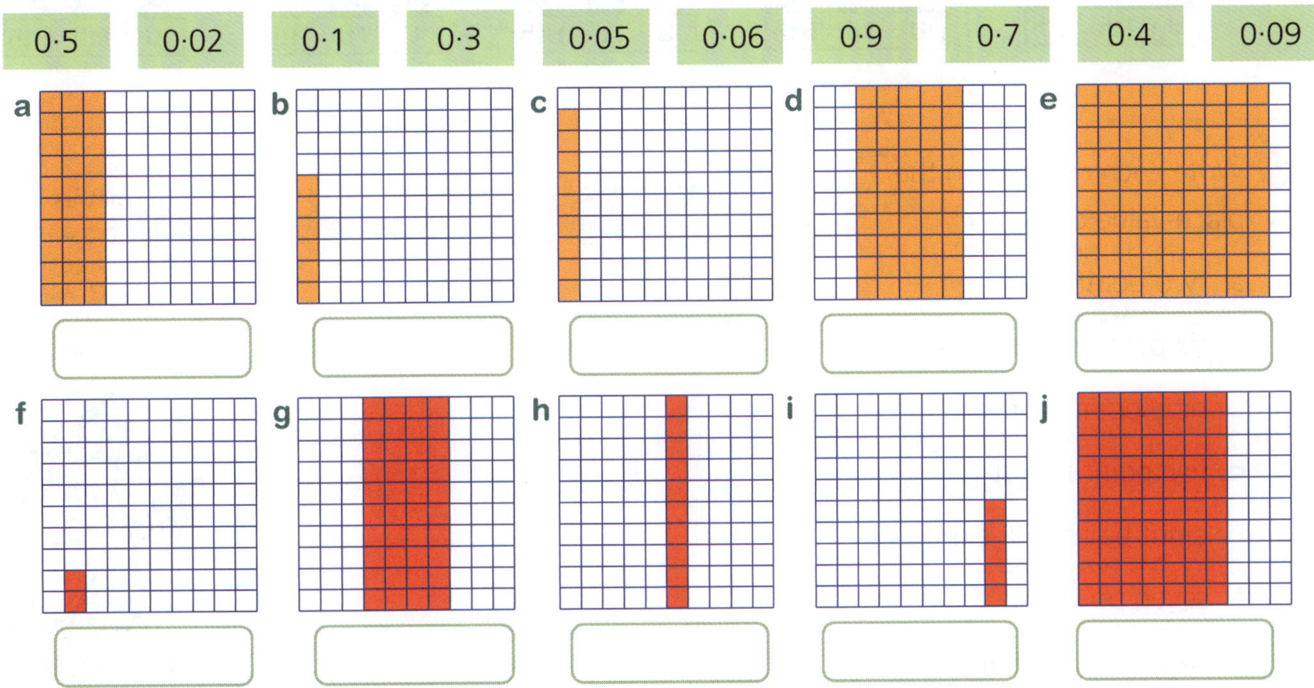

2 Colour part of each hundred square to match the given decimal.

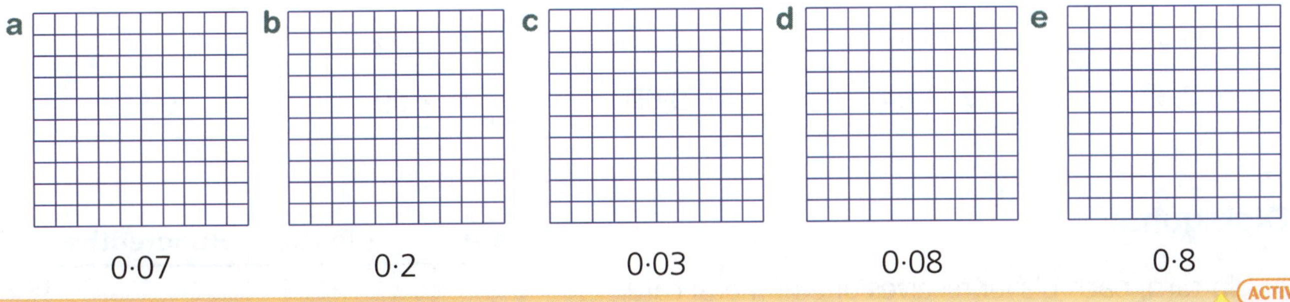

a 0·07 b 0·2 c 0·03 d 0·08 e 0·8

3 Use place-value blocks to model:

a 5 tenths **b** 3 hundredths **c** 4 tenths and 7 hundredths

d 0·3 **e** 0·7 **f** 0·02 **g** 0·06 **h** 0·4

i 0·52 **j** 0·89 **k** 0·72 **l** 0·67 **m** 0·99

ACTIVITY

1·12

1:20 Place value of hundedths

$16\frac{8}{100} = 16{\cdot}08$

$16\frac{80}{100} = 16{\cdot}80$ or $16{\cdot}8$

1 Write the numeral for:

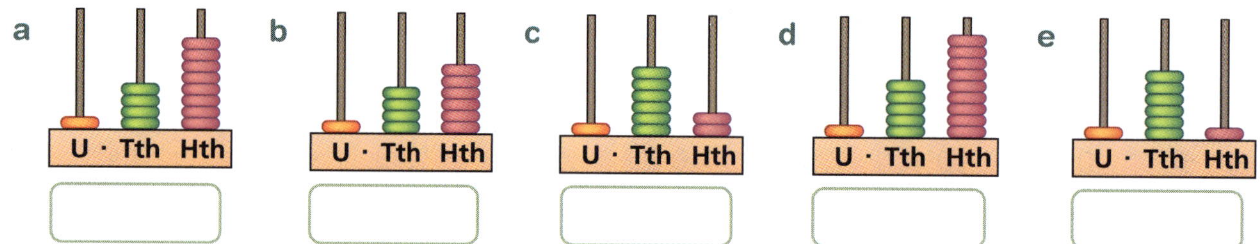

2 Write each number on the place-value chart.

	Units		Tenths	Hundredths
a two point five nine		·		
b six point seven three		·		
c nine point four one		·		
d five point two six		·		
e eight point four eight		·		
f seven point one three		·		
g six point seven nine		·		

2·59 metres is 2 metres and 59 hundredths of the next metre.

3 Write the value for each coloured digit.

a 4·3**2** b 8·**4**7 c **3**·95 d 5·3**8** e **1**·76

f 7·**5**1 g **2**·84 h 9·6**2** i 1·**6**9 j 6·5**1**

Digit game

- In turn, each player receives one numeral card from a dealer and places it in one column of a place-value chart.
- Two more cards are received and placed in the same way.
- The player with the largest number wins a point.

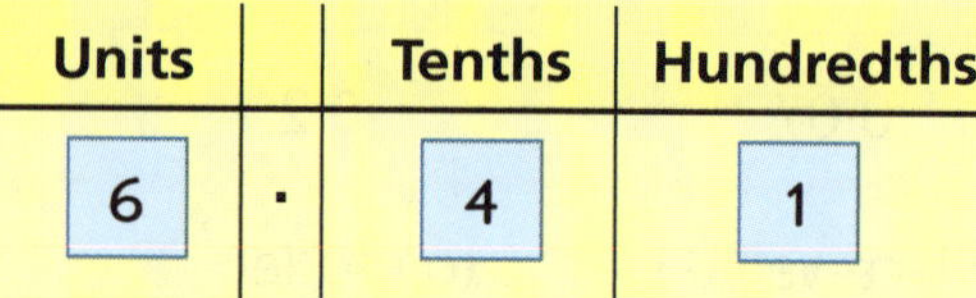

Units		Tenths	Hundredths
6	·	4	1

 • *AUSTRALIAN SIGNPOST MATHS 4* • ISBN 9780655708780

1:21 Reading and writing decimals

Is 1·25 larger than 1·5?

hundreds	tens	ones		tenths	hundredths
2	7	5	•	6	4
1	3	6	•	0	8
		9	•	4	0
	8	1	•	7	
		0	•	6	2

We can partition these decimals in different ways.

- 275·64 has 27 tens, 5 ones and 64 hundredths
- 136·08 has 136 ones and 8 hundredths
- 9·40 = 9·4 The zero is not necessary because 40 hundredths is the same as 4 tenths.
- 0·62 has 6 tenths and 2 hundredths

1 Use numerals to write:

a nineteen point seven five ☐
b forty point nine one ☐
c sixty-seven point eight two ☐
d thirty point zero six ☐
e fifty-two point one four ☐
f twenty-seven point four three ☐

2 Complete the following.

a 0·86 ☐ tenths and ☐ hundredths
b 0·09 ☐ tenths and ☐ hundredths
c 0·60 ☐ tenths and ☐ hundredths

3 Write the number represented by:

a 6 hundreds, 2 tens, 9 units, 3 tenths and 7 hundredths ☐
b 4 hundreds, 6 tens, 3 units, 0 tenths and 9 hundredths ☐
c 7 hundreds, 3 tens, 1 unit and 6 tenths ☐
d 9 hundreds, 5 tens, 7 units, 4 tenths and 2 hundredths ☐
e five and six tenths ☐
f ten and three tenths ☐
g two and eight tenths ☐
h seven and nine tenths ☐

$2.75 is read 'two dollars seventy-five'.
2·75 metres is read 'two point seven five metres.

4 Write the value for each coloured digit.

a 1**6**4·21 ☐
b 35**9**·73 ☐
c **8**47·35 ☐
d 652·**47** ☐
e 278·5**2** ☐
f 247·**38** ☐
g 5**1**6·69 ☐
h 7**5**9·57 ☐
i 316·**84** ☐
j 472·1**9** ☐
k 792·**62** ☐
l 134·**85** ☐

 • *AUSTRALIAN SIGNPOST MATHS 4* • ISBN 9780655708780

2:01 Number patterns

Skip counting helps you remember the multiplication tables.

Use skip counting to continue the patterns on this page. Add on the same number each time.

1 a 1, 2, 3, 4, ___, ___, ___, ___, ___, ___, ___

b 2, 4, 6, 8, ___, ___, ___, ___, ___, ___, ___

c 3, 6, 9, 12, ___, ___, ___, ___, ___, ___, ___

d 4, 8, 12, 16, ___, ___, ___, ___, ___, ___, ___

e 5, 10, 15, 20, ___, ___, ___, ___, ___, ___, ___

f 6, 12, 18, 24, ___, ___, ___, ___, ___, ___, ___

g 7, 14, 21, 28, ___, ___, ___, ___, ___, ___, ___

h 8, 16, 24, 32, ___, ___, ___, ___, ___, ___, ___

i 9, 18, 27, 36, ___, ___, ___, ___, ___, ___, ___

j 10, 20, 30, 40, ___, ___, ___, ___, ___, ___, ___

2 a 9, 10, 11, ___, ___ b 18, 20, 22, ___, ___

c 27, 30, 33, ___, ___ d 36, 40, 44, ___, ___

e 45, 50, 55, ___, ___ f 54, 60, 66, ___, ___

g 63, 70, 77, ___, ___ h 72, 80, 88, ___, ___

i 81, 90, 99, ___, ___ j 90, 100, 110, ___, ___

You could use me.

3 Consider your answers to Question 1. Describe the pattern made by the last digits of each number in part:

a b ___

b d ___

c e ___

d f ___

e h ___

f i ___

g j ___

4 Make two number patterns of your own.

a ___, ___, ___, ___ b ___, ___, ___, ___

Multiplication tables revision

Step 1: Have someone test you.

Step 2: For each table you don't know, make a card with the question on one side and the answer on the other.

Step 3: Carry these cards with you, testing yourself until you know them.

Use these steps to learn your 1, 2, 3, 5 and 10 times tables.

1 Use skip counting to complete.

×	0	1	2	3	4	5	6	7	8	9	10
1											
2											
3											
5											
10											

2 Complete these number wheels.

a

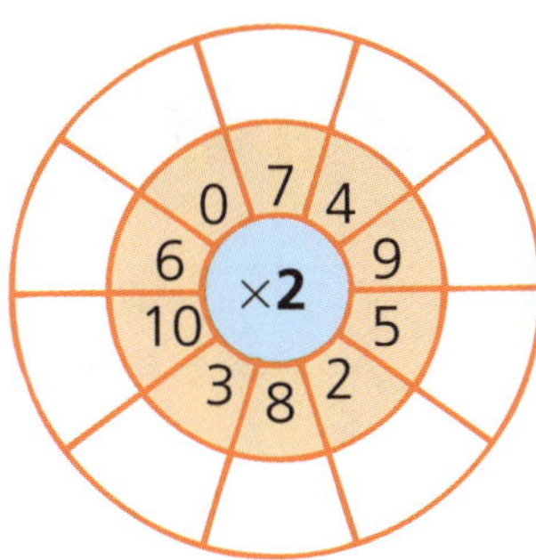

b

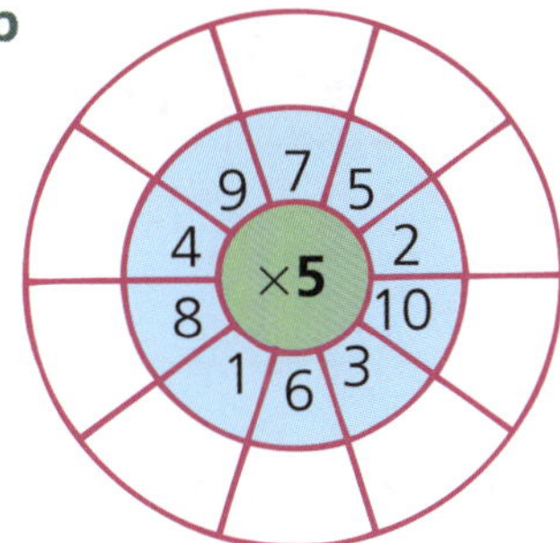

c

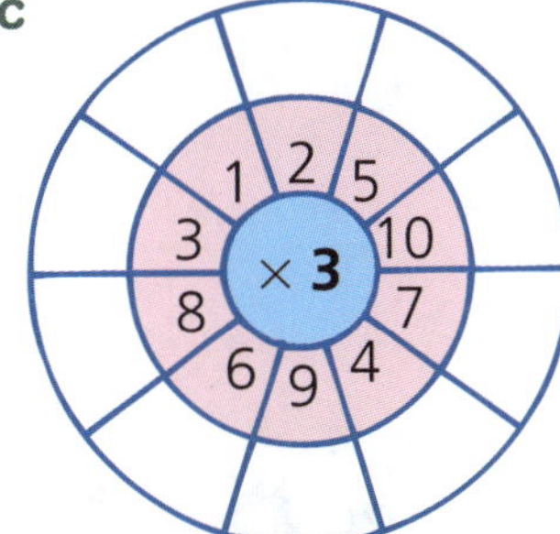

3

a $\begin{array}{r} 1 \\ \times\ 4 \\ \hline \end{array}$ **b** $\begin{array}{r} 5 \\ \times\ 6 \\ \hline \end{array}$ **c** $\begin{array}{r} 10 \\ \times\ 7 \\ \hline \end{array}$ **d** $\begin{array}{r} 2 \\ \times\ 5 \\ \hline \end{array}$

e $\begin{array}{r} 2 \\ \times\ 6 \\ \hline \end{array}$ **f** $\begin{array}{r} 1 \\ \times\ 8 \\ \hline \end{array}$ **g** $\begin{array}{r} 10 \\ \times\ 6 \\ \hline \end{array}$ **h** $\begin{array}{r} 2 \\ \times\ 7 \\ \hline \end{array}$

Multiplication cards

- Cards marked 1 to 10 are placed face down in a pile.
- One card is turned at a time. The first to correctly multiply the card by 5, keeps the card. The player with the most cards wins.

 AUSTRALIAN SIGNPOST MATHS 4 • ISBN 9780655708780

× 4 tables

4	4	4	4	4	4	4	4	4	4
× 1	× 2	× 3	× 4	× 5	× 6	× 7	× 8	× 9	× 10
4	8	12	16	20	24	28	32	36	40

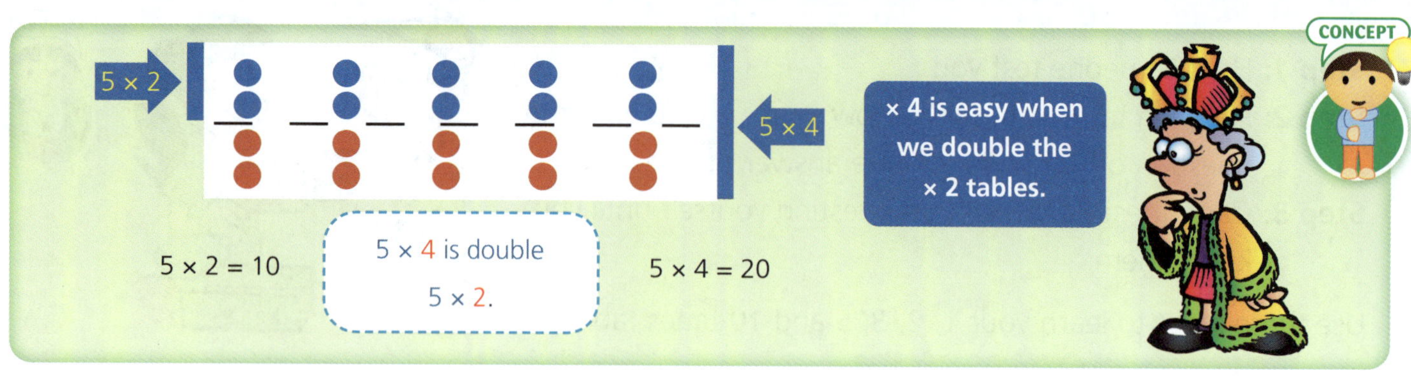

1 a 1 × 2 = ☐ 1 × 4 = ☐

b 7 × 2 = ☐ 7 × 4 = ☐

c 10 × 2 = ☐ 10 × 4 = ☐

d 8 × 2 = ☐ 8 × 4 = ☐

2 a

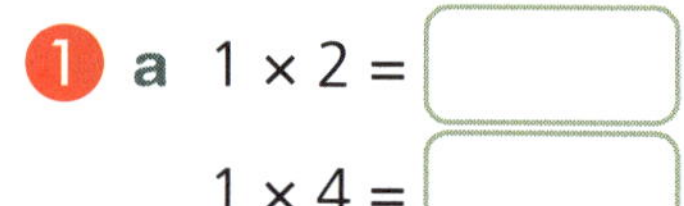

6 groups of 4 = ☐

b

7 groups of 4 = ☐

Use skip counting to complete.

c 4 groups of 4 = ☐

d 9 groups of 4 = ☐

e 8 groups of 4 = ☐

3 Complete the table.

×	0	1	2	3	4	5	6	7	8	9	10
2											
4											

4 a 3 groups of 4 cars

☐ × ☐ = ☐

b 5 groups of 4 cars

☐ × ☐ = ☐

c 10 groups of 4 cars

☐ × ☐ = ☐

d 11 groups of 4 cars

☐ × ☐ = ☐

5 Complete these number wheels.

a

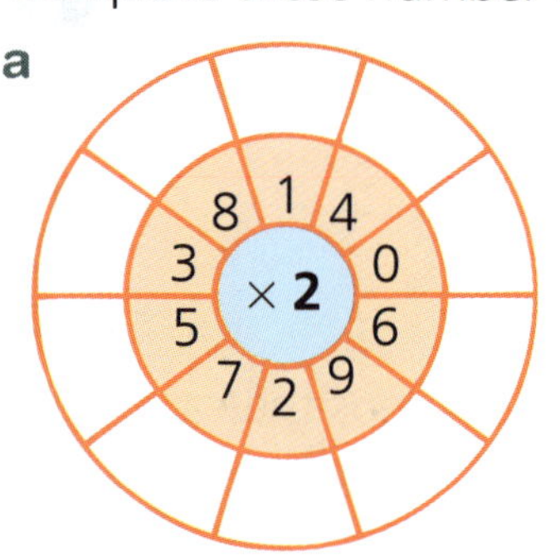

b

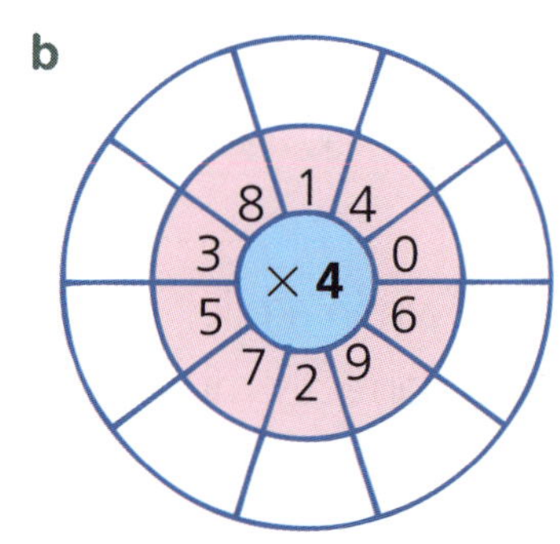

All answers to x 4 tables end in 2, 4, 6, 8 or 0.

2:04 Times tables review

If you know that $6 \times 5 = 30$ then $7 \times 5 = (6 \times 5) + 5 = 35$.

Start 4 8 10 12 16 20 24 28 30 32 36 40 44 48 50 60 70 80 90 100

CONCEPT

- Any number times 1 stays the same. $9 \times 1 = 9$
- Any number times 0 is equal to 0. $9 \times 0 = 0$
- To multiply by 4, we can double and double again.
  $6 \times 4 = (6 \times 2) \times 2 = 12 \times 2 = 24$
- To multiply by 10, place a zero at the end. $7 \times 10 = 70$
- To multiply by 5, you can multiply by 10 and halve the answer.
  $7 \times 5 = \text{half of } 7 \times 10 = 35$

$4 \times 5 = 5 \times 4$

1 Join each question to its answer, using a pencil and ruler.

a × 4

0 × 4	4
1 × 4	12
2 × 4	0
3 × 4	20
4 × 4	8
5 × 4	16
6 × 4	36
7 × 4	24
8 × 4	40
9 × 4	28
10 × 4	32

b × 4

3 × 4	0
0 × 4	12
5 × 4	4
1 × 4	28
7 × 4	20
2 × 4	32
8 × 4	40
4 × 4	8
6 × 4	36
10 × 4	24
9 × 4	16

c ×

6 × 10	0
3 × 1	10
4 × 0	2
5 × 2	3
2 × 1	60
7 × 2	12
4 × 10	10
6 × 2	80
10 × 1	14
9 × 2	40
8 × 10	18

x 2 answers end in: 0, 2, 4, 6, or 8.

x 10 answers end in: 0.

d × 5

1 × 5	15
2 × 5	25
3 × 5	20
4 × 5	5
5 × 5	10
6 × 5	40
7 × 5	30
8 × 5	0
9 × 5	50
10 × 5	35
0 × 5	45

e × 5

1 × 5	50
6 × 5	10
10 × 5	5
5 × 5	40
8 × 5	30
0 × 5	45
2 × 5	25
9 × 5	35
3 × 5	20
7 × 5	0
4 × 5	15

f ×

7 × 10	15
6 × 5	32
3 × 5	8
8 × 4	70
4 × 2	30
7 × 4	25
5 × 5	24
6 × 4	28
1 × 5	5
7 × 2	36
9 × 4	14

x 5 answers end in: 5 or 0.

40 **is:**
4 x 10
10 x 4
8 x 5

 • *AUSTRALIAN SIGNPOST MATHS 4* • ISBN 9780655708780

Addition, no trading

7 tens and 2 ones
+ 2 tens and 3 ones

CONCEPT

- 34 planes departed during the day and 12 during the night. How many planes departed?

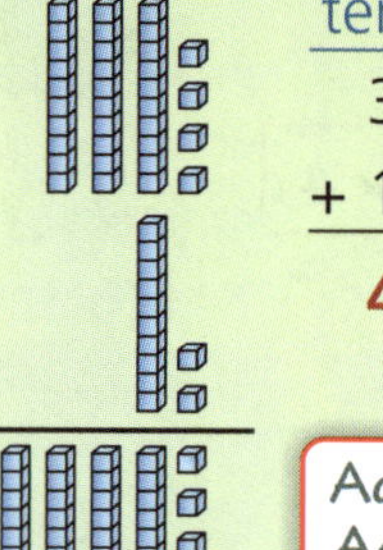

tens	ones
3	4
+ 1	2
4	**6**

Add the ones.
Add the tens.

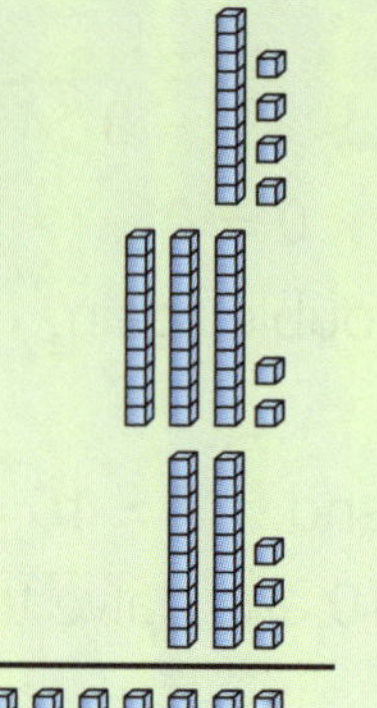

tens	ones
1	4
3	2
+ 2	3
6	**9**

This is the split strategy in columns.

1 Use the split strategy or place-value blocks to answer these.

a

tens	ones
9	2
+	6

b

tens	ones
4	2
+ 5	1

c

tens	ones
3	5
+ 6	2

d

tens	ones
1	5
+ 2	3

e

tens	ones
$5	0
+ $1	9

f

tens	ones
$2	3
+ $1	5

g

tens	ones
$4	4
+ $4	4

h

tens	ones
$2	7
+ $5	1

2 Use the split strategy or place-value blocks to answer these.

a

tens	ones
3	1
1	6
+ 2	2

b

tens	ones
2	3
4	2
+ 1	0

c

tens	ones
4	1
2	2
+ 1	3

d

tens	ones
2	4
1	4
+ 3	1

e

tens	ones
3	0
1	4
+ 3	2

f

tens	ones
4	2
1	5
+ 2	1

g

tens	ones
2	5
3	1
+ 1	3

h

tens	ones
3	2
4	1
+ 1	5

i

tens	ones
$5	1
$1	4
+ $2	2

j

tens	ones
$3	3
$4	0
+ $1	5

k

tens	ones
$2	0
$3	6
+ $2	1

l

tens	ones
$4	3
$3	1
+ $2	5

See *Extra Support 1* (Addition and subtraction facts).

 AUSTRALIAN SIGNPOST MATHS 4 • ISBN 9780655708780

Addition and subtraction, no trading

CONCEPT

- I bought 37 apples and sold 24. How many were left?

3 tens and 7 ones
− 2 tens and 4 ones

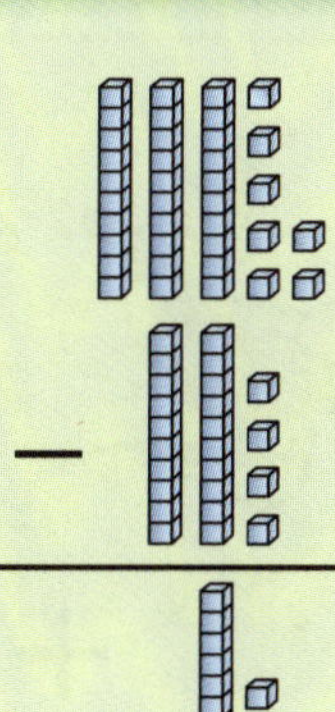

tens	ones
3	7
− 2	4
1	3

Subtract the ones.
Subtract the tens.

1

a

tens	ones
5	7
− 3	4

b

tens	ones
5	6
− 2	1

c

tens	ones
4	7
− 1	5

d

tens	ones
7	8
− 4	1

e

tens	ones
7	5
− 7	4

f

tens	ones
6	9
− 4	3

g

tens	ones
4	4
− 1	1

h

tens	ones
6	3
− 5	3

i

tens	ones
$8	4
− $8	0

j

tens	ones
$7	3
− $4	3

k

tens	ones
$9	9
− $3	2

l

tens	ones
$6	8
− $2	4

2 Model the question, write it as an algorithm, then find the answer.

a 23 candles
11 candles
54 candles
How many altogether?

tens	ones

b 30 lollies
25 lollies
14 lollies
How many altogether?

tens	ones

3 a I paid $23 for a shirt and $56 for pants. How much did I spend? ______

b There are 14 boys and 13 girls in our class. How many in our class? ______

4 Complete each number sentence.

a 47 birds, 35 fly away. How many remain?
______ = ______

b 56 books, 34 covered. How many more to cover?
______ = ______

c 74 needed, 61 collected. How many more to collect?
______ = ______

See *Extra Support 1* (Addition and subtraction facts).

 • *AUSTRALIAN SIGNPOST MATHS 4* • ISBN 9780655708780

2:07 Addition to 99 with trading

5 tens 14 ones
50 + 10 + 4
6 tens 4 ones

Thirty-eight ducks and twenty-six chickens were in the yard. How many birds were there altogether?

Find:
How many birds?

Number sentence:
38 + 26 = ☐

Answer:
64 birds were in the yard.

tens	ones
1	
3	8
+ 2	6
6	4

Show the trading on these algorithms.

1

a

tens	ones
2	2
+ 1	9

b

tens	ones
3	3
+ 5	7

c

tens	ones
1	5
+ 5	8

d

tens	ones
2	6
+ 5	8

e

tens	ones
1	6
+ 2	7

f

tens	ones
4	4
+ 3	8

g

tens	ones
6	2
+ 2	8

h

tens	ones
7	6
+ 1	9

i

tens	ones
	3
+ 8	9

j

tens	ones
8	1
+	9

k

tens	ones
2	5
+ 2	6

l

tens	ones
5	7
+ 2	7

2

a

tens	ones
$6	7
+ $	4

b

tens	ones
$	8
+ $5	4

c

tens	ones
$2	8
+ $3	8

d

tens	ones
$4	5
+ $1	7

3

a I have 42 English coins and 19 Turkish coins. How many coins do I have? ☐ coins

b We have 26 budgerigars and 58 finches. How many birds do we have? ☐ birds

c Hudson has 37 lizards and 18 snakes. How many reptiles does he have? ☐ reptiles

See *Extra Support 1* (Addition and subtraction facts).

2:08 Addition to 99 with trading

3 tens 12 ones
30 + 10 + 2
4 tens 2 ones

1

a
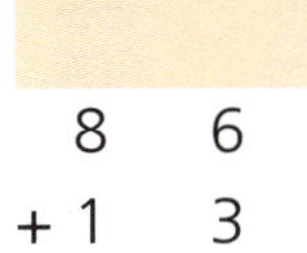

tens	ones
4	8
+ 4	6

b
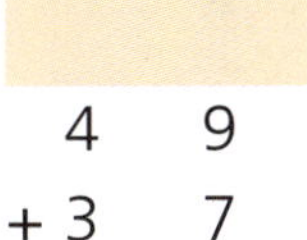

tens	ones
7	4
+ 1	6

c
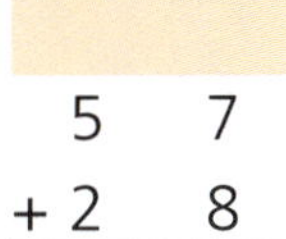

tens	ones
2	2
+ 7	5

d
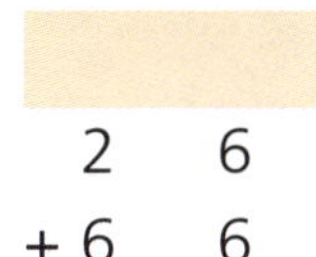

tens	ones
1	5
+ 5	9

e

tens	ones
8	6
+ 1	3

f

tens	ones
4	9
+ 3	7

g

tens	ones
5	7
+ 2	8

h
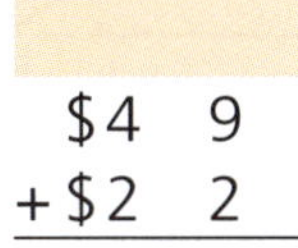

tens	ones
2	6
+ 6	6

i

tens	ones
$6	4
+ $2	9

j

tens	ones
$1	8
+ $5	3

k

tens	ones
$3	8
+ $3	8

l

tens	ones
$4	9
+ $2	2

CONCEPT

Example

How many rulers were in the classroom if 27 were on the desks and 35 were still in the cupboard?

Find:

How many rulers?

Number sentence:

27 + 35 = ☐

Answer:

There were 62 rulers in the classroom.

Working:

tens	ones
1	
2	7
+ 3	5
6	2

2 Answer these questions, following the process shown above.

a A group of emus has 13 females and 17 males. How many emus are there altogether?

Answer: ☐ emus

tens ones

b There were 37 kiwis in the zoo. 46 more hatched. How many kiwis are in the zoo now?

Answer: ☐ kiwis

tens ones

c A woman needed 20 metres of pink ribbon and 34 metres of blue ribbon. How much ribbon did she need?

Answer: ☐ metres

tens ones

d 28 finches and 12 doves were kept in a large aviary. How many birds were there altogether?

Answer: ☐ birds

tens ones

See *Extra Support 1* (Addition and subtraction facts).

 ISBN 9780655708780

2:09 Jump strategy, +

28 + 40 = ☐ 28 + 50 = ☐
28 + 10 = ☐ 28 + 20 = ☐
49 + 20 = ☐ 49 + 30 = ☐

CONCEPT

The jump strategy (addition)

28 + 57 = 28 + 50+ 2 + 5
= 85

Steps
1 Add the tens.
2 Jump to the next 10 if you can.
3 Add on anything left over.

To add 7, we add 2 then 5.

1. Use the jump strategy to answer these questions.

a 28 + 27 ☐ To add 7, we add 2 then 5.

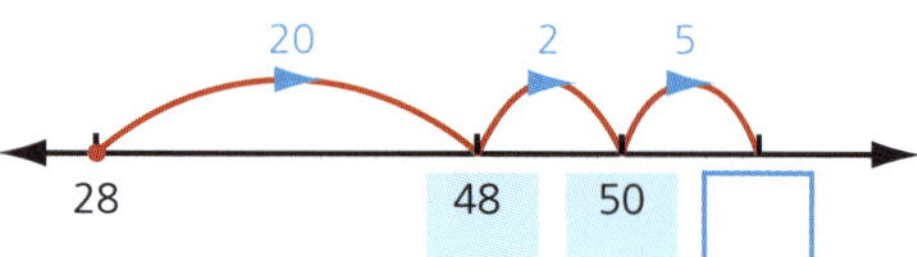

b 49 + 34 ☐ To add 4, we add 1 then 3.

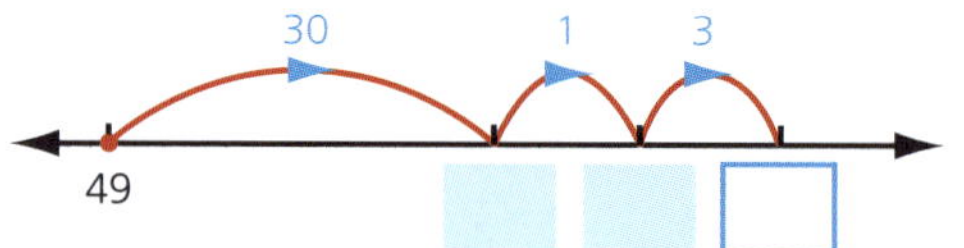

c 15 + 69 ☐

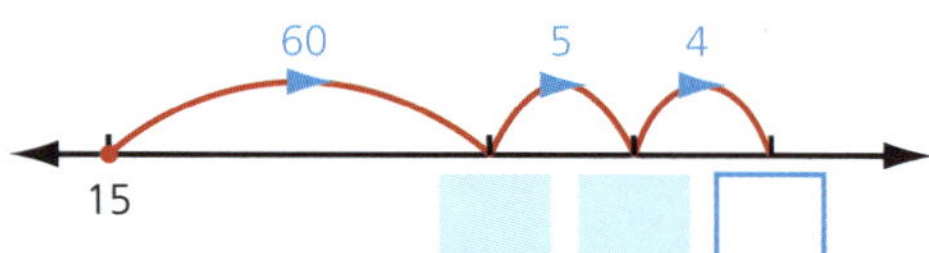

d 57 + 27 ☐

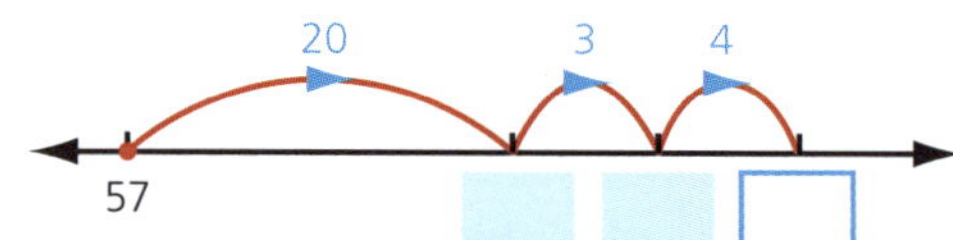

e 46 + 38 ☐

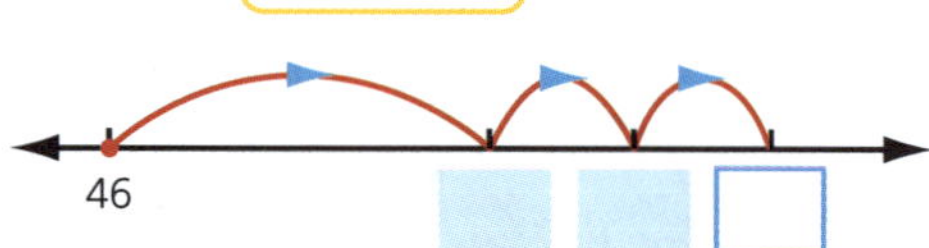

f 49 + 34 ☐

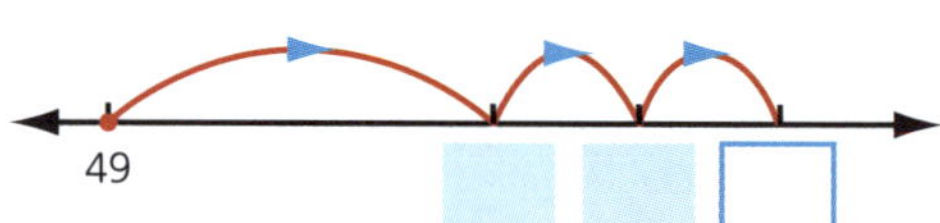

2. Use the jump strategy to answer these questions.

a 29 + 29 ☐

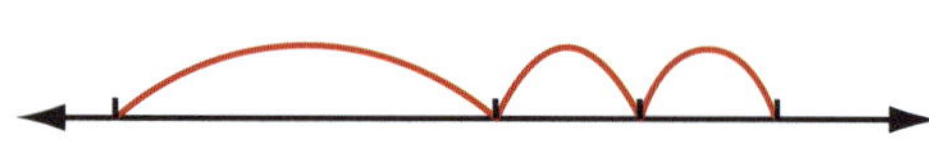

b 48 + 23 ☐

c 69 + 18 ☐

d 45 + 36 ☐

e 37 + 45 ☐

f 18 + 58 ☐

Do these on your own paper or in your head.

See Extra Support 2 (Building to the next 10).

2:10 Jump strategy, –

52 – 20 = ☐ 52 – 30 = ☐
72 – 10 = ☐ 72 – 20 = ☐
41 – 20 = ☐ 41 – 30 = ☐

CONCEPT

The jump strategy (subtraction)

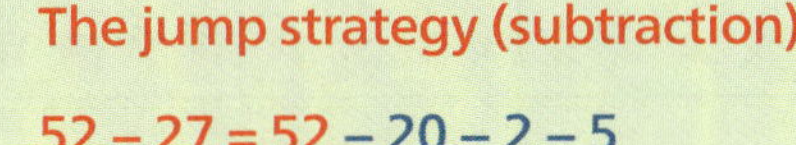

52 – 27 = 52 – 20 – 2 – 5
= 85

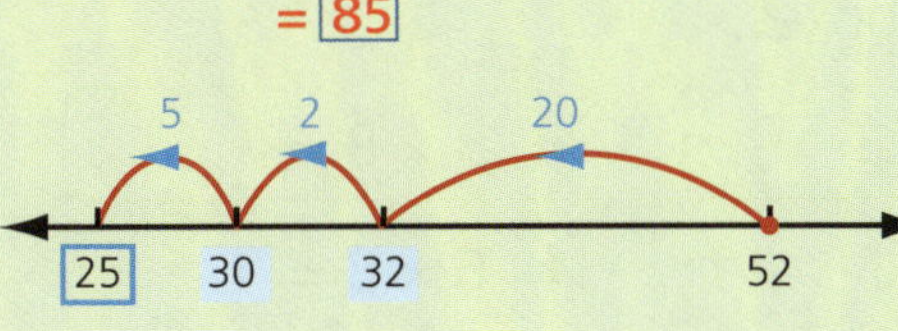

Steps
1 Subtract the tens.
2 Jump back to the next 10.
3 Take away anything left over.

To take away 7, we take away 2 then 5.

1 Use the jump strategy to answer these questions.

a 72 – 15 ☐ To take away 5, we take away 2 then 3.

b 41 – 28 ☐ To take away 8, we take away 1 then 7.

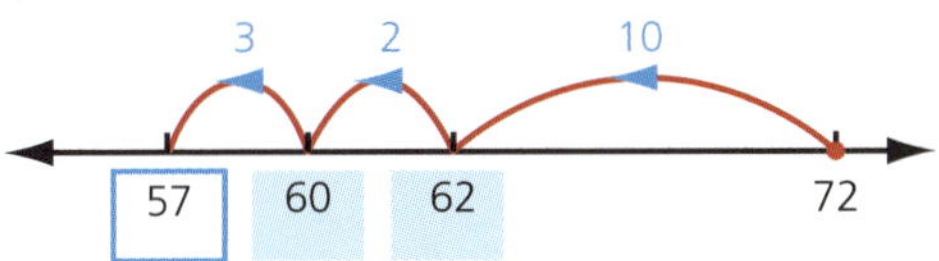
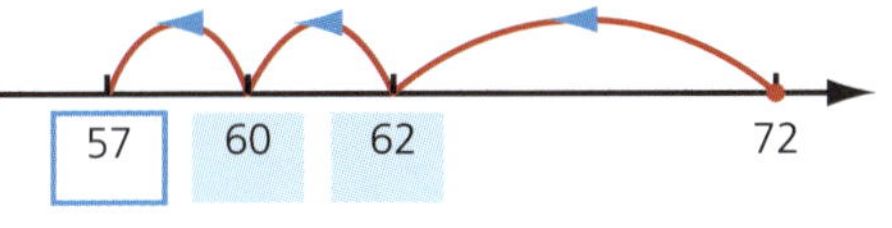

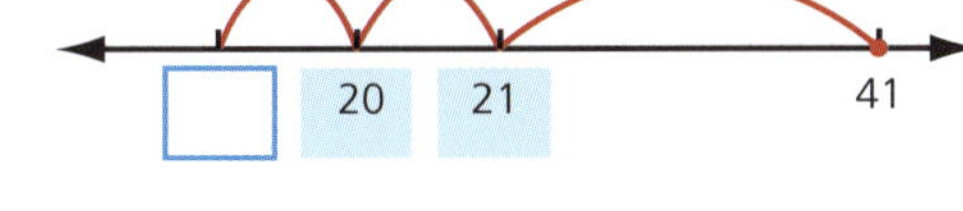

c 53 – 26 ☐ To take away 6, we take away 2 then 4.

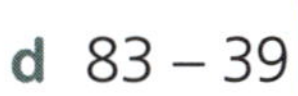

d 83 – 39 ☐ To take away 9, we take away 3 then 6.

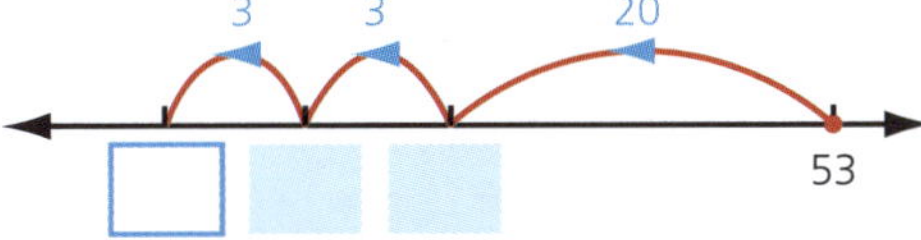

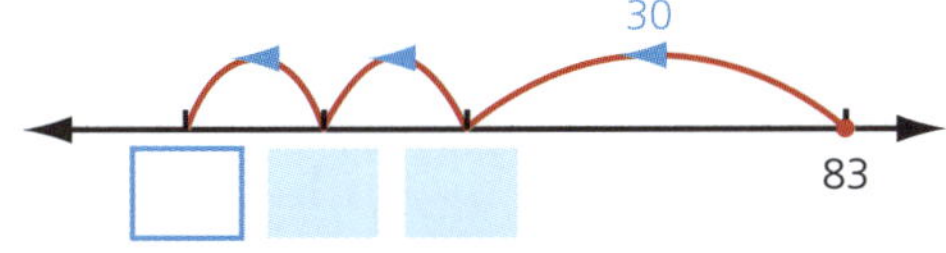

e 65 – 48 ☐

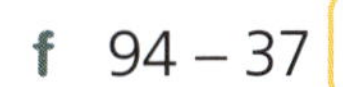

f 94 – 37 ☐

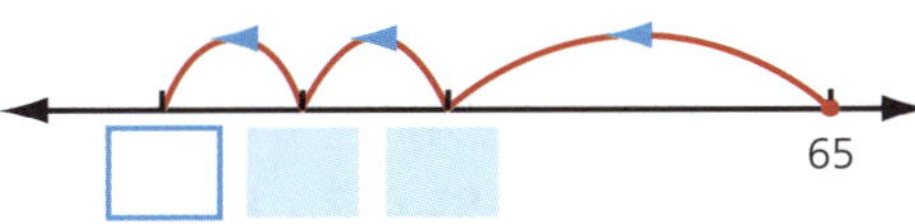

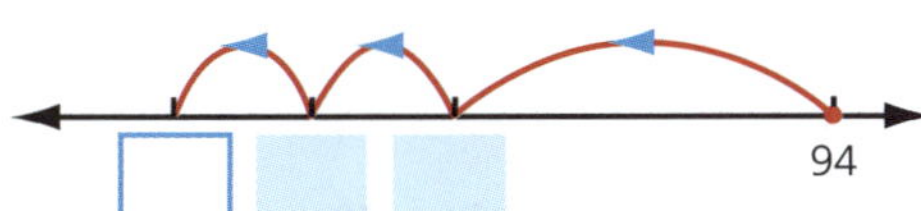

2 Use the jump strategy to answer these questions.

a 64 – 29 ☐

b 71 – 44 ☐

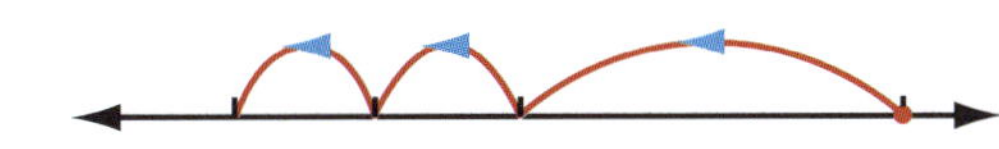

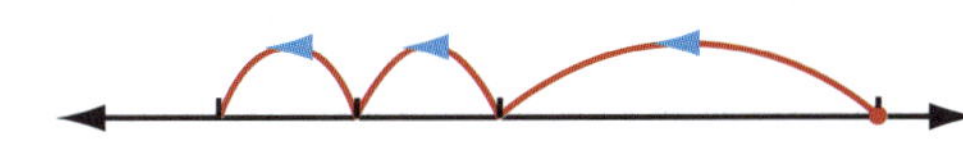

c 82 – 56 ☐

d 77 – 38 ☐

e 63 – 27 ☐

f 55 – 39 ☐

Do these on your own paper or in your head.

 • *AUSTRALIAN SIGNPOST MATHS 4* • ISBN 9780655708780

× 8 tables

Sing multiplication songs to learn your tables.

★★★★ ★★★★	★★★★ ★★★★	★★★★ ★★★★	★★★★ ★★★★	★★★★ ★★★★	★★★★ ★★★★	★★★★ ★★★★	★★★★ ★★★★	★★★★ ★★★★	★★★★ ★★★★

1 Count the groups of 8 to fill in the boxes.

Doubling the answers to '× 4' gives the answers to '× 8'.

a 1 × 8 = ☐ **b** 2 × 8 = ☐ **c** 3 × 8 = ☐

d 4 × 8 = ☐ **e** 5 × 8 = ☐ **f** 6 × 8 = ☐

g 7 × 8 = ☐ **h** 8 × 8 = ☐ **i** 9 × 8 = ☐

j 10 × 4 = ☐ so 10 × 8 = ☐ **k** 1 × 4 = ☐ so 1 × 8 = ☐

l 2 × 4 = ☐ so 2 × 8 = ☐ **m** 3 × 4 = ☐ so 3 × 8 = ☐

n 6 × 4 = ☐ so 6 × 8 = ☐ **o** 5 × 4 = ☐ so 5 × 8 = ☐

2 Complete:

a 3 groups of 8 = ☐ **b** 6 rows of 8 = ☐ **c** 5 eights = ☐

d 4 groups of 8 = ☐ **e** 7 lots of 8 = ☐ **f** 8 eights = ☐

g 1 group of 8 = ☐ **h** 9 rows of 8 = ☐ **i** 2 × 8 = ☐

j 0 groups of 8 = ☐ **k** 10 rows of 8 = ☐ **l** 11 × 8 = ☐

Skip counting by 3

3, 6, 9, 12, 15, 18, 21, 24, 27, 30, ...

Skip counting by 4

4, 8, 12, 16, 20, 24, 28, 32, 36, 40, ...

Skip counting by 8

8, 16, 24, 32, 40, 48, 56, 64, 72, 80, ...

Practise skip counting, just as you would learn a song.

7×8
$= (5 \times 8) + (2 \times 8)$
$= 40 + 16$
$= 56$

3 Do as many as you can without skip counting.

×	0	1	2	3	4	5	6	7	8	9	10
8											

×	5	3	7	4	2	9	10	1	8	6	0
2											
4											
8											
3											

 • *AUSTRALIAN SIGNPOST MATHS 4* • ISBN 9780655708780

× 8 tables

If you know that 6 × 5 = 30,
then 7 × 5 = (6 × 5) + 5 = 35.

CONCEPT

- The pattern of the last digit of the × 8 tables is 8, 6, 4, 2, 0. 8, 16, 24, 32, 40, 48, 56, ...
- To multiply by 4, we can double and double again. 6 × 4 = (6 × 2) × 2 = 12 × 2 = 24
- To multiply by 8, we can multiply by 4, then double. 6 × 8 = (6 × 4) × 2 = 24 × 2 = 48
- To multiply by 5, you can multiply by 10 and halve the answer. 7 × 5 = half of 7 × 10 = 35

1 Join each question to its answer, using a pencil and ruler.

a

	× 8	
0 × 8		16
1 × 8		24
2 × 8		0
3 × 8		48
4 × 8		8
5 × 8		32
6 × 8		56
7 × 8		80
8 × 8		40
9 × 8		64
10 × 8		72

b

	× 8	
3 × 8		0
0 × 8		24
5 × 8		56
1 × 8		64
7 × 8		32
2 × 8		8
8 × 8		40
4 × 8		80
6 × 8		16
10 × 8		72
9 × 8		48

c

	×	
10 × 6		72
3 × 4		40
9 × 8		30
5 × 6		60
5 × 8		16
7 × 8		12
4 × 4		64
8 × 4		24
8 × 8		56
3 × 8		48
6 × 8		32

x 8 answers end in: 8, 6, 4, 2, or 0.

x 10 answers end in: 0.

d

	× 5	
1 × 5		10
2 × 5		20
3 × 5		5
4 × 5		35
5 × 5		0
6 × 5		15
7 × 5		30
8 × 5		25
9 × 5		50
10 × 5		40
0 × 5		45

e

	× 3	
1 × 3		24
6 × 3		30
10 × 3		0
5 × 3		3
8 × 3		18
0 × 3		15
2 × 3		27
9 × 3		21
3 × 3		12
7 × 3		6
4 × 3		9

f

	× 4	
7 × 4		24
6 × 4		28
3 × 4		32
8 × 4		16
4 × 4		32
8 × 4		20
5 × 4		12
6 × 4		36
1 × 4		28
7 × 4		4
9 × 4		24

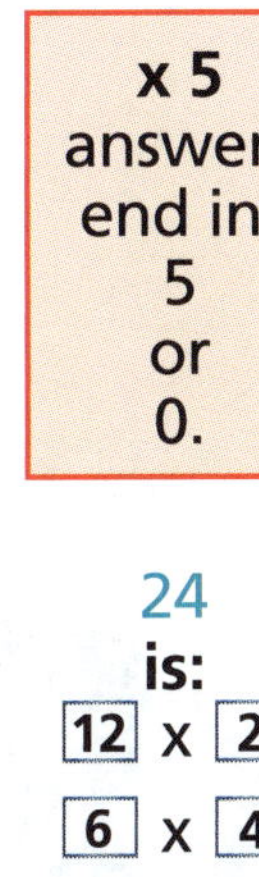

x 5 answers end in: 5 or 0.

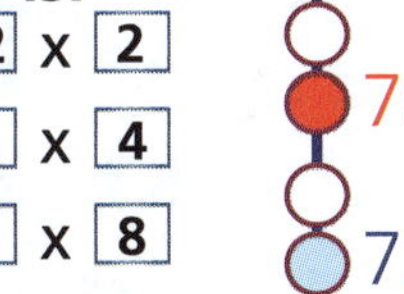

32 40 48 50 56 60 64 70 72 80 88 90 96 100

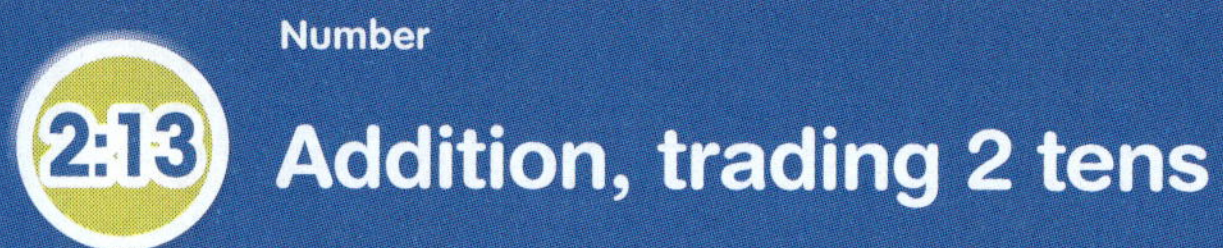

2:13 Addition, trading 2 tens

4 tens 24 ones
40 + 20 + 4
6 tens 4 ones

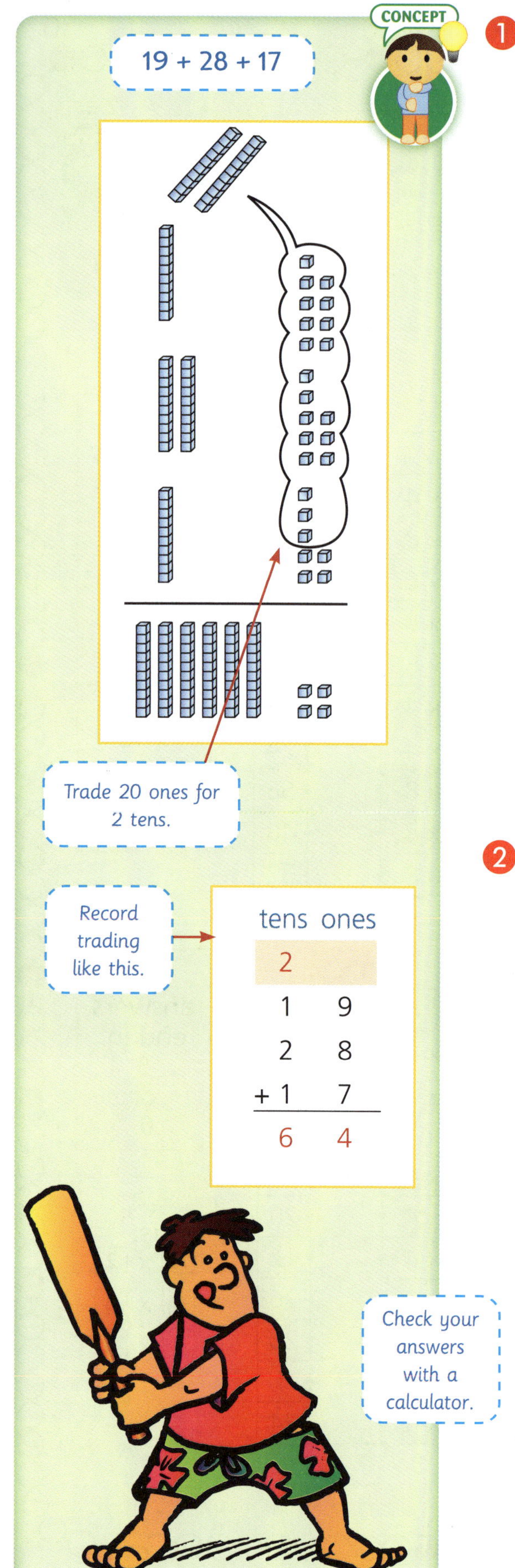

1

a

tens	ones
1	3
2	4
+ 2	5

b

tens	ones
2	6
3	3
+ 1	5

c

tens	ones
1	5
3	7
+ 2	9

d

tens	ones
3	8
2	7
+ 3	8

e

tens	ones
2	3
1	4
+ 3	6

f

tens	ones
	9
3	8
+ 2	9

g

tens	ones
4	4
3	4
+ 1	8

h

tens	ones
3	9
2	8
+ 1	5

i

tens	ones
2	8
2	8
+ 2	8

2

a

tens	ones
3	9
2	4
+ 1	3

b

tens	ones
2	8
3	6
+ 1	5

c

tens	ones
2	7
3	7
+ 2	8

d

tens	ones
3	7
2	9
+ 1	6

e

tens	ones
$1	4
$1	8
$2	6
+ $3	3

f

tens	ones
$1	2
$2	5
$1	7
+ $2	6

INVESTIGATION

- Adding 3 odd numbers gives an ______ number.

 • *AUSTRALIAN SIGNPOST MATHS 4* • ISBN 9780655708780

2:14 Addition involving hundreds

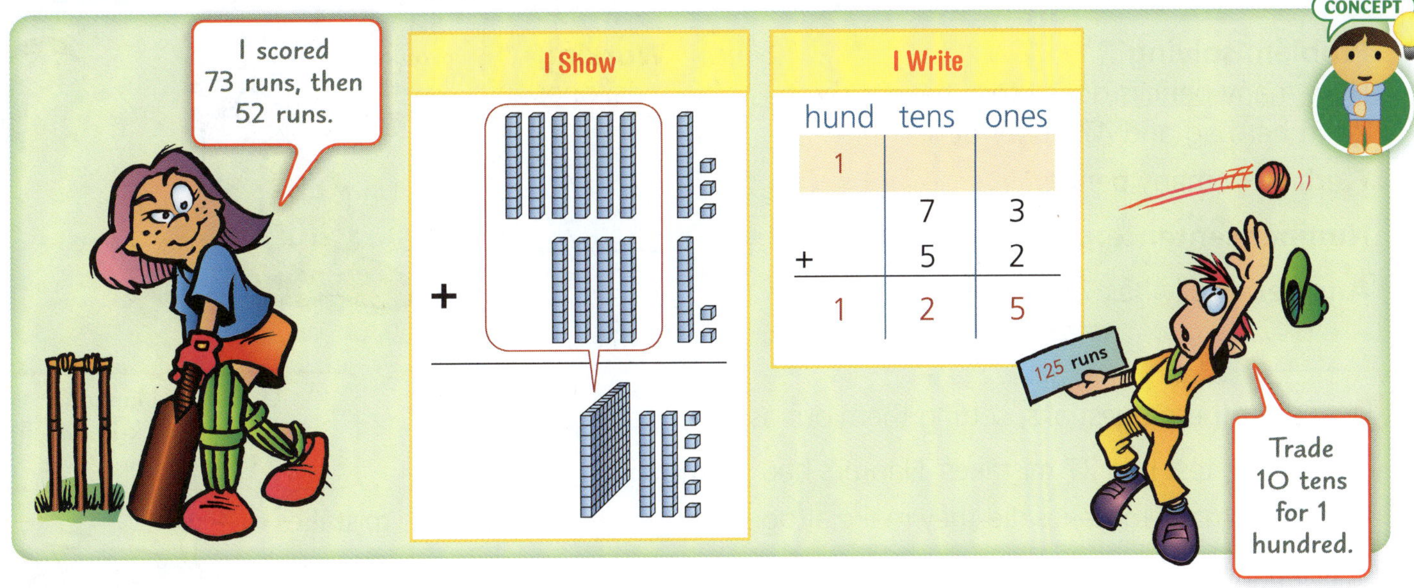

1. Model these with place-value blocks, then fill in the boxes.

a 61 books ☐ + ☐ = ☐
88 books
How many books altogether? ☐

b 94 stickers ☐ + ☐ = ☐
53 stickers
How many stickers altogether? ☐

2.

a

	hund	tens	ones
		5	8
+		6	0

b

	hund	tens	ones
		9	2
+		4	6

c

	hund	tens	ones
		8	5
+		7	2

d

	hund	tens	ones
		6	3
+		4	3

e

	hund	tens	ones
		7	4
+		8	5

f

	hund	tens	ones
		3	7
+		9	1

g

	hund	tens	ones
		9	4
+		6	1

h

	hund	tens	ones
		6	3
+		6	4

i

	hund	tens	ones
		7	2
+		5	7

3. In each part of Questions 1 and 2, estimate the answer by rounding off each number to the nearest ten and then adding.
In each case, ask: 'Is my answer reasonable?' If it is not, do the question again.

2:15 Addition problems to 99

Underline important words in the problem.

Problem solving
How many pencils does Molly have if she has 24 in her bag and 47 in her desk?

Find: How many pencils?

Number sentence: 24 + 47 = ☐

Answer: Molly has 71 pencils.

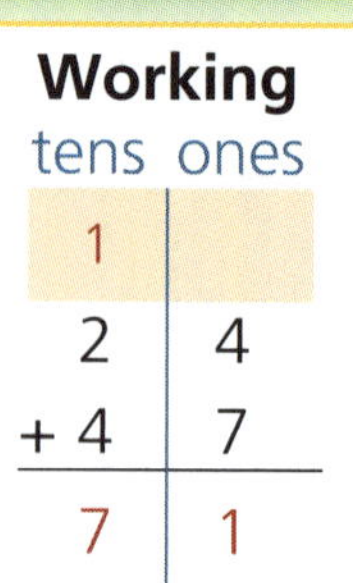

Working	
tens	ones
1	
2	4
+ 4	7
7	1

Use these blanks for working. Work in pencil so they can be reused.

1 Answer these questions, setting them out as shown above.

a Luke's test had 27 mistakes. Naomi's had 22 mistakes. How many mistakes did they make altogether? ☐ mistakes

b Brianna had 56 pet ants. Jordan caught 8 more and gave them to her. How many does she have now? ☐ ants

c Wen, an ancient Chinese king, began the first zoo 3000 years ago. He received 56 animals from the north and 27 from the south. How many animals did he receive altogether? ☐ animals

d At night, an owl can see about 100 times better than a human. In one week an owl caught 53 mice. In the next week it caught 38. How many mice did it catch altogether? ☐ mice

e At a waterhole, Michelle photographed 31 magpie geese, 12 Burdekin ducks and 8 pied herons. How many birds did she photograph altogether? ☐ birds

f A family of 18 bandicoots lived near 13 possums and 6 native rats. How many animals were there altogether? ☐ animals

2 a Alan saw three varieties of finch in one paddock. There were 35 zebra finches, 15 double-bar finches and 27 spice finches. How many were there altogether? ☐ finches

b On Phillip Island, 37 penguins came ashore before 6 pm. In the next hour 8 more arrived. How many had arrived by 7 pm? ☐ penguins

c Consecutive numbers follow one after the other. Find the sum of the consecutive numbers 28, 29 and 30. ☐ is the sum

d In a Test cricket series, Eric batted three times. His scores were 44, 28 and 19. What was his total score? ☐ runs

tens	ones

tens	ones

tens	ones

× 3, × 6 tables

Carry cards with you, so you can learn your tables.

★★★★ ★★	★★★★ ★★	★★★★ ★★	★★★★ ★★	★★★★ ★★	★★★★ ★★	★★★★ ★★	★★★★ ★★	★★★★ ★★	★★★★ ★★

1 Count the groups of 6 to fill in the boxes.

a 1 × 6 = ☐ **b** 2 × 6 = ☐ **c** 3 × 6 = ☐
d 4 × 6 = ☐ **e** 5 × 6 = ☐ **f** 6 × 6 = ☐
g 7 × 6 = ☐ **h** 8 × 6 = ☐ **i** 9 × 6 = ☐

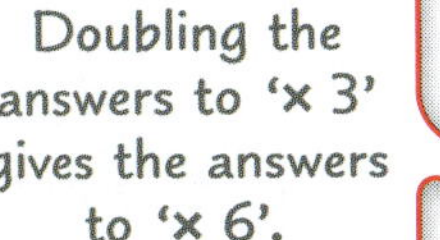

j 10 × 3 = ☐ so 10 × 6 = ☐ **k** 1 × 3 = ☐ so 1 × 6 = ☐
l 2 × 3 = ☐ so 2 × 6 = ☐ **m** 3 × 3 = ☐ so 3 × 6 = ☐
n 6 × 3 = ☐ so 6 × 6 = ☐ **o** 5 × 3 = ☐ so 5 × 6 = ☐

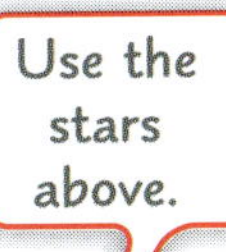

2 Complete:

a 3 groups of 6 = ☐ **b** 6 rows of 6 = ☐ **c** 5 sixes = ☐
d 4 groups of 6 = ☐ **e** 7 lots of 6 = ☐ **f** 8 sixes = ☐
g 1 group of 6 = ☐ **h** 9 rows of 6 = ☐ **i** 2 × 6 = ☐
j 0 groups of 6 = ☐ **k** 10 rows of 6 = ☐ **l** 11 × 6 = ☐

- The numbers in Skip counting by 6 are double the numbers in Skip counting by 3.

Skip counting by 3

3, 6, 9, 12, 15, 18, 21, 24, 27, 30, ...

Skip counting by 6

6, 12, 18, 24, 30, 36, 42, 48, 54, 60, ...

Practise skip counting, just as you would learn a song.

7×6
$= (5 \times 6) + (2 \times 6)$
$= 30 + 12$
$= 42$

3 Do as many as you can without skip counting.

×	0	1	2	3	4	5	6	7	8	9	10
3											
6											

×	5	3	7	4	2	9	10	1	8	6	0
3											
6											

 • *AUSTRALIAN SIGNPOST MATHS 4* • ISBN 9780655708780

2:17 × 3 and × 6 tables

Rub out the pencil lines and do the questions again.

CONCEPT

- When multiplying by 3 or 6, the sum of the digits will be in the pattern 3, 6, 9, 12, ...
  8 × 3 = 24 (2 + 4 = 6), 8 × 6 = 48 (4 + 8 = 12), 9 × 6 = 54 (5 + 4 = 9).
- To multiply by 6, you could multiply by 3, then double. 6 × 3 = 18 so 6 × 6 = 2 × 18 = 36.
- If you know that 3 × 6 = 18, then you know that 6 × 3 = 18. 6 × 8 = 8 × 6 = 48.

1 Join each question to its answer, using a pencil and ruler.

a

	× 3	
0 × 3		6
1 × 3		9
2 × 3		0
3 × 3		18
4 × 3		3
5 × 3		12
6 × 3		21
7 × 3		30
8 × 3		15
9 × 3		24
10 × 3		27

b

	× 3	
3 × 3		0
0 × 3		9
5 × 3		21
1 × 3		24
7 × 3		12
2 × 3		3
8 × 3		15
4 × 3		30
6 × 3		6
10 × 3		27
9 × 3		18

c

	×	
8 × 5		27
7 × 2		80
9 × 3		56
7 × 8		40
8 × 10		0
6 × 1		14
4 × 0		24
9 × 5		35
8 × 3		6
7 × 5		72
9 × 8		45

× 2
× 4
× 8
answers end in: 8, 6, 4, 2, or 0.

× 10 answers end in: 0.

× 5 answers end in: 5 or 0.

d

	× 6	
1 × 6		12
2 × 6		24
3 × 6		6
4 × 6		42
5 × 6		0
6 × 6		18
7 × 6		36
8 × 6		30
9 × 6		60
10 × 6		48
0 × 6		54

e

	× 6	
1 × 6		48
6 × 6		60
10 × 6		0
5 × 6		6
8 × 6		36
0 × 6		30
2 × 6		54
9 × 6		42
3 × 6		24
7 × 6		12
4 × 6		18

f

	×	
7 × 3		42
7 × 6		21
6 × 3		36
6 × 6		24
8 × 3		48
8 × 6		15
5 × 3		18
5 × 6		12
9 × 3		54
9 × 6		27
4 × 3		30

24 **is:**
8 × 3
4 × 6
3 × 8

33 36 40 42 48 50 54 60 66 70 72 80 90 100

 • *AUSTRALIAN SIGNPOST MATHS 4* • ISBN 9780655708780

Subtraction with trading

7 tens and 2 ones is the same as 6 tens and 12 ones.

CONCEPT

When adding, we trade 10 ones for 1 ten.

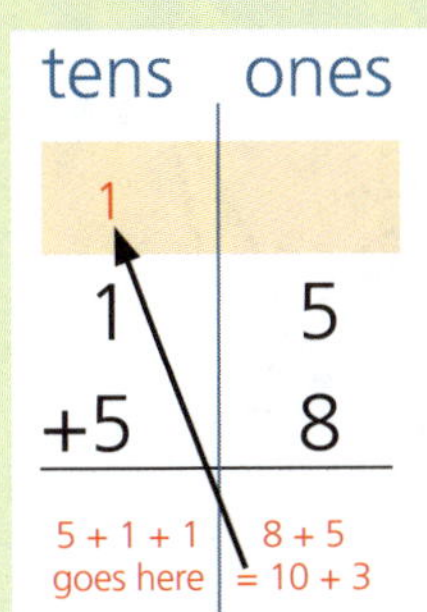

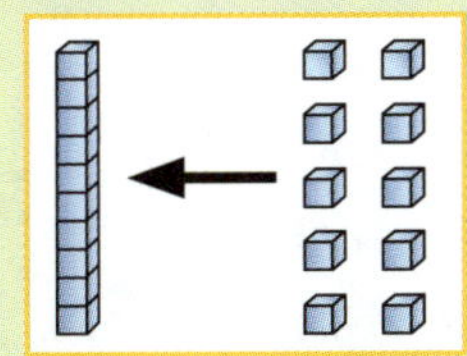

We change ten of the 13 ones into 1 ten. That leaves 3 in the ones place.

When subtracting, we trade 1 ten for 10 ones.

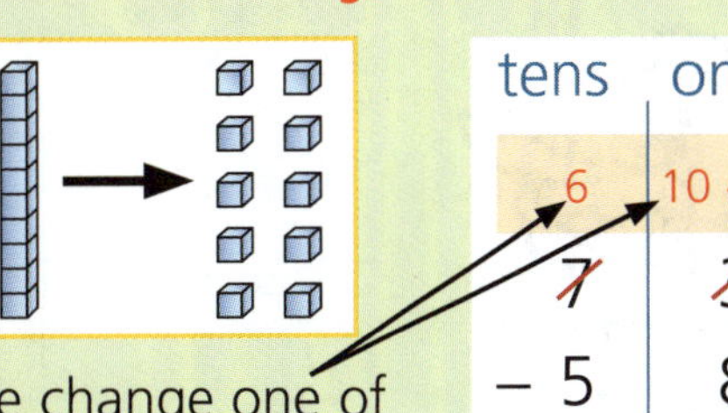

We change one of the 7 tens into 10 ones. That leaves 6 in the tens place.

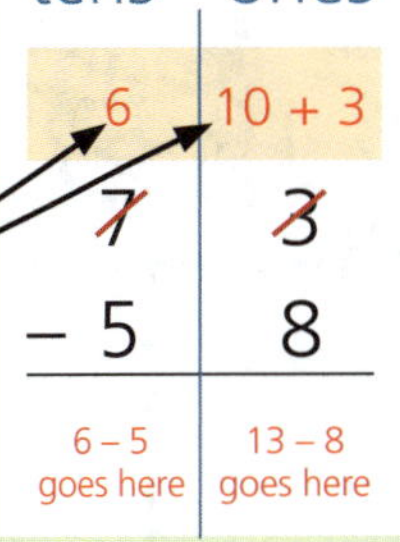

Trading down

1 34 cakes, 18 eaten. How many left?

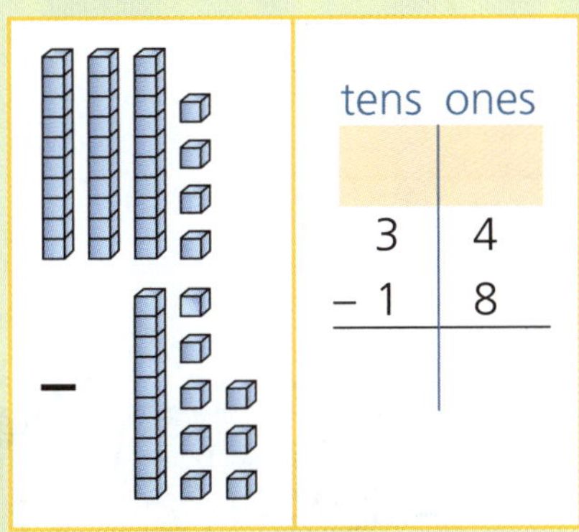

tens	ones
3	4
– 1	8

2 I can't take 8 ones from 4 ones. Trade 1 ten for 10 ones.

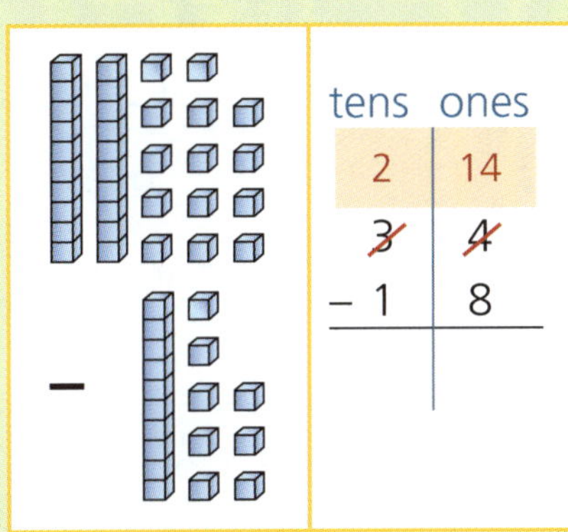

tens	ones
2	14
~~3~~	~~4~~
– 1	8

3 14 ones take away 8 ones leaves 6 ones. 2 tens take away 1 ten leaves 1 ten.

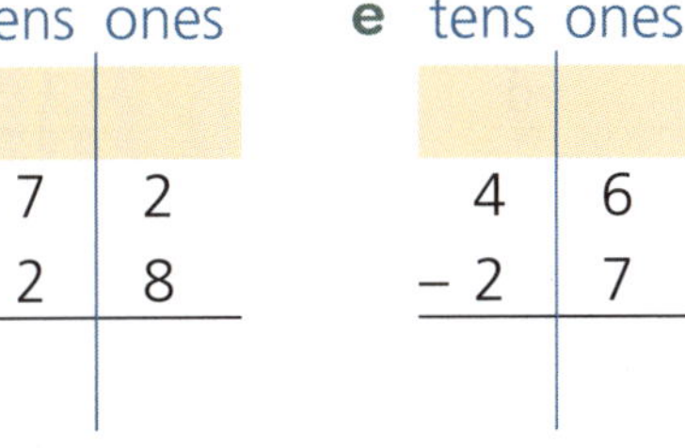

Answer
16 cakes were left uneaten.

tens	ones
2	14
~~3~~	~~4~~
– 1	8
1	6

1 You may use place-value blocks to do these. Estimate your answer first.

a

tens	ones
4	3
– 1	7

b

tens	ones
6	5
– 2	9

c

tens	ones
9	1
– 5	4

d

tens	ones
7	2
– 2	8

e

tens	ones
4	6
– 2	7

f

tens	ones
5	6
– 3	8

g

tens	ones
9	1
– 1	8

h

tens	ones
8	6
– 3	9

i

tens	ones
7	2
– 3	4

j

tens	ones
6	1
– 4	3

2 **a** Paul has 43 animal cards. I have 17 cards. How many more cards does Paul have?

b Rachel had $83. Felicity spent 2 hours cleaning the home. If Rachel gave Felicity $38 for the work done, how much does Rachel have left?

 • *AUSTRALIAN SIGNPOST MATHS 4* • ISBN 9780655708780

2:19 Subtracting from tens

1 Show trading down to 1 ten.

	tens	ones
a	5	0
b	7	0
c	4	0
d	9	0

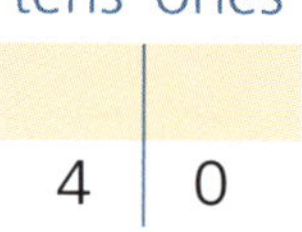

2

	tens	ones
a	6	0
	–	8
b	5	0
	–	4
c	9	0
	–	7

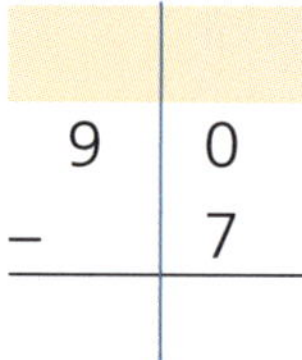

We don't need to write 'tens' and 'ones'.

	tens	ones
d	4	0
	– 1	6
e	3	0
	– 2	1
f	7	0
	– 3	5
g	8	0
	– 6	2
h	2	0
	– 1	3
i	6	0
	– 4	4
j	9	0
	– 5	9
k	$7	0
	– $5	6
l	$4	0
	– $2	7
m	$8	0
	– $3	5
n	$9	0
	– $4	2

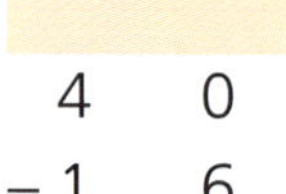

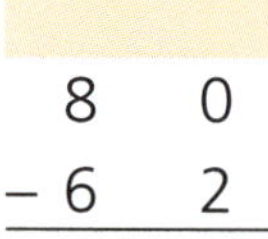

3 Scott had $90. Lachlan spent 2 hours cleaning the home. Scott gave Lachlan $28 for the work he did. How much does Scott have left?

 • *AUSTRALIAN SIGNPOST MATHS 4* • ISBN 9780655708780

2:20 Subtracting with trading

3 tens 3 ones is the same as 2 tens and 13 ones.

1

	tens	ones
a	3	1
	– 2	5
b	2	3
	– 1	6
c	4	6
	– 3	8
d	3	4
	– 2	7
e	5	2
	– 3	4
f	7	5
	– 5	9
g	6	7
	– 4	8
h	5	2
	– 3	7
i	8	4
	– 6	8
j	6	8
	– 4	9
k	9	1
	– 5	3
l	7	3
	– 2	9
m	3	7
	–	9
n	4	4
	– 1	5
o	3	8
	– 1	9
p	6	2
	–	7
q	\$5	5
	– \$2	9
r	\$7	2
	– \$5	4
s	\$8	0
	– \$4	3

Use a calculator to check your answers.

× 9 tables

To add 9, add 10 then take away 1.

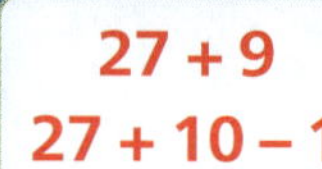

Skip counting by 9. (The 2 digits add to make 9 each time.)

9, 18, 27, 36, 45, 54, 63, 72, 81, 90, . . .

As the tens digit goes up by 1, the ones digit comes down by 1.

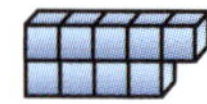     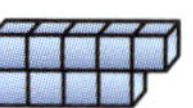 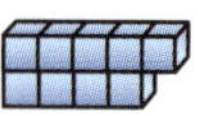 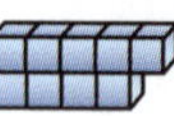 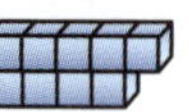 

1 Use the blocks above to complete these × 9 tables.

a 1 × 9 = ☐
b 2 × 9 = ☐
c 3 × 9 = ☐
d 4 × 9 = ☐
e 5 × 9 = ☐
f 6 × 9 = ☐
g 7 × 9 = ☐
h 8 × 9 = ☐
i 9 × 9 = ☐
j 10 × 9 = ☐

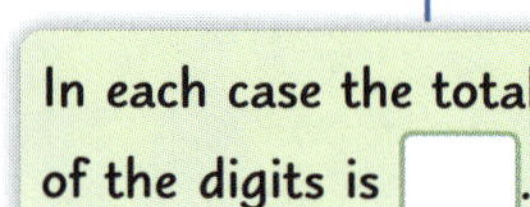

2 Use the method in the concept box to do these.

a 10 × 9 = ☐
b 9 × 9 = ☐
c 8 × 9 = ☐
d 7 × 9 = ☐
e 6 × 9 = ☐
f 5 × 9 = ☐
g 4 × 9 = ☐
h 3 × 9 = ☐
i 2 × 9 = ☐
j 1 × 9 = ☐

CONCEPT

4 × 9 is 4 × 10 take away 4.
4 × 9 = 40 − 4

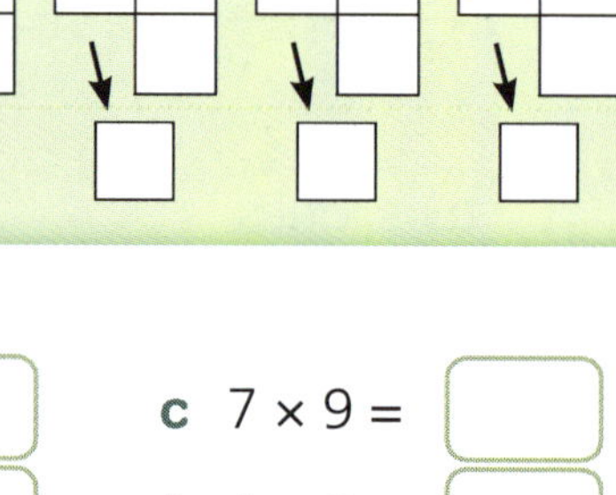

3

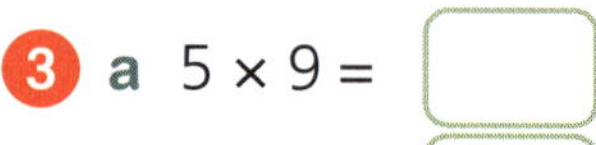

a 5 × 9 = ☐ b 9 × 9 = ☐ c 7 × 9 = ☐
d 8 × 9 = ☐ e 4 × 9 = ☐ f 1 × 9 = ☐
g 3 × 9 = ☐ h 6 × 9 = ☐ i 2 × 9 = ☐

4 Do as many as you can without skip counting.

×	0	1	2	3	4	5	6	7	8	9	10
3											
9											

×	5	3	7	4	2	9	10	1	8	6	0
3											
9											

 • *AUSTRALIAN SIGNPOST MATHS 4* • ISBN 9780655708780

× 9 tables

3 × 9 = 9 × 3   4 × 9 = 9 × 4   5 × 9 = 9 × 5

36 40 45 50 54 60 63 70 72

CONCEPT

- When multiplying by 9, you could multiply by 10, then subtract the original number.
  6 × 9 = (6 × 10) − 6 = 60 − 6 = 54,   7 × 9 = (7 × 10) − 7 = 70 − 7 = 63
- When multiplying by 9, the sum of the digits in the answer will be 9 (or 18 with larger numbers).
  6 × 9 = 54, ... (5 + 4 = 9),   8 × 9 = 72, ... (7 + 2 = 9),   11 × 9 = 99, ... (9 + 9 = 18)

1 Join each question to its answer, using a pencil and ruler.

a × 9

× 9	
0 × 9	18
1 × 9	27
2 × 9	0
3 × 9	54
4 × 9	9
5 × 9	36
6 × 9	63
7 × 9	90
8 × 9	45
9 × 9	72
10 × 9	81

b × 9

× 9	
3 × 9	0
0 × 9	27
5 × 9	63
1 × 9	72
7 × 9	36
2 × 9	9
8 × 9	45
4 × 9	90
6 × 9	18
10 × 9	81
9 × 9	54

c ×

×	
8 × 4	27
7 × 5	72
9 × 3	56
7 × 8	32
8 × 9	16
6 × 9	35
4 × 4	24
9 × 5	63
8 × 3	54
7 × 9	48
6 × 8	45

× 2
× 4
× 8
answers end in: 8, 6, 4, 2, or 0.

× 10
answers end in: 0.

d × 9

× 9	
6 × 9	9
1 × 9	90
3 × 9	54
10 × 9	18
5 × 9	0
7 × 9	27
2 × 9	63
8 × 9	45
4 × 9	81
9 × 9	72
0 × 9	36

e × 9

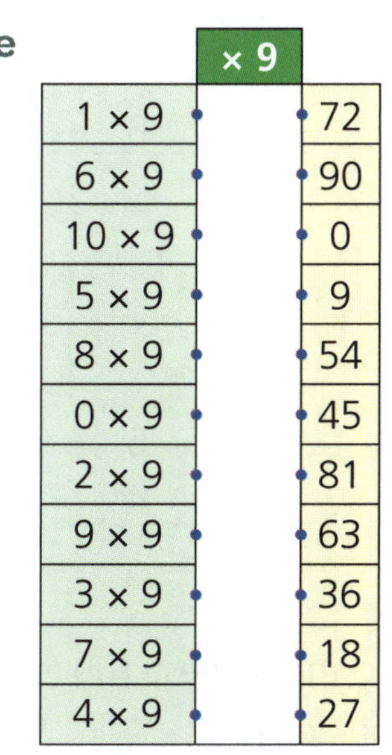

× 9	
1 × 9	72
6 × 9	90
10 × 9	0
5 × 9	9
8 × 9	54
0 × 9	45
2 × 9	81
9 × 9	63
3 × 9	36
7 × 9	18
4 × 9	27

f ×

×	
7 × 2	42
7 × 6	14
6 × 3	30
6 × 5	8
8 × 1	72
8 × 9	20
5 × 4	18
5 × 10	36
9 × 0	54
9 × 6	0
4 × 9	50

× 5
answers end in: 5 or 0.

36 **is:**
4 × 9
9 × 4
6 × 6

81 80

 • *AUSTRALIAN SIGNPOST MATHS 4* • ISBN 9780655708780

Addition to 999

Trade 10 ones for 1 ten.
Trade 10 tens for 1 hundred.

CONCEPT

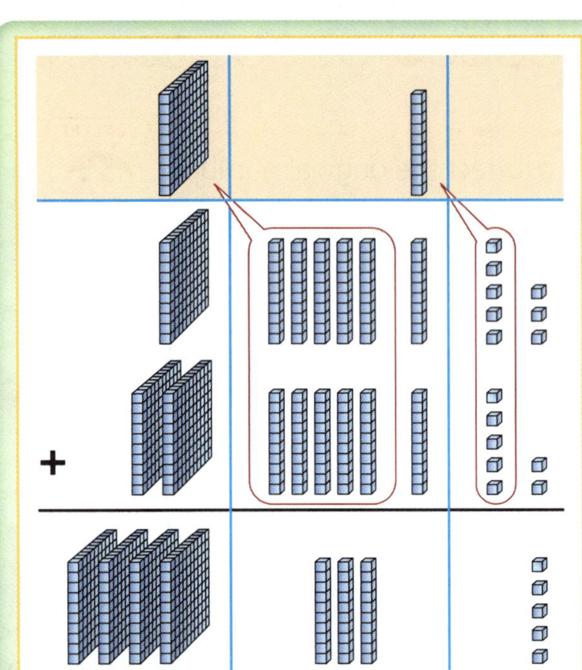

- 168 sheep and 267 cattle are on sale.
  How many animals are there altogether?

hund	tens	ones
1	1	
1	6	8
+ 2	6	7
4	3	5

There are 435 animals altogether.
We can check the answer by rounding to the nearest 100 (or 10).
200 + 300 = 500
435 is reasonably close to 500.

1

a

hund	tens	ones
	6	1
+	9	3

b

hund	tens	ones
	7	2
+	4	5

c

hund	tens	ones
	3	0
+	7	8

d

hund	tens	ones
2	5	8
+	2	5

e

hund	tens	ones
	7	6
+ 7	1	4

f

hund	tens	ones
3	6	9
+	1	9

g

hund	tens	ones
4	3	6
+	8	0

h

hund	tens	ones
4	2	5
+	8	5

i

hund	tens	ones
	8	7
+ 3	4	1

j

hund	tens	ones
1	8	8
+ 1	4	3

k

hund	tens	ones
3	6	5
+ 1	4	9

l

hund	tens	ones
4	5	9
+ 2	7	4

2 Check your answer by rounding each number to the nearest 100 (or 10) then adding.
If your answer is not reasonable, do the question again.

See *Extra Support* 5 (Addition of money), *Extra Support* 6 and 7 (Addition to 9999), *Extra Support* 8 (Addition to 999 999).

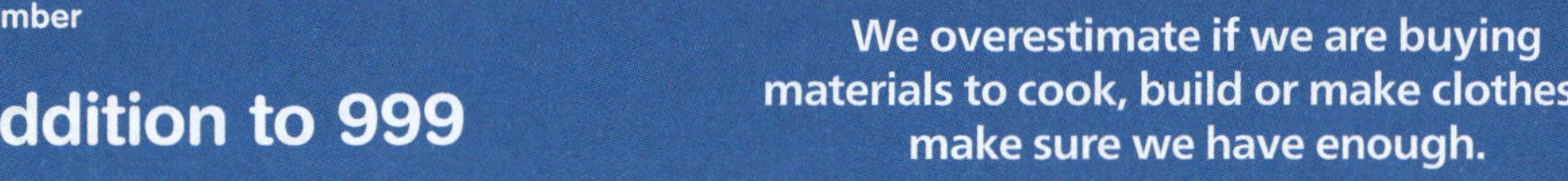

Addition to 999

We overestimate if we are buying materials to cook, build or make clothes to make sure we have enough.

CONCEPT

- We can round off to check our answers.
  We round down if the digit is 4 or less. We round up if the digit is 5 or more.
- When both numbers are rounded up, the answer is an **overestimate**.
  482 + 257 = 739
  500 + 300 = 800
  Here the estimate is more than the answer.
- When both numbers are rounded down, the answer is an **underestimate**.
  319 + 443 = 762
  300 + 400 = 700
  Here the estimate is less than the answer.

1 **a**

H	T	U
2	8	3
+	4	5

b

H	T	U
5	3	1
+	7	0

c

H	T	U
	8	2
+ 7	3	3

d

H	T	U
6	5	4
+	5	9

e

H	T	U
	8	7
+ 4	7	4

f

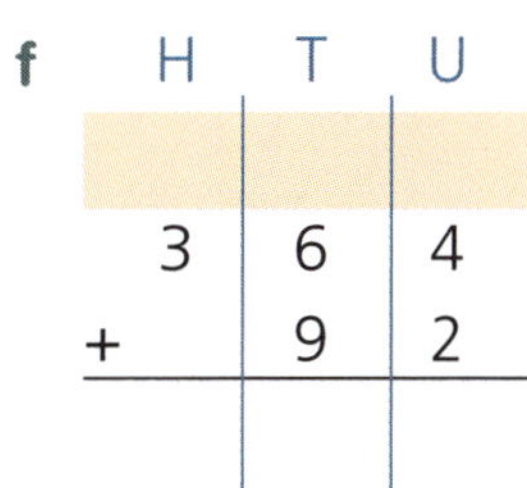

H	T	U
3	6	4
+	9	2

g

H	T	U
1	3	8
+ 2	0	4

h

H	T	U
3	1	6
+ 1	4	7

i

H	T	U
3	4	6
+ 2	2	4

j

H	T	U
1	8	4
+ 1	0	9

2 **a**

H	T	U
2	4	8
+ 1	1	7

b

H	T	U
	7	4
+ 5	3	1

c

H	T	U
4	1	9
+ 2	0	9

d

H	T	U
1	6	8
+ 6	1	1

e

H	T	U
2	4	8
+ 1	6	6

f

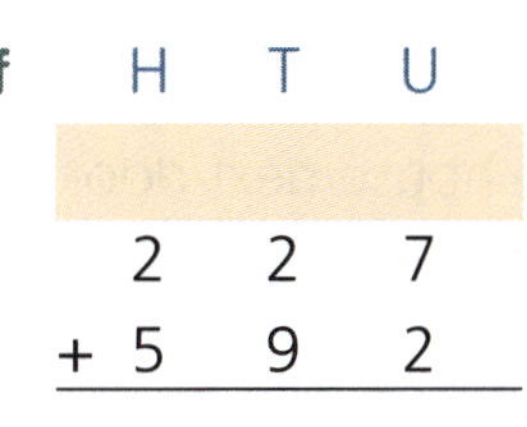

H	T	U
2	2	7
+ 5	9	2

See *Extra Support* 5 (Addition of money), *Extra Support* 6 and 7 (Addition to 9999), *Extra Support* 8 (Addition to 999 999).

Writing algorithms

To estimate, round each number to the nearest hundred, then add.

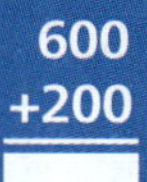

	hund	tens	ones
	1	1	
	5	8	3
+	1	7	9
	7	6	2

	hund	tens	ones
	1	1	
	5	8	3
+	1	7	9
	7	6	2

	H	T	U
	1	1	
	5	8	3
+	1	7	9
	7	6	2

```
   1  1
   5  8  3
+  1  7  9
   7  6  2
```

762 pieces of fruit were sold altogether.

1

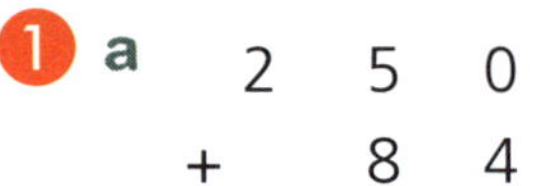

a	b	c	d	e
2 5 0	5 3 4	1 5 4	9 2	2 4 5
+ 8 4	+ 1 2 8	+ 2 0 7	+ 3 4 0	+ 3 7 0

f	g	h	i	j
3 6 5	2 0 9	3 4 5	5 0 7	3 6 5
+ 1 6 6	+ 5 8 3	+ 3 1 2	+ 2 2 0	+ 3 9 7

k	l	m	n	o
1 8 8	3 6 5	5 0 9	3 8 1	7 7 7
+ 1 3 3	+ 3 6 6	+ 2 9 6	+ 2 5 9	+ 1 8 5

2 Estimate each answer and use the estimate to check your answers.

a Luke watched 287 minutes of television on Saturday and 145 minutes on Sunday. How much did he watch altogether? Give your answer in minutes.  minutes

b Attendances at two concerts on Sunday were 156 and 218. How many people attended altogether?  people

c This year farmer McDonald sold 180 bags of corn. Last year he sold 17 bags more than this. How many bags were sold in the two years?  bags

d Rex and Lyn bought the house next door and added 346 square metres to their original block of 575 square metres. How large is the block now?  square metres

3 Use mental strategies and estimation to check your answers to Question 1.

See *Extra Support* 5 (Addition of money), *Extra Support* 6 and 7 (Addition to 9999), *Extra Support* 8 (Addition to 999 999).

 • *AUSTRALIAN SIGNPOST MATHS 4* • ISBN 9780655708780

What's the rule?

The rule is applied to each number to get the next one in the pattern.

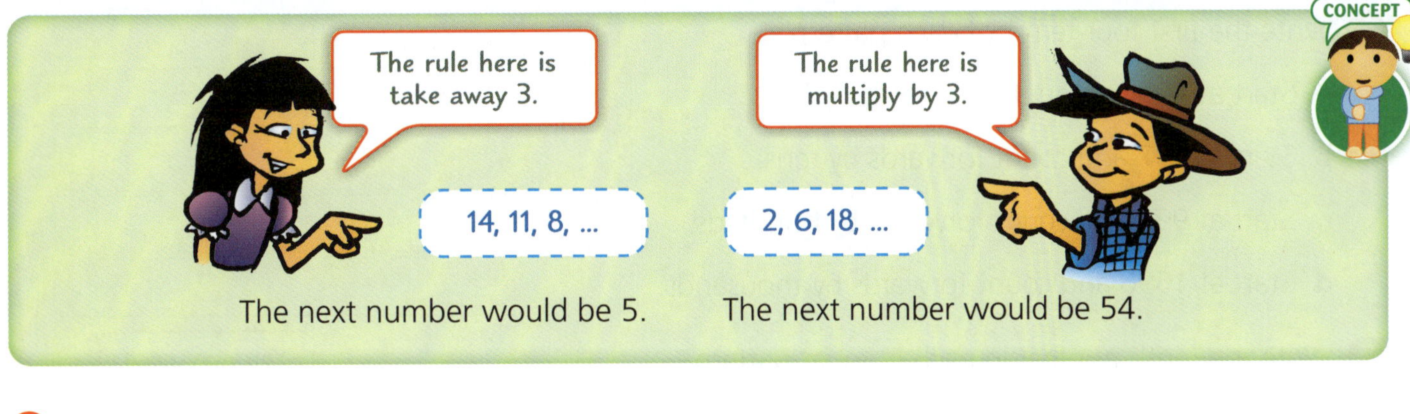

1. Write the next number in each pattern.

a	2, 4, 6, ☐	**b**	1, 5, 9, ☐	**c**	20, 18, 16, ☐
d	3, 6, 12, ☐	**e**	27, 9, 3, ☐	**f**	1, 5, 25, ☐
g	99, 98, 97, ☐	**h**	9, 16, 23, ☐	**i**	80, 40, 20, ☐

2. Write the rule for each part of Question 1.

a	☐	**b**	☐	**c**	☐
d	☐	**e**	☐	**f**	☐
g	☐	**h**	☐	**i**	☐

3. Continue each pattern by following the rule.

a	Add 7.	0, ☐, ☐, ☐	**b**	Subtract 5.	26, ☐, ☐, ☐
c	Multiply by 4.	1, ☐, ☐, ☐	**d**	Divide by 2.	88, ☐, ☐, ☐
e	Add 11.	23, ☐, ☐, ☐	**f**	Subtract 9.	47, ☐, ☐, ☐
g	Multiply by 2.	6, ☐, ☐, ☐	**h**	Divide by 3.	27, ☐, ☐, ☐

4. Write the pattern for the number of lines used in the pictures and write the rule used (e.g. 'add 3').

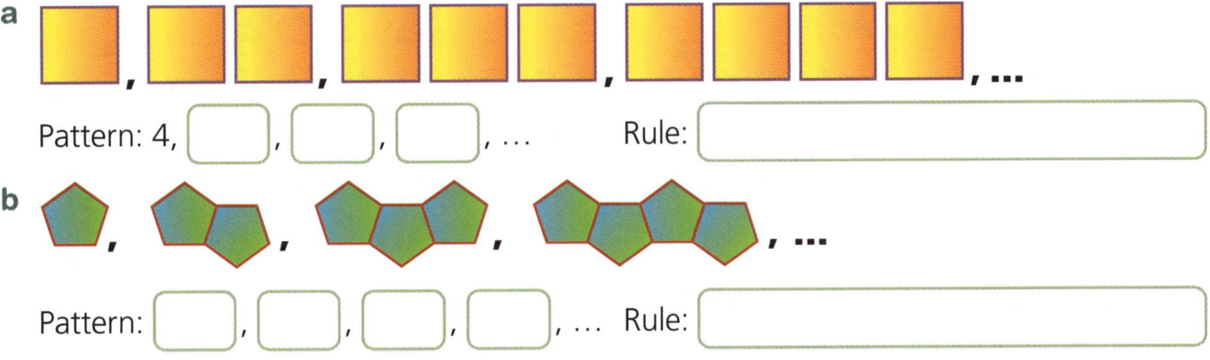

a Pattern: 4, ☐, ☐, ☐, … Rule: ☐

b Pattern: ☐, ☐, ☐, ☐, … Rule: ☐

 • *AUSTRALIAN SIGNPOST MATHS 4* • ISBN 9780655708780

2:27 Number patterns

Each pattern has a rule.

1 Write the first four terms of each pattern.

a Start at 40 and count backwards by fives.

b Start at 137 and count forwards by tens.

c Start at 995 and count forwards by hundreds.

d Start at 1696 and count forwards by thousands.

2 Write the tenth number in each number pattern.

You may need to write the pattern.

a 14, 21, 28, 35, …

b 189, 179, 169, 159, …

c 40, 80, 120, 160, …

d 16, 24, 32, 40, …

e 643, 743, 843, 943, …

f 950, 900, 850, 800, …

g $1\frac{1}{4}$, $1\frac{1}{2}$, $1\frac{3}{4}$, 2, …

h $6\frac{1}{2}$, 6, $5\frac{1}{2}$, 5, …

3 Complete each number pattern.

a

b 479, 489, ___, ___, 519, ___

c

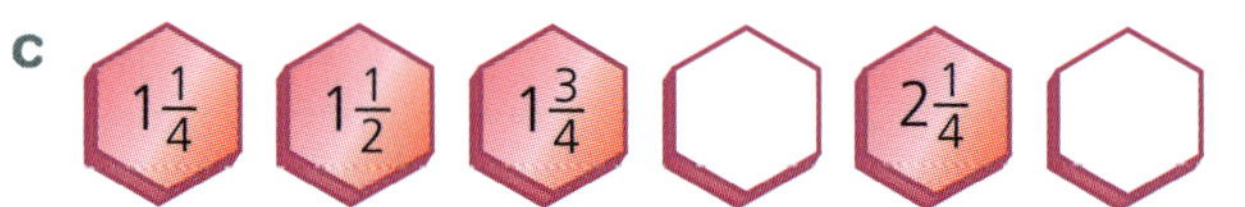

d 16, 24, 32, ___, 48, ___

4 Fill in the missing measurements for each bottle.

a

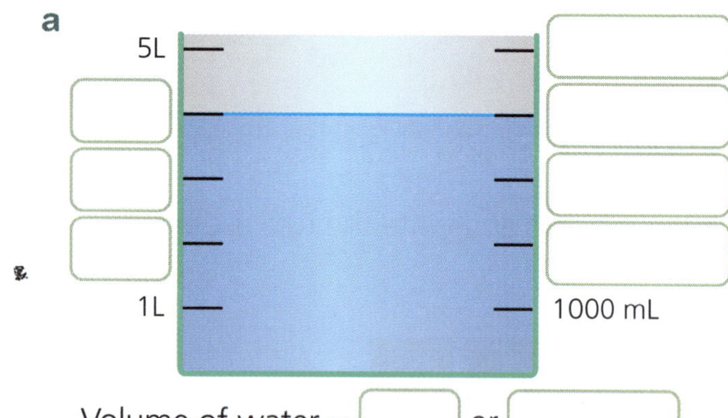

Volume of water = ___ or ___.

b

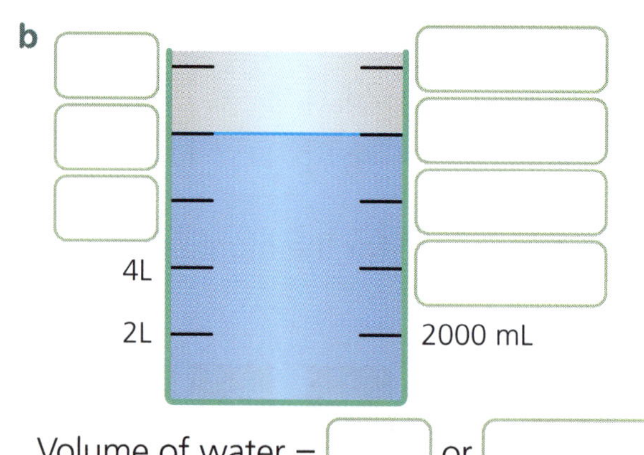

Volume of water = ___ or ___.

5 Continue each pattern.

a 1 kg, 2 kg, 3 kg, ___, ___

b 1000 g, 2000 g, 3000 g, ___, ___

c 5 km, 6 km, 7 km, ___, ___

d 5000 m, 6000 m, 7000 m, ___, ___

e 2 kg, 4 kg, 6 kg, ___, ___

f 2000 g, 4000 g, 6000 g, ___, ___

× 7 tables

$7 \times 7 = (5 \times 7) + (2 \times 7)$
$= 35 + 14$
$= 49$

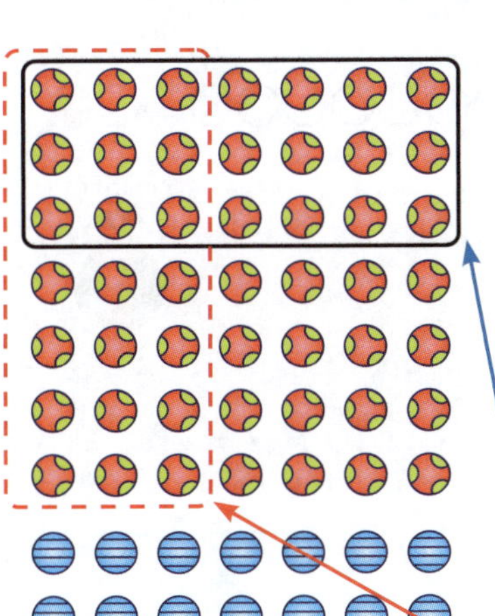

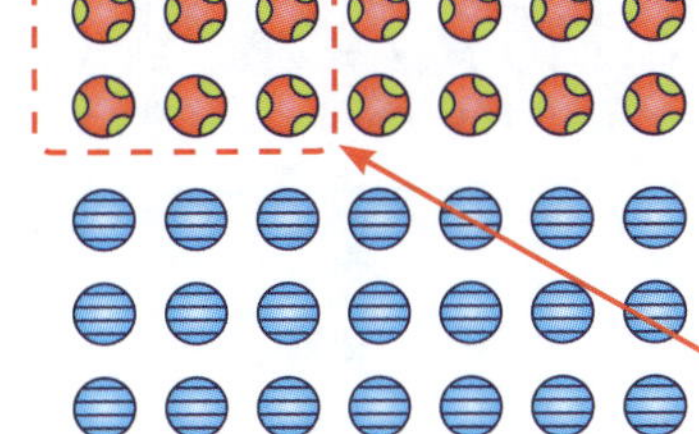

3 rows of 7

7 rows of 3

1 Count the rows and fill in the boxes.

a 7 rows of 3 = ☐ **b** 3 rows of 7 = ☐

c 7 × 4 = ☐ **d** 4 × 7 = ☐

e 7 × 5 = ☐ **f** 5 × 7 = ☐

g 7 × 6 = ☐ **h** 6 × 7 = ☐

i 7 × 8 = ☐ **j** 8 × 7 = ☐

k 9 × 7 = ☐

l 7 × 7 = ☐

Changing the order does not change the answer.

2 **a** 7 × 0 = ☐ **b** 0 × 7 = ☐ **c** 7 × 1 = ☐ **d** 1 × 7 = ☐

e 7 × 2 = ☐ **f** 2 × 7 = ☐ **g** 7 × 3 = ☐ **h** 3 × 7 = ☐

i 5 × 8 = ☐ **j** 9 × 8 = ☐ **k** 6 × 8 = ☐ **l** 8 × 8 = ☐

3

a $\begin{array}{r} 7 \\ \times\ 4 \\ \hline \end{array}$ **b** $\begin{array}{r} 7 \\ \times\ 6 \\ \hline \end{array}$

c $\begin{array}{r} 7 \\ \times\ 8 \\ \hline \end{array}$ **d** $\begin{array}{r} 7 \\ \times\ 7 \\ \hline \end{array}$

e $\begin{array}{r} 7 \\ \times\ 10 \\ \hline \end{array}$ **f** $\begin{array}{r} 7 \\ \times\ 9 \\ \hline \end{array}$

g $\begin{array}{r} 6 \\ \times\ 7 \\ \hline \end{array}$ **h** $\begin{array}{r} 9 \\ \times\ 7 \\ \hline \end{array}$

×	0	1	2	3	4	5	6	7	8	9	10
4											
2											
5											
8											
1											
6											
3											
0											
9											
10											
7											

4 Try to memorise the answers.

×	0	1	2	3	4	5	6	7	8	9	10
7											

×	5	3	7	4	2	9	10	1	8	6	0
7											

2:29

× 7 tables

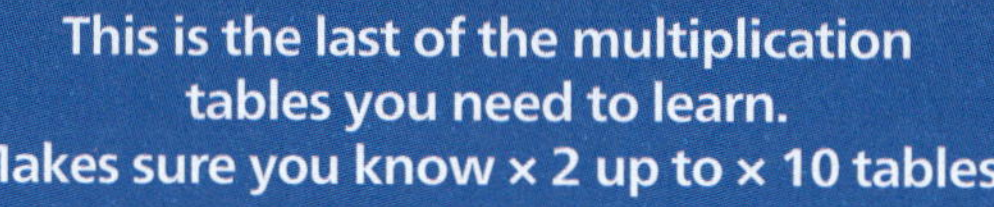

Start 7 10 14 20 21 28 30 35 40 42 49 50 56 60 63 70 77 80 84 90 100

CONCEPT

- If we know the other times tables we have met so far, the only new one would be $7 \times 7 = 49$

$7 \times 2 = 2 \times 7 = 14$, $7 \times 3 = 3 \times 7 = 21$ $7 \times 4 = 4 \times 7 = 28$ $7 \times 5 = 5 \times 7 = 35$

$7 \times 6 = 6 \times 7 = 42$, $7 \times 8 = 8 \times 7 = 56$, $7 \times 9 = 9 \times 7 = 63$, $7 \times 10 = 10 \times 7 = 70$

1 Join each question to its answer, using a pencil and ruler.

a

× 7	
0 × 7	14
1 × 7	21
2 × 7	0
3 × 7	42
4 × 7	7
5 × 7	28
6 × 7	49
7 × 7	70
8 × 7	35
9 × 7	56
10 × 7	63

b

× 7	
3 × 7	0
0 × 7	21
5 × 7	49
1 × 7	56
7 × 7	28
2 × 7	7
8 × 7	35
4 × 7	70
6 × 7	14
10 × 7	63
9 × 7	42

c

×	
9 × 4	21
6 × 7	72
7 × 3	32
4 × 8	36
8 × 9	28
7 × 7	42
4 × 7	56
9 × 5	63
8 × 7	49
7 × 9	24
6 × 4	45

d

× 7	
6 × 7	7
1 × 7	70
3 × 7	42
10 × 7	14
5 × 7	0
7 × 7	21
2 × 7	49
8 × 7	35
4 × 7	63
9 × 7	56
0 × 7	28

e

× 7	
1 × 7	56
6 × 7	70
10 × 7	0
5 × 7	7
8 × 7	42
0 × 7	35
2 × 7	63
9 × 7	49
3 × 7	28
7 × 7	14
4 × 7	21

f

×	
7 × 8	42
7 × 6	56
3 × 7	30
6 × 5	70
10 × 7	72
8 × 9	20
5 × 4	21
5 × 7	36
9 × 7	54
9 × 6	63
4 × 9	35

× 2
× 4
× 8
answers end in: 8, 6, 4, 2, or 0.

× 10
answers end in: 0.

× 5
answers end in: 5 or 0.

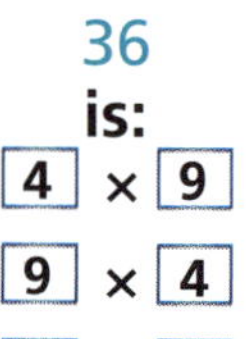

2:30 Multiplication tables review

Let's learn them all.

1 Complete these multiplication webs.

a

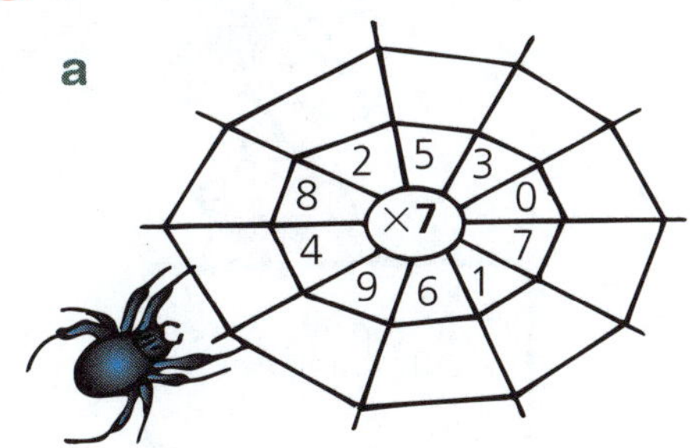

b

×6
10, 8, 1, 7, 2, 9, 4, 6, 3, 5

c

2

a 4 × 7 = ☐	**b** 7 × 4 = ☐	**c** 5 × 9 = ☐
d 10 × 9 = ☐	**e** 9 × 10 = ☐	**f** 3 × 9 = ☐
g 6 × 9 = ☐	**h** 9 × 6 = ☐	**i** 4 × 9 = ☐
j 8 × 9 = ☐	**k** 7 × 9 = ☐	**l** 9 × 9 = ☐
m 9 × 3 = ☐	**n** 7 × 7 = ☐	**o** 9 × 8 = ☐
p 9 × 7 = ☐	**q** 9 × 5 = ☐	**r** 9 × 4 = ☐

For x 9 tables, do the digits always add up to 9?

3

a 6 × 2

b 6 × 5

c 6 × 3

d 3 × 4

e 3 × 10

f 3 × 6

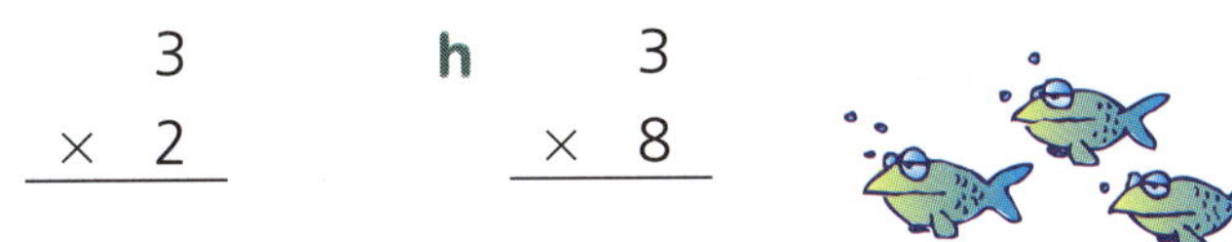

g 3 × 2

h 3 × 8

3 × 9 = 27 → 2 + 7 = 9

4 × 9 = 36 → 3 + 6 = 9

The answer to a multiplication question is called the **product**.

4

a The product of 7 and 6 = ☐	**b** The product of 0 and 6 = ☐
c The product of 7 and 3 = ☐	**d** The product of 5 and 9 = ☐
e The product of 6 and 6 = ☐	**f** The product of 8 and 6 = ☐

5

×	5	3	7	4	2	9	10	1	8	6	0
3											
9											

 • *AUSTRALIAN SIGNPOST MATHS 4* • ISBN 9780655708780

2:31 Subtraction without trading to 999

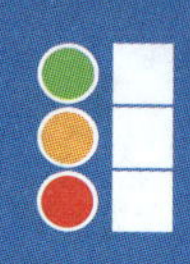

438 students.
216 were in uniform.
How many were out of uniform?

I Show

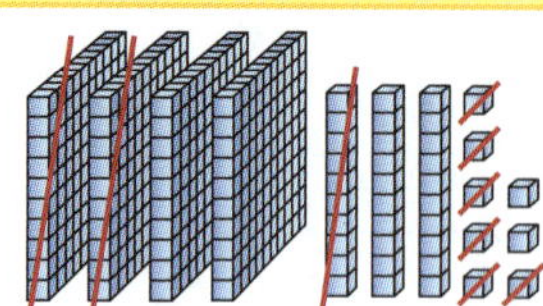

Take away 6 ones.
Take away 1 ten.
Take away 2 hundreds.

I Write

	hund	tens	ones
	4	3	8
−	2	1	6
	2	2	2

222 students were out of uniform.

CONCEPT

1 **a**

	4 hundreds	7 tens	6 ones
−	2 hundreds	3 tens	1 one

b

	8 hundreds	9 tens	7 ones
−	2 hundreds	5 tens	2 ones

c

	hund	tens	ones
	8	5	2
−	7	2	1

d

	hund	tens	ones
	9	6	7
−	2	3	4

e

	hund	tens	ones
	9	9	8
−	4	6	5

f

	hund	tens	ones
	3	4	2
−		1	1

g

	hund	tens	ones
	6	9	8
−		2	4

h

	hund	tens	ones
	9	4	5
−		1	1

i

	hund	tens	ones
	6	8	6
−			4

j

	hund	tens	ones
	7	4	7
−			4

k

	hund	tens	ones
	3	6	9
−			7

l

	hund	tens	ones
	5	5	9
−	4	3	0

m

	hund	tens	ones
	1	7	3
−		5	0

n

	hund	tens	ones
	6	4	6
−	2	0	3

o

	H	T	O
	7	7	8
−	6	0	0

p

	H	T	O
	5	2	9
−	1	0	0

q

	H	T	O
	1	8	3
−	1	1	3

r

	H	T	O
	5	8	7
−	3	8	2

2 Use mental strategies and estimation to check each answer in Question 1.

- Make up a problem to match each of the sums in parts **c**, **d**, **e** and **f**.

FUN SPOT

2:32 Subtraction with trading to 999

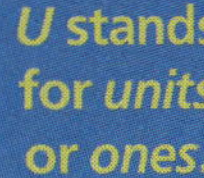

CONCEPT

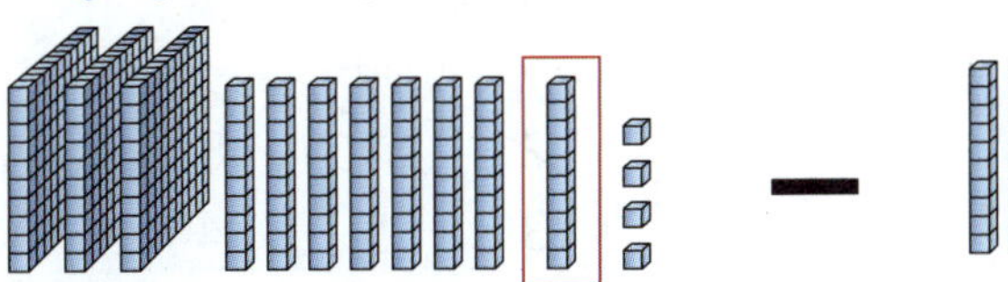

We can't take 8 ones from 4 ones, so trade 1 ten for 10 ones.

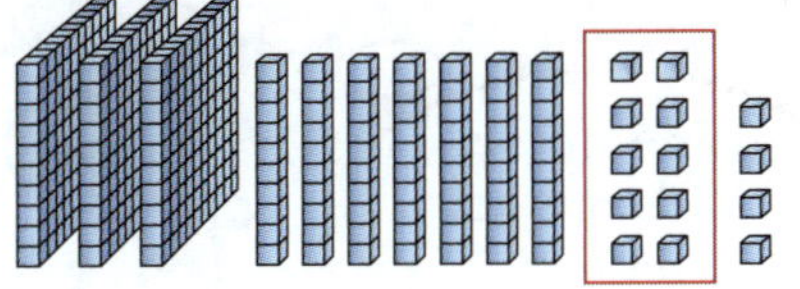

From this we take 2 tens and 8 ones.

$300 + \overset{70}{\cancel{80}} + \overset{14}{\cancel{4}}$

	hund	tens	ones
		7	14
	3	~~8~~	~~4~~
–		2	8
	3	5	6

1

a

	H	T	U
	5	8	1
–		5	3

b

	H	T	U
	3	4	3
–		2	8

c

	H	T	U
	2	9	6
–		6	7

d

	H	T	U
	4	6	0
–		3	9

e

	H	T	U
	2	7	3
–			9

f

	H	T	U
	1	6	6
–		5	8

g

	H	T	U
	8	4	4
–			8

h

	H	T	U
	9	7	3
–		6	5

i

	H	T	U
	7	5	0
–		3	9

j

	H	T	U
	3	4	1
–		2	6

k

	H	T	U
	2	8	0
–		3	2

l

	H	T	U
	6	4	7
–		1	9

m

	8	3	5
–	1	0	8

n

	8	9	1
–	8	3	6

o

	5	2	0
–	4	1	5

p

	6	8	4
–		7	6

q

	2	1	4
–	2	0	8

r

	7	8	4
–		5	0

s

	3	9	1
–	3	7	5

Use estimation or mental strategies to check your answers.

See *Extra Support 9* (Subtraction of money), *Extra Support 10* and *11* (Subtraction to 10 000, *Extra Support 12* (– to 999 999).

Subtraction with trading to 999

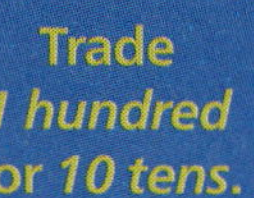
Trade 1 hundred for 10 tens.

CONCEPT

354 of the 718 birds in the zoo are parrots. How many are not parrots?

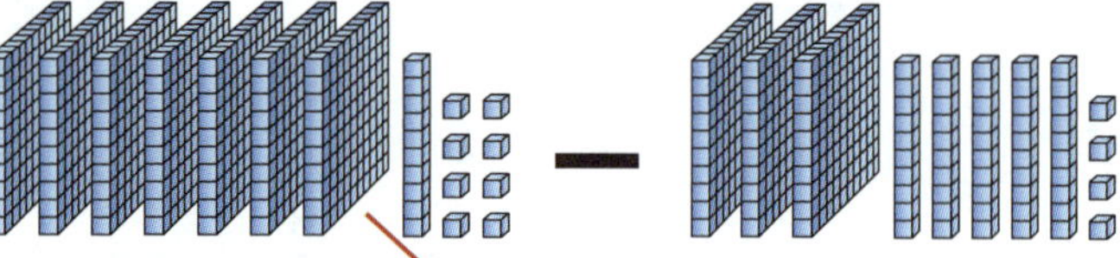

We can't take 5 tens from 1 ten, so trade 1 hundred for 10 tens.

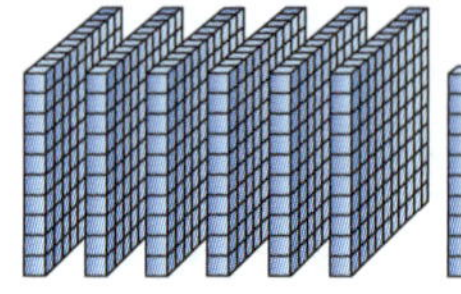

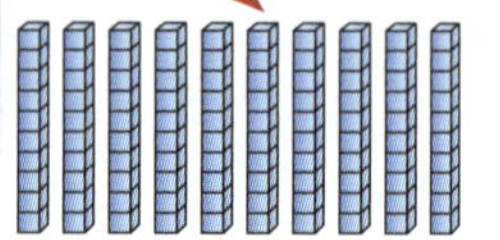

600 110
~~700~~ + ~~10~~ + 8

From this we take 3 hundreds, 5 tens and 4 ones.

Hund	Tens	Ones
6	11	
~~7~~	~~1~~	8
− 3	5	4
3	6	4

1

a

H	T	U
6	1	7
− 1	5	3

b

H	T	U
8	2	6
− 5	7	1

c

H	T	U
4	3	4
− 2	4	0

d

H	T	U
7	2	9
−	3	8

e

H	T	U
5	2	8
− 1	5	2

f

H	T	U
6	0	7
− 3	5	2

g

H	T	U
6	8	5
−	9	1

h

H	T	U
2	1	5
− 1	7	5

i

H	T	U
4	5	0
− 1	3	9

j

H	T	U
6	1	7
− 3	2	6

k

H	T	U
5	0	4
− 1	9	2

l

H	T	U
9	4	7
− 3	0	9

m

7	3	3
− 1	0	8

n

9	1	6
− 8	3	6

o

6	0	8
− 4	1	5

p

4	1	4
− 2	0	8

q

9	8	4
− 5	5	0

r

8	6	6
− 3	7	5

Estimate before you calculate.

See *Extra Support 9* (Subtraction of money), *Extra Support 10* and *11* (Subtraction to 10 000, *Extra Support 12* (– to 999 999).

Subtraction with 2 trades to 999

Trade *twice.*

CONCEPT

I had $524 and spent $245. How much do I have left?

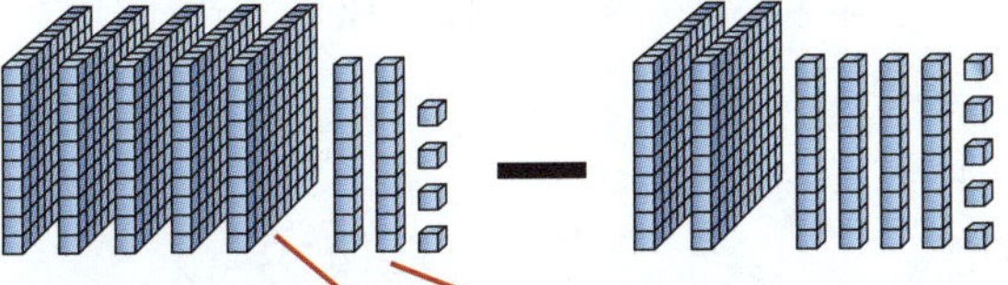

Trade 1 ten for 10 ones, and 1 hundred for 10 tens.

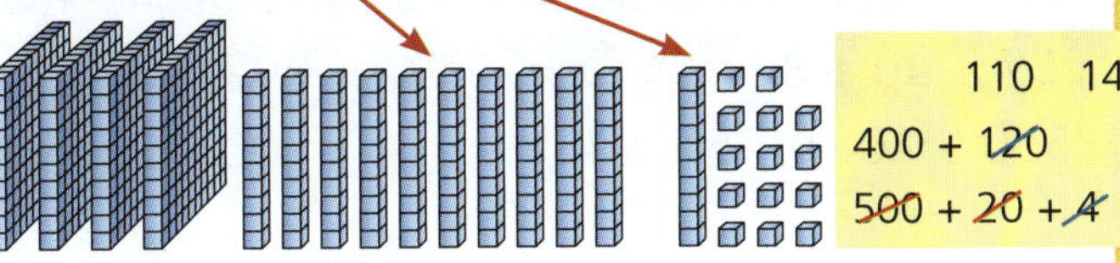

110 14
400 + 120
500 + 20 + 4

From this we take 2 hundreds, 4 tens and 5 ones.

hund	tens	ones
	11	
4	1	14
5	2	4
– 2	4	5
2	7	9

Use rounding to check your answers.

1

a
H	T	U
3	1	4
–	5	6

b
H	T	U
2	4	6
–	6	7

c
H	T	U
1	3	2
–	9	8

d
H	T	U
7	3	5
–	8	9

e
H	T	U
4	3	0
– 1	5	6

f
H	T	U
3	4	1
– 2	7	8

g
H	T	U
6	2	4
– 1	3	5

h
H	T	U
9	2	2
– 3	3	3

i
H	T	U
7	1	5
– 5	7	7

j
H	T	U
4	7	0
– 2	9	3

k
H	T	U
8	4	2
– 1	8	3

l
H	T	U
9	1	1
– 3	4	4

m
```
  6 1 4
– 5 8 5
```

n
```
  5 2 8
– 4 2 9
```

o
```
  7 5 5
– 6 6 8
```

p
```
  4 1 5
– 3 8 7
```

q
```
  7 0 6
– 2 4 9
```

r
```
  6 0 1
– 1 8 4
```

s
```
  5 0 6
– 2 7 8
```

In Questions 1q–1s, start by trading 1 hundred for 10 tens.

See *Extra Support 9* (Subtraction of money), *Extra Support 10* and *11* (Subtraction to 10 000, *Extra Support 12* (– to 999 999).

 • *AUSTRALIAN SIGNPOST MATHS 4* • ISBN 9780655708780

2:35 Mental strategies, + and –

Know these strategies.

CONCEPT

Look at the question and ask, 'Which strategy will work best?'

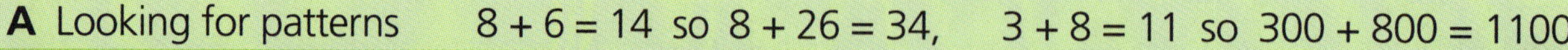

A	Looking for patterns	8 + 6 = 14 so 8 + 26 = 34,	3 + 8 = 11 so 300 + 800 = 1100	
B	Changing the order	115 + 137 + 15 = 115 + 15 + 137		= 130 + 137
C	Bridging to 10s	148 + 7	= 148 + 2 + 5	= 150 + 5
D	Compensation	318 + 98	= 318 +100 – 2	= 418 – 2
E	Split strategy	316 + 432	= (300 + 400) + (10 + 30) + (6 + 2)	= 700 + 40 + 8
F	Jump strategy	257 + 48	= 257 + 40 + 8	= 297 + 8
G	Compatible numbers	560 + 162	= (550 + 10) + (150 + 12)	= 700 + 22

1 Look for patterns. (**A**)

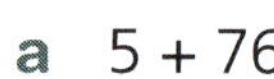

a 5 + 76 ____ **b** 7 + 83 ____ **c** 400 + 800 ____

2 Change the order. (**B**)

a 199 + 59 + 11 ____ **b** 630 + 9 + 70 ____ **c** 176 + 59 + 4 ____

3 Bridge to 10. (**C**)

a 538 + 6 ____ **b** 788 + 7 ____ **c** 844 + 8 ____

Make sure you know addition facts.

See Extra Support page 1.

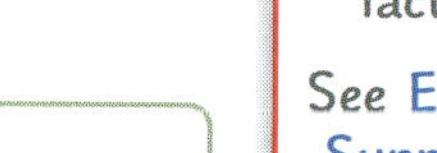

4 Round off then compensate. (**D**)

a 362 + 39 ____ **b** 288 + 98 ____ **c** 603 + 49 ____

5 Use the split strategy. (**E**)

a 426 + 113 ____ **b** 235 + 662 ____ **c** 714 + 263 ____

d 934 + 51 ____ **e** 63 + 725 ____ **f** 72 + 806 ____

6 Use the jump strategy. (**F**)

a 238 + 56 ____ **b** 418 + 38 ____ **c** 369 + 47 ____

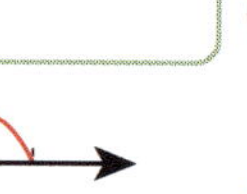

7 Look for compatible numbers. (**G**)

a 452 + 259 ____ **b** 185 + 723 ____ **c** 564 + 259 ____

INVESTIGATION

8 Complete the additions. Write the strategy you used (from **A** to **G** above).

a 342 + 57 ____ ____ **b** 72 + 9 + 18 ____ ____ **c** 424 + 7 ____ ____

d 65 + 19 ____ ____ **e** 800 + 900 ____ ____ **f** 537 + 46 ____ ____

Discuss how and why you chose each strategy.

See *Extra Support 2* (Building to the next 10).

2:36 Mental strategies, + and –

Practise looking for the best strategy.

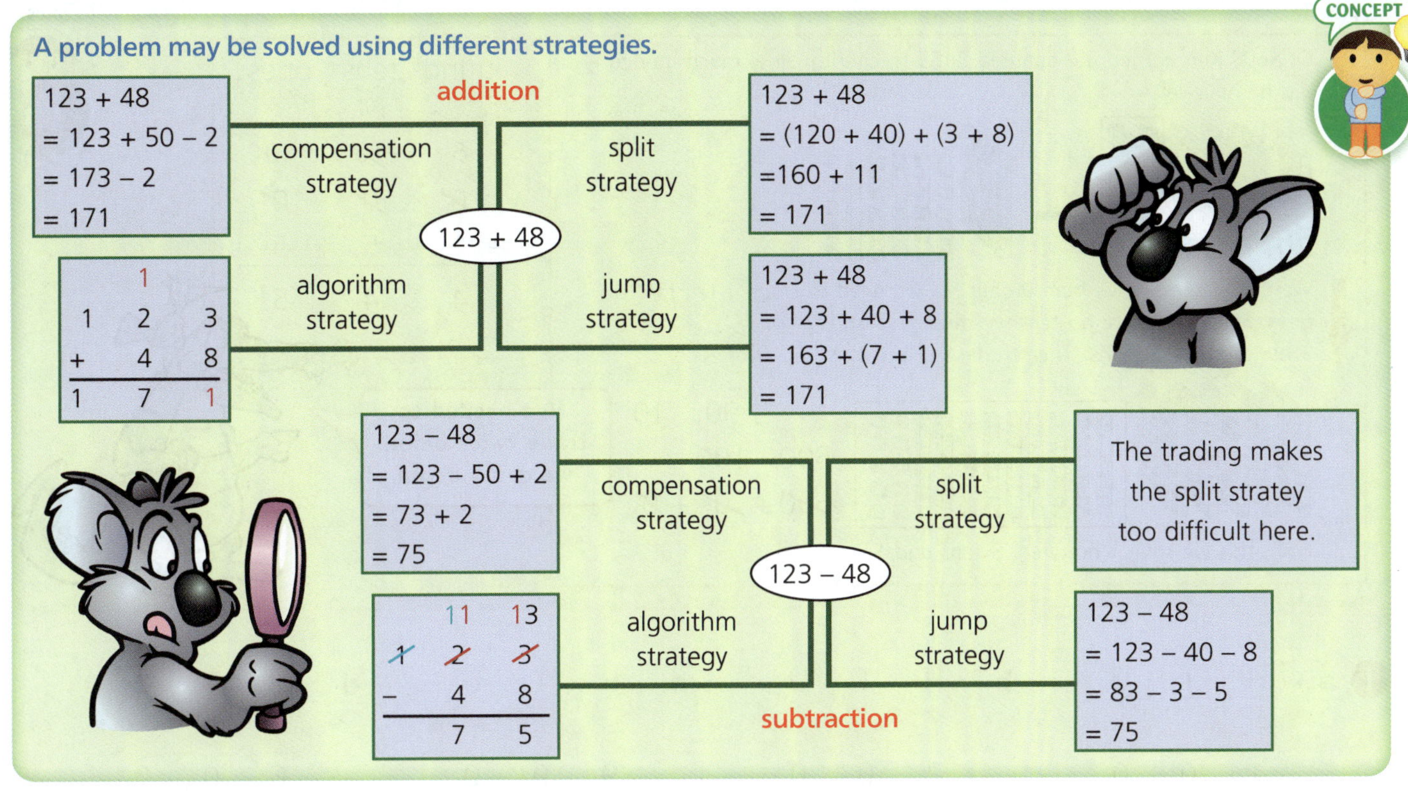

1 Compensation strategy (Round off the addition, then compensate.)

a 241 + 48 ____ b 513 + 9 ____ c 537 + 98 ____
d 374 + 49 ____ e 732 + 48 ____ f 277 + 95 ____
g 543 + 98 ____ h 587 + 95 ____ i 429 + 97 ____

To add 95, add 100 and subtract 5.

2 Building to 100 (Combine tens to make 100.)

a 745 + 63 ____ b 154 + 54 ____ c 842 + 69 ____
d 473 + 42 ____ e 735 + 80 ____ f 436 + 75 ____
g 823 + 94 ____ h 712 + 95 ____ i 663 + 65 ____

3 Compensation strategy (Round off the subtraction, then compensate.)

a 783 – 49 ____ b 260 – 48 ____ c 667 – 98 ____
d 374 – 48 ____ e 732 – 47 ____ f 277 – 99 ____
g 543 – 98 ____ h 587 – 49 ____ i 429 – 96 ____

To subtract 96, take away 100 and add 4.

4 Choose your own strategy.

a 783 – 59 ____ b 163 – 42 ____ c 627 – 19 ____
d 555 – 19 ____ e 664 – 490 ____ f 852 – 39 ____
g 548 – 36 ____ h 283 – 47 ____ i 892 – 48 ____

2:37 Subtraction from hundreds

1 hundred is the same as 9 tens and 10 ones.

CONCEPT

Of $600 Kim earned, he donated $155 to charity. How much money did he have left?

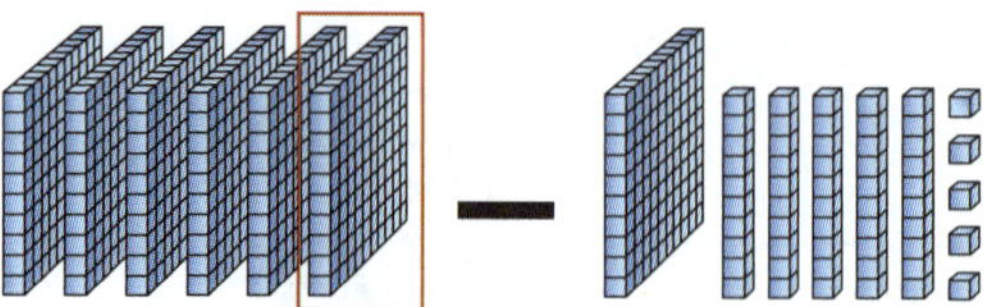

We can't take 5 ones from 0 ones, so we need to trade 1 ten for 10 ones. Since there are no tens we must first trade 1 hundred for 10 tens. Then trade 1 of the tens for 10 ones.

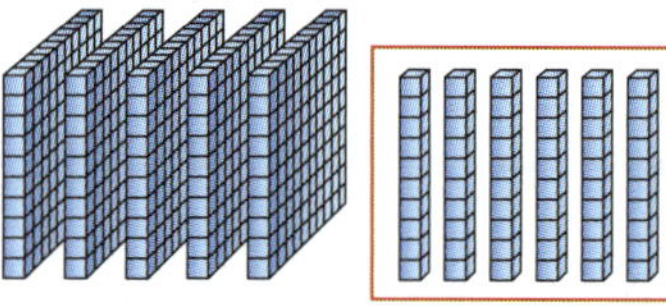

	90	10
500	~~100~~	
~~600~~ +	~~0~~ +	~~0~~

From this we take 1 hundred, 5 tens and 5 ones.

1

	H	T	U
a	1	0	0
	−	2	7

	H	T	U
b	2	0	0
	−	3	8

	H	T	U
c	9	0	0
	−	6	1

	H	T	U
d	6	0	0
	−	5	5

e 700 − 302

f 900 − 793

g 400 − 106

h 300 − 253

2

a 600 − 534

b 500 − 399

c 800 − 674

d 700 − 668

3 Estimate each answer and use the estimates to check your answers.

a Chloe needed 600 points to qualify for a state team. She earned only 487. How far short of her target was she? ☐ points

b Blackburn Post Office was sent 900 stamp albums to sell. If 481 were sold in the first month, how many were left? ☐ albums

c In our class library we have 400 books. I have read 147. How many have I not read? ☐ books

 • *AUSTRALIAN SIGNPOST MATHS 4* • ISBN 9780655708780

2:38 Subtraction from hundreds strategy

CONCEPT

700 – 137
= 699 + 1 – 137
= 699 – 137 + 1
= 562 + 1
= 563

OR

700 – 137 563	699 + 1 – 137 562 + 1 = 563

1

a H T U 9 9 +1 ~~1 0 0~~ – 3 7 + 1 = ___	**b** H T U 2 9 9 +1 ~~3 0 0~~ – 4 8 + 1 = ___	**c** H T U 8 9 9 +1 ~~9 0 0~~ – 7 1 + 1 = ___
d +1 ~~7 0 0~~ – 4 6 9 + 1 = ___	**e** +1 ~~5 0 0~~ – 2 8 5 + 1 = ___	**f** +1 ~~2 0 0~~ – 1 3 7 + 1 = ___
g +1 4 0 0 – 3 2 1 + 1 = ___	**h** +1 6 0 0 – 2 9 3 + 1 = ___	**i** +1 8 0 0 – 5 4 6 + 1 = ___
j 6 0 0 – 2 7 1 + = ___	**k** 9 0 0 – 3 4 9 + = ___	**l** 5 0 0 – 1 5 6 + = ___

2 I took $1000 to the show. How much would I have left if I spent:

a $297? ___ **b** $174? ___ **c** $856? ___ **d** $324? ___

 • *AUSTRALIAN SIGNPOST MATHS 4* • ISBN 9780655708780

2:39 Division as repeated subtraction

1 How many groups of 3 could be made from each of these?

a  ☐ groups b ☐ groups c  ☐ groups

2
a How many groups of 5 mushrooms are in 15? ☐ groups. So 15 ÷ 5 = ☐
b How many groups of 5 candles are in 30? ☐ groups. So 30 ÷ 5 = ☐
c How many groups of 3 mushrooms are in 15? ☐ groups. So 15 ÷ 3 = ☐
d How many groups of 6 tacks are in 36? ☐ groups. So 36 ÷ 6 = ☐
e How many groups of 3 candles are in 30? ☐ groups. So 30 ÷ 3 = ☐
f How many groups of 4 tacks are in 36? ☐ groups. So 36 ÷ 4 = ☐
g How many groups of 4 footballs are in 24? ☐ groups. So 24 ÷ 4 = ☐
h How many groups of 6 notes are in 48? ☐ groups. So 48 ÷ 6 = ☐
i How many groups of 9 tacks are in 36? ☐ groups. So 36 ÷ 9 = ☐
j How many groups of 8 footballs are in 24? ☐ groups. So 24 ÷ 8 = ☐
k How many groups of 8 notes are in 48? ☐ groups. So 48 ÷ 8 = ☐

3 Use counters or place-value blocks to answer these.
a 42 apples are put in groups of 6. How many groups are there? ☐, 42 ÷ 6 = ☐
b 5 cakes fill one box. How many boxes can be filled with 35 cakes? ☐, 35 ÷ 5 = ☐
c A table seats 4 people. How many tables are needed to seat 32? ☐, 32 ÷ 4 = ☐

 ISBN 9780655708780

Algebra

2:40 Understanding division

How many groups?
or
How many in each share?

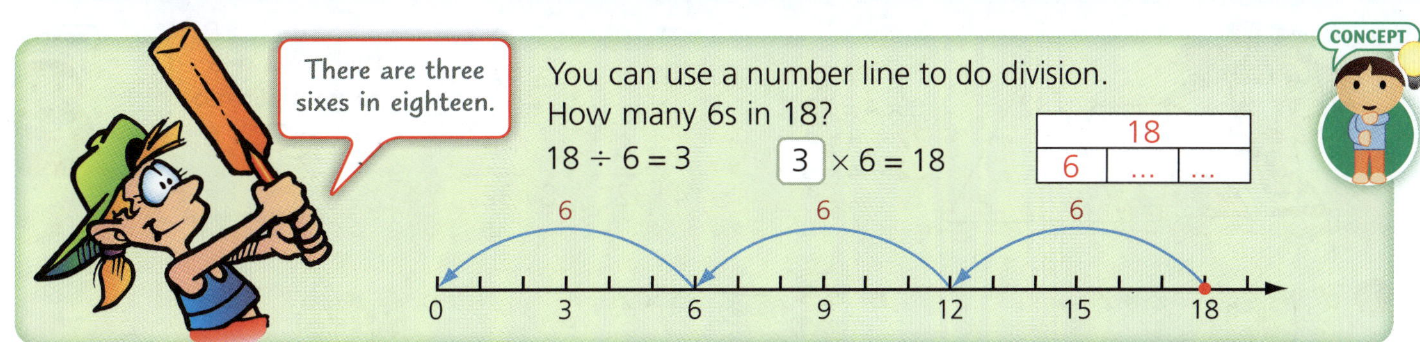

1 Use the number line above to find the answers.

a How many 3s are in 18?

18 ÷ 3 = ☐

b How many 9s are in 18?

18 ÷ 9 = ☐

c How many 2s are in 18?

18 ÷ 2 = ☐

d How many 18s are in 18?

18 ÷ 18 = ☐

2 Use this number line to find the answers.

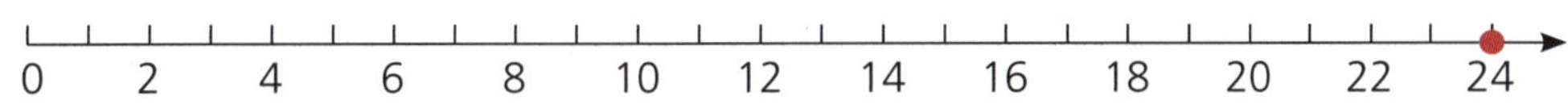

a How many 4s in 24?

24 ÷ 4 = ☐

b How many 8s in 24?

24 ÷ 8 = ☐

c How many 2s in 24?

24 ÷ 2 = ☐

d How many 3s in 24?

24 ÷ 3 = ☐

e How many 6s in 24?

24 ÷ 6 = ☐

f How many 12s in 24?

24 ÷ 12 = ☐

3 Use this number line to find the answers.

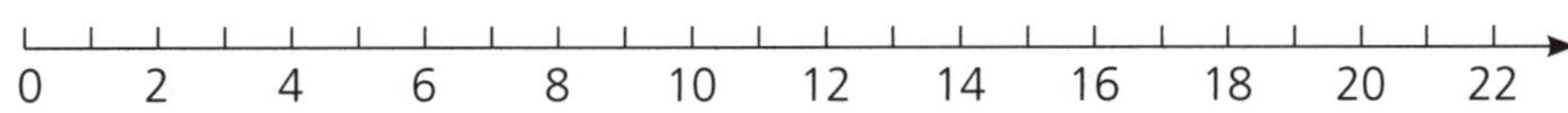

a How many 5s in 15?

15 ÷ 5 = ☐

b How many 6s in 18?

18 ÷ 6 = ☐

c How many 1s in 18?

18 ÷ 1 = ☐

d How many 3s in 15?

15 ÷ 3 = ☐

e How many 4s in 16?

16 ÷ 4 = ☐

f How many 8s in 16?

16 ÷ 8 = ☐

4 Write a number sentence for each sharing problem.

a 20 stickers, 4 students

b 16 bones, 8 dogs

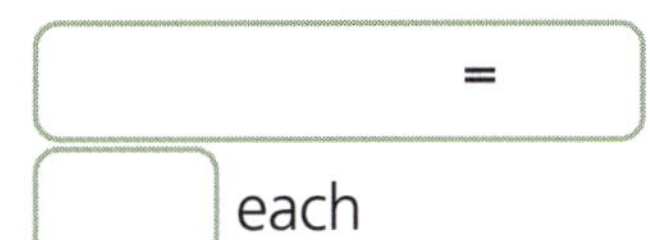

c 20 toys, 2 children

☐ = ☐

☐ each

Division facts

$4 \times 8 = 32$

$32 \div 8 = \square$ so or $32 \div 4 = \square$

$4 \times 8 = 32$
$8 \times 4 = 32$
$32 \div 8 = 4$
$32 \div 4 = 8$

$8 \times 4 = 32$

$4\overline{)32}$ = 8 $\quad$ $8\overline{)32}$ = 4

Division is related to multiplication.

CONCEPT

1 **a** 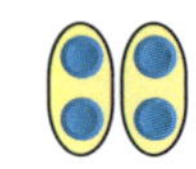 $2 \times 2 = \square$ $4 \div 2 = \square$

b 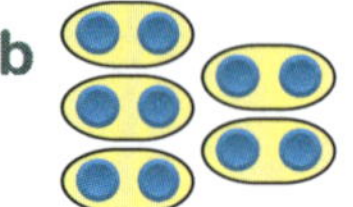 $5 \times 2 = \square$ $10 \div 5 = \square$

c 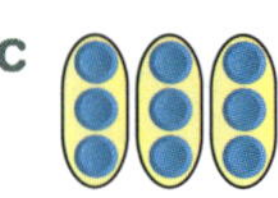 $3 \times 3 = \square$ $9 \div 3 = \square$

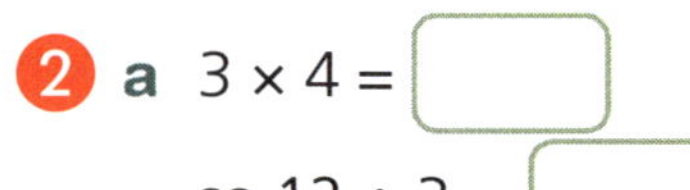

2 **a** $3 \times 4 = \square$ so $12 \div 3 = \square$

b $2 \times 8 = \square$ so $16 \div 2 = \square$

c $7 \times 4 = \square$ so $28 \div 7 = \square$

d $9 \times 3 = \square$ so $27 \div 9 = \square$

e $6 \times 5 = \square$ so $30 \div 6 = \square$

f $5 \times 3 = \square$ so $15 \div 5 = \square$

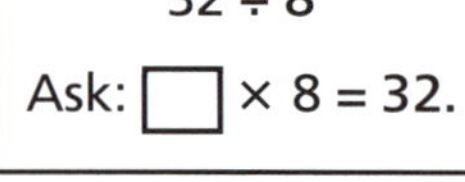

$32 \div 8$
Ask: $\square \times 8 = 32$.

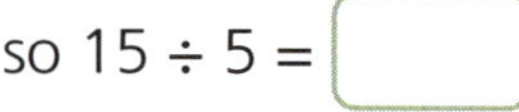

3 Use the multiplication table to answer the division questions.

a $3 \times 4 = 12$ $\quad 4\overline{)12} \quad 3\overline{)12}$

b $8 \times 5 = 40$ $\quad 5\overline{)40} \quad 8\overline{)40}$

c $10 \times 9 = 90$ $\quad 9\overline{)90} \quad 10\overline{)90}$

d $6 \times 10 = 60$ $\quad 10\overline{)60} \quad 6\overline{)60}$

e $7 \times 8 = 56$ $\quad 8\overline{)56} \quad 7\overline{)56}$

f $5 \times 9 = 45$ $\quad 9\overline{)45} \quad 5\overline{)45}$

4 **a** $12 \div 6 = \square$ or $\square \times 6 = 12$

b $18 \div 3 = \square$ or $\square \times 3 = 18$

c $35 \div 5 = \square$ or $\square \times 5 = 35$

d $30 \div 5 = \square$ or $\square \times 5 = 30$

e $20 \div 2 = \square$ or $\square \times 2 = 20$

f $24 \div 8 = \square$ or $\square \times 8 = 24$

5 **a** We bought 80 oranges and put the same number in each of 8 buckets. How many did we put in each bucket? $\square$

b We decided to give 4 toys to each girl. If we gave out 32 toys, how many girls were there? $\square$

c Four boys shared 28 keys. How many did each boy get? $\square$

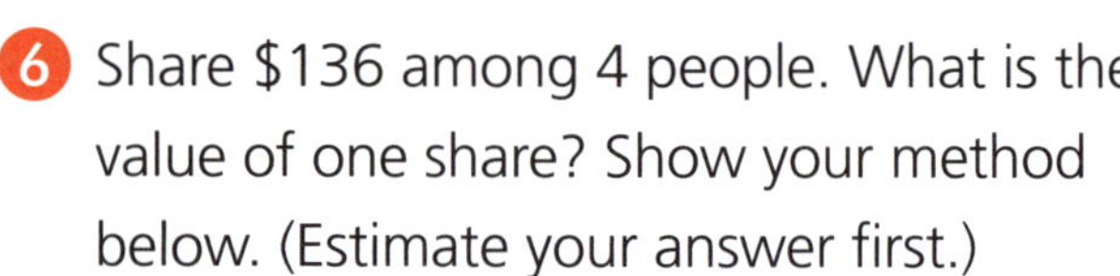

6 Share \$136 among 4 people. What is the value of one share? Show your method below. (Estimate your answer first.)

Is the answer close to your estimate?

 • *AUSTRALIAN SIGNPOST MATHS 4* • ISBN 9780655708780

Division facts

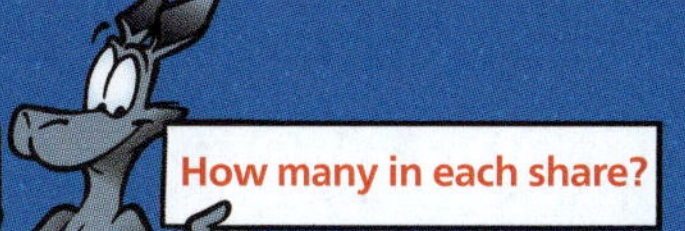

CONCEPT

- Six friends shared \$42. How much did each receive?

Find: How much did each receive?

Number sentence: $42 \div 6 = \square$

Ask: $\square \times 6 = 42$

Answer: Each received \$7.

Multiplication and division are related.

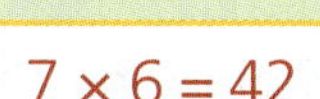

$7 \times 6 = 42$

so

$42 \div 7 = 6$ or $42 \div 6 = 7$

1 Use the first number sentence to fill in the other two.

a $8 \times 3 = 24$
$24 \div 3 = \square$
$24 \div 8 = \square$

b $4 \times 9 = 36$
$36 \div 4 = \square$
$36 \div 9 = \square$

c $5 \times 6 = 30$
$30 \div 6 = \square$
$30 \div 5 = \square$

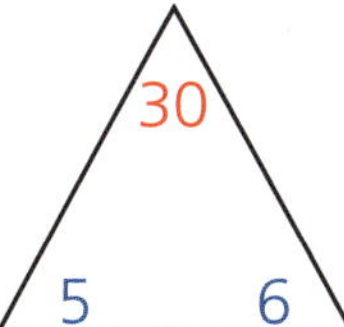

2
a $\square \times 9 = 18$ **b** $\square \times 10 = 20$ **c** $\square \times 3 = 21$
d $\square \times 5 = 25$ **e** $\square \times 3 = 9$ **f** $\square \times 6 = 12$
g $3 \times \square = 6$ **h** $2 \times \square = 10$ **i** $7 \times \square = 14$

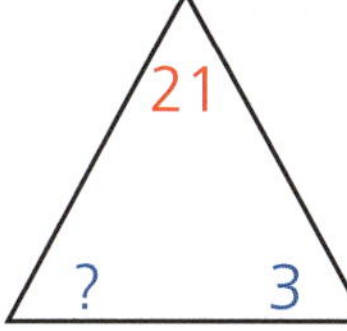

3
a $40 \div 5 = \square$ **b** $63 \div 9 = \square$ **c** $48 \div 8 = \square$
d $32 \div 4 = \square$ **e** $3 \div 3 = \square$ **f** $90 \div 10 = \square$
g $54 \div 9 = \square$ **h** $35 \div 5 = \square$ **i** $16 \div 4 = \square$
j $27 \div 3 = \square$ **k** $72 \div 8 = \square$ **l** $40 \div 8 = \square$

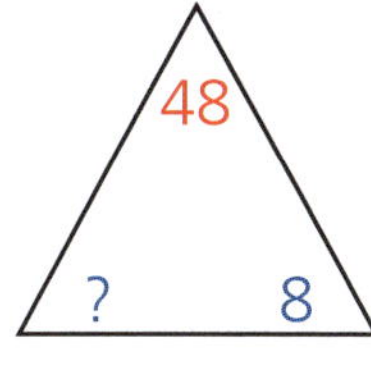

4

a

18	÷ 2	=	
	÷ 3	=	
	÷ 6	=	
	÷ 9	=	

b

24	÷ 3	=	
	÷ 4	=	
	÷ 6	=	
	÷ 8	=	

c

30	÷ 3	=	
	÷ 5	=	
	÷ 6	=	
	÷ 10	=	

5 Use a calculator to check all your answers.

ACTIVITY

Find the number sentences

- One person draws a number line which shows several equal jumps, starting at zero.
- The other person writes multiplication and division number sentences to match the picture.

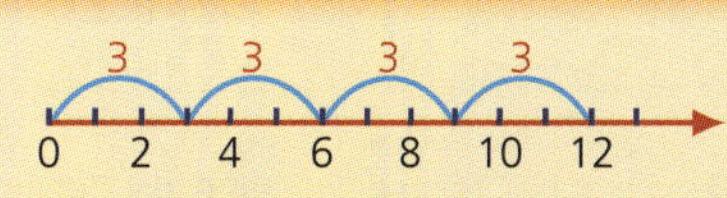

This shows:
$4 \times 3 = 12$
so $12 \div 3 = 4$
and $12 \div 4 = 3$.

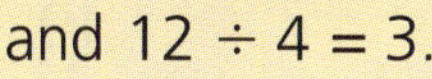

 • *AUSTRALIAN SIGNPOST MATHS 4* • ISBN 9780655708780

2:43 Odd and even numbers

Is the total even or odd?

CONCEPT

- Odd numbers end in 1, 3, 5, 7 or 9.
  87 is an odd number.
- Even numbers end in 2, 4, 6, 8 or 0.
  34 is an even number.

An odd number of items can't be drawn in pairs.

Examples:

569, 12 721, 1163

An even number of items can be drawn in pairs.

Examples:

1690, 724, 6928

1 Colour the odd numbers red and the even numbers blue.

83 100 109 111 118 120 125 127 130 3005 6112

2 Why are numbers ending in 1, 3, 5, 7 or 9 odd numbers?

3 Circle the even numbers. Underline the odd numbers.

38 53 75 14 87 92 66 36 29 41 50 35 74 100
482 764 2221 3106 988 3825 24 000

4 **a** What is the largest even number less than 80?

b What is the largest odd number less than 67?

c What is the largest even number less than 95?

d What is the largest odd number less than 100?

61	62	63	64	65	66	67	68	69	70
71	72	73	74	75	76	77	78	79	80
81	82	83	84	85	86	87	88	89	90
91	92	93	94	95	96	97	98	99	100

5 Find the rules for operating with two even numbers. Try to use mental strategies.

a

6 + 14	10 + 8	100 + 84
16 + 12	32 + 16	104 + 58
28 + 4	92 + 20	94 + 94

even number plus even number =

b

44 – 42	56 – 56	36 – 8
28 – 16	86 – 20	958 – 602
32 – 14	198 – 8	600 – 2

even number minus even number =

Odd and even

Odd numbers end in 1, 3, 5, 7, or 9.
Even numbers end in 2, 4, 6, 8 or 0.

1 Find the rules for operating with two odd or two even numbers.

a

7 + 7		11 + 3		75 + 25	
1 + 99		17 + 17		133 + 27	
5 + 83		87 + 21		77 + 33	

odd number plus odd number =

b

9 – 3		11 – 5		15 – 9	
21 – 11		33 – 19		17 – 15	
65 – 43		73 – 15		49 – 37	

odd number minus odd number =

c

12 × 2		8 × 6		4 × 2	
8 × 4		2 × 20		6 × 6	
6 × 4		4 × 10		2 × 8	

even number times even number =

d

48 ÷ 2		10 ÷ 10		80 ÷ 2	
40 ÷ 4		24 ÷ 4		40 ÷ 8	
18 ÷ 6		24 ÷ 8		36 ÷ 6	

even number divided by even number = odd or even

Use other pairs of odd or even numbers to check these rules.

2 Use many different examples of each case to complete this table.
In each case write whether the answer would be odd or even.

Number types	+	–	×	÷
Even and Even				odd or even
Odd and Odd				
Odd and Even				

Flow chart

Start with a number.

Does it end in 1, 3, 5, 7 or 9? Yes → The number is odd.

No ↓

Does it end in 2, 4, 6, 8 or 0? Yes → The number is even.

3 Use the rules above to cross (✗) the answers that must be wrong.

6248 + 396 = 6645		8104 – 7998 = 106		366 × 47 = 17 201	
6107 ÷ 31 = 196		7319 + 2997 = 10 313		2817 – 199 = 2617	
283 × 654 = 28 353		173 × 881 = 152 416		68 019 ÷ 79 = 862	

2:45 Division using a grid

CONCEPT

×	0	1	2	3	4	5	6	7	8	9	10
0	0	0	0	0	0	0	0	0	0	0	0
1	0	1	2	3	4	5	6	7	8	9	10
2	0	2	4	6	8	10	12	14	16	18	20
3	0	3	6	9	12	15	18	21	24	27	30
4	0	4	8	12	16	20	24	28	32	36	40
5	0	5	10	15	20	25	30	35	40	45	50
6	0	6	12	18	24	30	36	42	48	54	60
7	0	7	14	21	28	35	42	49	56	63	70
8	0	8	16	24	32	40	48	56	64	72	80
9	0	9	18	27	36	45	54	63	72	81	90
10	0	10	20	30	40	50	60	70	80	90	100

Use the multiplication grid above to answer these division questions.

1
- **a** 15 ÷ 3 = ☐ **b** 20 ÷ 5 = ☐ **c** 16 ÷ 8 = ☐ **d** 90 ÷ 10 = ☐
- **e** 42 ÷ 6 = ☐ **f** 10 ÷ 10 = ☐ **g** 24 ÷ 6 = ☐ **h** 24 ÷ 4 = ☐
- **i** 64 ÷ 8 = ☐ **j** 45 ÷ 5 = ☐ **k** 36 ÷ 6 = ☐ **l** 25 ÷ 5 = ☐
- **m** 72 ÷ 9 = ☐ **n** 16 ÷ 4 = ☐ **o** 10 ÷ 5 = ☐ **p** 81 ÷ 9 = ☐
- **q** 18 ÷ 6 = ☐ **r** 54 ÷ 9 = ☐ **s** 40 ÷ 8 = ☐ **t** 36 ÷ 4 = ☐
- **u** 40 ÷ 8 = ☐ **v** 50 ÷ 10 = ☐ **w** 48 ÷ 6 = ☐ **x** 21 ÷ 3 = ☐

2
- **a** 2)8 **b** 5)5 **c** 2)6 **d** 10)30 **e** 6)12
- **f** 4)12 **g** 10)80 **h** 3)9 **i** 9)45 **j** 8)32
- **k** 5)30 **l** 5)15 **m** 5)40 **n** 3)24 **o** 9)27

3 Follow this track, putting an answer in every empty place.

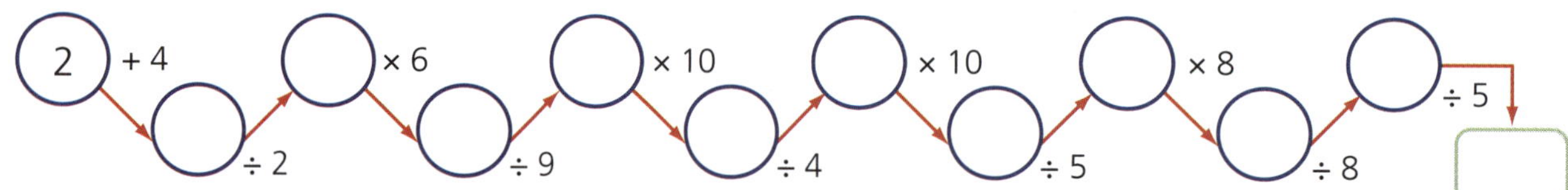

 • *AUSTRALIAN SIGNPOST MATHS 4* • ISBN 9780655708780

× and ÷ tables (by 2, 4, 8)

4 × 8 = 32 so
32 ÷ 4 = 8
and 32 ÷ 8 = 4.

CONCEPT

If 8 × 4 = 32 then
- 32 ÷ 4 (How many 4s in 32?) = 8
- 32 ÷ 8 (32 shared by 8) = 4 (each)

32 ÷ 4 = ☐
- We can ask ☐ × 4 = 32
- We can ask 8 × 4 = 32 so ☐ = 8.

1 Join each question to its answer using a pencil and ruler.

a

× 2	
3 × 2	8
4 × 2	6
7 × 2	12
6 × 2	14
8 × 2	18
9 × 2	16
5 × 2	20
10 × 2	10

÷ 2	
8 ÷ 2	6
6 ÷ 2	9
12 ÷ 2	10
14 ÷ 2	4
18 ÷ 2	3
16 ÷ 2	7
20 ÷ 2	5
10 ÷ 2	8

b

× 4	
3 × 4	16
4 × 4	28
7 × 4	12
6 × 4	32
8 × 4	24
9 × 4	20
5 × 4	40
10 × 4	36

÷ 4	
16 ÷ 4	7
28 ÷ 4	3
12 ÷ 4	6
32 ÷ 4	4
24 ÷ 4	8
20 ÷ 4	10
40 ÷ 4	9
36 ÷ 4	5

c

× 8	
3 × 8	32
4 × 8	24
7 × 8	56
6 × 8	48
8 × 8	64
9 × 8	72
5 × 8	80
10 × 8	40

÷ 8	
32 ÷ 8	7
24 ÷ 8	6
56 ÷ 8	4
48 ÷ 8	9
64 ÷ 8	3
72 ÷ 8	10
80 ÷ 8	5
40 ÷ 8	8

d

×	
3 × 4	28
4 × 8	32
7 × 4	12
6 × 8	64
8 × 8	48
9 × 4	80
5 × 8	40
10 × 8	36

÷	
28 ÷ 4	3
32 ÷ 8	4
12 ÷ 4	8
64 ÷ 8	10
48 ÷ 8	7
80 ÷ 8	9
40 ÷ 8	6
36 ÷ 4	5

e

×	
3 × 8	8
4 × 2	24
7 × 8	56
6 × 8	48
8 × 8	18
9 × 2	64
5 × 8	80
10 × 8	40

÷	
8 ÷ 2	3
24 ÷ 8	8
56 ÷ 8	4
48 ÷ 8	9
18 ÷ 2	6
64 ÷ 8	7
80 ÷ 8	5
40 ÷ 8	10

f

×	
9 × 2	28
7 × 4	48
6 × 8	18
4 × 4	24
3 × 8	16
11 × 2	64
10 × 4	22
8 × 8	40

÷	
28 ÷ 4	6
48 ÷ 8	3
18 ÷ 2	7
24 ÷ 8	11
16 ÷ 4	9
64 ÷ 8	10
22 ÷ 2	4
40 ÷ 4	8

2:47 Mental strategies, × and ÷

18 × 3
= (10 × 3) + (8 × 3)
= 30 + 24 = 54

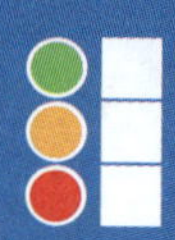

These are some of the strategies that can be used to solve problems.

A	Using × to answer ÷	6 × 4 = 24 so 24 ÷ 6 = 4 and 24 ÷ 4 = 6			
B	Extending known facts	12 × 7	= 11 × 7 + 7	= 77 + 7	= 84
C	Break up a number	5 × 18	= 5 × 2 × 9	= 10 × 9	= 90
D	Multiply in parts	16 × 4	= (10 × 4) + (6 × 4)	= 40 + 24	= 64
E	Multiplying 10s	7 × 40	= 7 × 4 × 10	= 28 × 10	= 280
F	Multiplying 100s	3 × 800	= 3 × 8 × 100	= 24 × 100	= 2400
G	Halve twice to divide by 4	128 ÷ 4 Halve 128, then halve again. (128 ÷ 2) ÷ 2 = 32			

1 (**A**) Use 7 × 9 = 63, 8 × 4 = 32 and 8 × 6 = 48 to answer:

a 63 ÷ 7 ☐ **b** 63 ÷ 9 ☐ **c** 32 ÷ 8 ☐
d 32 ÷ 4 ☐ **e** 48 ÷ 6 ☐ **f** 48 ÷ 8 ☐

2 (**B**) Use 11 × 6 = 66, 11 × 4 = 44 and 11 × 8 = 88 to answer **a** to **c**.

a 12 × 6 ☐ **b** 12 × 4 ☐ **c** 12 × 8 ☐
d 20 × 4 = 80, 21 × 4 = ☐ **e** 40 × 3 = 120, 41 × 3 = ☐

3 (**C**) Break up a number into one number times another.

a 5 × 16 ☐ **b** 5 × 14 ☐ **c** 5 × 18 ☐
d 18 × 50 ☐ **e** 14 × 50 ☐ **f** 40 × 25 ☐

4 (**D**) Multiply in two easier parts.

a 14 × 4 ☐ **b** 16 × 6 ☐ **c** 15 × 6 ☐
d 12 × 14 ☐ **e** 13 × 15 ☐ **f** 11 × 21 ☐

Multiply in parts

16 threes is 10 threes plus 6 threes.

10

6

3

16 × 3 = (10 × 3) + (6 × 3)
= 30 + 18
= 48

5 (**E**) Multiply tens numbers.

a 8 × 20 ☐ **b** 7 × 30 ☐ **c** 8 × 40 ☐
d 60 × 7 ☐ **e** 20 × 9 ☐ **f** 70 × 4 ☐

6 (**F**) Multiply hundreds numbers.

a 7 × 200 ☐ **b** 4 × 400 ☐ **c** 7 × 500 ☐
d 600 × 3 ☐ **e** 900 × 6 ☐ **f** 800 × 9 ☐

7 (**G**) Halve and halve again to divide by 4. Halve three times to divide by 8.

a 64 ÷ 4 ☐ **b** 148 ÷ 4 ☐ **c** 160 ÷ 4 ☐
d 160 ÷ 8 ☐ **e** 808 ÷ 8 ☐ **f** 240 ÷ 8 ☐

Working with numbers

An estimate is a good guess.

1. Estimate the number of stickers to the nearest ten. ☐
2. What two multiplication tables are shown by this array?

☐ × ☐ = ☐ and ☐ × ☐ = ☐

3. What two division tables are shown by this array?

42 ÷ ☐ = ☐ and 42 ÷ ☐ = ☐

4. How many children could be given 5 stickers? ☐
5. How many more stickers are needed to make 60? ☐

6. Halve the number and keep halving for as long as you can.

a 400 ☐ ☐ ☐ ☐ ☐ **b** 160 ☐ ☐ ☐ ☐ ☐

c 256 ☐ ☐ ☐ ☐ ☐ ☐ ☐ ☐ ☐ ☐

Double the number and keep doubling until you have filled the boxes.

d 3 ☐ ☐ ☐ ☐ ☐ ☐

e 9 ☐ ☐ ☐ ☐ ☐ ☐

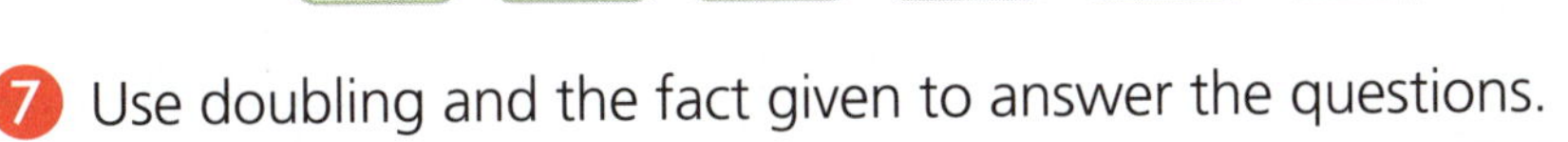

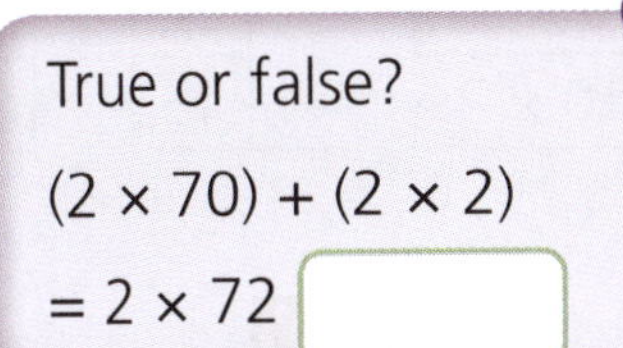

INVESTIGATION

True or false?

(2 × 70) + (2 × 2)

= 2 × 72 ☐

7. Use doubling and the fact given to answer the questions.

a 2 × 12 = 24 4 × 12 = ☐, 8 × 12 = ☐, 16 × 12 = ☐

b 6 × 3 = 18 12 × 3 = ☐, 24 × 3 = ☐, 48 × 3 = ☐

c 7 × 9 = 63 14 × 9 = ☐, 28 × 9 = ☐, 56 × 9 = ☐

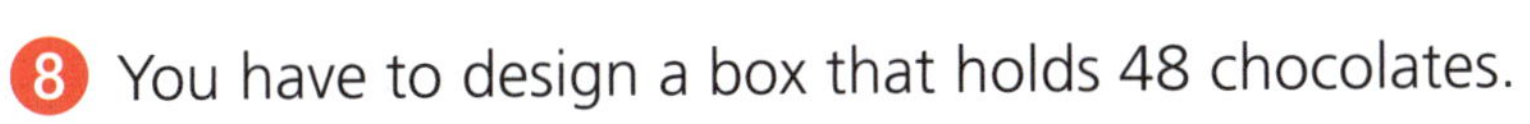

8. You have to design a box that holds 48 chocolates.
There can be one or two layers, and on each layer the chocolates are arranged in equal rows.
How many ways could you arrange the chocolates in a box? ☐

9. Show the method that you would use to answer each of these questions.

a 18 × 23 Estimate = ☐

b 852 ÷ 4 Estimate = ☐

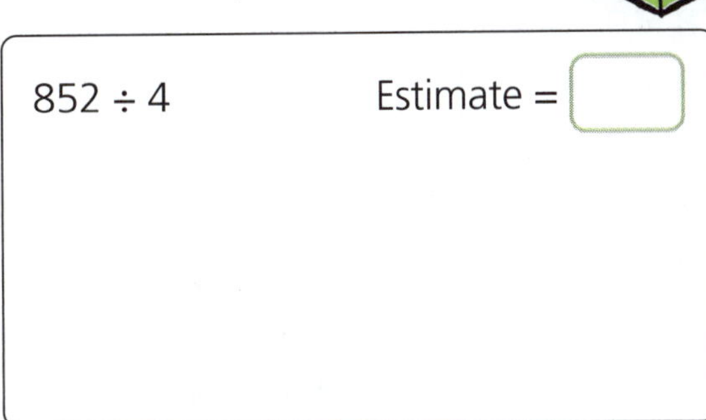

× and ÷ tables (by 3, 6, 9)

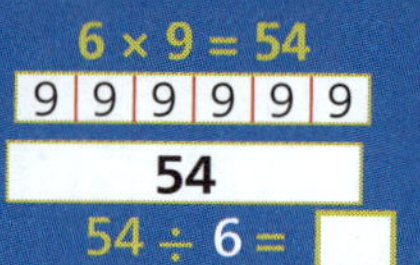

CONCEPT

If 6 × 3 = 18 then
- 18 ÷ 3 (How many 3s in 18?) = 6
- 18 ÷ 6 (18 shared by 6) = 3 (each)

18 ÷ 3 = ☐
- We can ask ☐ × 3 = 18
- We know that 6 × 3 = 18 so ☐ = 6.

1 Join each question to its answer using a pencil and ruler.

a

× 3	
3 × 3	12
4 × 3	9
7 × 3	18
6 × 3	21
8 × 3	27
9 × 3	24
5 × 3	30
10 × 3	15

÷ 3	
12 ÷ 3	6
9 ÷ 3	9
18 ÷ 3	10
21 ÷ 3	4
27 ÷ 3	3
24 ÷ 3	7
30 ÷ 3	5
15 ÷ 3	8

b

× 6	
3 × 6	24
4 × 6	42
7 × 6	18
6 × 6	48
8 × 6	36
9 × 6	30
5 × 6	60
10 × 6	54

÷ 6	
24 ÷ 6	7
42 ÷ 6	3
18 ÷ 6	6
48 ÷ 6	4
36 ÷ 6	8
30 ÷ 6	10
60 ÷ 6	9
54 ÷ 6	5

c

× 9	
5 × 9	90
10 × 9	45
4 × 9	72
8 × 9	36
3 × 9	54
6 × 9	27
7 × 9	81
9 × 9	63

÷ 9	
90 ÷ 9	4
45 ÷ 9	8
72 ÷ 9	10
36 ÷ 9	3
54 ÷ 9	5
27 ÷ 9	9
81 ÷ 9	7
63 ÷ 9	6

d

× 6	
6 × 6	54
5 × 6	30
9 × 6	36
3 × 6	42
7 × 6	18
8 × 6	12
4 × 6	48
2 × 6	24

÷ 6	
54 ÷ 6	6
30 ÷ 6	5
36 ÷ 6	7
42 ÷ 6	2
18 ÷ 6	9
12 ÷ 6	4
48 ÷ 6	3
24 ÷ 6	8

e

× 9	
8 × 9	72
3 × 9	27
5 × 9	45
7 × 9	63
9 × 9	54
6 × 9	81
4 × 9	18
2 × 9	36

÷ 9	
72 ÷ 9	3
27 ÷ 9	9
45 ÷ 9	8
63 ÷ 9	6
54 ÷ 9	7
81 ÷ 9	5
18 ÷ 9	4
36 ÷ 9	2

f

×	
3 × 5	80
8 × 10	25
5 × 5	15
4 × 10	45
9 × 5	40
6 × 10	20
7 × 5	60
2 × 10	35

÷	
80 ÷ 10	5
25 ÷ 5	9
15 ÷ 5	8
45 ÷ 5	6
40 ÷ 10	3
20 ÷ 10	7
60 ÷ 10	4
35 ÷ 5	2

 • *AUSTRALIAN SIGNPOST MATHS 4* • ISBN 9780655708780

2:50 Division facts

2 kangaroos shared 12 balls.
6 × 2 = 12 so 12 ÷ 2 = 6

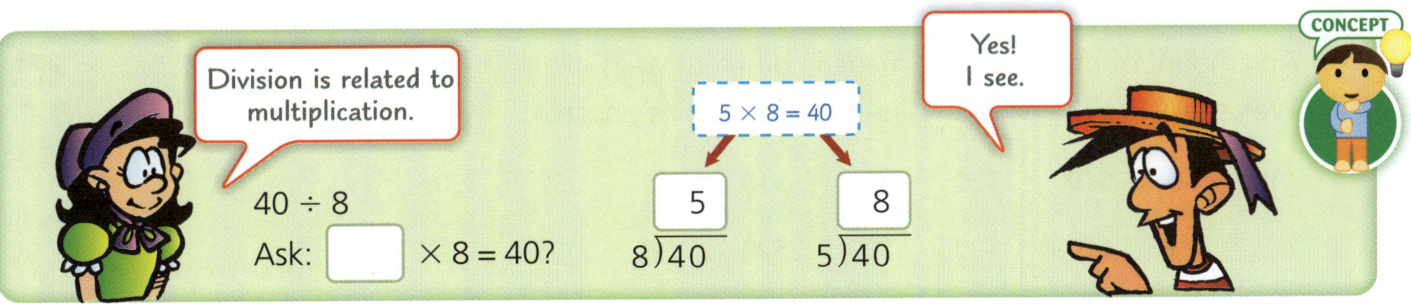

1. Use a multiplication table to answer the division questions.

a 6 × 10 = 60	**b** 5 × 8 = 40	**c** 6 × 9 = 54
6)60 10)60	8)40 5)40	9)54 6)54
d 9 × 8 = 72	**e** 7 × 6 = 42	**f** 4 × 9 = 36
8)72 9)72	6)42 7)42	9)36 4)36

2.

a ☐ × 2 = 12	**b** 6 × ☐ = 18	**c** ☐ × 4 = 20	**d** 5 × ☐ = 10
e ☐ × 3 = 18	**f** 7 × ☐ = 56	**g** ☐ × 9 = 9	**h** 6 × ☐ = 36
i ☐ × 5 = 35	**j** 4 × ☐ = 32	**k** ☐ × 4 = 16	**l** 3 × ☐ = 27

3.

a 16 ÷ 2 = ☐	**b** 25 ÷ 5 = ☐	**c** 30 ÷ 6 = ☐	**d** 24 ÷ 6 = ☐
e 30 ÷ 3 = ☐	**f** 24 ÷ 4 = ☐	**g** 35 ÷ 7 = ☐	**h** 90 ÷ 9 = ☐
i 24 ÷ 8 = ☐	**j** 48 ÷ 6 = ☐	**k** 64 ÷ 8 = ☐	**l** 36 ÷ 6 = ☐
m 27 ÷ 3 = ☐	**n** 50 ÷ 5 = ☐	**o** 63 ÷ 9 = ☐	**p** 30 ÷ 5 = ☐
q 45 ÷ 5 = ☐	**r** 72 ÷ 9 = ☐	**s** 54 ÷ 6 = ☐	**t** 90 ÷ 10 = ☐
u 81 ÷ 9 = ☐	**v** 48 ÷ 8 = ☐	**w** 16 ÷ 8 = ☐	**x** 30 ÷ 5 = ☐

For **81** ÷ 9 **ask**, 'What times 9 gives **81**'?

FUN SPOT

Dice multiplication

×	1	2	3	4	5	6
1						
2						
3						
4						
5						
6						

- Take turns to throw two dice.
- Multiply the numbers showing.
- Write the answer in the table (each player uses a different colour).
- The first to get 3 answers in a line wins.

Note: 3 × 1 and 1 × 3 are made by [dice] [dice].

Money

Use 20c and 10c coins to make 70c in two ways.

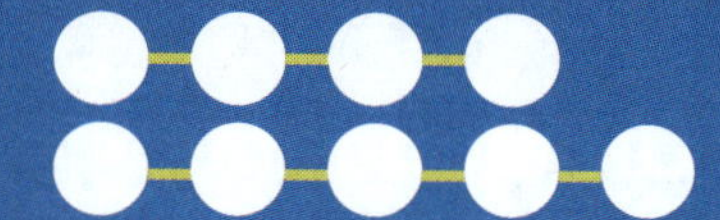

- An amount of money can be made in different ways.
- We usually use the highest value notes and coins possible.

$187.50 = $100 $50 $20 $10 $5 $2 50c

or $100 $20 $20 $20 $20 $5 $2 50c

The white boxes stand for coins.

1 Make each amount using the highest value of notes and coins possible.

a $57

b $51.50

c $23

d $60.30

e $188.60

f $96.95

g $133.80

h $165.75

i $65.35

j $153.35

k $275.40

l $212.80

m $107.25

ACTIVITY

2 From a collection of coins, choose 8. Write the value of each coin and the total. Repeat the process.

 • *AUSTRALIAN SIGNPOST MATHS 4* • ISBN 9780655708780

2:52 Rounding off money

If we pay cash, the cost is rounded to the nearest 5 cents.

CONCEPT

When paying by cash, the price is rounded to the nearest 5 cents.

Cost →

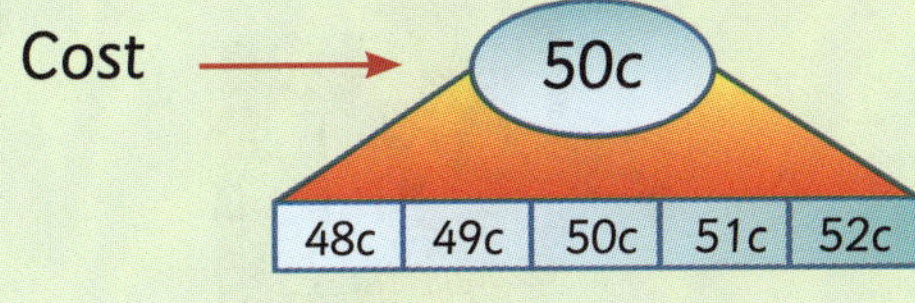

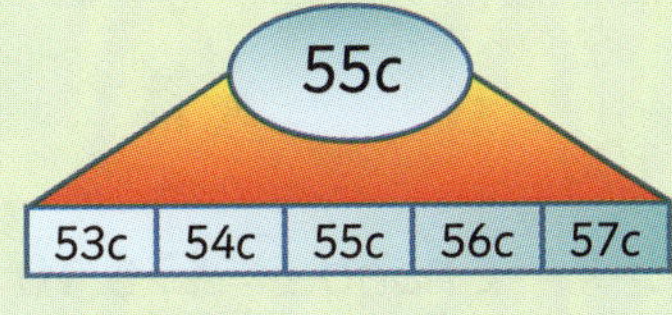

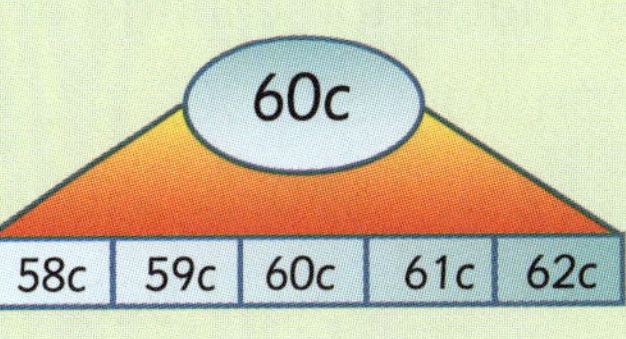

48c	49c	50c	51c	52c

53c	54c	55c	56c	57c

58c	59c	60c	61c	62c

1 Round these amounts to the nearest 5 cents.

a 87c		**b** $0.87		**c** $1.52	
d $6.88		**e** $3.26		**f** $9.45	
g $8.90		**h** $4.51		**i** $7.43	
j $5.04		**k** $0.59		**l** $8.74	
m $7.13		**n** $4.88		**o** $0.42	
p $8.77		**q** $3.56		**r** $8.04	

We no longer use 1 and 2 cent coins.

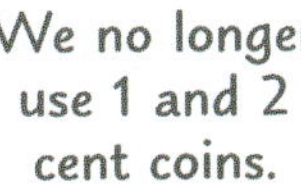

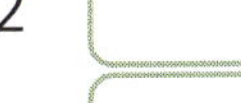

Round each to the nearest dollar to estimate.

2 Find the total cost of the items then round to the nearest 5c.

a ice cream ($5.86), milk ($2.33), chocolate ($3.58)

b biscuits ($3.35), nuts ($12.48), raisins ($3.96)

c tea ($12.47), scissors ($2.42), calculator ($45.11)

d pens ($3.71), paper ($6.15), cereal ($7.32)

CONCEPT

To find the change, follow these steps:

Step 1 Find the total cost using a calculator.

Step 2 Round to the nearest 5 cents.

Step 3 Count on, to determine the change.

Step 4 Write the amount of change.

3 Complete the table.

	Cost of items	Total	Total rounded	Amount given	Count on to give change	Change
a	$1.14, $6.35, $4.17	$11.66	$11.65	$50	5c, $11.70 30c, $12 $8, $20 $30	$38.35
b	$0.98, $7.93, $11.42			$50		
c	$12.56, $5.99, $3.04			$50		
d	$1.78, $4.29, $3.95			$20		
e	$0.75, $0.89, $1.13			$20		
f	$8.46, $12.18, $9.87			$100		
g	$37.54, $9.45, $6.69			$100		

2:53 Counting change

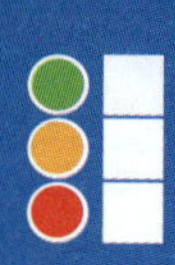

CONCEPT

To give change, we count on from the price paid.

Example: What is the change from $100 if the cost is $23.90?

- Count on from $23.90.

$24… $25… $30… $50… $100

10c | $1 | $5 | $20 | $50 Change = $76.10

1 Count on and write the change given in coins and notes.

	Cost	Money given	Count on ⟶ Coins and notes given as change	Total change
a	$6.50	$50	$7 → $8 → $10 → $30 → $50	
b	$1.20	$10	$1.30 → $1.50 → $2 → $3 → $5 → $10	
c	$8.70	$50	$8.80 → $9 → $10 → $30 → $50	
d	$3.00	$100	$5 → $10 → $30 → $50 → $100	
e	$36.40	$50		
f	$67.20	$100		

2 Find the change from $50 using only the boxes you need.

a $36.50 Change =

b $9.20 Change =

c $18.30 Change =

INVESTIGATION

3 Show three different ways of giving change from $50 if the cost is $41.95.

a

b

c

Practise giving change using play money.

 • *AUSTRALIAN SIGNPOST MATHS 4* • ISBN 9780655708780

2:54 Multiplying by 10, 100, 1000

CONCEPT

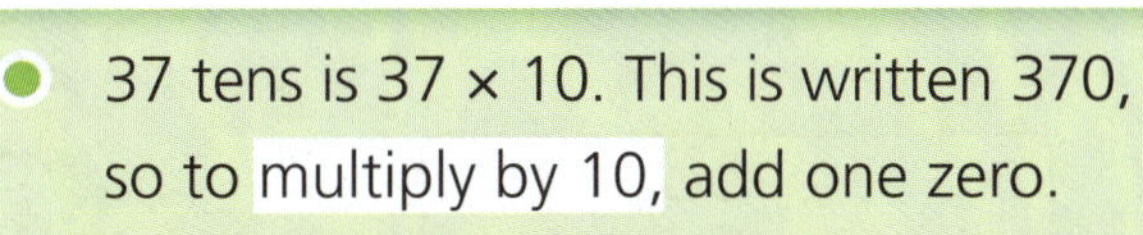

- 37 tens is 37 × 10. This is written 370, so to multiply by 10, add one zero.
  Examples: 93 × 10 = 930, 154 × 10 = 1540

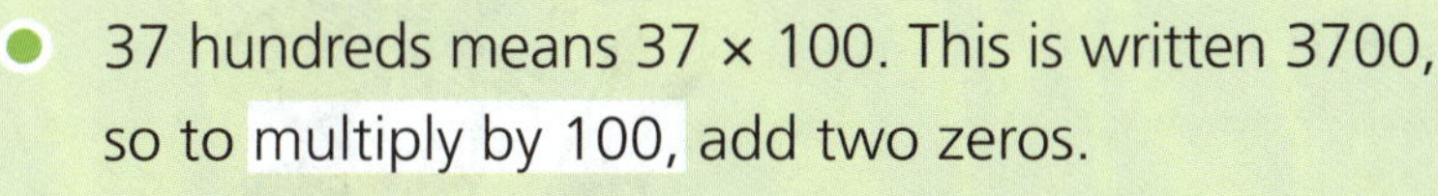

- 37 hundreds means 37 × 100. This is written 3700, so to multiply by 100, add two zeros.
  Examples: 93 × 100 = 9300, 154 × 100 = 15 400
- 37 thousands means 37 × 1000. This is written 37 000, so to multiply by 1000, add three zeros.
  Examples: 93 × 1000 = 93 000, 154 × 1000 = 154 000

Write the answer to each problem.

1
a 56 × 10 ☐ b 91 × 10 ☐ c 33 × 10 ☐
d 620 × 10 ☐ e 2917 × 10 ☐ f 44 188 × 10 ☐
g 78 × 100 ☐ h 15 × 100 ☐ i 48 × 100 ☐
j 913 × 100 ☐ k 4054 × 100 ☐ l 7500 × 100 ☐
m 79 × 1000 ☐ n 98 × 1000 ☐ o 80 × 1000 ☐
p 300 × 1000 ☐ q 5835 × 1000 ☐ r 60 000 × 1000 ☐

2
a 30 250 × 10 ☐ b 91 450 × 10 ☐ c 70 000 × 10 ☐
d 19 742 × 100 ☐ e 75 000 × 100 ☐ f 40 565 × 100 ☐
g 19 500 × 1000 ☐ h 60 300 × 1000 ☐ i 74 000 × 1000 ☐

3

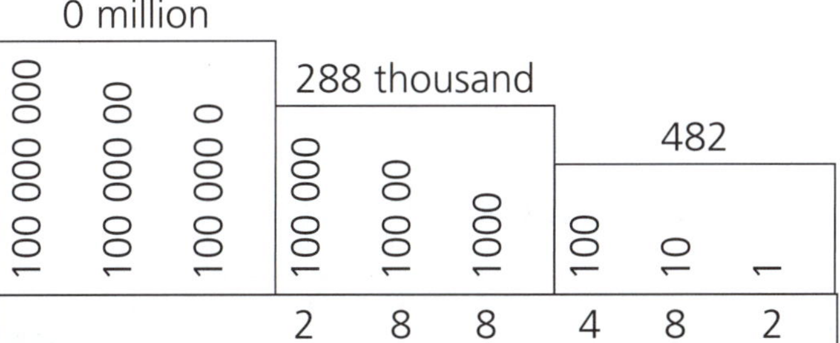

a 288 482 × 10 ☐
b 288 482 × 100 ☐
c 288 482 × 1000 ☐

× 10, × 100 and × 1000 move the digits 1, 2 an 3 places to the left.

Multiplying by 10 moves all digits one place to the left by adding a zero.
Multiplying by 100 moves all digits two places to the left by adding two zeros.
Multiplying by 1000 moves all digits three places to the left by adding three zeros.

 • *AUSTRALIAN SIGNPOST MATHS 4* • ISBN 9780655708780

2:55 Dividing by 10, 100, 1000

200 years is ☐ times as much as 20 years.

CONCEPT

- 810 × 10 = 8100, so 8100 ÷ 10 = 810.
  To divide by 10, remove one zero.
  Examples: 9300 ÷ 10 = 930, 75 000 ÷ 10 = 7500
- 810 × 100 = 81 000, so 81 000 ÷ 100 = 810.
  To divide by 100, remove two zeros.
  Examples: 56 000 ÷ 100 = 560, 114 000 ÷ 100 = 1140
- 810 × 1000 = 810 000, so 810 000 ÷ 1000 = 810.
  To divide by 1000, remove three zeros.
  Examples: 84 000 ÷ 1000 = 84, 4 190 000 ÷ 1000 = 4190

Write the answer to each problem.

1

a 660 ÷ 10		b 200 ÷ 10		c 830 ÷ 10	
d 6700 ÷ 10		e 85 370 ÷ 10		f 22 000 ÷ 10	
g 7800 ÷ 100		h 48 000 ÷ 100		i 41 400 ÷ 100	
j 33 300 ÷ 100		k 53 600 ÷ 100		l 50 000 ÷ 100	
m 19 000 ÷ 1000		n 31 000 ÷ 1000		o 80 000 ÷ 1000	
p 300 000 ÷ 1000		q 104 000 ÷ 1000		r 700 000 ÷ 1000	

2

a 110 000 ÷ 100		b 622 000 ÷ 1000		c 35 600 ÷ 100	
d 6 000 000 ÷ 10		e 291 700 ÷ 100		f 8 418 800 ÷ 100	
g 7 100 000 ÷ 10		h 900 000 ÷ 100		i 5 054 000 ÷ 1000	

3

95 million			200 thousand			000		
100 000 000	10 000 000	1 000 000	100 000	10 000	1000	100	10	1
	9	5	2	0	0	0	0	0

a 95 200 000 ÷ 10 ☐

b 95 200 000 ÷ 100 ☐

c 95 200 000 ÷ 1000 ☐

÷ 10, ÷ 100 and ÷ 1000 move the digits 1, 2 an 3 places to the right.

Dividing by 10 moves all digits one place to the right by removing a zero.
Dividing by 100 moves all digits two places to the right by removing two zeros.
Dividing by 1000 moves all digits three places to the right by removing three zeros.

Linking ÷ and ×

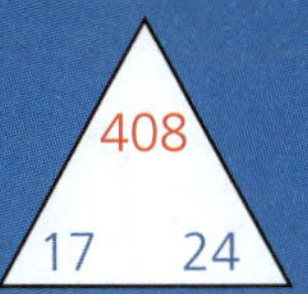

17 × 24 = 408
24 × 17 = 408
408 ÷ 17 = 24
408 ÷ 24 = 17

7 × 4 = 28	17 × 24 = 408
so	so
28 ÷ 7 = 4	408 ÷ 17 = 24
and	and
28 ÷ 4 = 7	408 ÷ 24 = 17

If 17 × ☐ = 408
then 408 ÷ 17 = ☐
and
If ☐ × 24 = 408
then 408 ÷ 24 = ☐

What is each share if $270 is shared among 9?

In each case, use a calculator to find the missing number.

Example
9 × ☐ = $270
Answer = $270 ÷ 9
= $30
Calculator keys used:
270 ÷ 9 =

1
a 8 × ☐ = 168
168 ÷ 8 = ☐
b 5 × ☐ = 225
225 ÷ 5 = ☐
c 7 × ☐ = 245
245 ÷ 7 = ☐
d 4 × ☐ = 504
504 ÷ 4 = ☐
e 3 × ☐ = 435
435 ÷ 3 = ☐
f 9 × ☐ = 351
351 ÷ 9 = ☐

How many $8 hats can I buy with $192?

Example
☐ × $8 = $192
Answer = $192 ÷ $8
= 24 hats
Calculator keys used:
192 ÷ 8 =

2
a ☐ × 7 = 476
476 ÷ 7 = ☐
b ☐ × 3 = 486
486 ÷ 3 = ☐
c ☐ × 5 = 835
835 ÷ 5 = ☐
d ☐ × 8 = 296
296 ÷ 8 = ☐
e ☐ × 9 = 504
504 ÷ 9 = ☐
f ☐ × 6 = 648
648 ÷ 6 = ☐

3
a 14 × ☐ = 224
Answer = ☐
b 17 × ☐ = 884
Answer = ☐
c 24 × ☐ = 1632
Answer = ☐
d ☐ × 35 = 4410
Answer = ☐
e ☐ × 62 = 1550
Answer = ☐
f ☐ × 27 = 729
Answer = ☐
g 38 × ☐ = 988
Answer = ☐
h 63 × ☐ = 1701
Answer = ☐
i 75 × ☐ = 1875
Answer = ☐

24 times what number gives 1632? We divide 1632 by 24.

2:57 Missing number strategies

True or false?
13 + 5 = 9 + 9

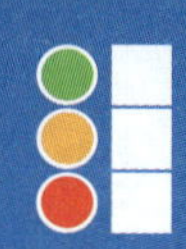

1 Linking addition and subtraction

a 8 – ☐ = 1 b 9 – ☐ = 0 c 15 – ☐ = 10 d 10 – ☐ = 10

e ☐ – 3 = 7 f ☐ – 10 = 10 g ☐ – 7 = 8 h ☐ – 5 = 4

2 Finding the difference

a ☐ + 8 = 10 b ☐ + 3 = 7 c ☐ + 8 = 15

d 9 + ☐ = 12 e 8 + ☐ = 17 f 10 + ☐ = 10

g ☐ + 11 = 15 h ☐ + 9 = 14 i ☐ + 12 = 12

j 14 + ☐ = 20 k 18 + ☐ = 23 l 17 + ☐ = 19

m ☐ + 9 = 20 n ☐ + 15 = 25 o ☐ + 11 = 40

40	
	11

3 Each side of an = sign has the same value. Find the missing numbers.

a 5 – ☐ = 10 – 7 b 18 + ☐ = 15 + 8 c 21 – ☐ = 19 – 7

d 16 – 7 = ☐ + 6 e 24 + ☐ = 35 – 6 f 30 – 15 = 6 + ☐

4 Compensation strategy

a 887 + 96 = 887 + 100 – ☐ = ☐ b 416 + 49 = 416 + 50 – ☐ = ☐

c 1076 + 97 = 1076 + 100 – ☐ = ☐ d 253 + 89 = 476 + 90 – ☐ = ☐

5 Linking multiplication and division

a ☐ × 6 = 18 b ☐ × 5 = 35 c ☐ × 4 = 24 d ☐ × 3 = 27

e 4 × ☐ = 20 f 7 × ☐ = 21 g 9 × ☐ = 90 h 8 × ☐ = 40

i ☐ × 10 = 80 j ☐ × 6 = 36 k ☐ × 4 = 28 l ☐ × 5 = 35

m ☐ ÷ 2 = 8 n ☐ ÷ 4 = 3 o ☐ ÷ 5 = 8

p 24 ÷ ☐ = 3 q 24 ÷ ☐ = 4 r 24 ÷ ☐ = 8

24 ÷ ☐ = 8.
Ask, '24 divided by what number gives 8?'

6 Mixed operations

a 6 + 7 + ☐ = 15 b 3 – 1 + ☐ = 12 c 8 + 7 + ☐ = 20

d 4 × 2 + ☐ = 10 e 6 × 5 – ☐ = 26 f 21 ÷ 3 + ☐ = 13

g 2 × ☐ + 1 = 9 h 3 × ☐ + 2 = 17 i 2 × ☐ + 1 = 7

Partitioning, + and –

These strategies help you work it out in your head.

When we partition, adding larger numbers is easier.

36 + 25

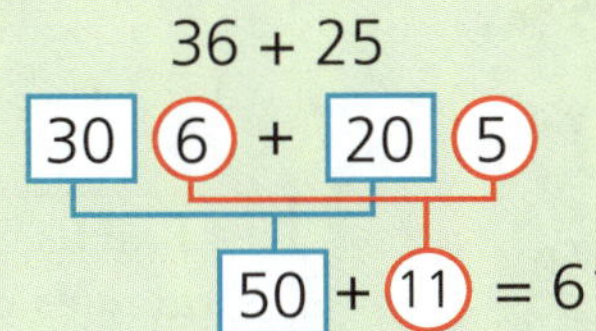

518 + 74

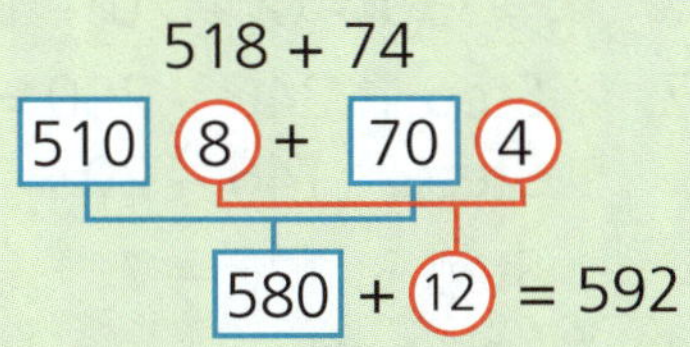

CONCEPT

1 Use partitioning to add these numbers.

a 47 + 36

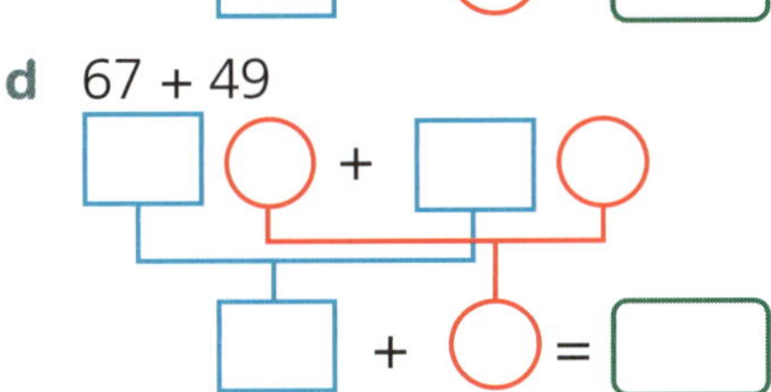

b 25 + 29

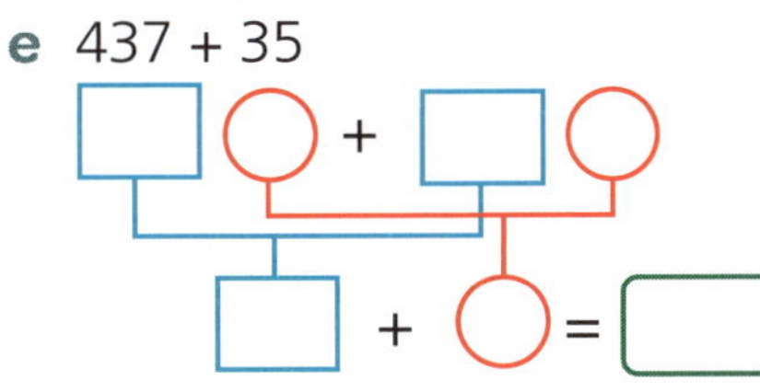

c 648 + 45

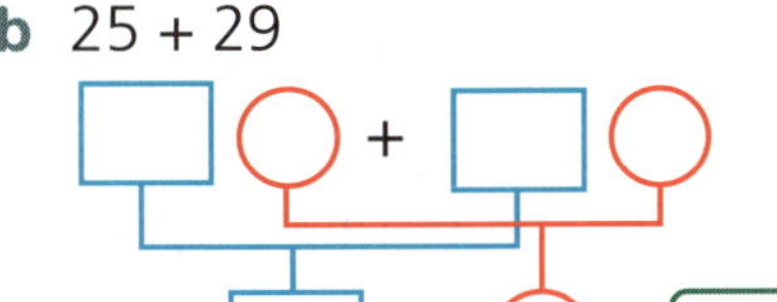

d 67 + 49

e 437 + 35

f Try these in your head.

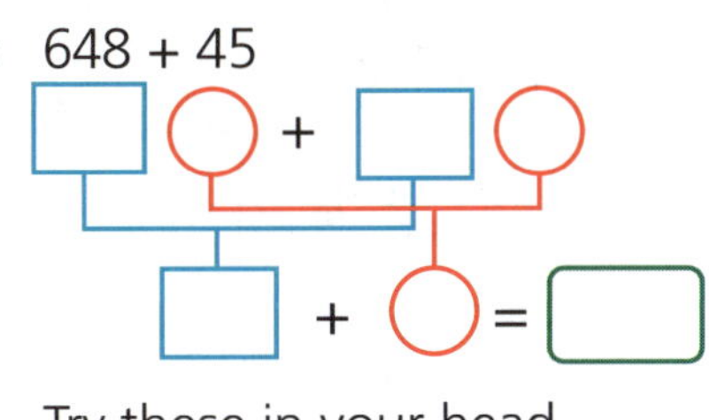

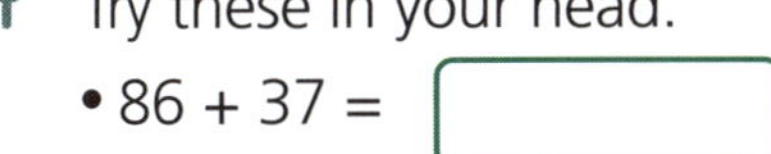

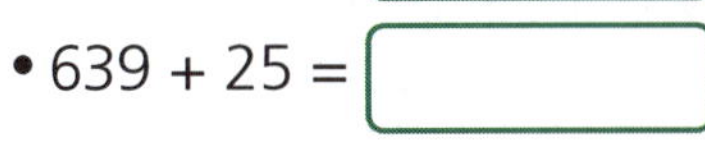

- 86 + 37 =
- 639 + 25 =
- 427 + 37 =

When we partition to subtract we must make sure we can subtract the second number.

CONCEPT

86 – 39

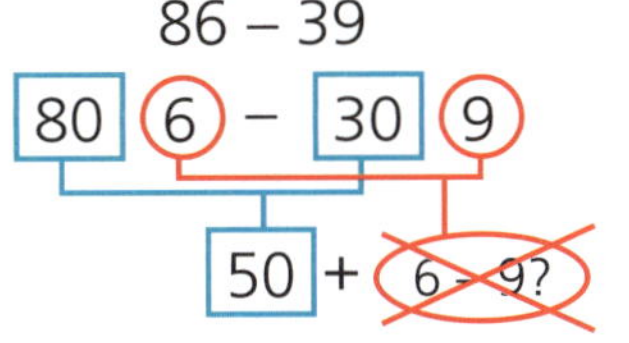

86 – 39

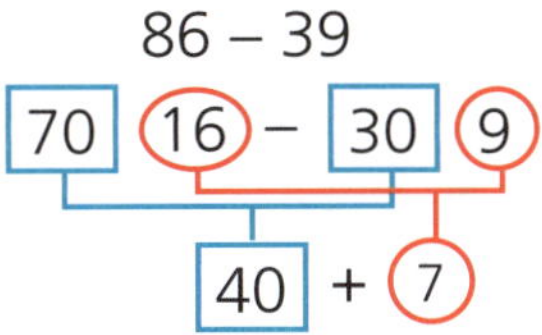

We cannot subtract 9 from 6 so we break up 86 into 70 + 16.

473 – 45

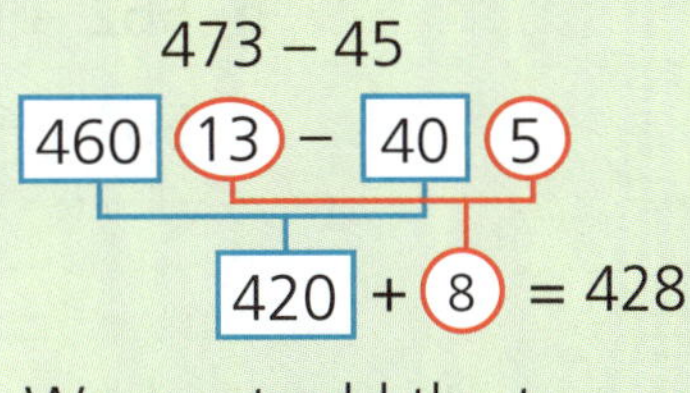

We must add the two parts we have subtracted.

2 Use partitioning to subtract these numbers.

a 52 – 28

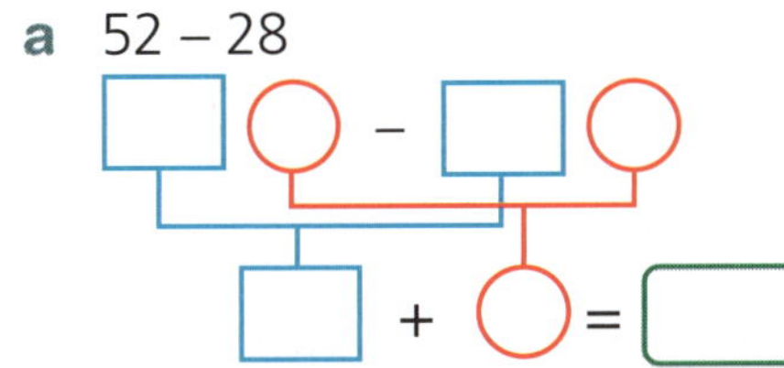

b 73 – 46

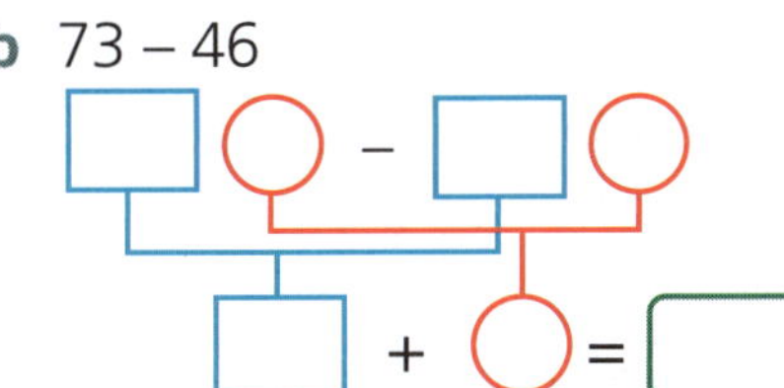

c 273 – 46

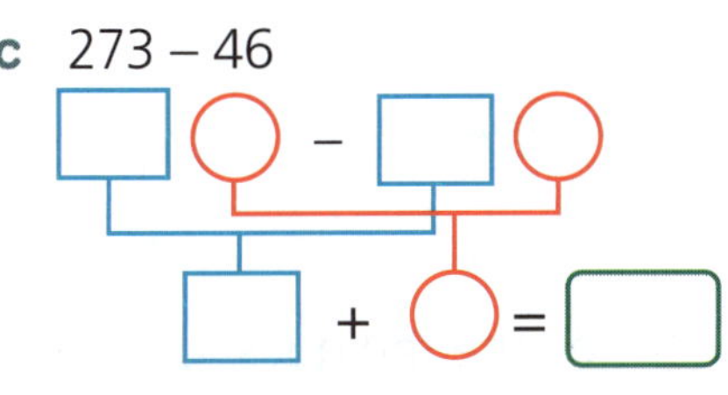

d 114 – 37

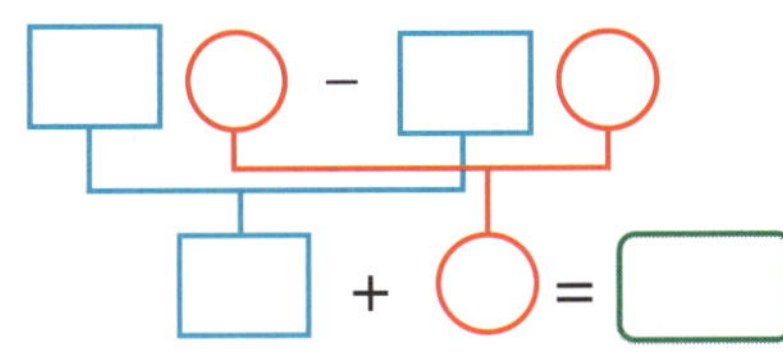

e 313 – 47

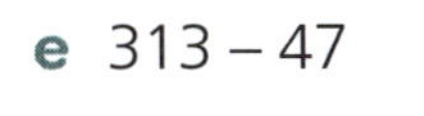

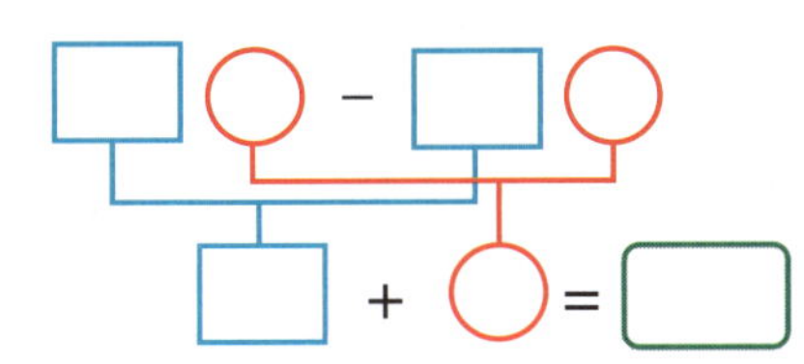

f Try these in your head.

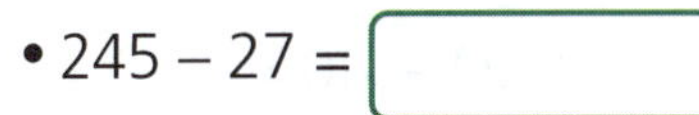

- 245 – 27 =
- 461 – 58 =
- 314 – 45 =

 • *AUSTRALIAN SIGNPOST MATHS 4* • ISBN 9780655708780

2:59 Mental strategies, + and –

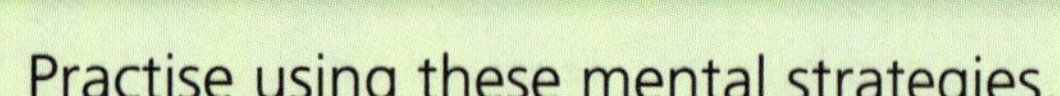

Choose a strategy that makes it easier.

CONCEPT

Practise using these mental strategies.

A	Bridging to 10s	338 + 23	= 338 + (2 + 20 + 1)	= 361
B	Break up the number	346 – 227	Step 1: 346 – 200 = 146 Step 2: 146 – 20 = 126 Step 3: 126 – 7	= 119
C	Constant difference	18 – 11 (–1, –1)	=17 – 10	= 7
		623 – 398 (+2, +2)	= 625 – 400	= 225
D	Levelling	6 + 19 (–1, +1)	= 5 + 20	= 25
	Take one from the right and put it on the left.	143 + 36 (–3, +3)	= 140 + 39	= 179

Practise these strategies on easier questions if you find them difficult.

1 Bridge to 10s. (**A**)

a 26 + 35 ☐ b 48 + 24 ☐ c 55 + 38 ☐

d 336 + 56 ☐ e 237 + 47 ☐ f 618 + 67 ☐

2 Use place value to break up the number. (**B**)

a 356 – 127
- 356 – 100 =
- 256 – 20 =
- 236 – 7 =

b 562 – 134
- 562 – 100 =
- – 30 =
- – 4 =

c 472 – 145
- ☐
- ☐
- ☐

3 Rewrite the question. Add or subtract from both numbers. Keep the difference constant. (**C**)

a 51 – 25: 56 – 30 =
b 62 – 37: .... – 40 =
c 71 – 38: .... – 40 =
d 381 – 202: .... – 200 =
e 562 – 397 ☐
f 467 – 304 ☐
g 531 – 496 ☐
h 671 – 404 ☐

4 Rewrite the question. Take from one number and add to the other to make the question easier. (**D**)

a 23 + 38: 21 + 40 =
b 69 + 32: 70 +
c 58 + 43 ☐
d 158 + 25: 160 +
e 245 + 38 ☐
f 459 + 34 ☐
g 347 + 96 ☐
h 461 + 195 ☐

3:01 Analog time

10 minutes after 25 past the hour, would be ... ______ to the next hour.

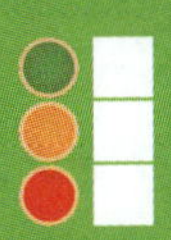

CONCEPT

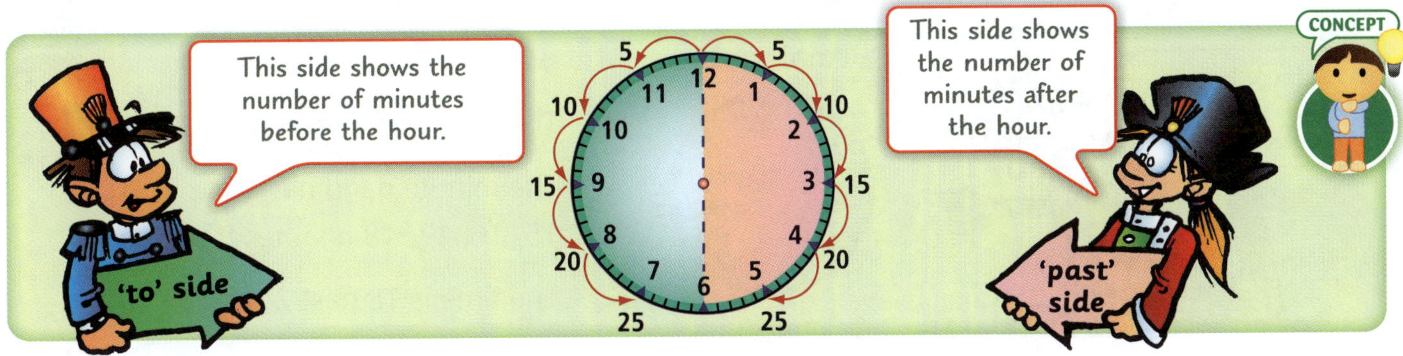

1 Complete the label for each time shown.

a  5 to 2

b  25 to 6

c  10 past 10

d  20 to 5

e  ______

f  ______

g  ______

h  ______

i  ______

j  ______

2 Complete the clocks to show the given times.

a 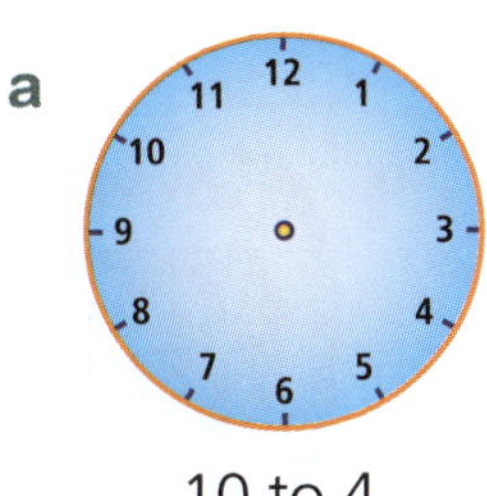
10 to 4

b 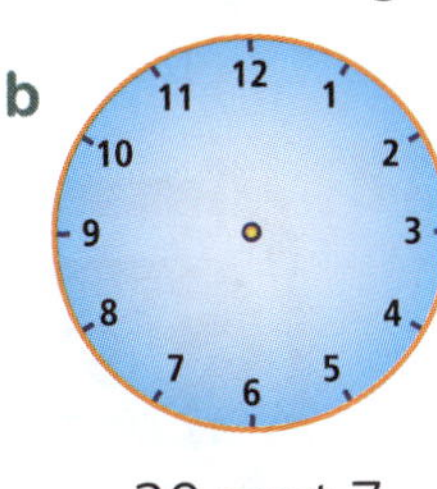
20 past 7

c 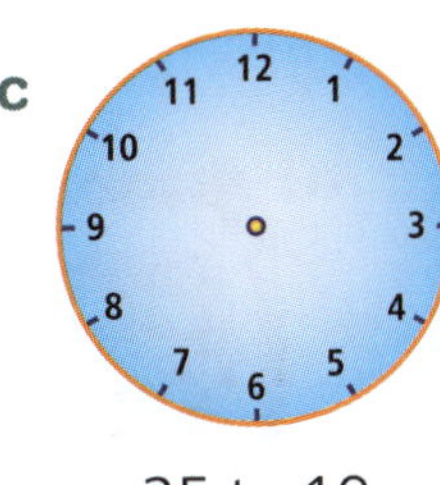
25 to 10

d 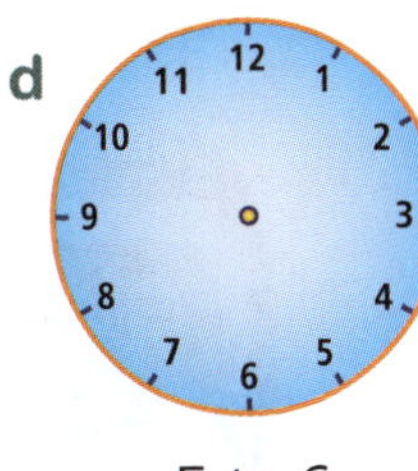
5 to 6

e 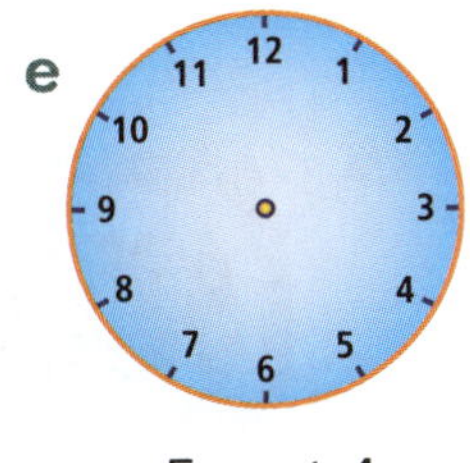
5 past 4

3 Write the time that is five minutes after:

a 5 past 8		**b** 10 past 7		**c** 10 to 12	
d 15 past 6		**e** 20 to 8		**f** 15 to 3	
g 20 past 3		**h** 25 to 3		**i** 5 to 9	

4 Write the time that is five minutes before:

a 25 past 1		**b** 10 past 4		**c** 15 to 4	
d 10 to 5		**e** 20 past 6		**f** 25 to 8	
g 15 past 10		**h** 20 to 11		**i** 5 past 2	

3:02 Analog and digital time

Digital time shows how many minutes past the hour.

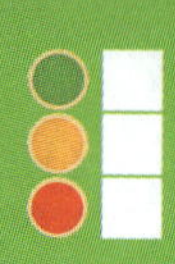

CONCEPT

The hour hand has passed 2.

The minute hand has gone 5, 10, 15, 16, 17, 18 minutes from 12.

The time is 18 past 2 or 2:18.

1 Complete the labels for each time shown.

a 11 : ☐ ☐ past ☐

b 7 : ☐ ☐ past ☐

c 4 : ☐ ☐ to ☐

d 5 : ☐ ☐ past ☐

e 3 : ☐ ☐ to ☐

f 12 : ☐ ☐ to ☐

g 9 : ☐ ☐ past ☐

h 6 : ☐ ☐ to ☐

i 10 : ☐ ☐ past ☐

j 8 : ☐ ☐ to ☐

k 2:42 ☐ to ☐

l 4:58 ☐ to ☐

m 9:19 ☐ past ☐

n 7:09 ☐ past ☐

o 11:38 ☐ to ☐

2 Write the time that is one minute after:

a 3:16 ☐ b 2:47 ☐ c 7:28 ☐
d 9:03 ☐ e 11:41 ☐ f 4:39 ☐
g 12:24 ☐ h 5:20 ☐ i 6:55 ☐

3 Write the time that is five minutes after:

a 4:13 ☐ b 9:41 ☐ c 7:32 ☐
d 10:54 ☐ e 8:16 ☐ f 5:58 ☐

3:03 Analog and digital time

If the hair cutting began at 17 past 5 and finished at 17 to 6, how long did it take?

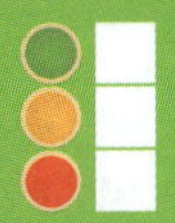

1 Complete the label for each time shown.

a ☐ past ☐ b ☐ to ☐ c ☐ past ☐ d ☐ past ☐ e ☐ to ☐

2 Complete the label for each time shown.

a ☐ past ☐ b ☐ past ☐ c ☐ past ☐ d ☐ past ☐ e ☐ past ☐

3 The cross-country run began at 10:15. I finished at 10:58. How long did I take? ☐ min

Ron, who was also in the race, finished at 10:50. How long did he take? ☐ min

The winner of the race finished the run at 10:43. By how much did he beat me? ☐ min

At 1:37, I walked back to school. It took me 9 minutes. When did I reach school? ☐

Ron did not reach school until 14 minutes later. When did he get there? ☐

4 We left Griffith at 9:13 and arrived in Hillston at 11:30. How long did we take? ☐

5 Jindi, Jedda and Maali walked from the waterhole to the river to meet their father's boat.

They left at 7:15. It took them 1 hour 23 minutes. When did they reach the river? ☐

Their father's boat arrived 20 minutes after them. When did the boat arrive? ☐

 • *AUSTRALIAN SIGNPOST MATHS 4* • ISBN 9780655708780

3:04 Using a ruler

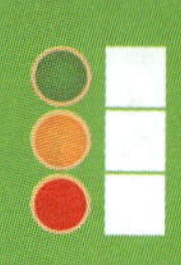

10 millimetres = 1 centimetre
100 centimetres = 1 metre

10 mm = 1 cm	
100 cm = 1 m	1000 mm = 1 m

- When measuring, use the closest mark on the scale to give the answer, unless you are told to use a different unit. (e.g. Answer correct to the nearest cm.)

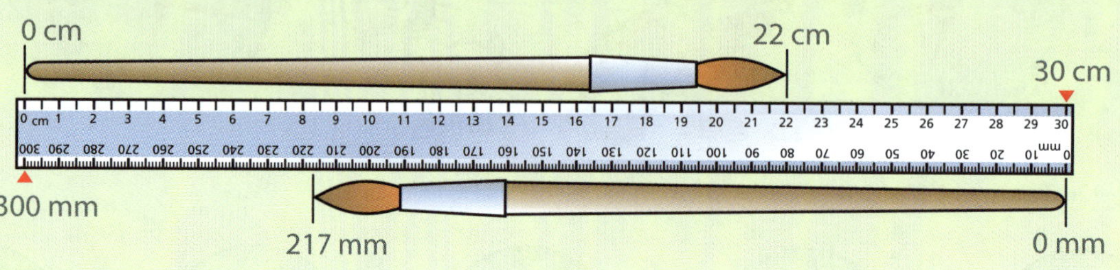

1 Use the closest mark on the scale to write the length of the pen in each case.

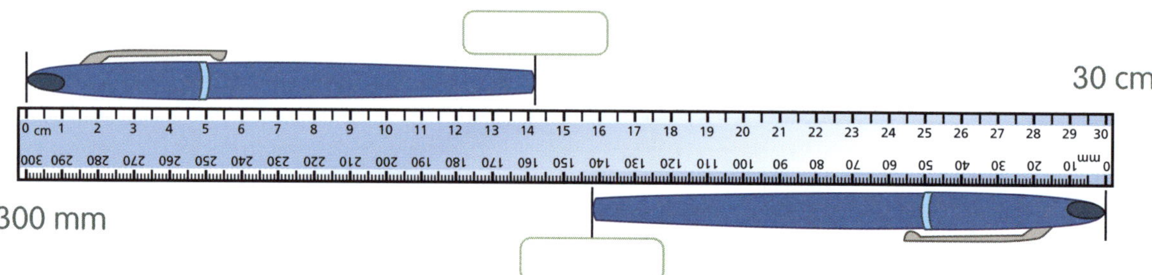

2 Measure the length of each line correct to the nearest millimetre.

a ____
b ____
c ____
d ____
e ____
f ____
g ____
h ____

3 Use a ruler marked in cm and mm to measure the length of four objects.

	Object	Length correct to the nearest centimetre (cm)	Length correct to the nearest millimetre (mm)
a			
b			
c			
d			

3:05 Centimetres and millimetres

10 mm = 1 cm
100 cm = 1 m
1000 mm = 1 m

CONCEPT

This ruler is marked in millimeters.

34 mm = 3 cm 4 mm

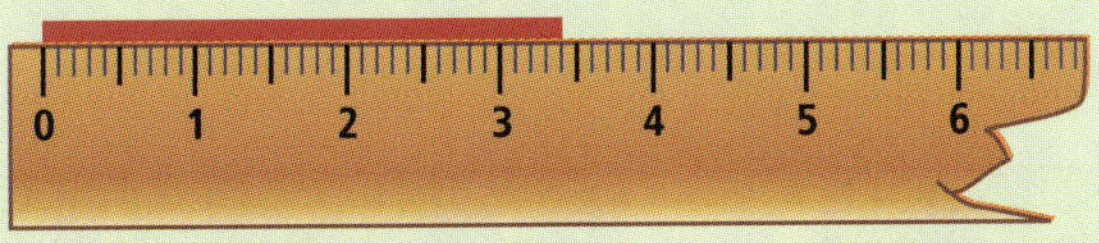

1 centimetre is divided into 10 millimetres.

mm is short for millimetres.

1 Estimate, then measure the length of each bar.

a ☐ mm b ☐ mm
c ☐ mm d ☐ mm
e ☐ mm f ☐ mm

2 Write these as millimetres.

a 1 cm 9 mm ☐ mm b 4 cm 7 mm ☐ mm c 6 cm 1 mm ☐ mm
d 3 cm 6 mm ☐ mm e 5 cm 5 mm ☐ mm f 7 cm 2 mm ☐ mm
g 2 cm 8 mm ☐ mm h 9 cm 3 mm ☐ mm

3 Write these as centimetres and millimetres.

a 25 mm ☐ b 68 mm ☐ c 51 mm ☐
d 92 mm ☐ e 43 mm ☐ f 87 mm ☐

ACTIVITY

- Estimate, then use a ruler to measure these objects to the nearest millimetre.

Object	Estimated length	Actual length
length of a finger		
height of a cup		
width of an eraser		
thickness of a book		

- Use a tape measure to measure these objects to the nearest centimetre.
  - the length of a brick ☐
  - the width of your desk ☐
  - the height of your chair ☐

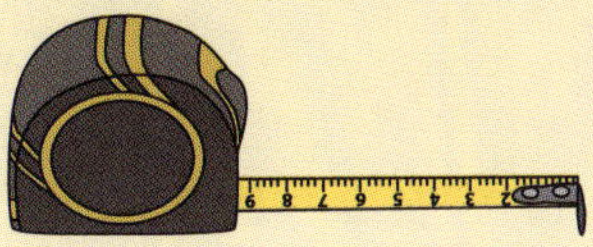

Not all rulers measure right from the end.

3:06 Using millimetres

The width of my thumb is  mm.

The length of my finger is mm.

1. Record the length of each bar.

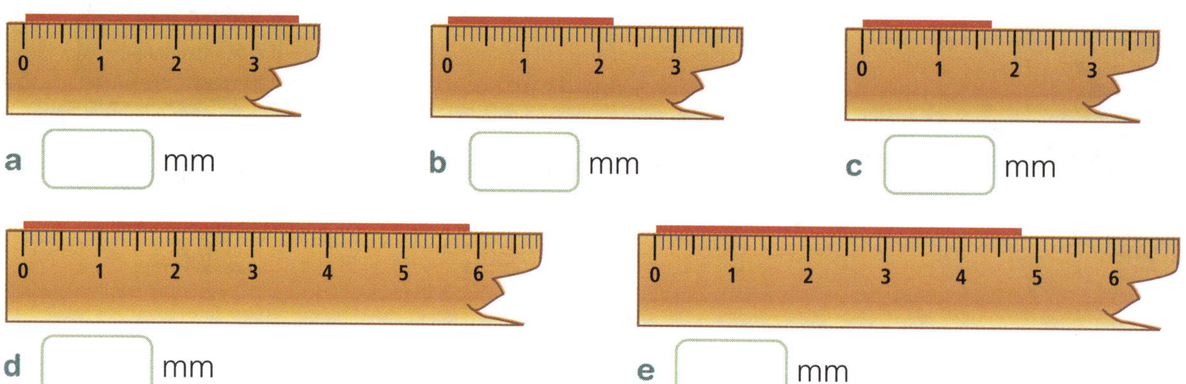

a mm b mm c mm

d mm e mm

2. Estimate, then measure the length of each bar.

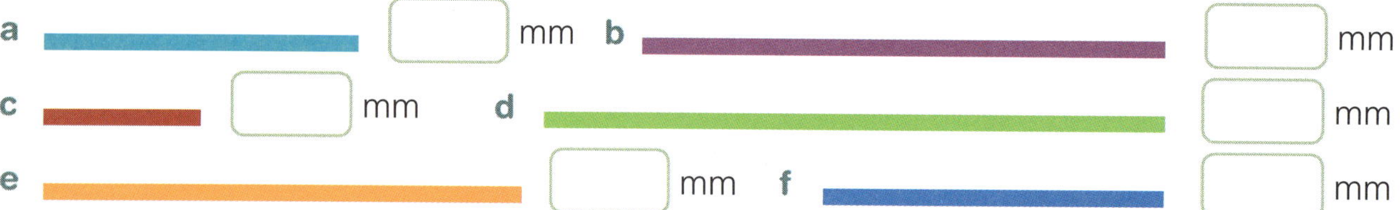

a mm b mm

c mm d mm

e mm f mm

3. Write these as millimetres.

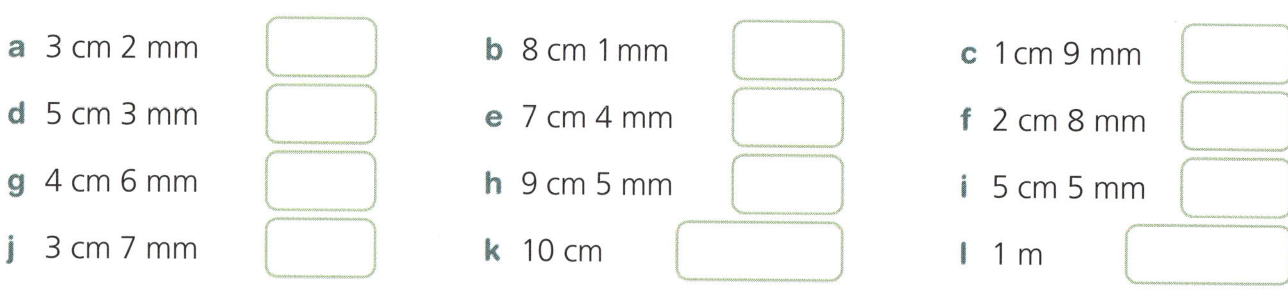

a 3 cm 2 mm	b 8 cm 1 mm	c 1 cm 9 mm
d 5 cm 3 mm	e 7 cm 4 mm	f 2 cm 8 mm
g 4 cm 6 mm	h 9 cm 5 mm	i 5 cm 5 mm
j 3 cm 7 mm	k 10 cm	l 1 m

4. Write these as centimetres and millimetres.

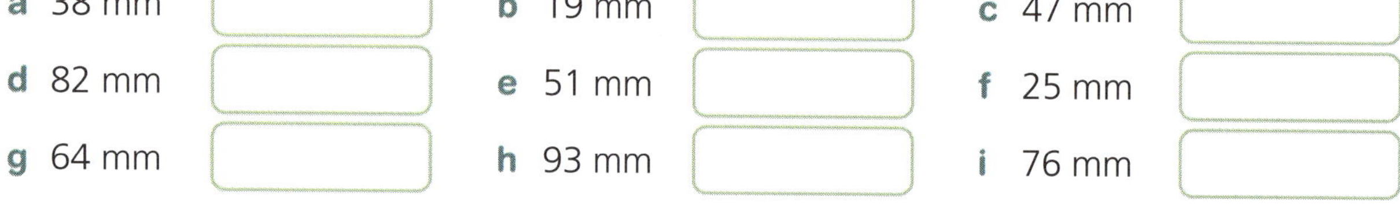

a 38 mm	b 19 mm	c 47 mm
d 82 mm	e 51 mm	f 25 mm
g 64 mm	h 93 mm	i 76 mm

5. Estimate then find the perimeter of each shape

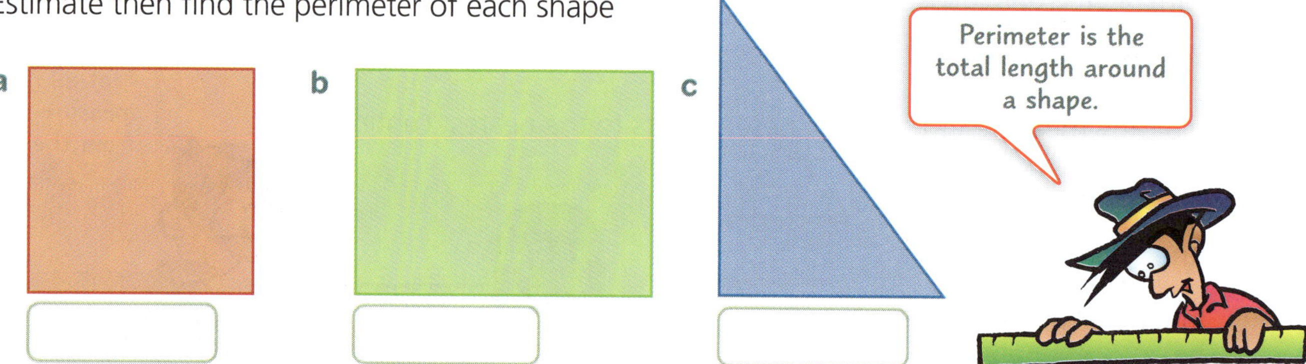

 • *AUSTRALIAN SIGNPOST MATHS 4* • ISBN 9780655708780

Square centimetres

I am going to cut some wood 10 cm wide and 30 cm long.

CONCEPT

- Area is the **space enclosed** by the boundary of a shape or the **surface of an object**.
- Small areas can be measured in **square centimetres**. A square centimetre is a square with each side 1 cm long. The short way to write square centimetre is **cm²**.

1. Record the area of each shape.

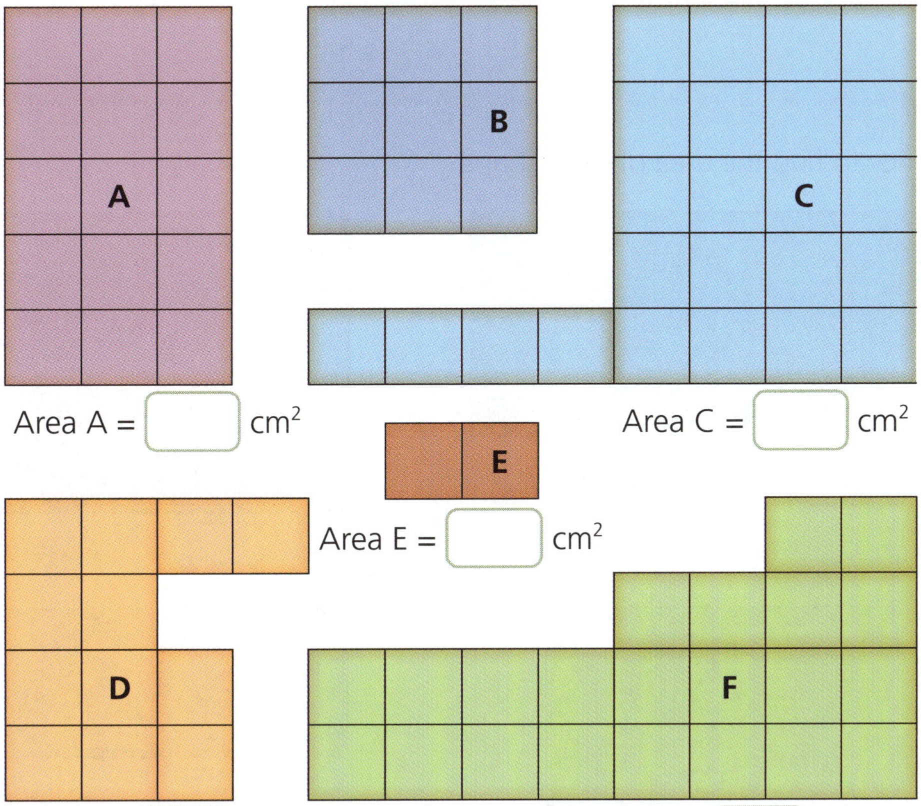

Area A = ☐ cm^2

Area B = ☐ cm^2

Area C = ☐ cm^2

Area D = ☐ cm^2

Area E = ☐ cm^2

Area F = ☐ cm^2

Area C is the largest. Area E is the smallest.

There must not be any gaps or overlaps.

2. Write the areas in Question 1 in order, smallest to largest. ☐

ACTIVITY

- On 1 cm grid paper, trace around some small objects. Count the number of square centimetres. **Count the squares that are more than half covered.**
- Overlay some small surfaces with a 1 cm grid transparency. Count the number of square centimetres covered. Label each area measured.

Area: 5 cm^2, 6 cm^2, 7 cm^2 or 8 cm^2?

Estimate the area of each small surface before measuring.

© PEARSON AUSTRALIA 2024 • *AUSTRALIAN SIGNPOST MATHS 4* • ISBN 9780655708780

3:08 The square centimetre

This is 3 rows of 4.
$3 \times 4 = 12$
(12 square units)

INVESTIGATION

- Use a 1 cm grid transparency to measure and compare the areas of different surfaces.
- Discuss ways to find the area when some squares are not fully covered.
- List items that have an area between 20 cm^2 and 50 cm^2.

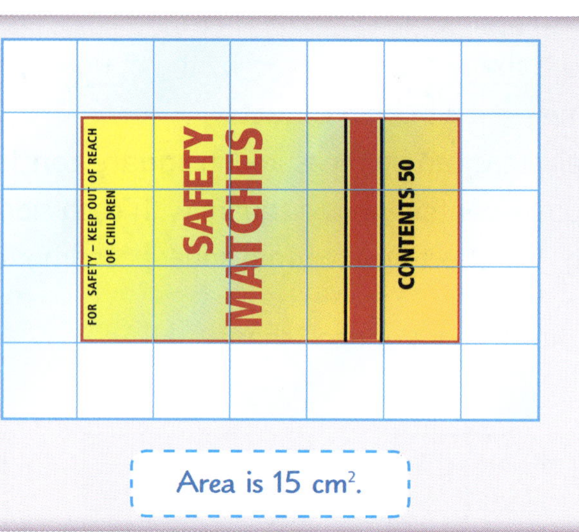

Area is 15 cm^2.

1 Use a 1 cm grid transparency to find the area of each shape.

a

2 rows of 2 = 2 × 2

b

3 rows of 6 = 3 × 6

c

d

e

f

2 rows of 5 = 2 × 5

2 Draw your own grid to find the area of each shape.

a

b

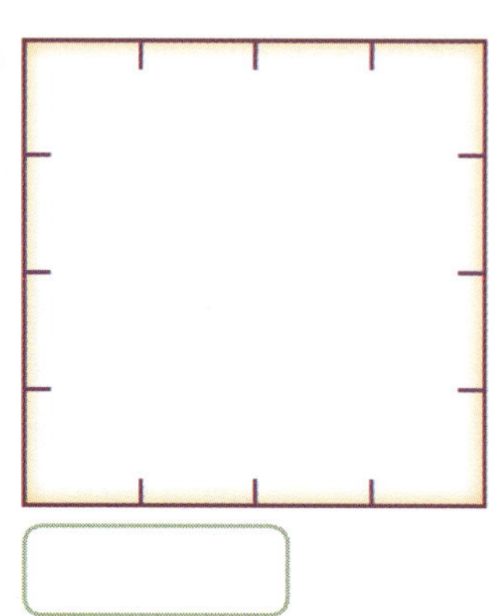

c

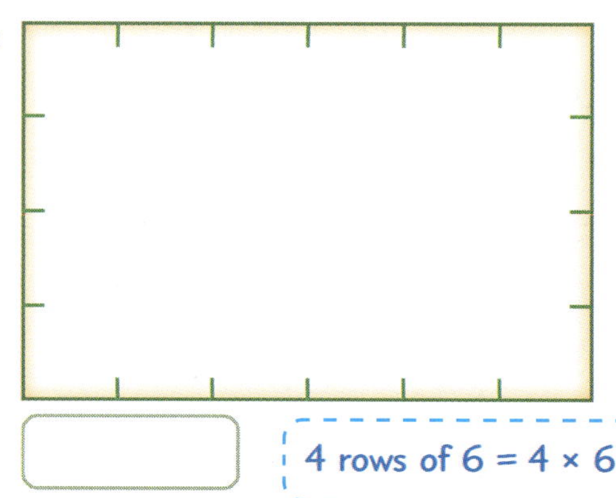

4 rows of 6 = 4 × 6

3:09 The square centimetre

On 1 cm grid paper, trace your hand. Estimate the area by counting squares that are more than half used.

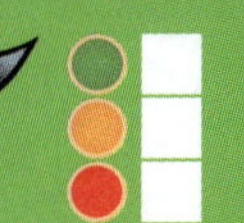

1. Use a 1 cm grid transparency, or draw a grid, to find the area of each shape.

Remember it's 1 cm^2.

2. Draw your own grid and find the area (A) and perimeter (P) of each shape.

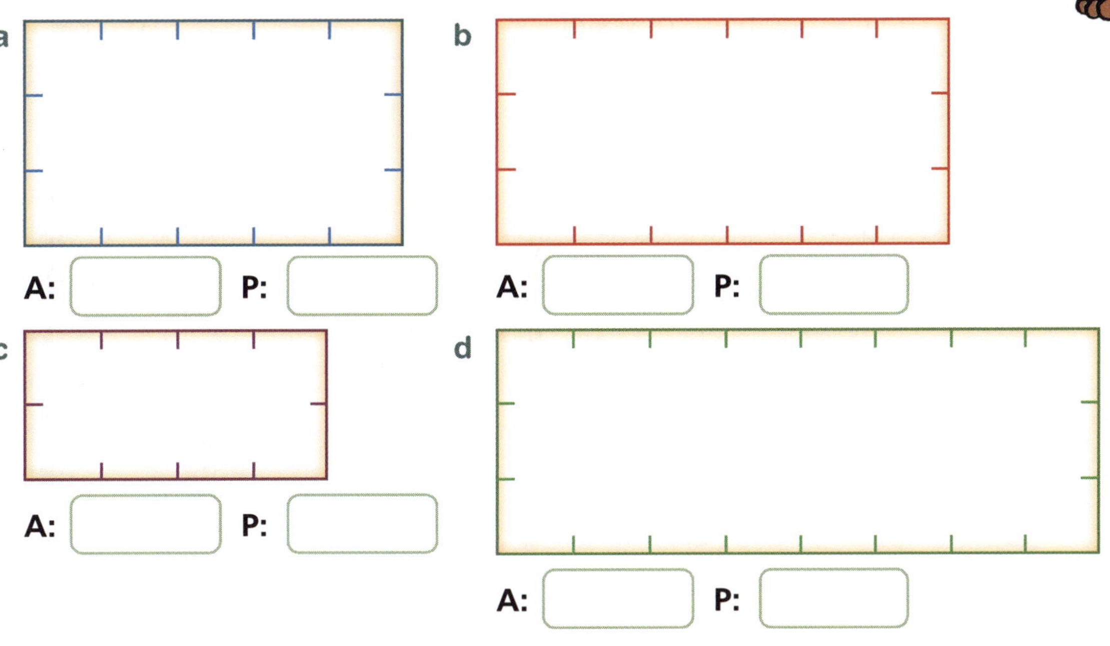

ACTIVITY

- Use a 10 cm by 10 cm grid transparency to find areas:
  - less than 100 cm^2
  - about 100 cm^2
  - more than 100 cm^2
- Record three surfaces with areas of more than 100 cm^2.

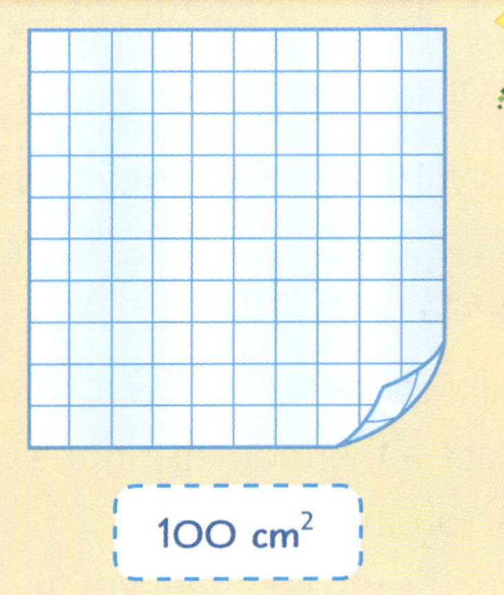

 • *AUSTRALIAN SIGNPOST MATHS 4* • ISBN 9780655708780

3:10 Temperature

Hottest time of year: December, January, February
Coldest time of year: June, July, August

CONCEPT

To read temperature we use the Celsius temperature scale.

0°C is the freezing point of water.
100°C is the boiling point of water.

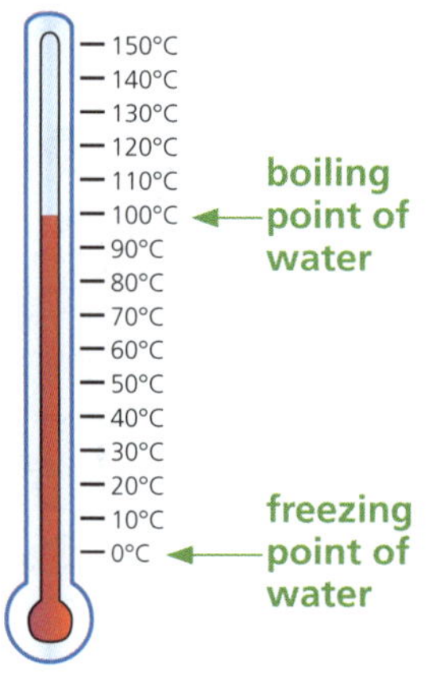

1 Draw lines to make each statement true.

The boiling point of water •	• is cool to warm weather.
35°C to 45°C •	• is cold weather.
25°C to 35°C •	• is 100°C.
15°C to 25°C •	• is 0°C.
5°C to 15°C •	• is very hot weather.
The freezing point of water •	• is warm to hot weather.

2 What temperature is shown on each thermometer?

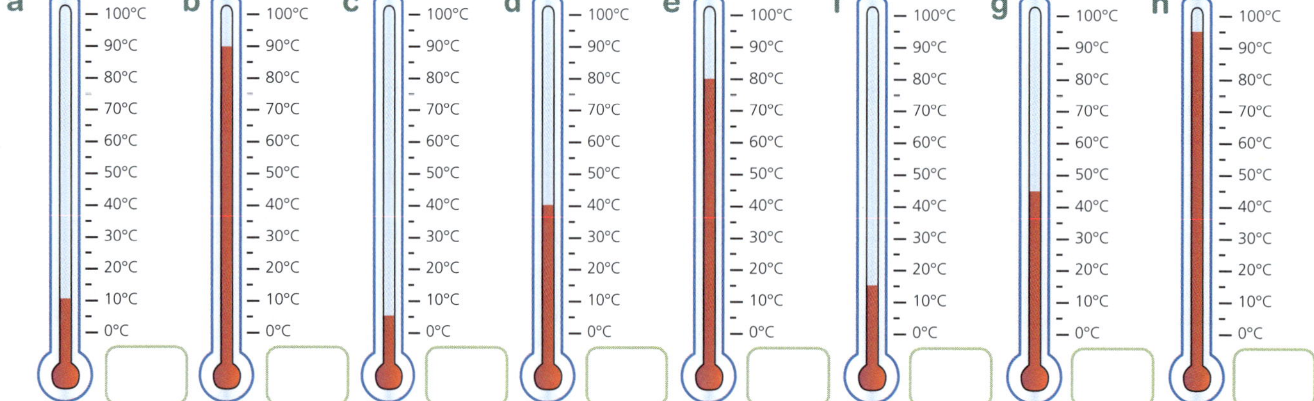

3 Each thermometer above is measuring the temperature of water.

a Which three thermometers show the water is hot?

b Which three thermometers show the water is cold?

c Which two thermometers show it is warm?

Temperature chart

ACTIVITY

- Fill a container with warm water.
- Place a thermometer in the water and record the temperature every five minutes.
- Graph the results.
- Discuss why the temperature dropped quickly at the beginning of the experiment.

 • *AUSTRALIAN SIGNPOST MATHS 4* • ISBN 9780655708780

3:11 Recording temperature

36·5° is halfway between 36° and 37° Celsius.

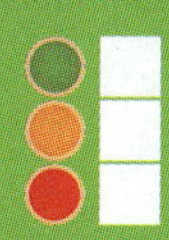

ACTIVITY

- When reading a thermometer use the nearest graduation mark.
- Read aloud these temperatures.
  - 42°C • 27°C • 19°C • 63°C • 100°C • 37°C • 84°C • 34°C
  - 16°C • 0°C • 96°C • 21°C • 39°C • 72°C • 55°C • 25°C

1 Write these measurements of temperature in short form.

a twenty-five degrees Celsius ☐
b zero degrees Celsius ☐
c eighteen degrees Celsius ☐
d fifty-eight degrees Celsius ☐
e eighty-six degrees Celsius ☐
f thirty-seven degrees Celsius ☐
g forty-one degrees Celsius ☐
h seventy-three degrees Celsius ☐

2 On each thermometer, colour the mercury to match the given temperature.

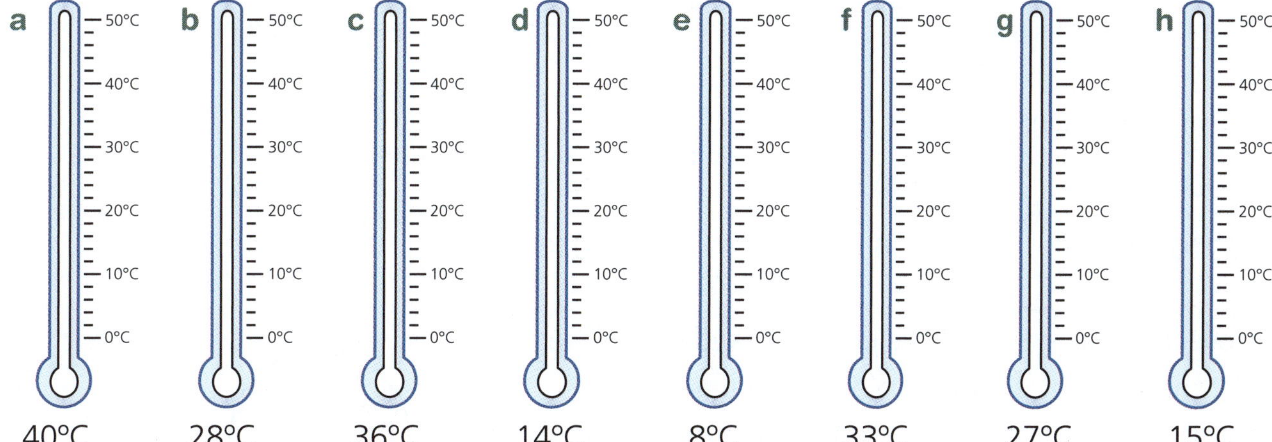

40°C 28°C 36°C 14°C 8°C 33°C 27°C 15°C

3 Draw lines to match to the most suitable temperature.

a	a cold glass of milk	40°C
b	a very hot day	96°C
c	a warm day	70°C
d	a bowl of hot soup	26°C
e	a pot of very hot tea	2°C

f	a very cold day	100°C
g	water boiling	17°C
h	body temperature	67°C
i	a cup of coffee	9°C
j	a cool day	37°C

3:12 Using millilitres

We write 7 litres as 7 L
We write half a litre as 0·5 L
or 500 mL.

A bottle of water holds about 600 mL.

1. Which measure (**L** or **mL**) has been left off each label?

2. Would we use litres (**L**) or millilitres (**mL**) to measure:

   a drink in a cup? ☐ **b** water in a bath? ☐
   c medicine in a teaspoon? ☐ **d** juice in a glass? ☐
   e water in a fish pond? ☐ **f** petrol in our car? ☐
   g cream in a small carton? ☐ **h** ice cream in a large container? ☐

3. How many litres in:

   a 1000 mL? ☐ **b** 4000 mL? ☐ **c** 2000 mL? ☐ **d** 6000 mL? ☐
   e 5000 mL? ☐ **f** 7000 mL? ☐ **g** 9000 mL? ☐ **h** 3000 mL? ☐

ACTIVITY

- Collect containers that have labels marked in millilitres. List the kinds of products sold in millilitres. Discuss the most common shape found in the containers.
- Pour 100 mL of water from a standard measure into a large plastic bottle. Mark the level of water with a pen. Pour in another 100 mL of water and mark that level. Repeat until 1 litre has been reached. This is a **calibrated measure**.
- Check the accuracy of the calibrated measure by pouring in 500 mL of water.
- Pour water from different containers into the calibrated one. Check that the capacity shown on each label is correct.

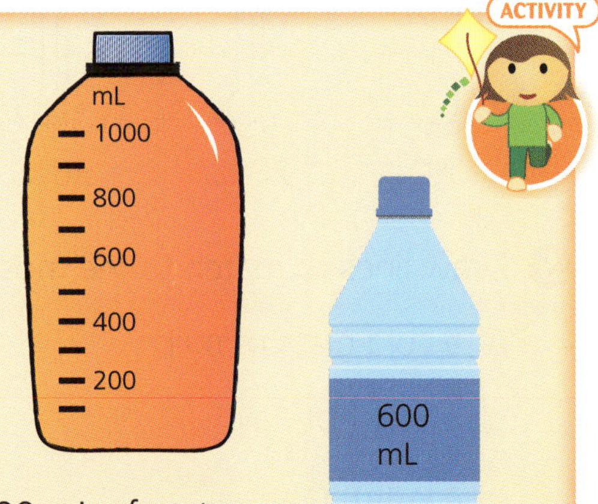

 ISBN 9780655708780

3:13 Using millilitres

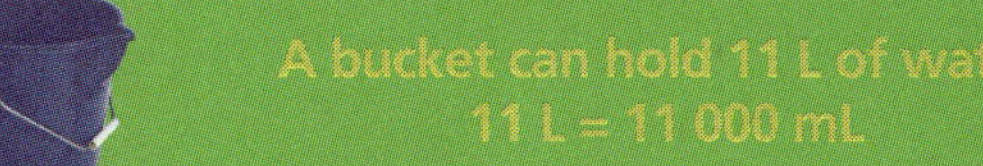

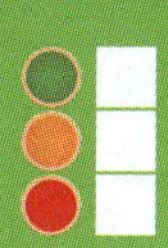

1. Use a medicine glass to measure the capacity of these small containers.
Fill the medicine glass to a mark that you estimate will fill the container.
Pour water into the small container until it is full.
Calculate how much water you used to fill the container to complete the table.

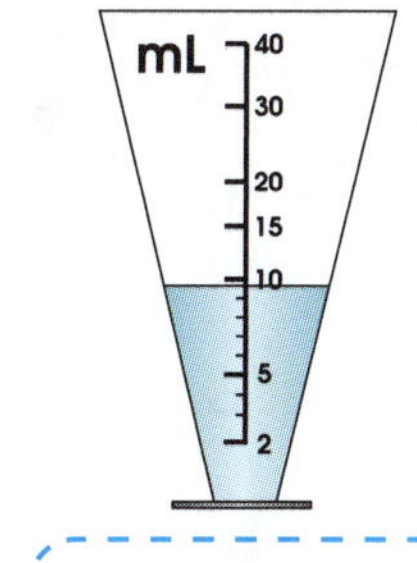

	Container	Estimated capacity	Measurement	Description of estimate	Difference
A	teaspoon	15 mL	5 mL	too big	10 mL
B	tablespoon				
C	bottle lid				
D					

1 mL has the same volume as a ones block.

2. Order containers **A** to **D** from smallest to largest capacity.

3. Would we use litres or millilitres to measure:

a a bowl of soup? **b** a sink full of water? **c** a spoonful of sauce?
d a cup of coffee? **e** a drum of oil? **f** a can of drink?

4. How many millilitres are there in:

a 2 L? **b** 7 L? **c** 3 L? **d** 5 L?
e 8 L? **f** 4 L? **g** $6\frac{1}{2}$ L? **h** $9\frac{1}{2}$ L?
i 3·5 L? **j** 8·5 L? **k** 2·5 L? **l** $3\frac{1}{2}$ L?
m $7\frac{1}{2}$ L? **n** 8·3 L? **o** 5·25 L? **p** 7·25 L?

5. How many litres are there in:

a 1000 mL? **b** 7000 mL? **c** 5000 mL? **d** 3000 mL?
e 6000 mL? **f** 4000 mL? **g** 2000 mL? **h** 8000 mL?

6. Record the measure shown.

a
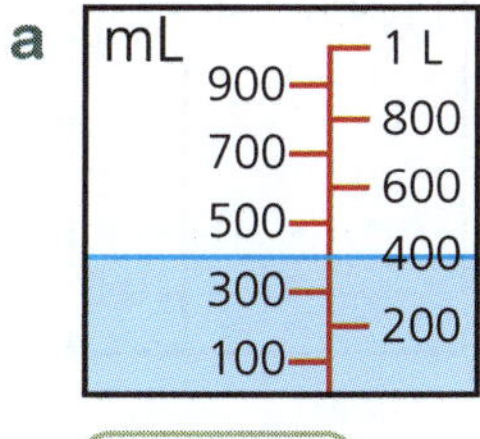

b
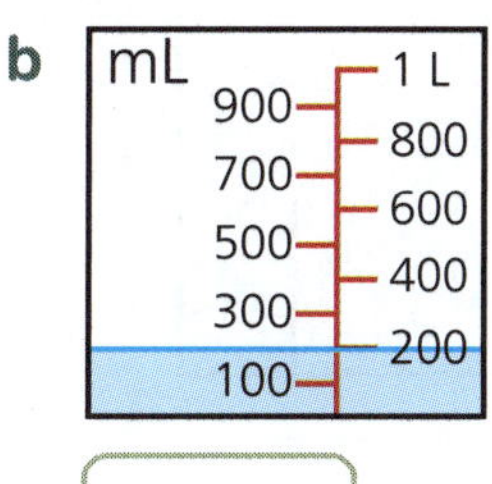

c
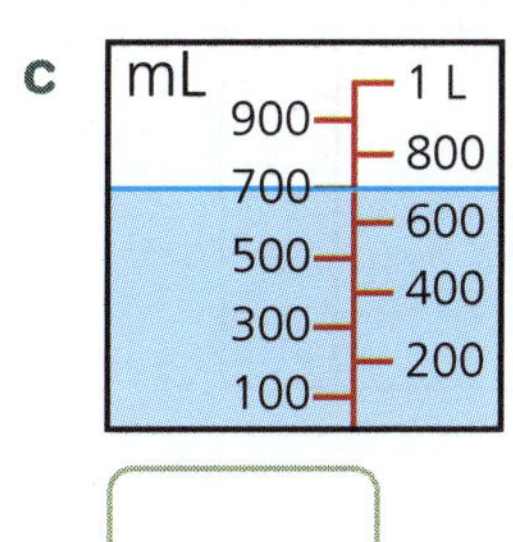

d
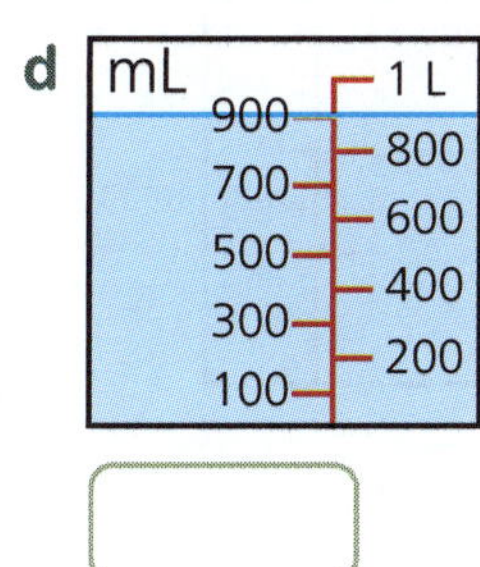

Using L and mL

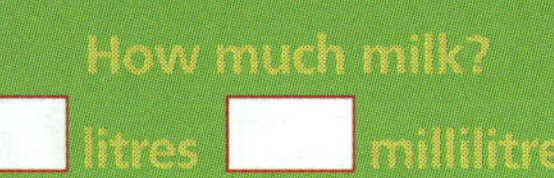

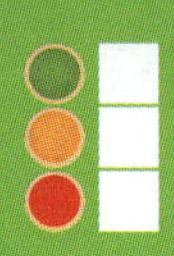

1 What is the total capacity of each set of containers?

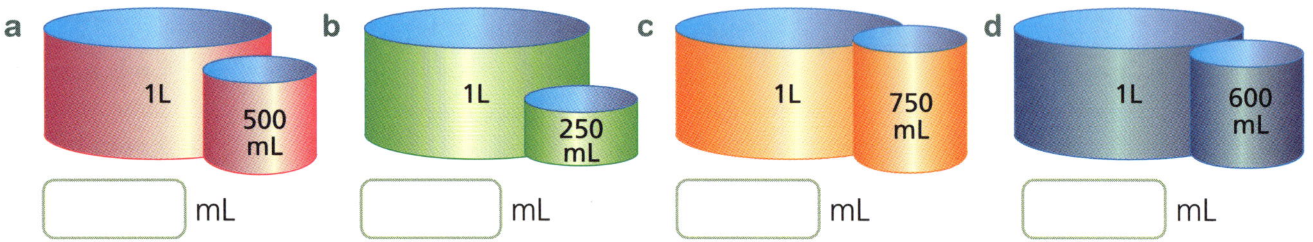

a ☐ mL b ☐ mL c ☐ mL d ☐ mL

2 Write these as millilitres.

a 1 L 300 mL ☐ b 1 L 490 mL ☐ c 1 L 875 mL ☐
d 1 L 625 mL ☐ e 1 L 750 mL ☐ f 2 L 500 mL ☐

3 Write these as litres and millilitres.

a 1600 mL ☐ b 1900 mL ☐ c 1350 mL ☐
d 1250 mL ☐ e 1425 mL ☐ f 2750 mL ☐

4 Would you use litres or millilitres to measure:

a water in a bucket? ☐ b water in a teacup? ☐
c ice cream in a cone? ☐ d milk in a small carton? ☐
e liquid parts of an egg? ☐ f petrol in a car? ☐
g medicine in a dessertspoon? ☐ h liquid in an eye-dropper? ☐

5 Record the measure shown.

a
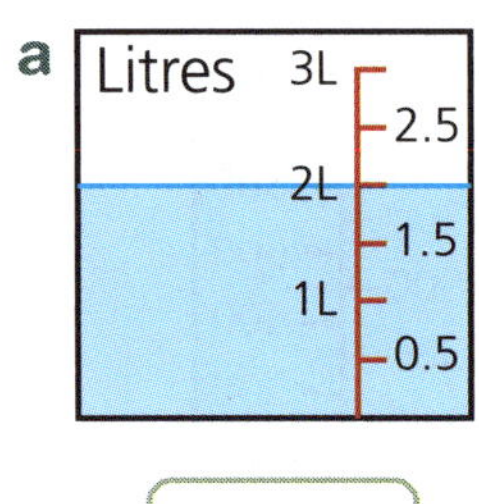

b
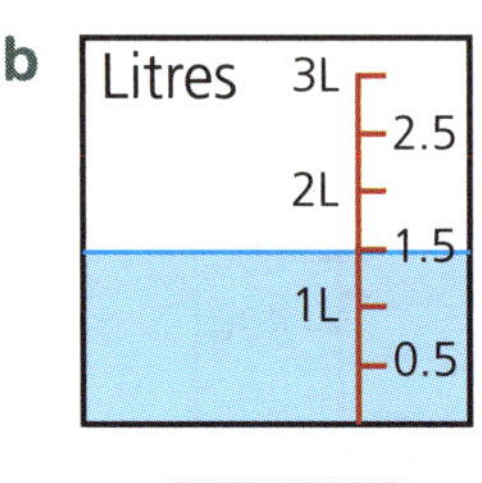

c
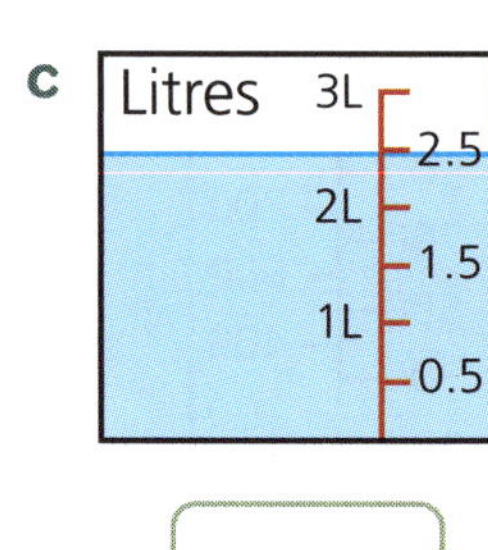

d
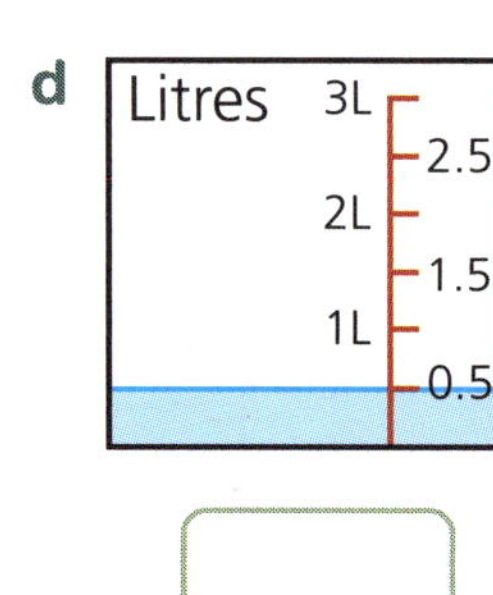

Measuring mass

The one in my right hand feels heavier than one kilogram.

1. Use the short form to write:

a 60 grams		b 1 kilogram		c 350 grams	
d 700 grams		e 500 grams		f 3 kilograms	
g 9 kilograms		h 900 grams		i 16 kilograms	

2. Which unit of measurement (**g** or **kg**) has been left off each item?

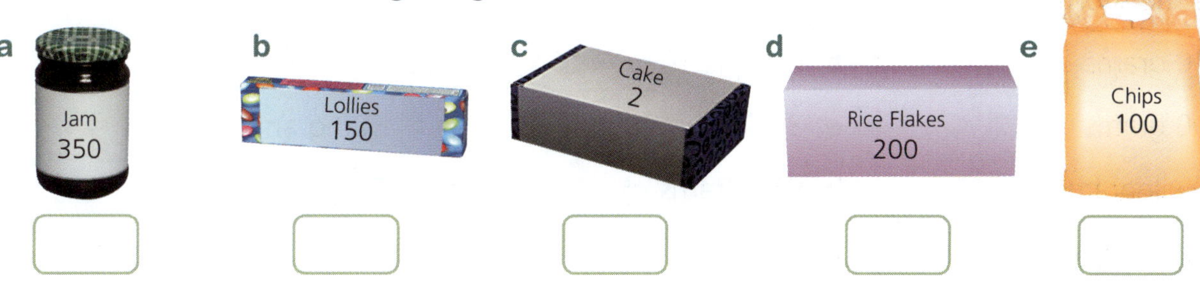

3. How many grams are there in:

a 1 kilogram? ☐ b 3 kilograms? ☐ c 5 kilograms? ☐ d 9 kilograms? ☐

4. How many kilograms are there in:

a 1000 g? ☐ b 4000 g? ☐ c 6000 g? ☐ d 8000 g? ☐

ACTIVITY

- Use scales to measure objects that are heavier than 1 kg (correct to the nearest 100 g).
- Complete the table.

	Object	Estimated mass	Actual mass
A			
B			
C			
D			
E			

- Order objects **A** to **E** from lightest to heaviest. ☐

3:16 Using grams

The mass of 1 mL of water is very close to 1 gram.

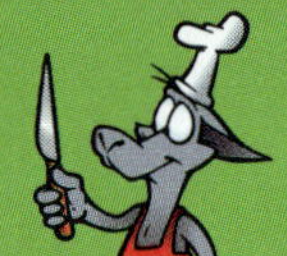

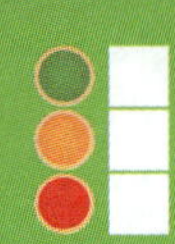

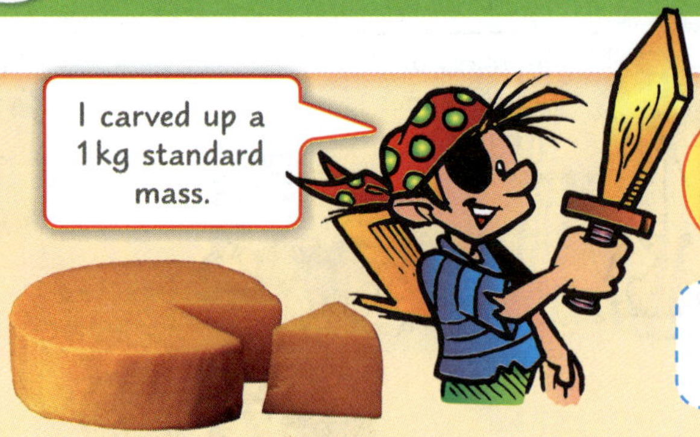

I carved up a 1 kg standard mass.

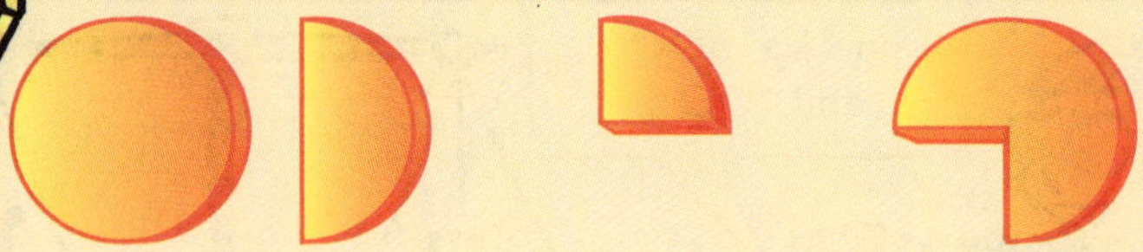

1 kg	$\frac{1}{2}$ kg	$\frac{1}{4}$ kg	$\frac{3}{4}$ kg
1000 g	500 g	250 g	750 g

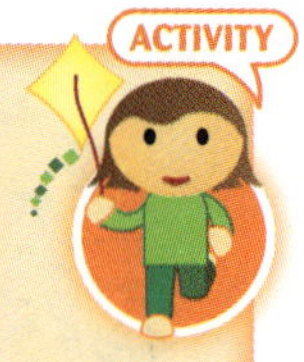

ACTIVITY

- Use scales to find objects that are these sizes.

Mass	Objects
about $\frac{1}{4}$ kg	
about $\frac{1}{2}$ kg	
about $\frac{3}{4}$ kg	
about 1 kg	

1 Write the short form for:

a 100 grams ☐ b 600 grams ☐ c 1 kilogram ☐

d 500 grams ☐ e 3 kilograms ☐ f 300 grams ☐

g 10 kilograms ☐ h 956 grams ☐ i 875 grams ☐

2 How many kilograms are there in:

a 3000 g? ☐ b 7000 g? ☐ c 2000 g? ☐

d 5000 g? ☐ e 9000 g? ☐ f 4000 g? ☐

3 How many grams are there in:

a 2 kg? ☐ b 1 kg 200 g? ☐ c 3 kg? ☐

d 1 kg 600 g? ☐ e 5 kg? ☐ f 1 kg 450 g? ☐

g 1 kg 980 g? ☐ h 1 kg 500 g? ☐ i 7 kg? ☐

4 How many grams are there in:

a $\frac{1}{2}$ kg? ☐ b $\frac{3}{4}$ kg? ☐ c $\frac{1}{4}$ kg? ☐ d $1\frac{1}{2}$ kg? ☐

e $1\frac{3}{4}$ kg? ☐ f $1\frac{1}{4}$ kg? ☐ g $2\frac{1}{2}$ kg? ☐ h $3\frac{1}{2}$ kg? ☐

5 Order these objects from least mass to most mass.

A
$\frac{1}{2}$ kg
B
$\frac{3}{4}$ kg
C
$\frac{1}{4}$ kg
D
$1\frac{1}{2}$ kg

☐

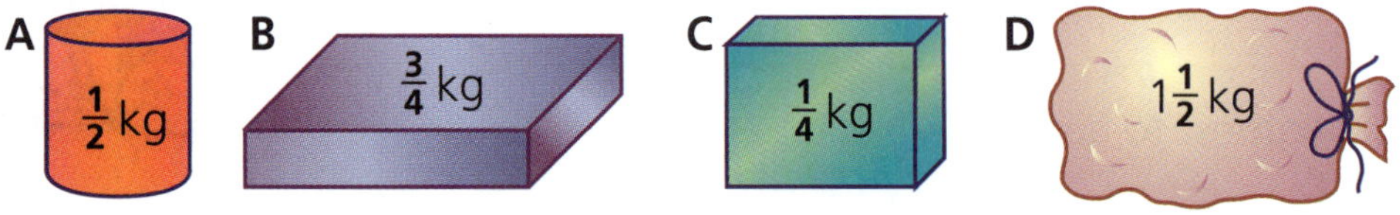

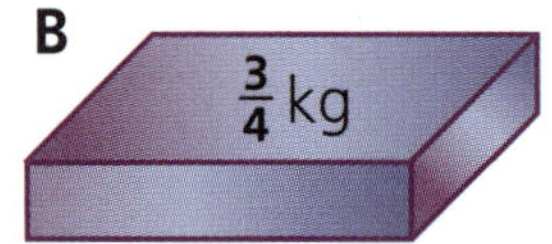

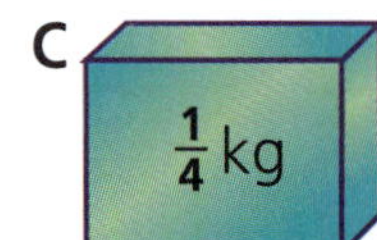

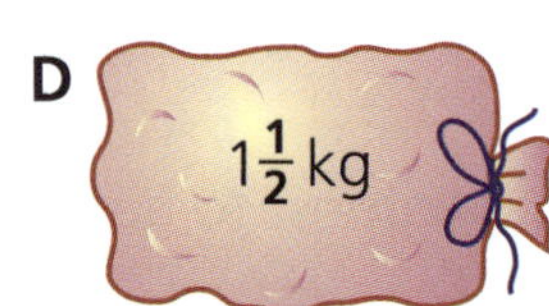

5:20 means 20 minutes past 5.
5:40 means 40 minutes past 5 or 20 minutes to 6.

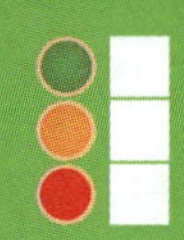

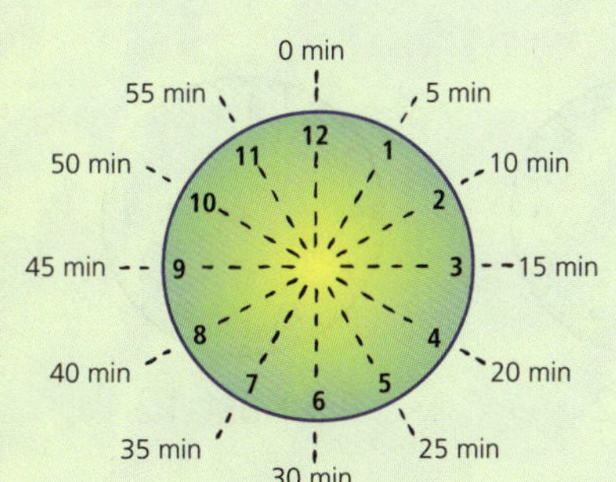

It takes 5 minutes for the minute hand to move from one numeral to the next.

- The hour hand has passed 7.
- The minute hand has moved 5, 10, 15, 20 minutes from 12.
- The time is ______ past ______ or ____ : ____

- The hour hand has passed 1.
- The minute hand has moved 5, 10, 15, 20, 21, 22 minutes from 12.
- The time is ____________

60 minutes = 1 hour

- The hour hand is approaching 6.
- The minute hand has 5, 10, 11, 12, 13, 14 minutes to go before it reaches 12.
- The time is ____________.

60 – 14 = 46 | 5:46

- The hour hand is approaching 11.
- The minute hand has 5, 10, 15, 20, 21, 22, 23 minutes to go before it reaches 12.
- The time is ____________.

60 – 23 = 37 | 10:37

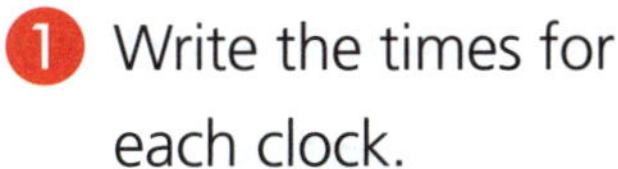

1 Write the times for each clock.

a

____ past ____
____ : ____

b

____ to ____
____ : ____

c

____ past ____
____ : ____

d

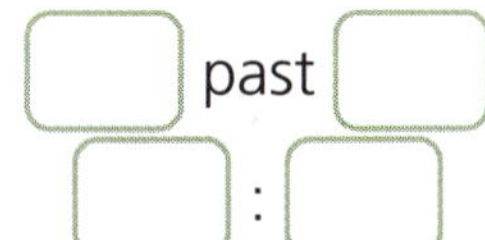

____ to ____
____ : ____

e

____ to ____
____ : ____

f

____ to ____
____ : ____

3:18 Time

A fortnight is 14 days.
365 days = 1 year
366 days = 1 leap year

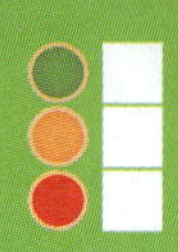

1 On each face show the time given.

a 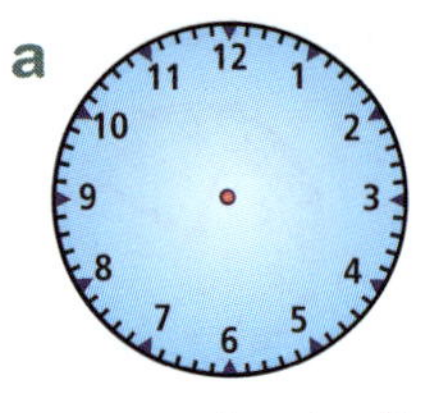 a quarter to 8

b 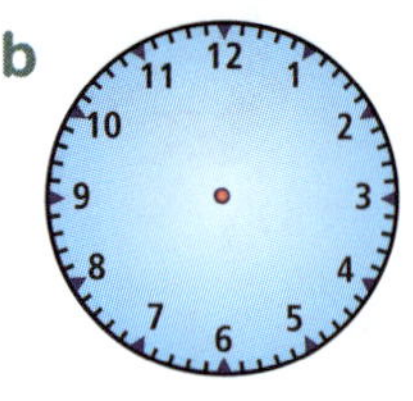 7 past 4

c 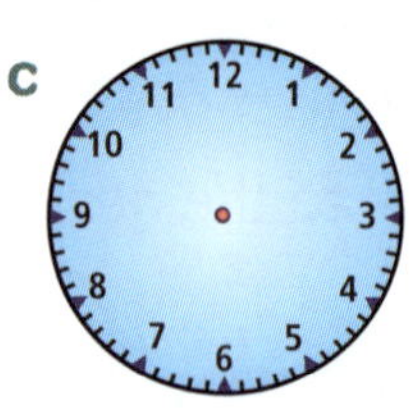 20 to 11

d 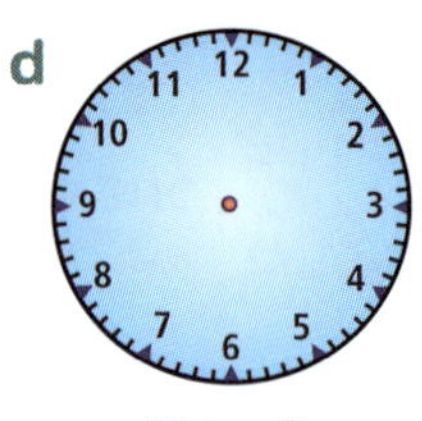 5 to 2

e 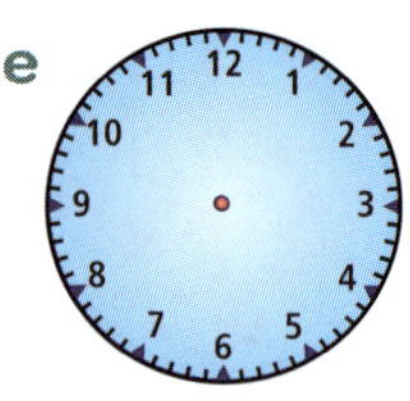 19 past 12

2 Complete the label for each time shown.

a 

☐ to ☐

b 

☐ past ☐

c 

☐ to ☐

d 

☐ past ☐

e 

☐ to ☐

3 How many more minutes will it take for the minute hand to reach the 12?

a  ☐ minutes The time is: ☐

b  ☐ minutes The time is: ☐

c 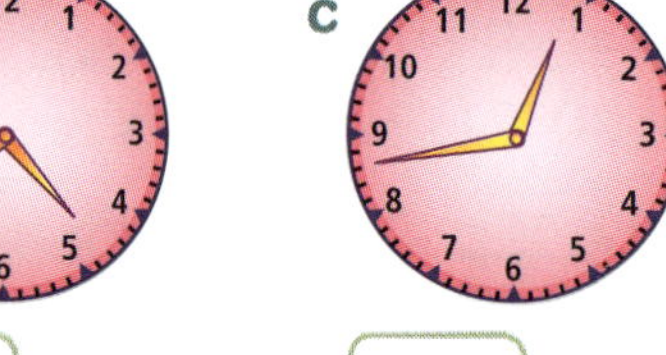 ☐ minutes The time is: ☐

d  ☐ minutes The time is: ☐

e  ☐ minutes The time is: ☐

4 Complete:

a 7 weeks = ☐ days **b** 3 fortnights = ☐ days **c** 28 days = ☐ fortnights

d 3 weeks = ☐ days **e** 77 days = ☐ weeks **f** 14 weeks = ☐ fortnights

g 21 days = ☐ weeks **h** 35 days = ☐ weeks **i** 14 days = ☐ weeks

5 Complete:

a 4 consecutive years would include ☐ normal years and ☐ leap year.

b 3 years = ☐ days **c** 3 years = ☐ months **d** 730 days = ☐ years

e 60 months = ☐ years **f** 3 years = ☐ weeks **g** 208 weeks = ☐ years

6 I started training at 3:37. I finished after 25 minutes. When did I finish? ☐

My friend continued for 8 minutes after I stopped. When did he finish? ☐

 • *AUSTRALIAN SIGNPOST MATHS 4* • ISBN 9780655708780

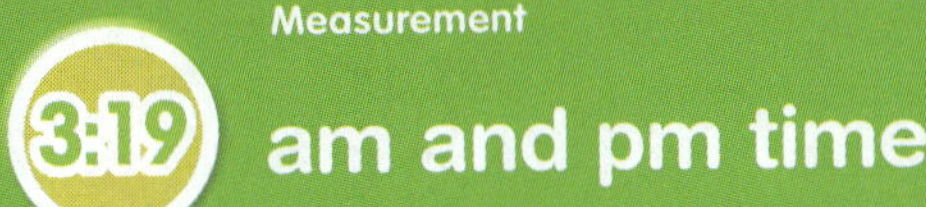

am and pm time

am: From midnight until noon
pm: From noon until midnight

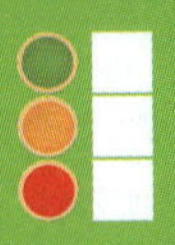

1 hour 20 minutes is written 1 h 20 min

When we write digital time we usually add **am** or **pm**.

Ante meridiem (am), is Latin for before midday.

7:35 am

Post meridiem (pm), is Latin for after midday.

10:46 pm

1 Write a digital label for each time shown.

a 
afternoon
___ : ___ pm

b 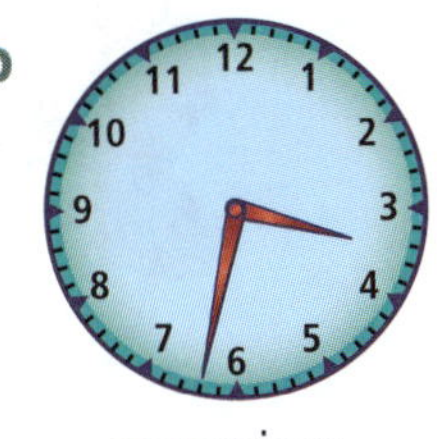
morning
___ : ___ am

c 
evening
___ : ___

d 
morning
___ : ___

e 
evening
___ : ___

2 For each digital time, write **before** midday or **after** midday.

a 

b 

c 

d 

e 

3 How long is it from 7 am till 10 pm?

How long is it from 7:35 am till 10:46 pm?

Count the hours from 7 to 12 noon and then from 12 onwards.

4 I started working at 8:30 am. Write down how long I have been working if it is now:

a 11:00 am
b 10:10 am
c 12:30 pm
d 3:30 pm
e 5 pm
f 4:15 pm

5 My assignment was given to me at 10 am on 13 June. It was due at 3 pm on 20 June. How much time did I have to do the assignment?

It is now 7 pm on 19 June. How much time do I have left?

It is now 9:30 am on 20 June. How much time do I have left?

 • *AUSTRALIAN SIGNPOST MATHS 4* • ISBN 9780655708780

3:20 Recording length

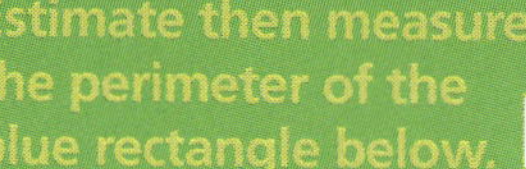

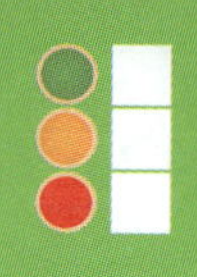

1 Write these as centimetres.

1 m equals 100 cm.

a 2 m 56 cm ☐ b 3 m 16 cm ☐
c 5 m 40 cm ☐ d 7 m 81 cm ☐
e 4 m 95 cm ☐ f 1 m 79 cm ☐
g 8 m 63 cm ☐ h 6 m 28 cm ☐

I can write it like this.
1 m 34 cm

This is shorter.
134 cm

2 Write these as metres and centimetres.

a 119 cm ☐ b 853 cm ☐
c 582 cm ☐ d 697 cm ☐
e 935 cm ☐ f 374 cm ☐

3 Write these as centimetres and millimetres.

a 27 mm ☐ b 36 mm ☐ c 51 mm ☐
d 19 mm ☐ e 42 mm ☐ f 85 mm ☐

4 Write these as millimetres.

a 5 cm 4 mm ☐ b 6 cm 9 mm ☐ c 1 cm 1 mm ☐
d 8 cm 7 mm ☐ e 4 cm 3 mm ☐ f 2 cm 6 mm ☐
g 45 cm ☐ h 104 cm ☐ i 3 m ☐

5 Which unit (**m**, **cm** or **mm**) has been left off each measurement of length?

a tree **5**
b battery **5**
c window **3**
d sharpener **25**
e pencil **14**
f door **1**
g finger **12**
h ruler **300**

SIZE C
centimetres

 • *AUSTRALIAN SIGNPOST MATHS 4* • ISBN 9780655708780

Comparing measurements

25 mm	
18 mm	?

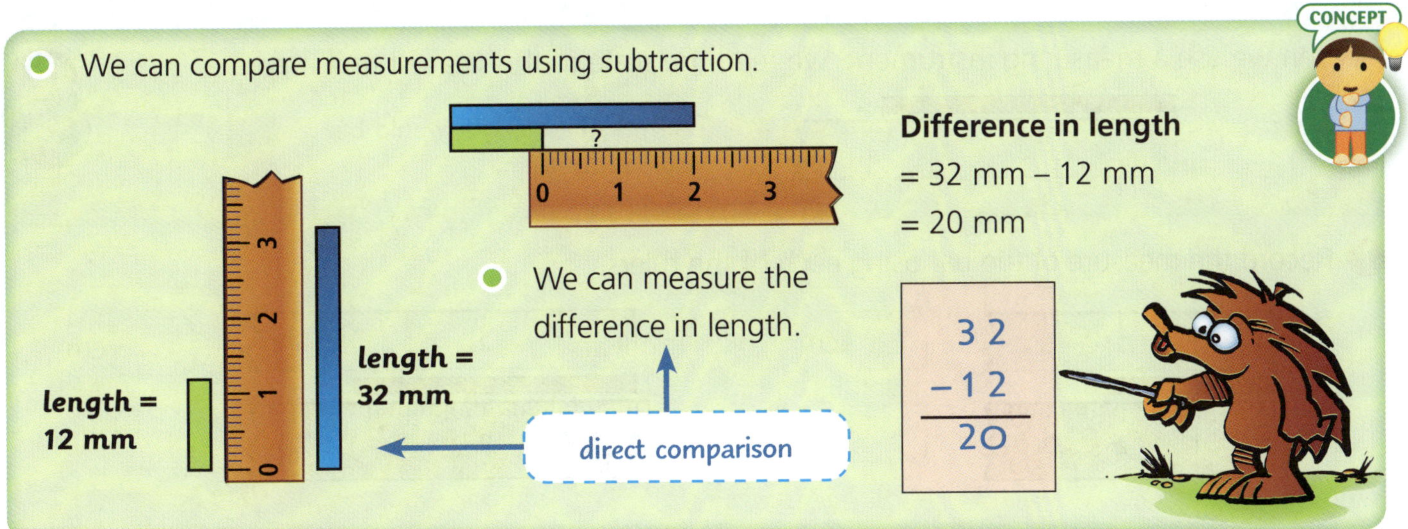

1 What is the difference in length of the rectangles:

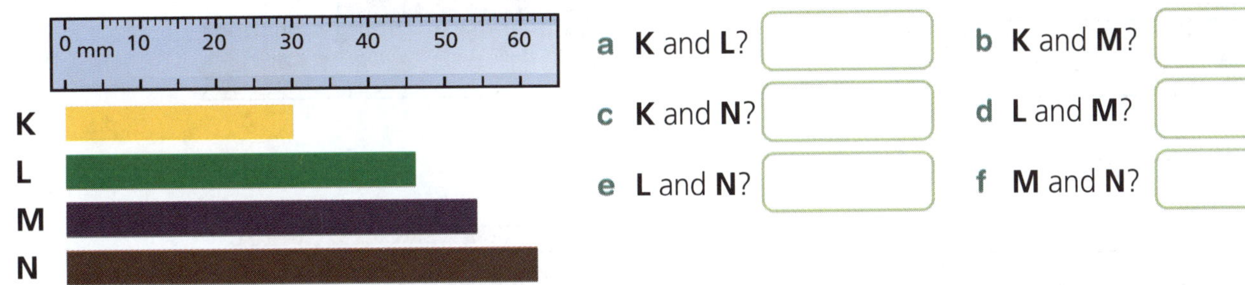

a **K** and **L**? ______ b **K** and **M**? ______
c **K** and **N**? ______ d **L** and **M**? ______
e **L** and **N**? ______ f **M** and **N**? ______

2 Measure the length of each rod in millimetres.

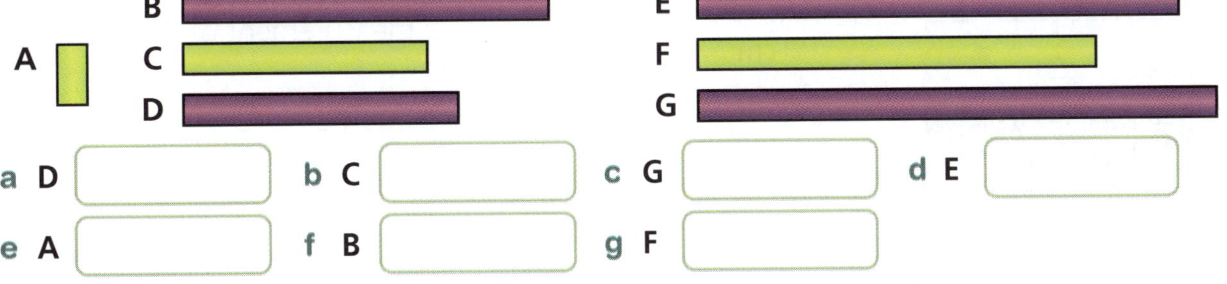

a **D** ______ b **C** ______ c **G** ______ d **E** ______
e **A** ______ f **B** ______ g **F** ______

3 On your own paper, calculate the difference in length of:

a **A** and **B** ______ b **C** and **D** ______ c **E** and **F** ______
d **G** and **A** ______ e **E** and **C** ______ f **D** and **G** ______
g **C** and **A** ______ h **D** and **E** ______ i **B** and **C** ______

INVESTIGATION

Explain how you would find the difference between the distance around a tree and the thickness of the tree.

 • *AUSTRALIAN SIGNPOST MATHS 4* • ISBN 9780655708780

Using measurement scales

When we use a measuring instrument, we read the scale to the nearest unit mark.

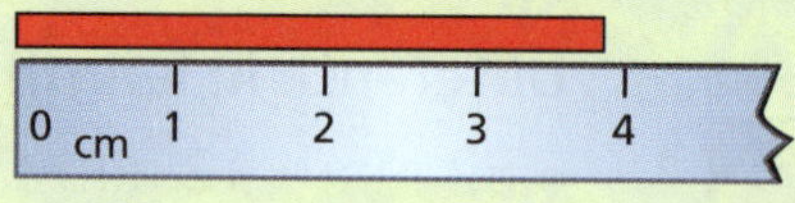

The measured length would be recorded as 4 cm.

1 Record the measure of the bar using each of the rulers.

a
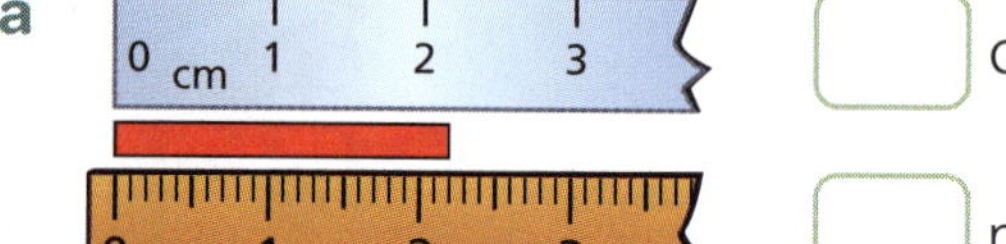

cm

mm

b
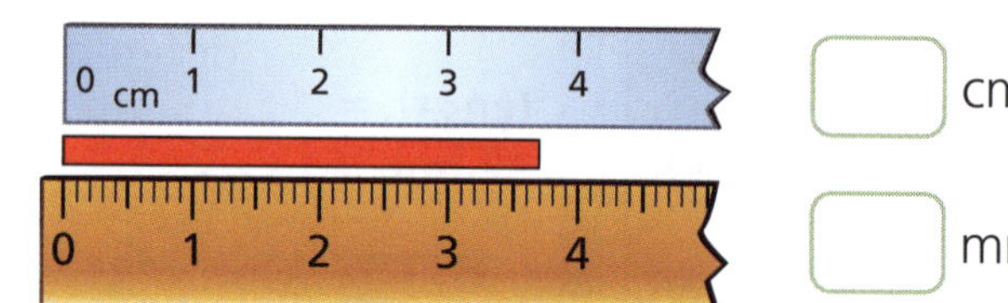

cm

mm

c
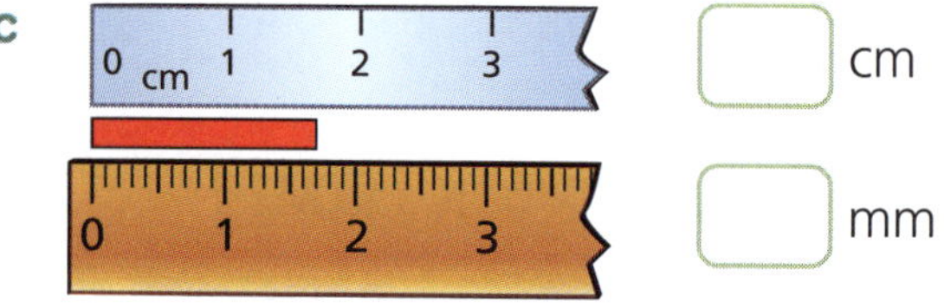

cm

mm

d
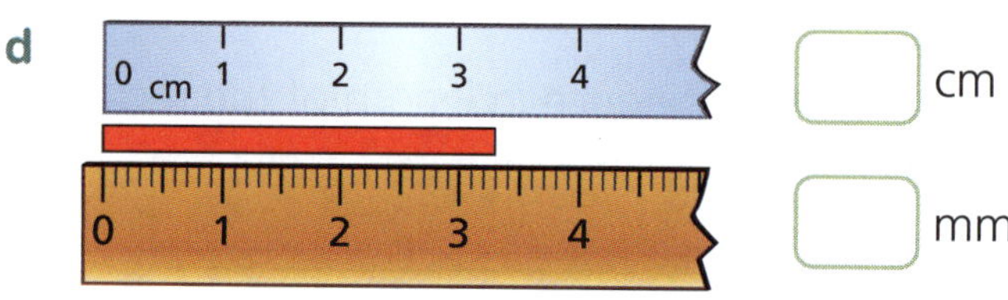

cm

mm

e

cm

mm

f
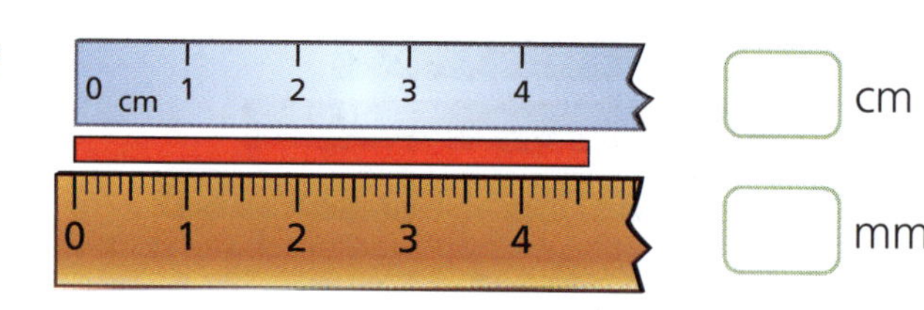

cm

mm

g
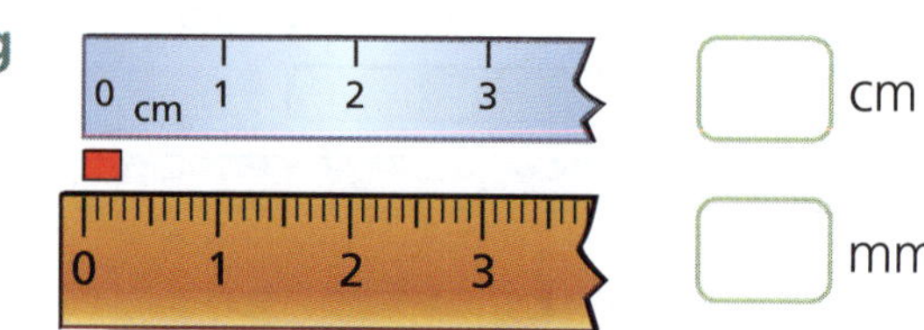

cm

mm

h What does a measurement of 0 cm mean?

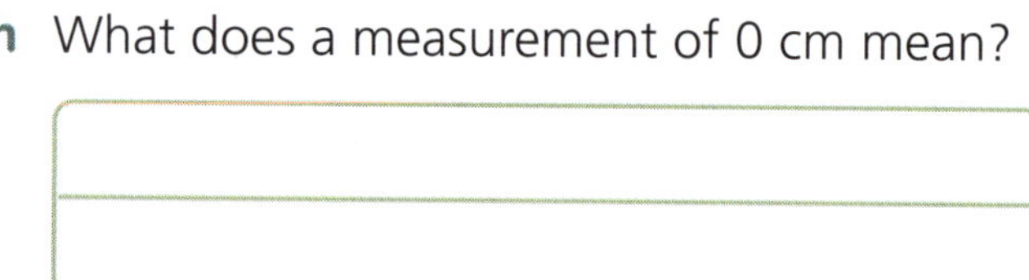

2 Record the measure shown on each scale.

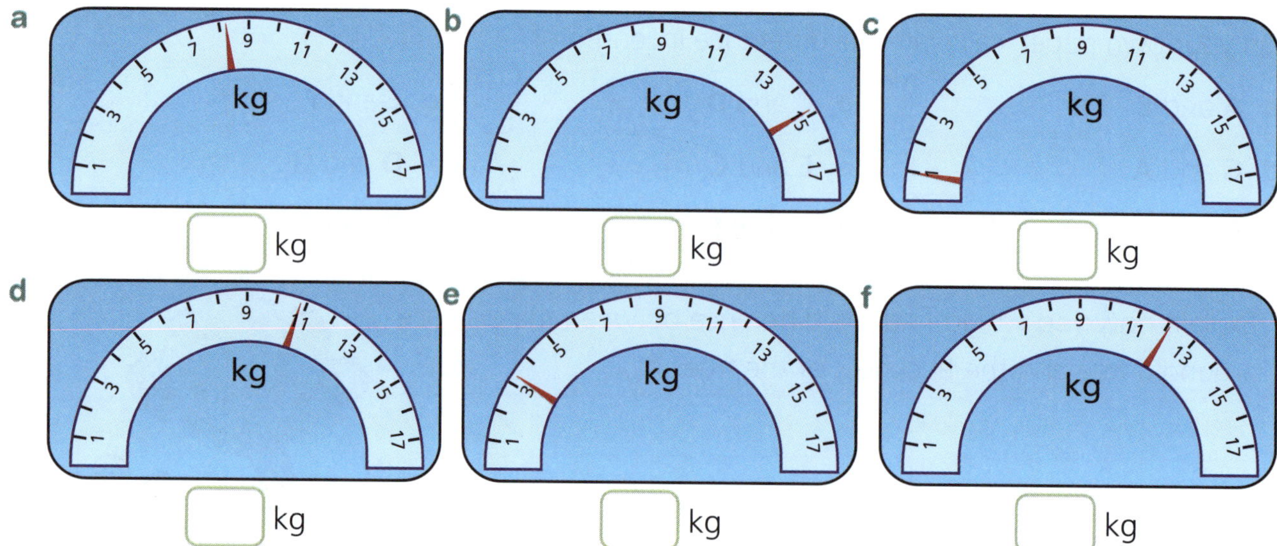

a kg

b kg

c kg

d kg

e kg

f kg

 • *AUSTRALIAN SIGNPOST MATHS 4* • ISBN 9780655708780

Recording length

When rounding to the nearest cm, round up for 5 mm and above, round down for less than 5 mm.

1 Complete this table.

Millimetres	cm and mm	Rounded to the nearest cm
39 mm		
	6 cm 3 mm	
56 mm		
	7 cm 2 mm	
81 mm		
	4 cm 5 mm	
	9 cm 4 mm	
26 mm		

2 Use a strip of 1 cm grid paper to measure the distance around:

a a pen ______ cm

b drink bottle ______ cm

c a pencil ______ cm

d your head ______ cm

e your arm ______ cm

3 Measure the length of each line correct to the nearest millimetre.

a ______ mm

b ______ mm

c ______ mm

d ______ mm

e ______ mm

f ______ mm

g ______ mm

h ______ mm

4 Estimate then measure the perimeter of each shape.

a ______ mm

b 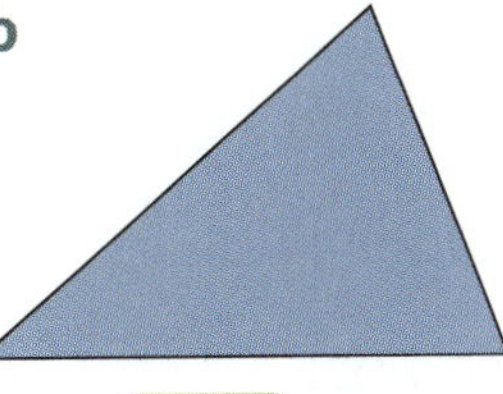 ______ mm

c  ______ mm

- Use a trundle wheel to measure:
  - the length of a path
  - the length of a hose
  - the length of the classroom
  - the length of a car
- Use a tape measure to measure:
  - the height of a door
  - the width of a window
  - the distance around a tree
  - the distance around a bottle

3:24 The square metre

My garden has an area of about 8 square metres.

Making a square metre

- Tape large sheets of newspaper together.
- Use a metre ruler to draw a square with side lengths of 1 m on the paper.
- Cut out your square.

Because this square has side lengths of one metre, it is a square metre.

1. List things in your classroom that are bigger than a square metre.

2. List things in your classroom that are smaller than a square metre.

3. Estimate and then check to find how many:

I have cut my square metre into four parts.

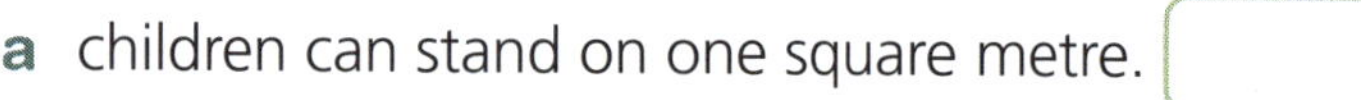

a children can stand on one square metre.

b children can sit on one square metre.

c children can lie on one square metre.

4. Estimate and then check to find how many:

a books are needed to cover one square metre.

b school bags are needed to cover one square metre.

c boxes are needed to cover one square metre.

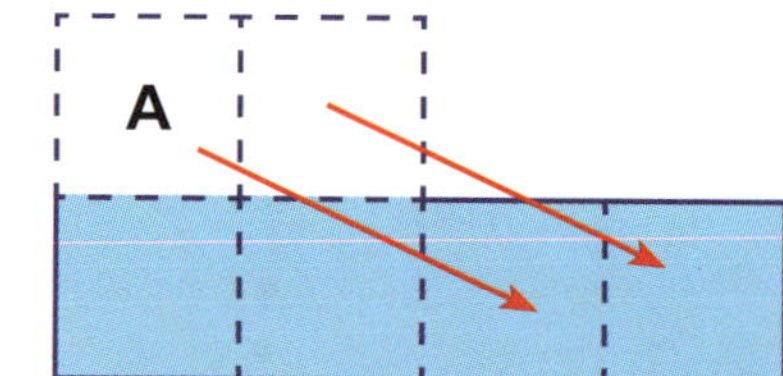

5. Estimate and then check to find how many:

a square metres are needed to cover a teacher's desk.

b square metres are needed to cover a door.

c square metres are needed to cover the floor.

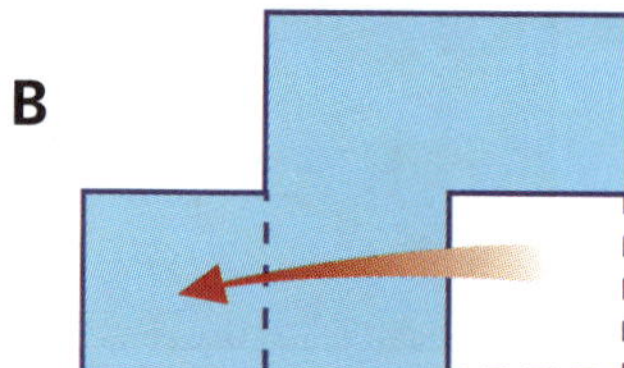

6. Cut, then join your square metre to make shapes like **A**, **B** and **C**.

a Does each still cover one square metre?

b Discuss how this could help us measure different surfaces.

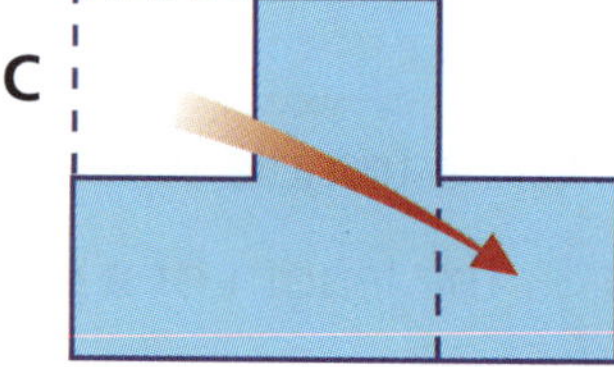

- Estimate, then measure, the size of a:

a table top ____ square metres

b window ____ square metres

c handball court ____ square metres

 • *AUSTRALIAN SIGNPOST MATHS 4* • ISBN 9780655708780

3:25 The square metre

Building blocks of land: 300 m^2
Cost: $600 000

ACTIVITY

- Make a 1 m^2 template from newspaper, plastic or cloth.
- Estimate, then measure surfaces of area:
  - less than 1 m^2.
  - about 1 m^2.
  - more than 1 m^2.
- Complete the table.

	Surface	
Less than 1 m^2		
About 1 m^2		
More than 1 m^2		

- Use your 1 m^2 template to measure bigger areas.

Work in groups for this activity.

Region or surface to be measured	Number of square metres	
	Estimate	Measure
classroom floor	m^2	m^2
a wall	m^2	m^2
whiteboard	m^2	m^2
section of path	m^2	m^2

1 Use the short form to write:

a 2 square metres ☐ b 6 square centimetres ☐
c 5 square metres ☐ d 12 square centimetres ☐
e 10 square metres ☐ f 15 square centimetres ☐

2 Which unit of measurement (**cm^2** or **m^2**) would you use to find the area of:

a the top of a brick? ☐ b a car park? ☐ c a keyboard? ☐
d a long path? ☐ e a playing card? ☐ f a bedroom floor? ☐
g a tennis court? ☐ h a book cover? ☐ i a sheet of notepaper? ☐

Timelines

You need a line showing time, and space to record what happened.

1. How many foreign cities did we visit?

2. Counting the days travelling, how long was our holiday? ______ days

3. Our travelling from Brisbane to London took 2 days. All other trips took 1 day. On how many days did we travel?

4. Which city did we visit on:
   - **a** 15 June?
   - **b** 28 June?
   - **c** 5 July?
   - **d** 20 June?

5. Not counting the days when we travelled, how many days did we spend in:
   - **a** Rome?
   - **b** Istanbul?
   - **c** Amman?
   - **d** Athens?

6. Where were we on:
   - **a** 12 June?
   - **b** 18 June?
   - **c** 30 June?
   - **d** 6 July?

7. We left Brisbane at 10 am on 9 June and arrived in London at 6:30 pm on 10 June. How long did it take us to travel to London?

8. Make a timeline for one school day, from the time you wake up till the time you go to bed.

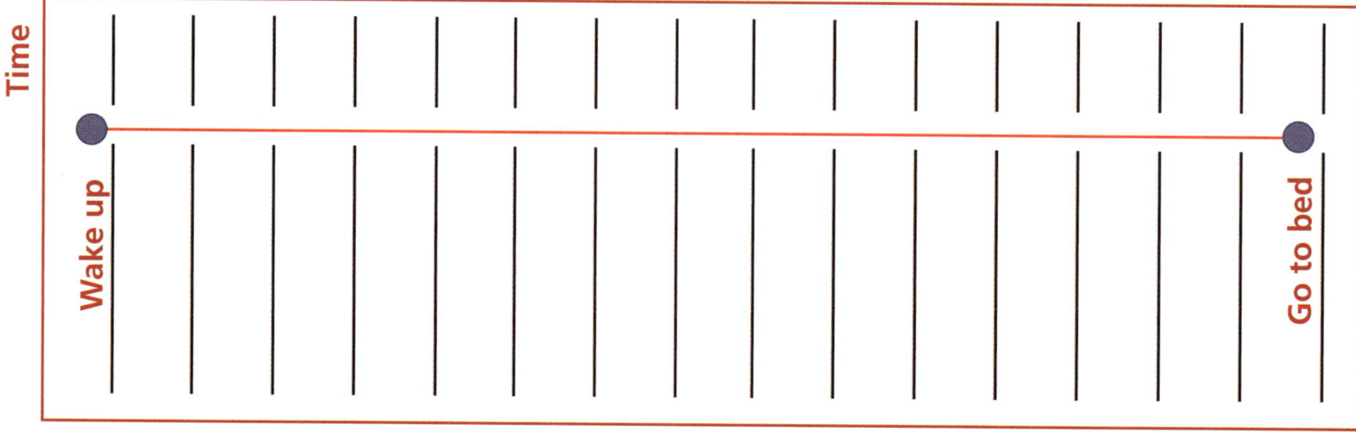

How did you make your timeline?

 • *AUSTRALIAN SIGNPOST MATHS 4* • ISBN 9780655708780

Timetables

Sometimes the am and pm are left out of timetables.

Use the timetable to answer the following questions.

Mulga Line timetable	
Arriving	
Ironbark	6:10
Christmas Ck	7:25
Mt Gordon	7:50
Richmond	8:45
Wandong	10:05
Carbor	11:40
Black Hill	12:30
Mulga	1:15

1 At what time does the train arrive in:

a Ironbark? ______ b Richmond? ______
c Carbor? ______ d Mt Gordon? ______
e Wandong? ______ f Mulga? ______

2 At which station does the train arrive at:

a 8:45 am ______ b 7:25 am ______
c 12:30 pm ______ d 6:10 am ______
e 1:15 pm ______ f 10:05 am ______

3 If the train is two hours late, at what time does it arrive in:

a Ironbark? ______ b Carbor? ______
c Mulga? ______ d Wandong? ______
e Black Hill? ______ f Richmond? ______

am means 'before noon' (from midnight until noon).

pm means 'after noon' (from noon until midnight).

4 If the train is half an hour early, at what time does it arrive in:

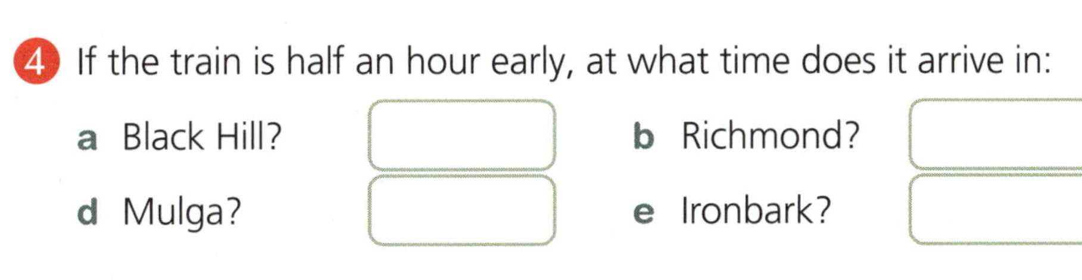
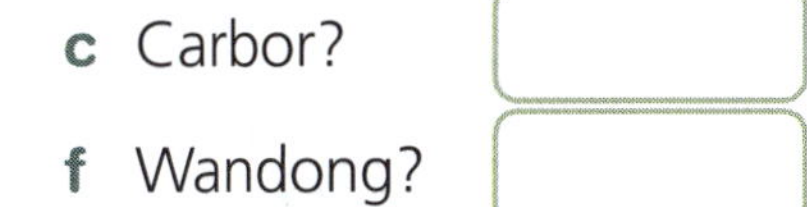

a Black Hill? ______ b Richmond? ______ c Carbor? ______
d Mulga? ______ e Ironbark? ______ f Wandong? ______

5 At which station does the train arrive at:

a half past 12? ______ b a quarter past 1? ______
c a quarter to 9? ______ d 5 past 10? ______
e 20 to 12? ______ f 10 to 8? ______

6 Complete the timeline for the Mulga Line train.

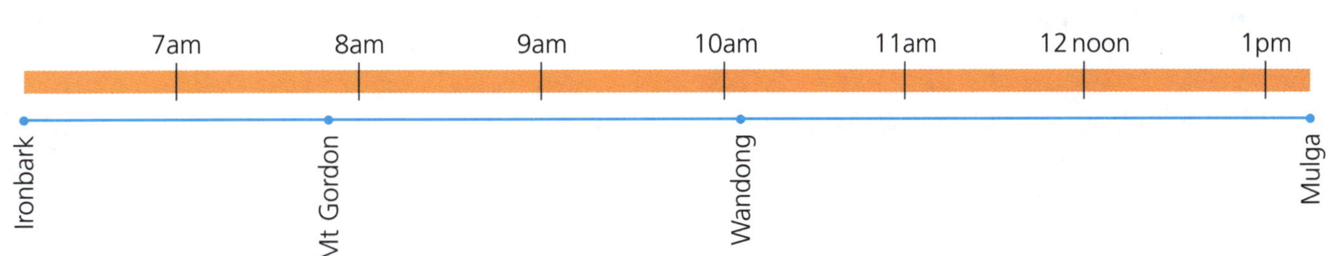

The calendar

A leap year happens once in every four years.

February						
Sun	Mon	Tues	Wed	Thur	Fri	Sat
		1	2	3	4	5
6	7	8	9	10	11	12
13	14	15	16	17	18	19
20	21	22	23	24	25	26
27	28	29				

Study the calendar then answer these questions.

1 a On what day of the week is the 18th?
  b Write the date of the first Thursday.
  c Write the date of the last Friday.
  d How many Saturdays are in February?
  e How many Tuesdays are there?
  f On what day does February begin?
  g How many days are in February on this calendar?
  h How many days are in February in most years?

7 days in a week
2 weeks in a fortnight
52 weeks in a year
365 days in a year
366 days in a leap year (one year in four)
12 months in a year

2 Write the date for:
  a the first Wednesday
  b the first Sunday
  c the last Saturday
  d the second Monday

3 Write the day of:
  a 10th February
  b 4th February
  c 19th February
  d 21st February

4 Write the dates for:
  a the first weekend
  b the second weekend
  c the third weekend
  d all the Wednesdays

INVESTIGATION

Research
Last year, what was the highest temperature in:
- February?
- July?

ACTIVITY

On this timeline, show events that happen on Saturday.

7 o'clock — midday — 10 o'clock

3:29 The calendar

The dictionary on page xxi shows another way to remember the days in each month.

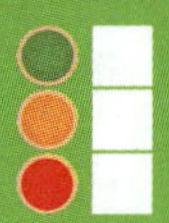

Thirty days has September, April, June and November.
All the rest have thirty-one, except for February alone,
Which has twenty-eight days clear,
and twenty-nine days each leap year.

There are 12 months in a year.

Here is a jingle to help you to remember how many days there are in each month.

A calendar shows the way a year is broken up into months, weeks and days.

January

S	M	T	W	T	F	S
		1	2	3	4	5
6	7	8	9	10	11	12
13	14	15	16	17	18	19
20	21	22	23	24	25	26
27	28	29	30	31		

February

S	M	T	W	T	F	S
					1	2
3	4	5	6	7	8	9
10	11	12	13	14	15	16
17	18	19	20	21	22	23
24	25	26	27	28		

March

S	M	T	W	T	F	S
31					1	2
3	4	5	6	7	8	9
10	11	12	13	14	15	16
17	18	19	20	21	22	23
24	25	26	27	28	29	30

April

S	M	T	W	T	F	S
	1	2	3	4	5	6
7	8	9	10	11	12	13
14	15	16	17	18	19	20
21	22	23	24	25	26	27
28	29	30				

May

S	M	T	W	T	F	S
			1	2	3	4
5	6	7	8	9	10	11
12	13	14	15	16	17	18
19	20	21	22	23	24	25
26	27	28	29	30	31	

June

S	M	T	W	T	F	S
30						1
2	3	4	5	6	7	8
9	10	11	12	13	14	15
16	17	18	19	20	21	22
23	24	25	26	27	28	29

July

S	M	T	W	T	F	S
	1	2	3	4	5	6
7	8	9	10	11	12	13
14	15	16	17	18	19	20
21	22	23	24	25	26	27
28	29	30	31			

August

S	M	T	W	T	F	S
				1	2	3
4	5	6	7	8	9	10
11	12	13	14	15	16	17
18	19	20	21	22	23	24
25	26	27	28	29	30	31

September

S	M	T	W	T	F	S
1	2	3	4	5	6	7
8	9	10	11	12	13	14
15	16	17	18	19	20	21
22	23	24	25	26	27	28
29	30					

October

S	M	T	W	T	F	S
		1	2	3	4	5
6	7	8	9	10	11	12
13	14	15	16	17	18	19
20	21	22	23	24	25	26
27	28	29	30	31		

November

S	M	T	W	T	F	S
					1	2
3	4	5	6	7	8	9
10	11	12	13	14	15	16
17	18	19	20	21	22	23
24	25	26	27	28	29	30

December

S	M	T	W	T	F	S
1	2	3	4	5	6	7
8	9	10	11	12	13	14
15	16	17	18	19	20	21
22	23	24	25	26	27	28
29	30	31				

1 Which month comes before:

a February ___ b November ___ c June ___ d October ___

2 How many days are in:

a April? ___ b August? ___ c December? ___ d March? ___

3 Look carefully at the month of May. Write the day of:

a the first Sunday ___ b the first Wednesday ___

4 Look at the month of September. What is the date:

a one week after 12th? ___ b two days before 27th? ___

5 What day is:

a 13th September? ___ b 21st June? ___ c 2nd February? ___
d 31st May? ___ e 29th August? ___ f 3rd January? ___

6 How many weeks and days is it from 12 July to:

a 25 July? ___ b 23 August? ___
c 2 October? ___ d 25 December? ___

7 How many weeks and days before 13 April, was:

a 1 January? ___ b 26 January? ___

3:30 The passage of time

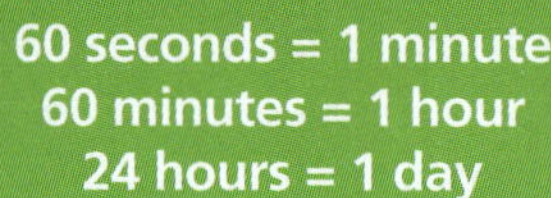

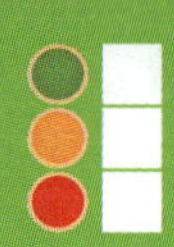

CONCEPT

Clocks sometimes have a second hand.
This clock, shows 21 minutes, 29 seconds past 1.
The time shown here can be writen as 1:21:29 pm.

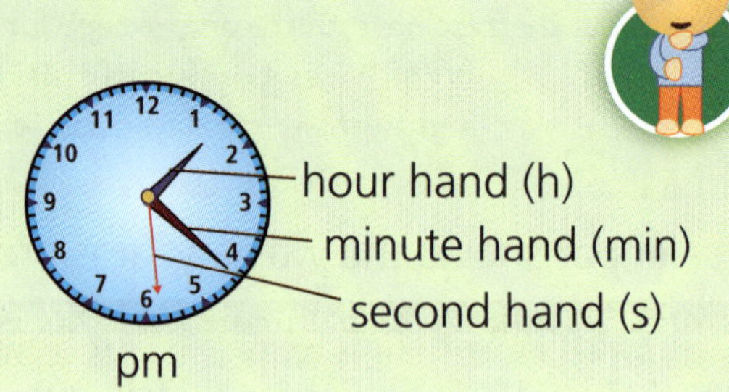

- While the second hand moves one full turn around the clock (60 s), the minute hand moves one small unit (1 min).
- While the minute hand moves one full turn around the clock (60 min), the hour hand moves from one number to the next (1 h).

1 These times were recorded on Thursday. Estimate the time to the nearest minute

A
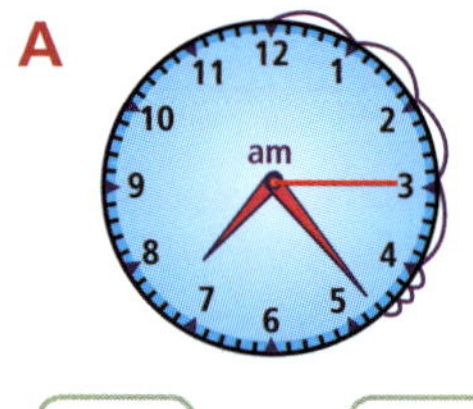

☐ past ☐
☐ : ☐

B

☐ past ☐
☐ : ☐

C

☐ to ☐
☐ : ☐

D

☐ to ☐
☐ : ☐

a Are the times in **A** to **D** shown in order, from earliest to latest? ☐

b Which clock has a second hand? ☐

c Which clocks show times that are before noon? ☐

d Which clocks show times that are after noon? ☐

To find how much time it is from 10:20 am to 2:12 pm, count forward.

From 10:20 to 11:00	40 min
From 11 :00 to 2:00	3 h
From 2:00 to 2:12	12 min
Total:	3 h 52 min

2 How much time elapsed between the times shown on clocks:

a **A** and **B**? ☐ **b** **B** and **C**? ☐

c **C** and **D**? ☐ **d** **A** and **D**? ☐

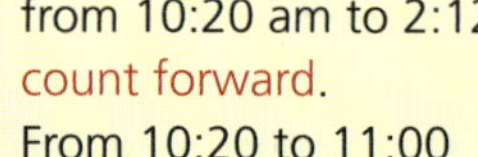

3 **a** Naomi began cooking at 3 pm, and put the cake in the oven at 5:15 pm. She took the cake out of the oven 30 minutes later. How long did it take to make the cake? ☐

b Luke left at 1:33 pm and returned at 4:29 pm. How long was he gone? ☐

c The movie started at 6:52 pm and ended at 9:08 pm. How long was it? ☐

d We started work at 9:17 am and finished at 4:05 pm. How long did we work? ☐

See Extra Support 13 (Comparing decimal measurements).

Measuring mass

3 kilograms 500 grams is 3 kg 500 g

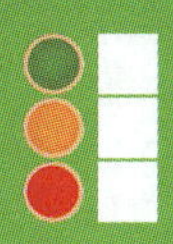

1. Use the short form to write:
   - a 1 kilogram
   - b 450 grams
   - c 3 kilograms
   - d 1 kilogram 560 grams
   - e 2 kilograms 125 grams

2. How many grams are in:
   - a 3 kilograms?
   - b 5 kilograms?
   - c 9 kilograms?
   - d 7 kilograms?
   - e 4 kilograms?
   - f 6 kilograms?

3. How many kilograms are in:
   - a 1000 grams?
   - b 8000 grams?
   - c 2000 grams?
   - d 4000 grams?
   - e 6000 grams?
   - f 5000 grams?

4. Write each measurement as kilograms (kg) using one decimal place.
   - a 100 g
   - b 300 g
   - c 900 g
   - d 500 g
   - e 700 g
   - f 1400 g

700 g

0·7 kg

Digital scales

Analog scales

0 kg 1 2 3 4

The measure next to the blue dot is 4 kg 750 g.

5. Write each measurement as grams (g).
   - a 0·5 kg
   - b 0·2 kg
   - c 0·8 kg
   - d 0·6 kg

6. There are three marks between 0 and 1 on these analog scales. These stand for 250 g, 500 g and 750 g. Write the measure that is shown by the:
   - a white dot
   - b black dot
   - c yellow dot
   - d green dot

ACTIVITY

- Use balance scales and standard masses to complete this table

Mass	Objects found
Less than 100 g	
About 500 g	
About 1 kg	
More than 1 kg	

1 litre of water weighs about 1 kilogram.

1 L 1.0 L 0.5 L 1kg

 • *AUSTRALIAN SIGNPOST MATHS 4* • ISBN 9780655708780

Measurement

3:32 Personal benchmarks

My weight (mass)

My height

Learn these benchmarks. They will help you estimate more accurately.

1 Match each oval with a rectangle.

the length of two of my steps

the length of a full-sized pool

the capacity of a bucket

the capacity of a small bottle of water

the capacity of this milk container

the mass of 1 L of milk

temperature of a hot day

- 600 mL
- 1 m
- 50 m
- the same as 1 L of water
- 100 cm^2
- 1 cm^2
- 11 L
- 2 L
- 10 cm
- 5°C
- 1 kg
- 600 cm^2
- 1 cm
- 35°C

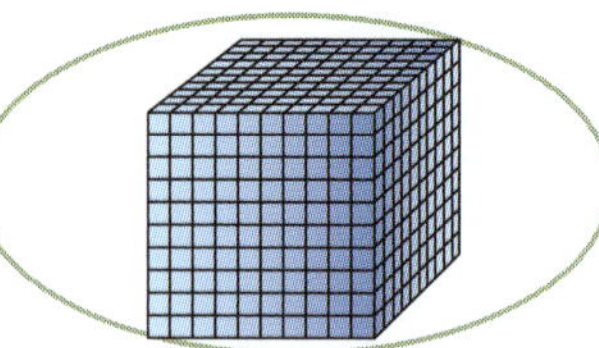
the volume (capacity) of a 1000s block

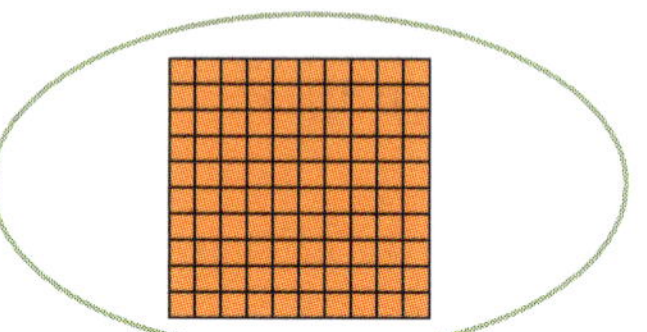
the area of the front of a 100s block

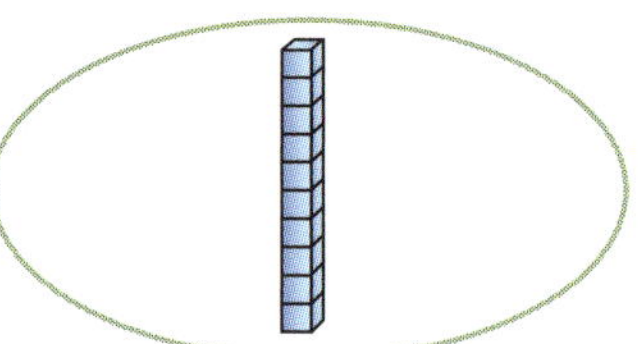
the height of a tens block

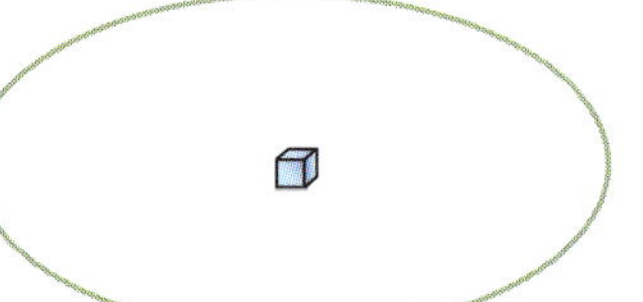
the front area of a ones block

the area of a page of this textbook

the width of my finger

temperature on a cold day

3:33 Finding area

Half of 1 cm² is $\frac{1}{2}$ cm².

We can cut squares into half squares.

1 What is the area of each coloured shape?

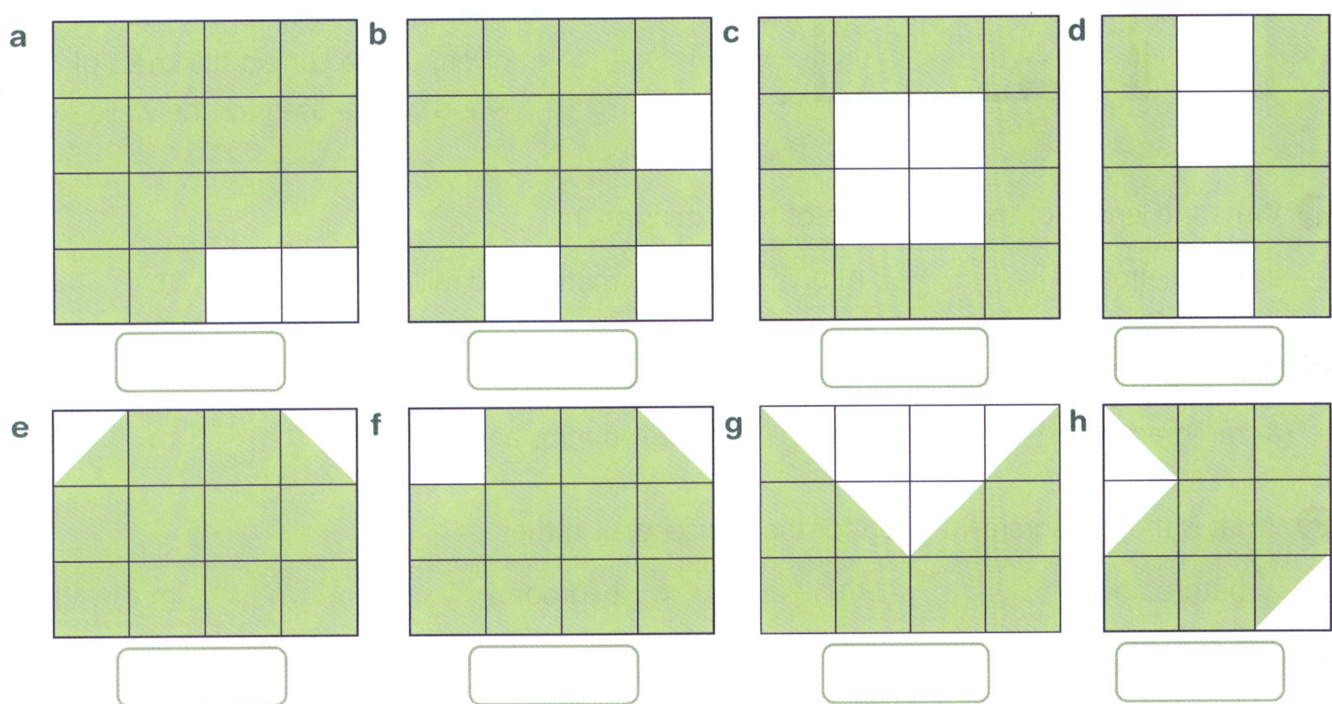

2 Find the area of each triangle.

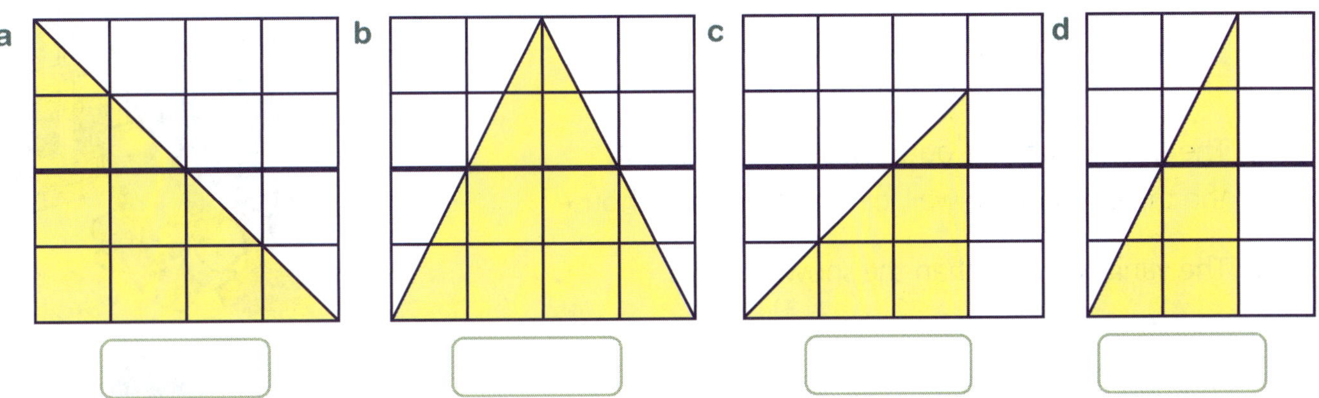

Cut and find area

- Cut a square with 4 cm sides from 1 cm grid paper. Find its area.
- Draw in the diagonals and cut along them to form four triangles.
- Rearrange them to make a rectangle (as shown) and find its area.

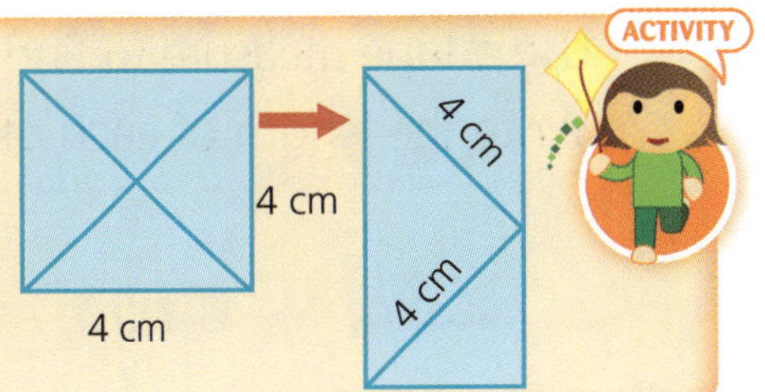

 • *AUSTRALIAN SIGNPOST MATHS 4* • ISBN 9780655708780

3:34 Using mm when building

The measurements shown on building plans are in millimetres.

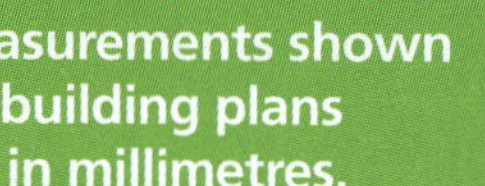

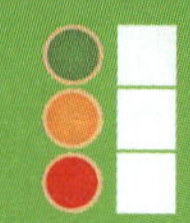

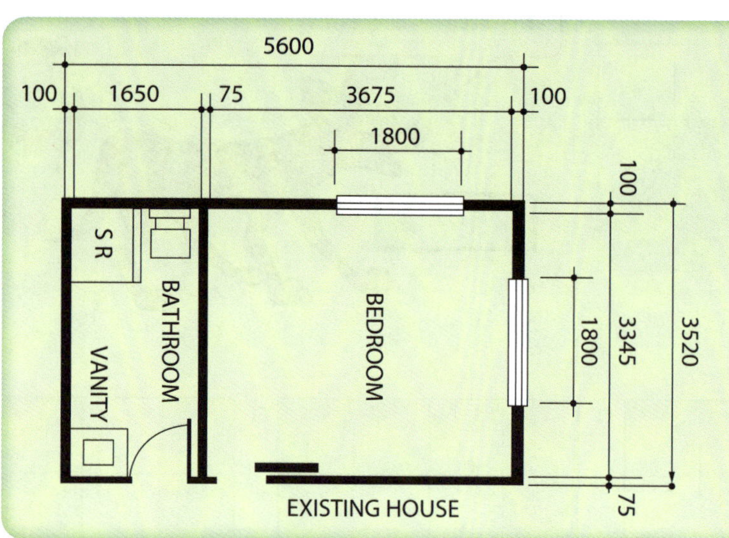

CONCEPT

- This is the building plan for an extension to Tom's house.
  - All measurements are in millimetres.
  - S R stands for shower recess. Vanity stands for a sink
  - There are two windows and a sliding door in the bedroom.
  - Even the thickness of the walls is given, so the correct thickness of wood will be used for the walls.

1. Write the length of the longer side of the extension in:
   a millimetres [ ] mm
   b metres and millimetres [ ] m [ ] mm

2. Write the length of the shorter side of the extension in:
   a millimetres [ ] mm
   b metres and millimetres [ ] m [ ] mm

3. What is the measurement given for the shorter wall in the:
   a bathroom? [ ] mm
   b bedroom? [ ] m [ ] mm

4. True or false?
   a The longer wall of the bathroom is the same length as the shorter wall of the bedroom. [ ]
   b The width of the shower recess is about 940 mm. [ ]
   c The thickness of the outer walls is greater than the thickness of the wall joining the existing house. [ ]
   d The vanity is wider than the shower recess. [ ]

INVESTIGATION

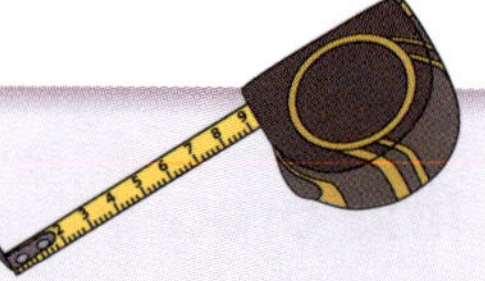

- Use a tape measure to find 3 objects that are longer than a metre. Write the length of each of these objects in millimetres.

[ ] [ ] [ ]

 • *AUSTRALIAN SIGNPOST MATHS 4* • ISBN 9780655708780

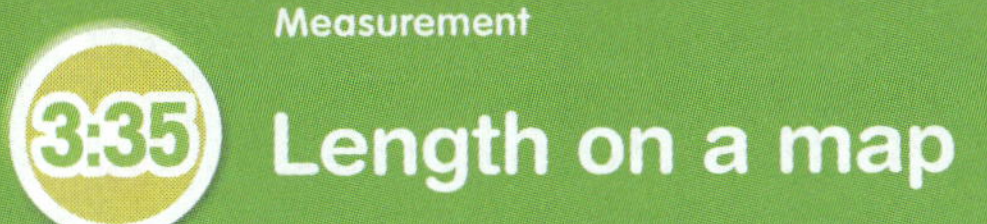

The scale tells us that one centimetre on the map represents one kilometre.

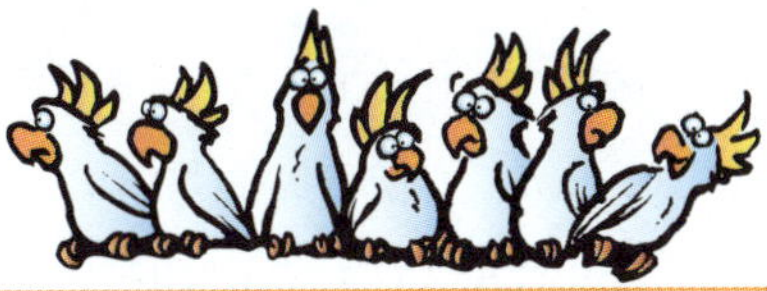

Country map

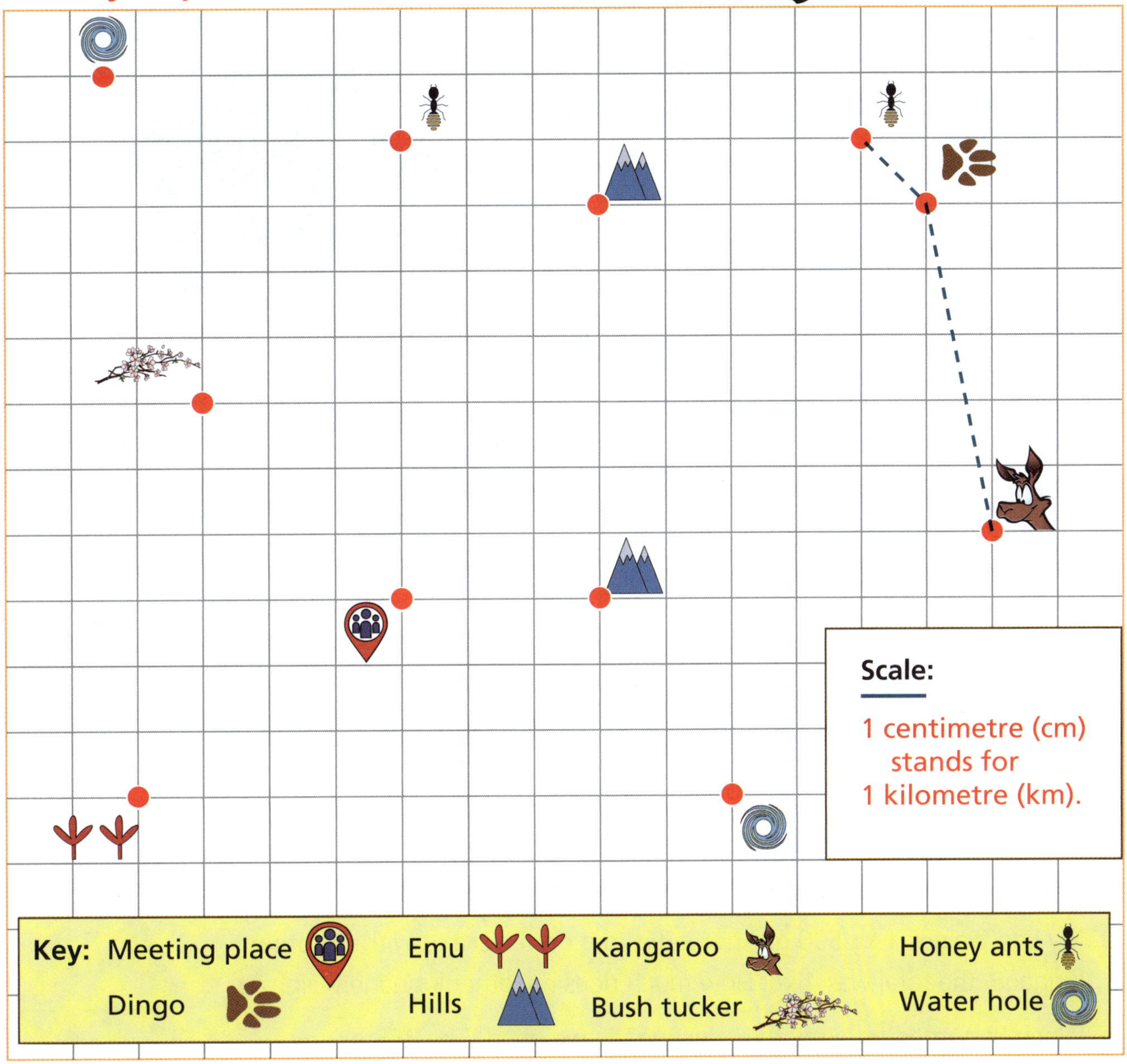

The **centres** of the red dots show the position of the places.

1. Find the distance to the nearest kilometre (km) between the meeting place and the nearest:
   a hills ☐ b honey ants ☐ c water hole ☐

2. Find the distance (to the nearest kilometre) between the meeting place and the:
   a emu ☐ b dingo ☐ c kangaroo ☐

3. Each millimetre on the map stands for 100 metres. Find the distance between the dingo and:
   a the kangaroo ☐ m b the nearest honey ants ☐ m

3:36 Problem solving

Don't forget to include units of measurement in your answer.

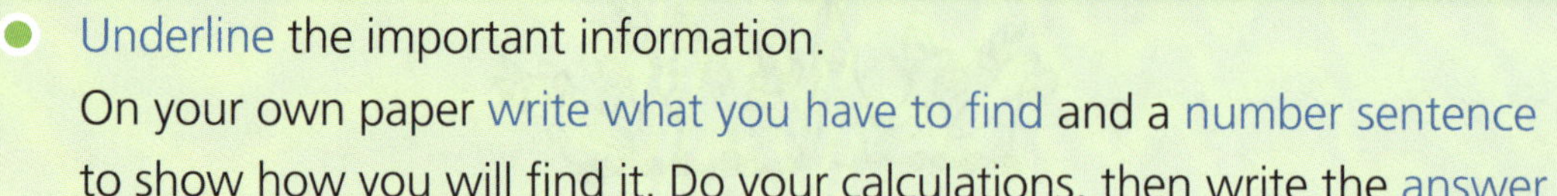

Underline the important information.
On your own paper write what you have to find and a number sentence to show how you will find it. Do your calculations, then write the answer.

1. The length of the tree's shadow was half of its real height. If the height of the tree was 36 m, how long was the shadow?

   Use the cartoon to estimate:

   a the width of the house

   b the length of the truck

2. The temperature at 5 pm on Monday was 27°C. On Tuesday at 5 pm, the temperature was 6°C higher. On Wednesday at 5 pm the temperature was 13°C less than Tuesday's. What was Wednesday's temperature?

3. The jug held one litre of water. It was full before I poured out 275 mL. How much water remained in the jug?

4. The jar of jam I bought weighed 350 g, the rice flakes weighed 200 g, the tissues 150 g and the cake 750 g. What was the total weight of these items?

5. a The show started at 6:45 pm. I arrived 37 minutes late. When did I arrive?

   b I left at 9:12 pm, when the show finished. How much of the show did I see?

6. I left on January 27 and returned home on February 2. What was the total number of days that I was away or travelling?

7. a My bag weighs 1 kg 500 g. After it was put on the scales with my other luggage, the total was 4 kg. How much does my other luggage weigh?

   b When I returned from my trip, my luggage weighed 7 kg 365 g. How much heavier was my luggage on the return trip?

8. The width of the wall is 3345 mm. Of this, the door takes up 1800 mm. How much width of the wall is left to hang up my photos?

9. My goal is to swim 800 m each day.

   a One lap of the pool is 50 m. How many laps should I swim each day?

   b I swam only 550 m on the first day. How far should I swim on the second day to make up for this shortfall?

 ISBN 9780655708780

Problem solving

20 – 19 + 18 – 17 + 16 – 15 + 14
= (1) + (1) + (1) + 14
= 17

List the pairs of numbers that make this algorithm true.

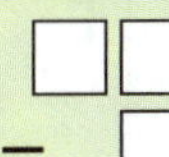

Clues:
One number has 2 digits.
The other one has 1 digit.
Their difference is 2.

The answers are:
------ and ------
or ------ and ------

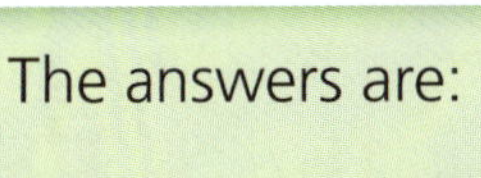

1 List the pairs of numbers that have the difference given.

a 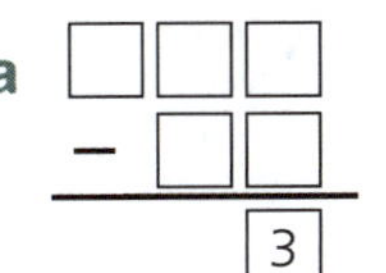

----

b 

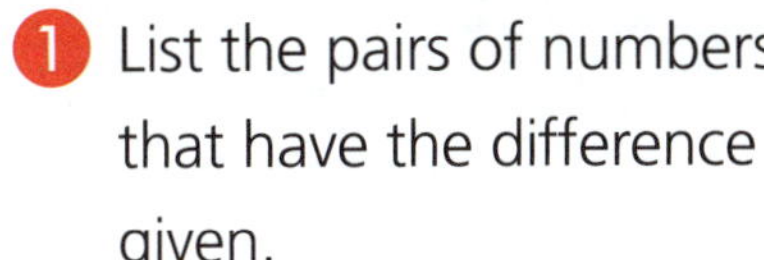
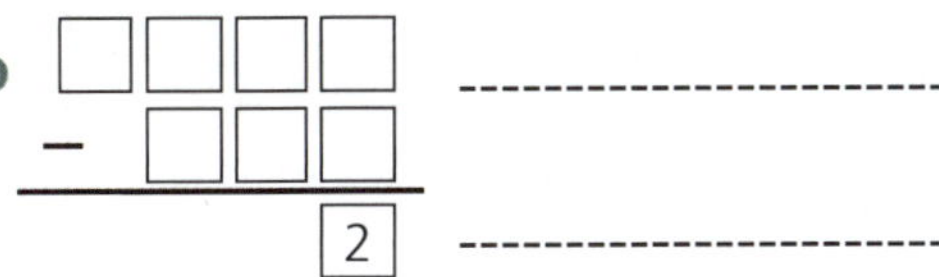
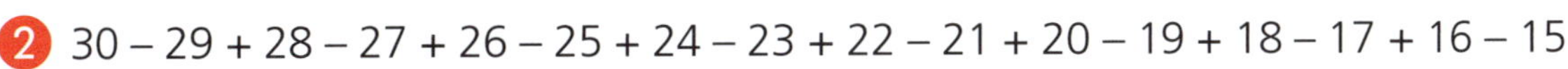

2 30 – 29 + 28 – 27 + 26 – 25 + 24 – 23 + 22 – 21 + 20 – 19 + 18 – 17 + 16 – 15

3 **a** Soft drink was for sale in 300 mL, 600 mL, 1250 mL and 2000 mL plastic bottles. I bought one of each. How many mL of soft drink did I buy?

b Write the answer to part **a** using litres and millilitres (L and mL).

c If each millilitre of soft drink has a mass of one gram and the four drink containers have a mass of 20 g altogether, what was the total mass?

4 I worked from 9:10 am until lunch at 12:30 pm. I took 30 minutes for lunch. I then worked until 5 pm. For how long did I work?

5 **a** I was walking along a path which was 850 m long. After travelling 247 m, I saw a snake. How far from the end of the path was the snake?

b 100 m before the end of the path I saw a bull-ant nest. How far was the nest from the start of the path?

c How far was the nest from the snake?

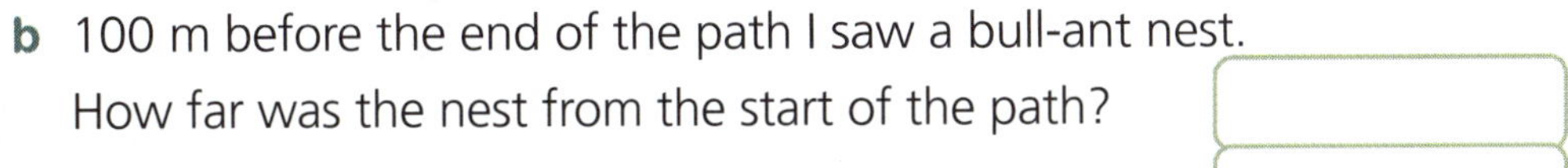

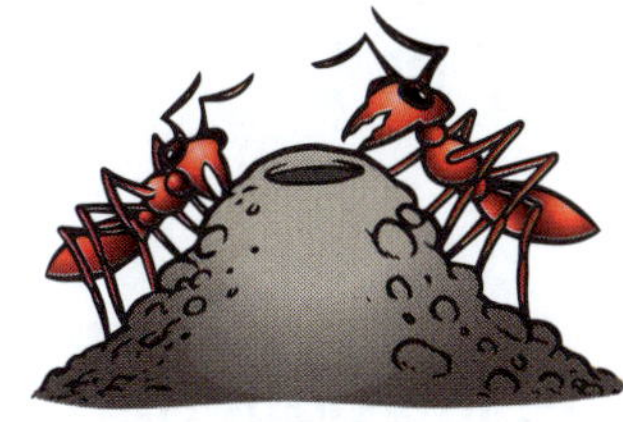

6 The area of the desk is 2600 cm^2. My book was covering 600 cm^2 of this area. What area of the desk was not covered by my book?

7 My table is 3 m 25 cm long and 2 m wide. My desk is 150 cm long and 45 cm wide.

a How much longer is my table than my desk?

b How much wider is the table than my desk?

8 I built a bird breeding box. All four sides are 10 cm wide and 20 cm long. The two square ends are 10 cm wide and 10 cm long. What was the total surface area of the box before I made a hole for the entrance?

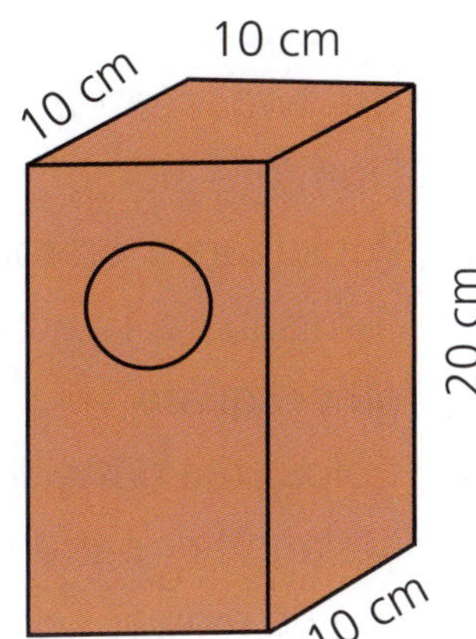

 • *AUSTRALIAN SIGNPOST MATHS 4* • ISBN 9780655708780

Flip, slide and turn

If you fold along a line of symmetry, the two halves will match.

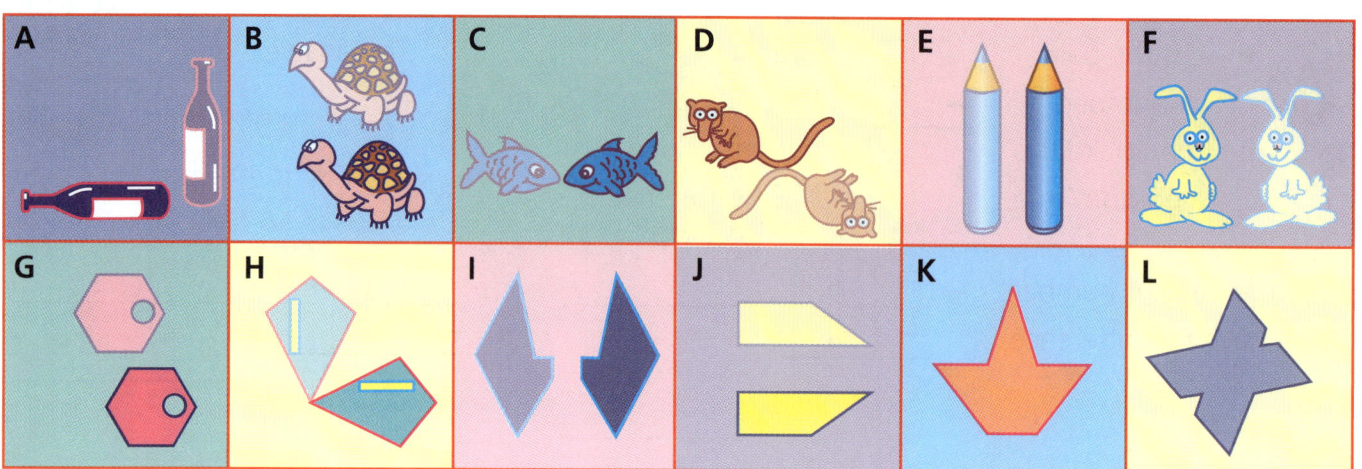

1 Which pictures (**A** to **J**) are samples of:

a flip (reflection)? b slide (translation)?

c turn (rotation)?

2 Which picture could be an example of a flip or a slide?

3 How many axes of symmetry has picture:

a **K**?	b **L**?	c **C**?
d **D**?	e **E**?	f **F**?
g **G**?	h **H**?	i **I**?

Try to draw pictures of your own that show flip, slide or turn.

Turning patterns

ACTIVITY

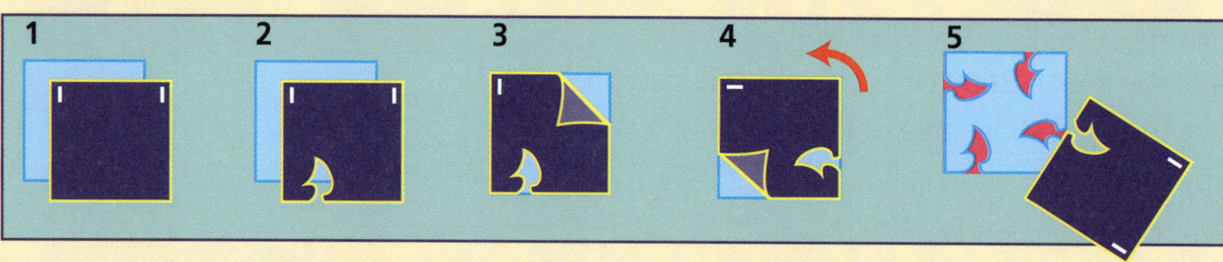

1 Use two identical cardboard squares.
2 From one side of square 1, cut out an interesting shape.
3 Put square 1 on top of the other square and trace the shape you have made.
4 Turn square 1 and trace the shape onto each side of the other square.
5 Colour the pattern you have made.

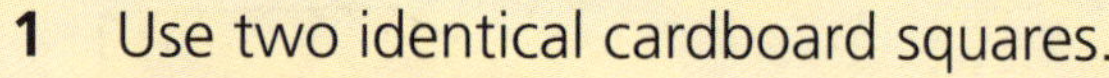

Make other patterns starting with:

a two regular hexagons b two regular octagons

See *Extra Support 3* (Tangrams) and *Extra Support 4* (Flip, slide and turn).

Angles and 2D shapes

The size of an angle is the amount of turn from one arm to the other.

a Are these angles the same size?

b Does an angle get bigger if you make its arms longer?

c The angle at the corner of a page is called a **right angle**. Is angle **B** bigger than a right angle?

2

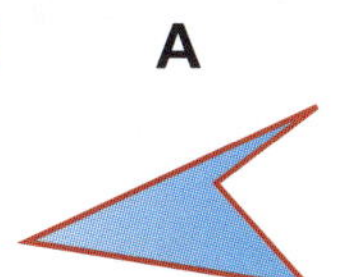
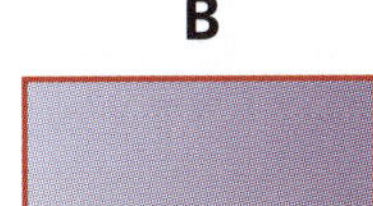
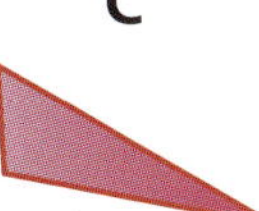
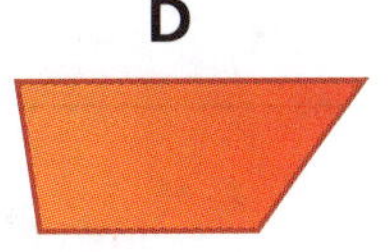

a Which of these shapes are not quadrilaterals?

b Which have parallel sides?

c Which shapes have symmetry?

d How many sides has shape **B**? How many angles?

e How many sides has shape **C**? How many angles?

f Do all of these shapes have the same number of sides as vertices?

3 Use the corner of a sheet of paper to test these angles.

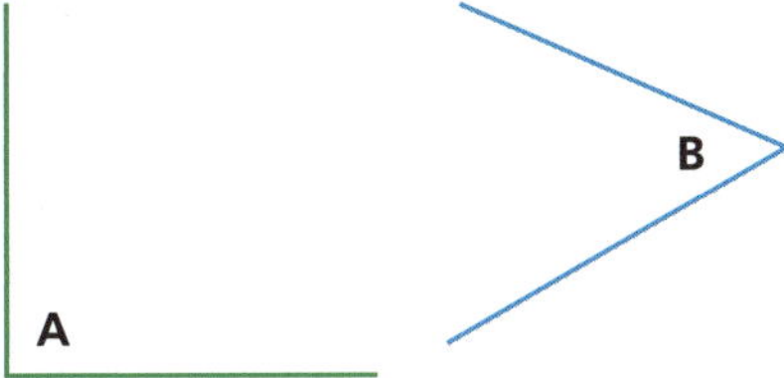

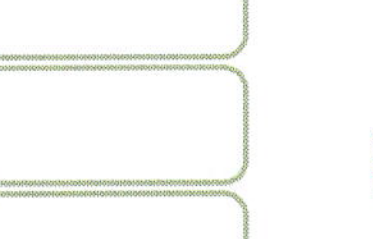

a Which of these angles are right angles?

b Which angle is less than a right angle?

c Which one is bigger than a right angle?

d Are the arms of a right angle perpendicular?

4 On your own paper, use a pencil and ruler to draw or trace:

a a square
b a rectangle
c a pentagon
d a trapezium
e a right angle
f an angle smaller than a right angle

5 Which triangle has:

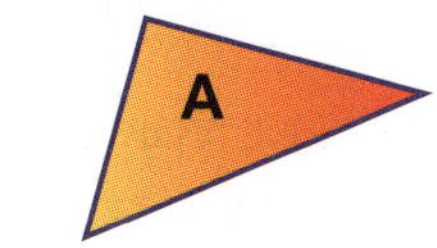
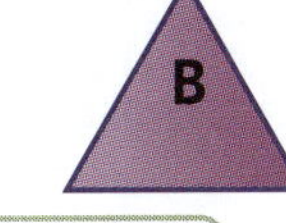

a all sides equal?

b two sides equal?

c no sides equal?

d a right angle?

 • *AUSTRALIAN SIGNPOST MATHS 4* • ISBN 9780655708780

Comparing angles

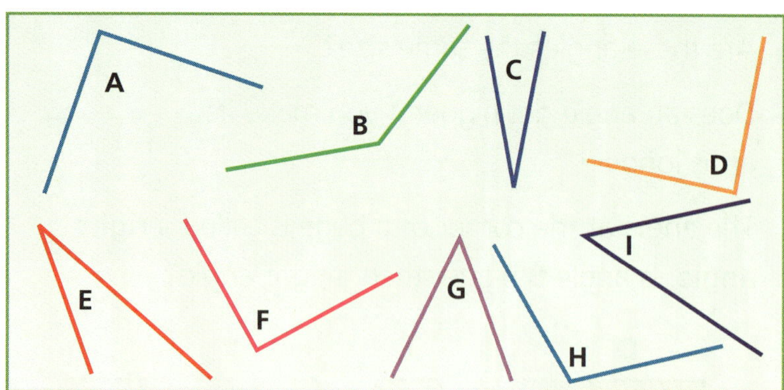

1 Use the corner of a page to test the angles above. Put the letter of each angle in the correct column.

My angle (Right angle)	Smaller	The same	Larger

2 Which angle is smaller:

a **A** or **B**? ☐ **b** **C** or **D**? ☐ **c** **E** or **F**? ☐ **d** **G** or **H**? ☐

3 Fold your paper right angle to make half a right angle. Use this new angle to test the angles at the top of the page. Put the letter of each angle in the correct column.

Half of a right angle	Smaller	The same	Larger

4 Draw each angle showing both arms and the vertex.

a the opening of a gate **b** the slope of a road **c** the swing of a bat

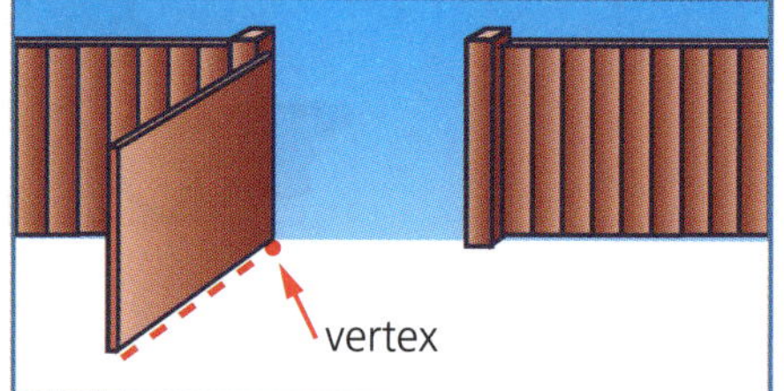

Name an angle in your classroom that is:

- smaller than a right angle ____________
- greater than a right angle ____________

Use computer software to create simple shapes that involve direction and angles.

 AUSTRALIAN SIGNPOST MATHS 4 • ISBN 9780655708780

3D objects

Are the cross-sections that are parallel to the base, the same size and shape as the base?

CONCEPT

Prisms have:
- ends that are the same shape
- sides that are rectangles.

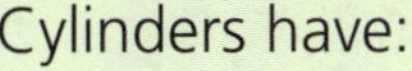

Cylinders have:
- ends that are circles
- one curved surface.

1 **a** Colour the prisms red, the cylinders blue and the pyramids green.

b What shapes are the surfaces of the objects in part **a**? Discuss.

2

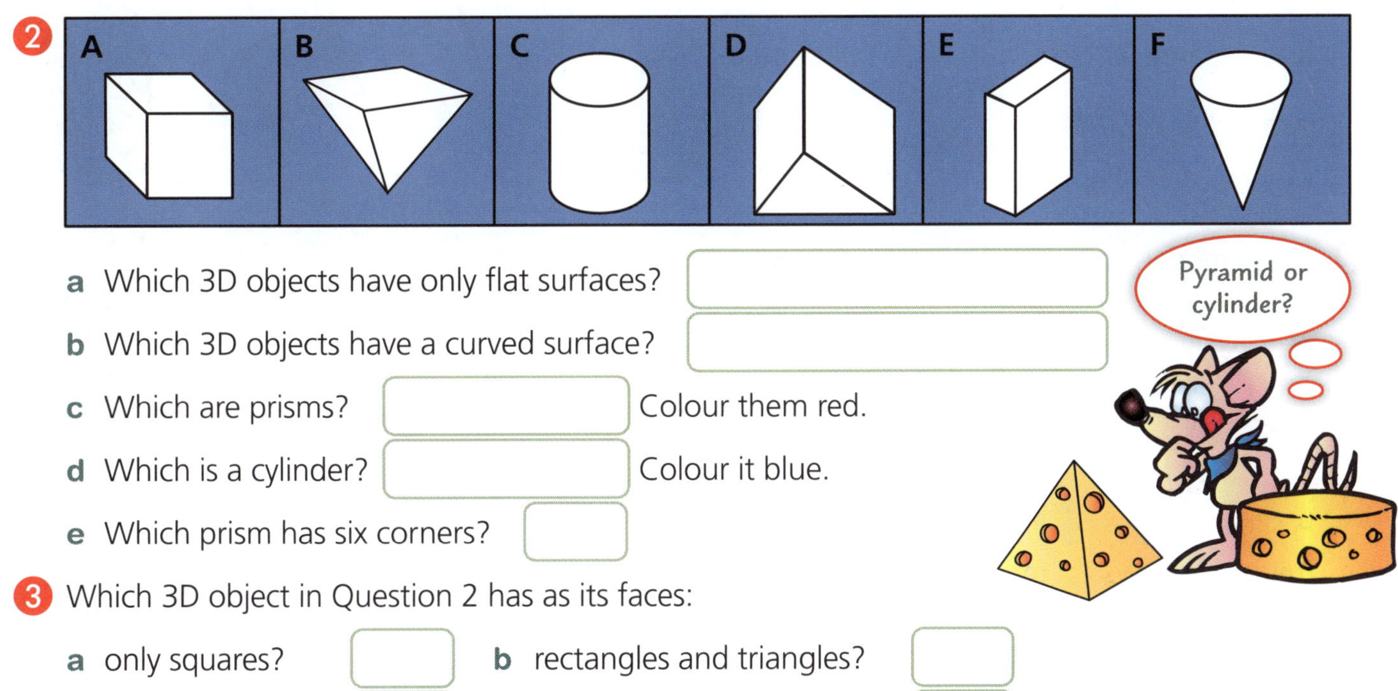

a Which 3D objects have only flat surfaces? ______

b Which 3D objects have a curved surface? ______

c Which are prisms? ______ Colour them red.

d Which is a cylinder? ______ Colour it blue.

e Which prism has six corners? ______

3 Which 3D object in Question 2 has as its faces:

a only squares? ______ **b** rectangles and triangles? ______

c only rectangles? ______ **d** triangles and a square? ______

INVESTIGATION

Make a list of real-life objects that are prisms.

4:05 Prisms and pyramids

A face is a flat surface that has straight sides.

A is a square

p

B is a hexagonal

p

1 Which of these 3D objects are:

a prisms?

b pyramids?

Which shapes have:

c a square base?

d a rectangular base?

e a triangular base?

f a hexagonal base?

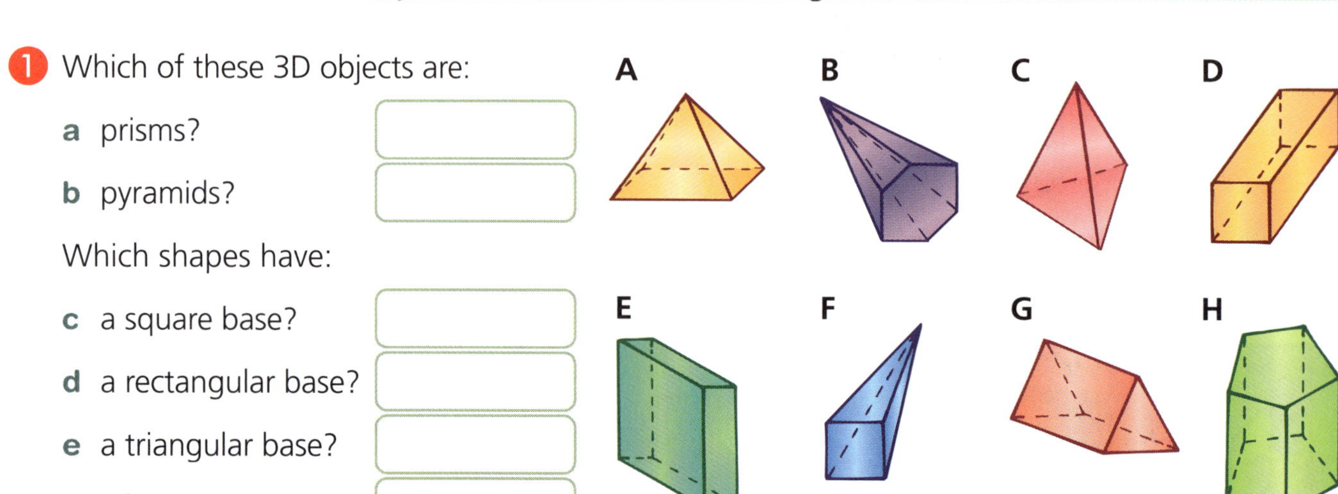

2 These models have been made by class 4B.

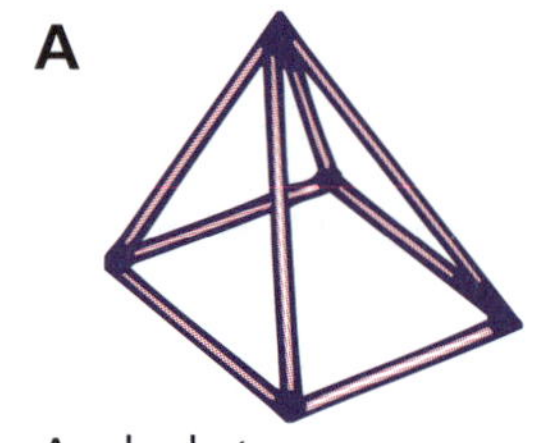

A skeleton made of straws and Plasticine.

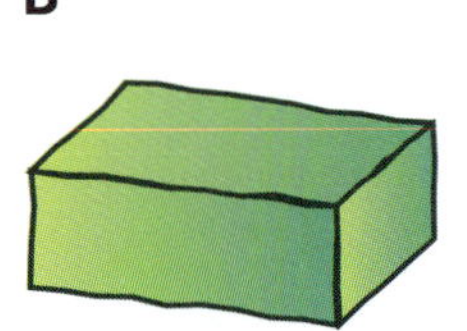

Plasticine modelled to make the solid.

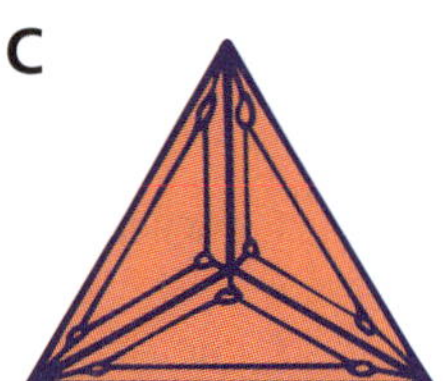

Cardboard shapes joined by elastic bands.

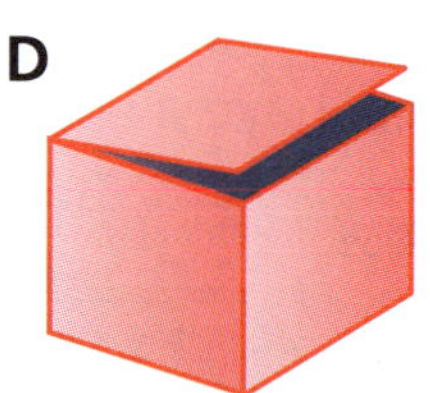

Folded net made of paper.

Plastic shapes fitted together.

Name the 3D object modelled in:

a A

b B

c C

d D

e E

- Choose at least two of the methods above to model:
  - a cube
  - a pyramid
  - a prism
- Try to make more prisms and pyramids using these methods.

Can you draw 3D objects on a computer?

 • *AUSTRALIAN SIGNPOST MATHS 4* • ISBN 9780655708780

Faces of prisms and pyramids

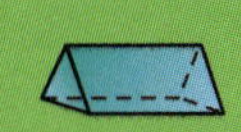
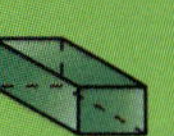

1. Would these faces make a prism (**A**) or a pyramid (**B**)?

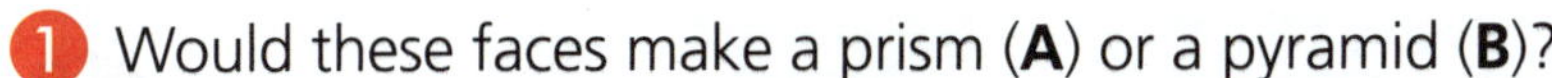

a
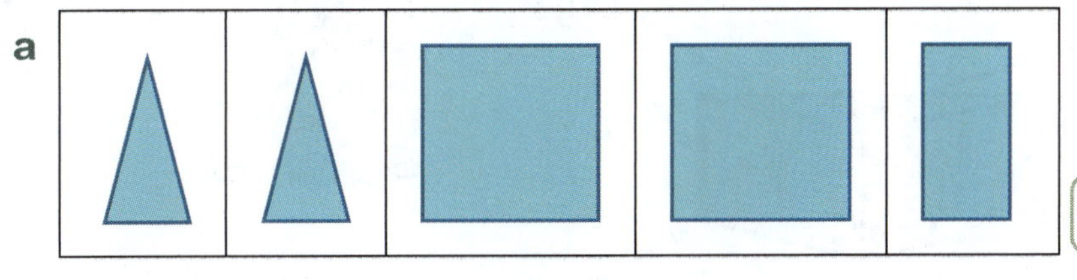

b
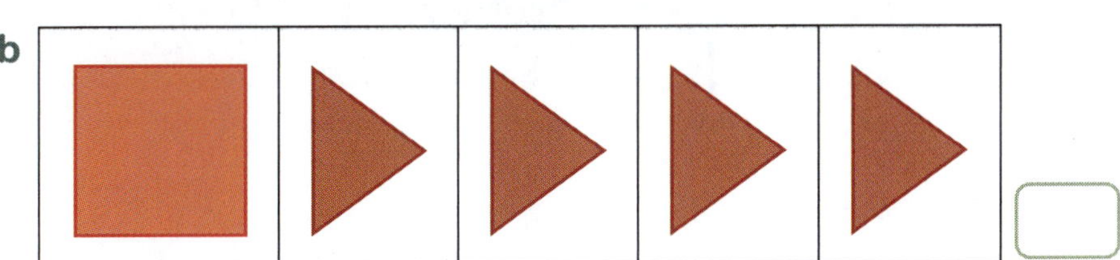

c
d
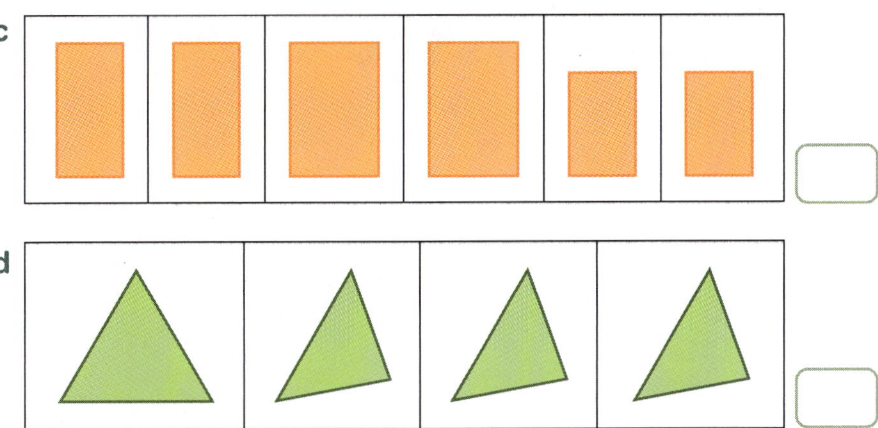

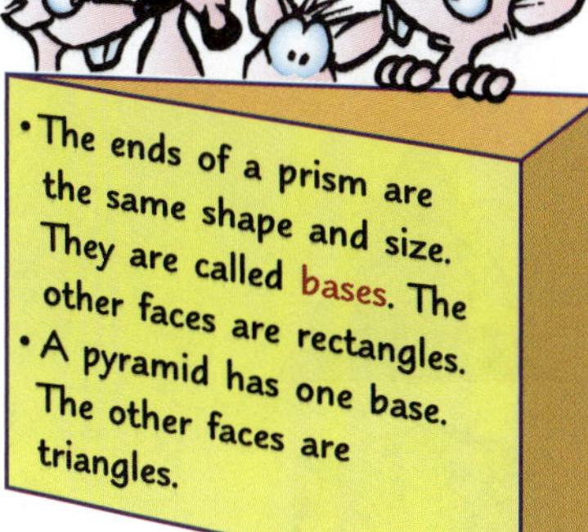

2. Would these nets make a prism or a pyramid? Discuss the reasons for your answers.

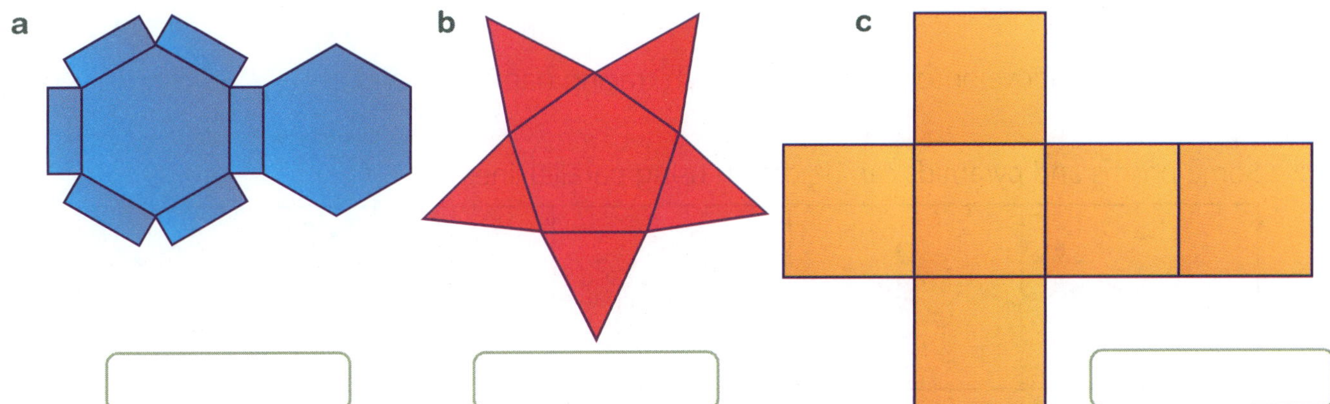

- Use cardboard shapes and elastic bands or plastic interlocking shapes to make a model of:
  - a prism
  - a cube
  - a pyramid.

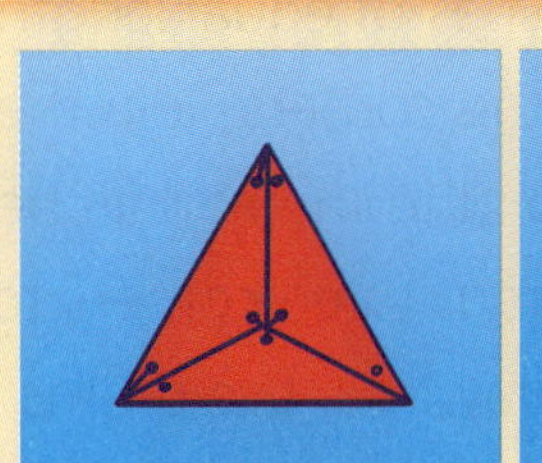

4:07 Prisms and pyramids

Is my cash register a prism?

A

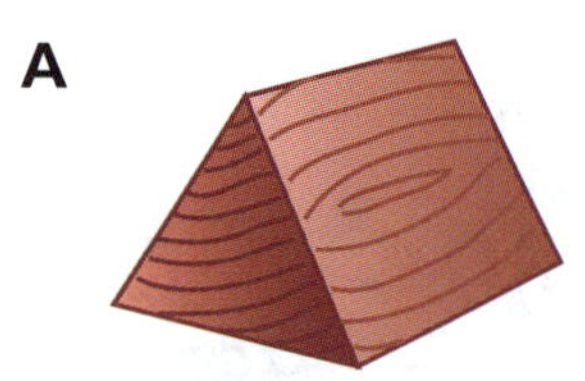

B

CONCEPT

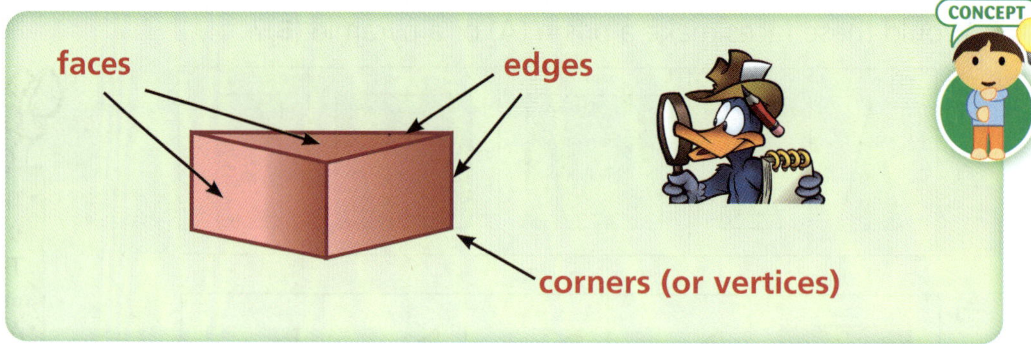

C

D

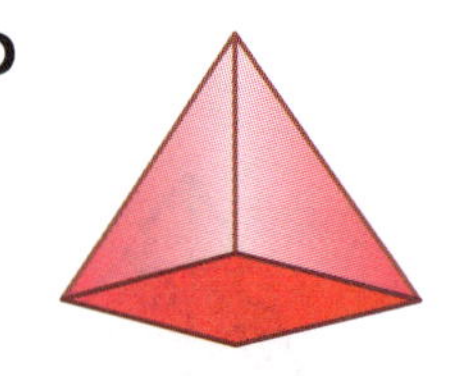

E

F

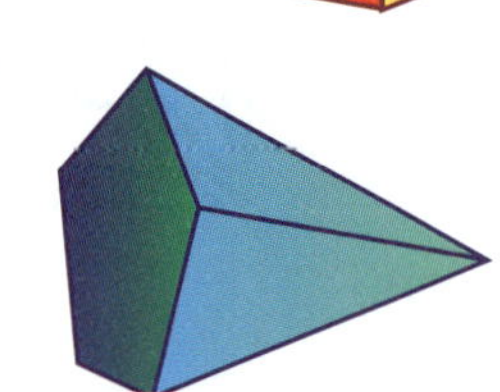

1 Describe each object.

	Name of the object	Number of faces	Number of corners	Number of edges
A				
B				
C				
D				
E				
F				

2 Trace each solid above onto paper. Under each tracing name the solid.

ACTIVITY

- Some prisms and pyramids can be drawn using parallel lines.

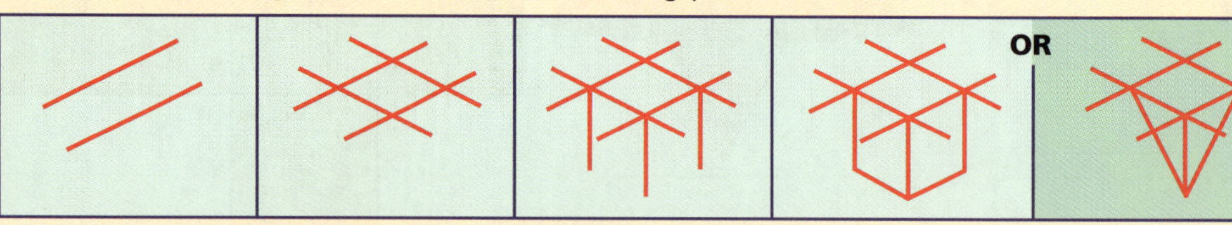

Step 1 Draw two pairs of parallel lines which cross.

Step 2 Draw three lines of equal length straight down from the corners. Join the ends to get a prism.

OR Choose a point in the middle below (or above) the figure. Draw lines from three corners to this point to get the pyramid.

- Use this method to draw: • five prisms • five pyramids

 • *AUSTRALIAN SIGNPOST MATHS 4* • ISBN 9780655708780

4:08 Drawing angles

Write 1, 2, 3 for smallest to largest.

- Julia took two geostrips and joined them to make a movable angle.
- By moving its arms, she made angles of different sizes.

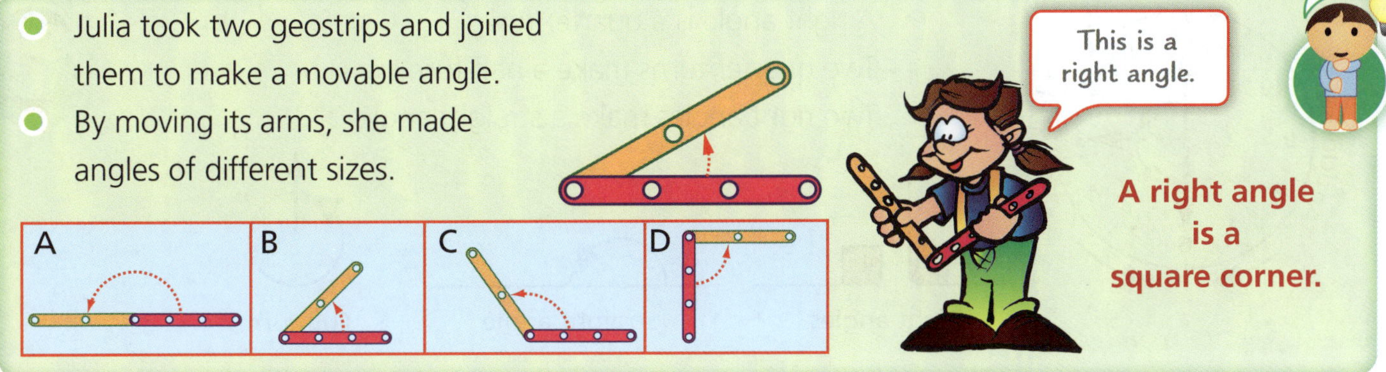

A right angle is a square corner.

1. Geostrips were used to make the angles in **A**, **B**, **C** and **D** above. Which is the larger angle:

   a **A** or **B**? ______ **b** **B** or **C**? ______

   c **C** or **D**? ______ **d** **A** or **C**? ______

   e Which angle is a right angle? ______

The size of an angle is the amount of turning between its arms.

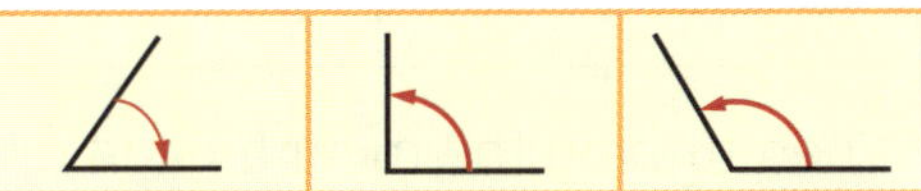

2. Trace these angles.

   a the corner of a book

   b blades of scissors

   c your choice

3. What is a right angle? ______

4. On your own paper, copy or trace these four angles in order of size. Put the smallest angle on the left and the largest angle on the right.

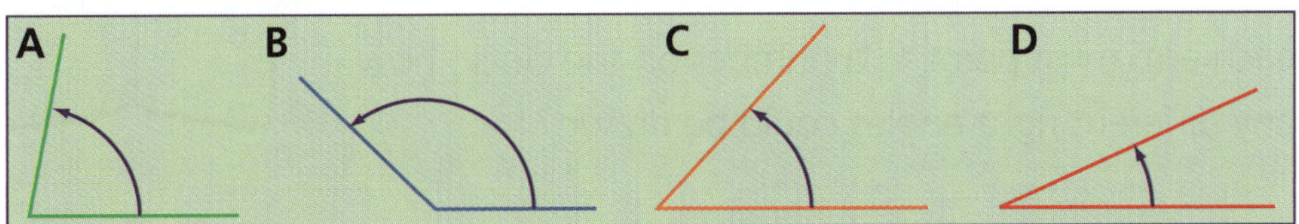

- Describe two angles in the room. Identify the smallest and the largest.

______

______

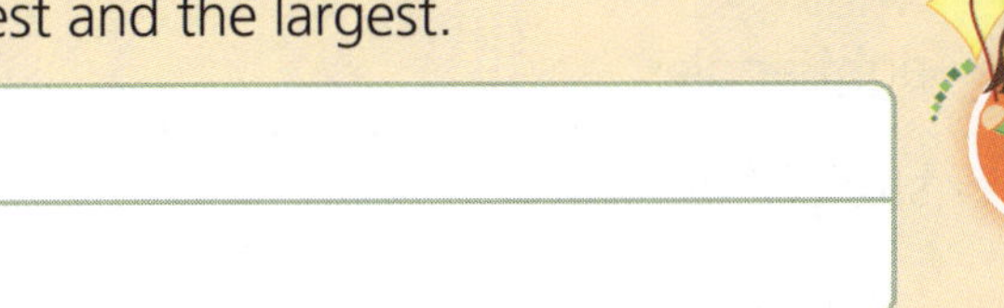

 • *AUSTRALIAN SIGNPOST MATHS 4* • ISBN 9780655708780

Angles as quarter and half turns

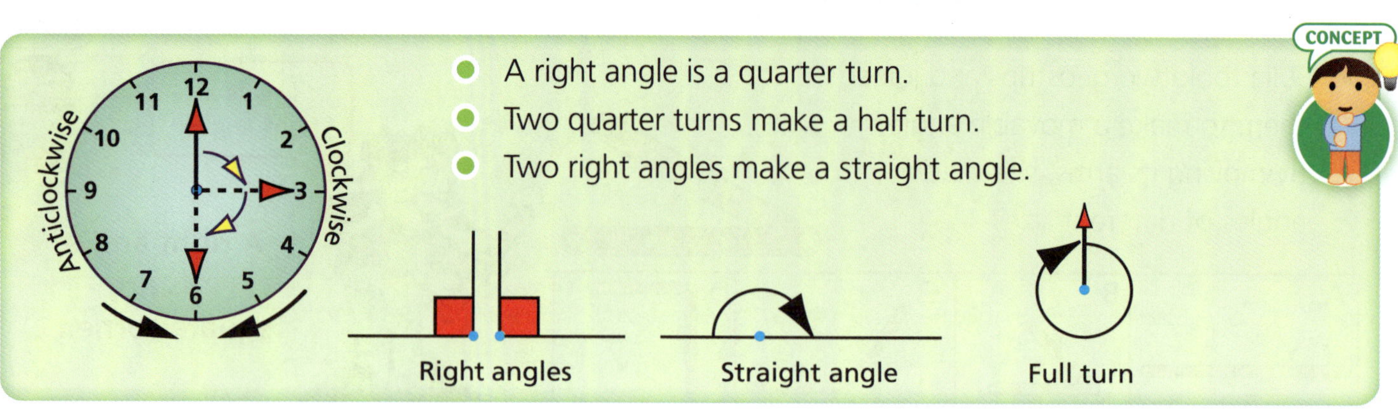

- A right angle is a quarter turn.
- Two quarter turns make a half turn.
- Two right angles make a straight angle.

1 Draw an angle that represents:

a quarter turn	a half turn	a full turn
•	•	•

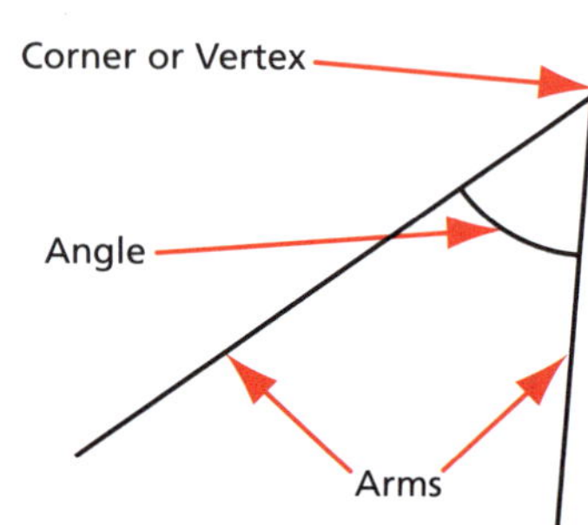

2 When turning the minute hand on a clock:

a a half turn anticlockwise is the same as...

b a three-quarter turn anticlockwise is the same as...

c two quarter turns clockwise is the same as...

3 **a** How many quarter turns make a full turn?

b How many right angles make a full turn?

c How many right angles make a straight angle?

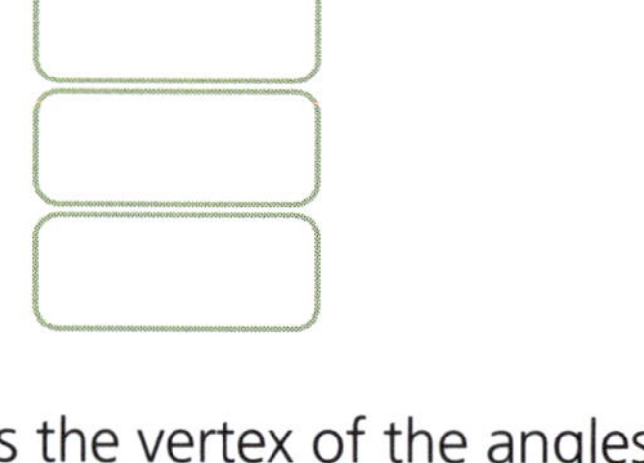

4

a Using the centre of the clock as the vertex of the angles, how many right angles can you draw at one time that do not overlap or share an arm?

b If each arm must point to a number on the clock, how many different right angles could be drawn?

- List places in real life that show:
  - right angles
  - straight angles
  - full turns.

 • *AUSTRALIAN SIGNPOST MATHS 4* • ISBN 9780655708780

4:10 Investigating polygons

Polygon is a Greek word meaning 'many sides'.

- A polygon is a figure made of three or more straight sides.
- In a regular polygon, all angles are equal and all sides are equal.
- Diagonals are lines drawn from one corner to another, across a polygon.

1 Draw all the diagonals that start at the red dot for each shape below.

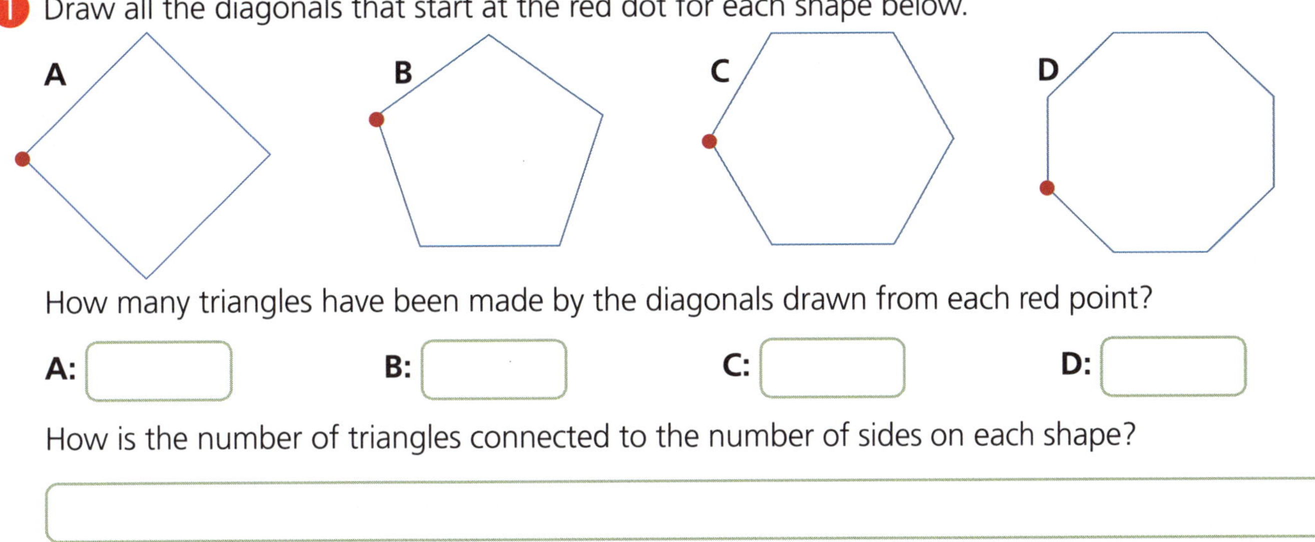

How many triangles have been made by the diagonals drawn from each red point?

A: ______ B: ______ C: ______ D: ______

How is the number of triangles connected to the number of sides on each shape?

______

2 Draw all of the lines of symmetry on each regular shape. Use a ruler and pencil.

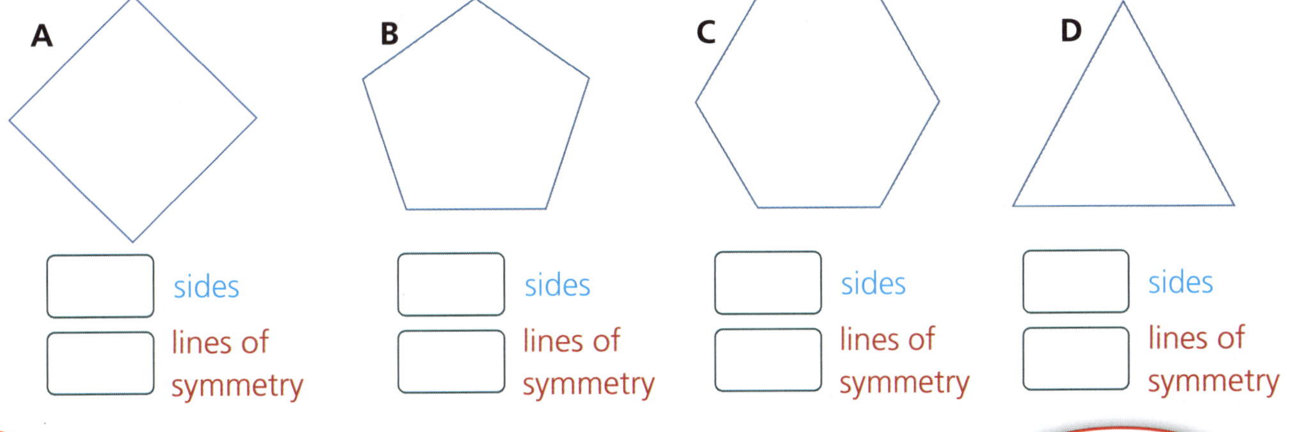

A: ______ sides ______ lines of symmetry

B: ______ sides ______ lines of symmetry

C: ______ sides ______ lines of symmetry

D: ______ sides ______ lines of symmetry

3 Complete this table.

Regular shape	Number of sides	Number of angles	Number of lines of symmetry
square			
pentagon			
hexagon			
triangle			

Visualising shapes

These are the same. I've turned one to get the other.

We can combine shapes in different ways.
Here a square and two triangles have been used.

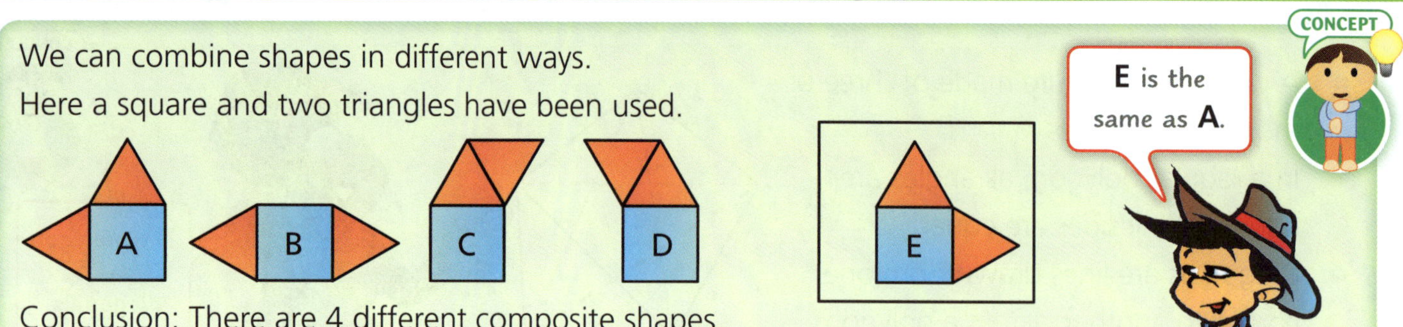

Conclusion: There are 4 different composite shapes.

1 **a** Draw as many different composite shapes (combinations) as you can using the two squares and the triangle. A combination is not different if it is turned.

b How many different combinations are possible using just three of the squares?

2

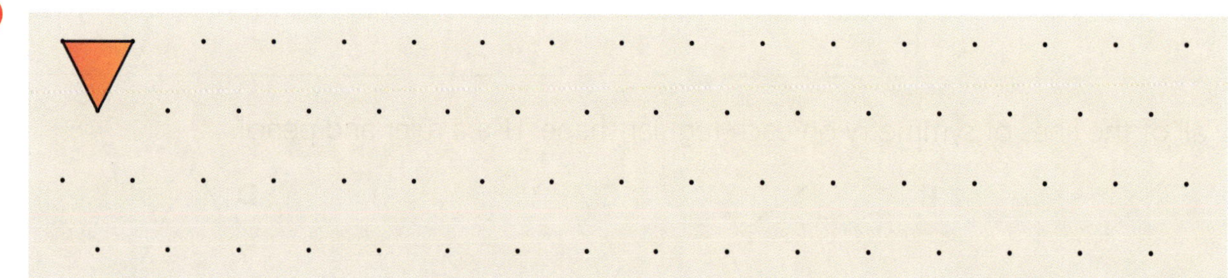

a How many different composite shapes are possible using three of these triangles?

b Draw four different composite shapes formed by using four of these triangles.

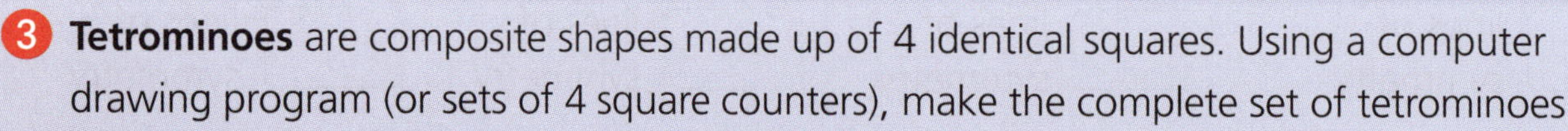

3 **Tetrominoes** are composite shapes made up of 4 identical squares. Using a computer drawing program (or sets of 4 square counters), make the complete set of tetrominoes.

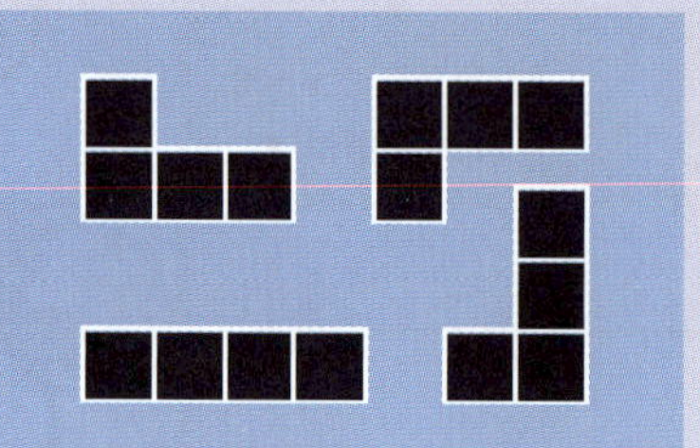

a Join the two tetrominoes that are the same.

b How many tetrominoes are there altogether?

 • *AUSTRALIAN SIGNPOST MATHS 4* • ISBN 9780655708780

4:12 Maps

When we look at a map we have a 'bird's-eye view'.

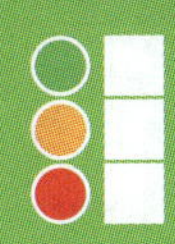

CONCEPT

- A scale of 1 cm = 1 km means that 1 cm on the map represents 1 km.
- The legend lists the features shown on the map.

Scale: 1 cm = 1 km

Legend:

School	Traffic lights
Hospital	Police station

Meg St, Warn St, Munn St, Joseph St, March St

1 On which street on the map above would you find the:

a school? ____ b traffic lights? ____

c hospital? ____ d police station? ____

What feature would you find on:

e Warn St? ____ f Joseph St? ____

g Meg St? ____ h March St? ____

2 Starting at the red arrow position, where will you be if you drive:

a 1 km forward, then turn left and drive 2 km, then turn right and drive 1 km? ____

b 3 km forward, then turn left and drive 1 km? ____

c 1 km forward, then turn right and drive 2 km, then turn left and drive 2 km? ____

3 Where are the traffic lights? ____

4 a How far is it from the school to the police station? ____

b How far is it from the school to the hospital? ____

ACTIVITY

- Draw a map using the scale 1 cm = 10 m and a legend.

SCHOOL, SHOPS, GYM

1cm = 10m

Scale

Legend	
	School
	Gym
	Shops

 • *AUSTRALIAN SIGNPOST MATHS 4* • ISBN 9780655708780

Creating a map

The vertical axis goes up and down.
The horizontal axis goes across.

1 Use the scale 2 cm = 1 m to draw a map of your room. Make up your own legend and icons to represent the features of the room. First record the dimensions of the room.

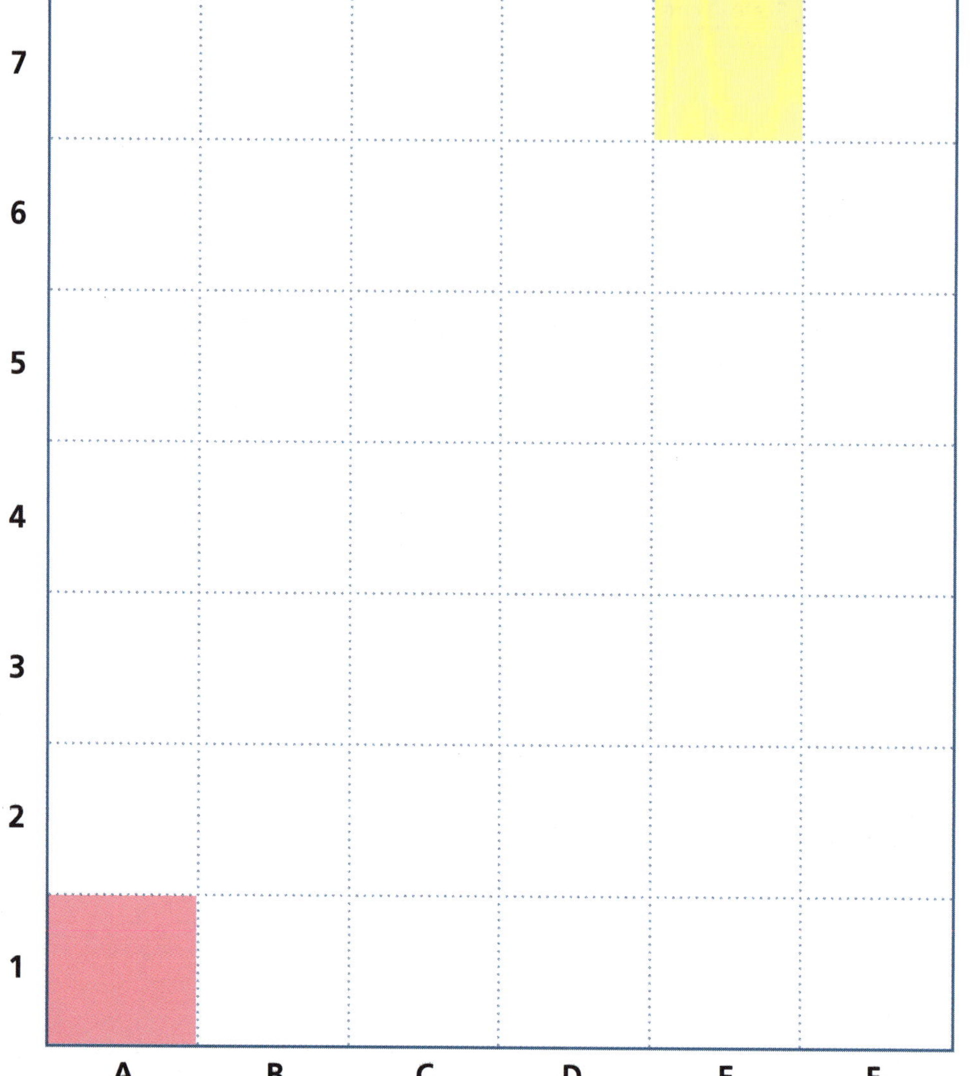

Scale

2 cm = 1 m

Legend

☒ desk

Grid references

- We call the yellow square E7.
- We call the pink square A1.

2 List the features in your room using grid references to describe where each feature is found.

 • *AUSTRALIAN SIGNPOST MATHS 4* • ISBN 9780655708780

Cones, cylinders and spheres

Why is the base of a cone not a face?

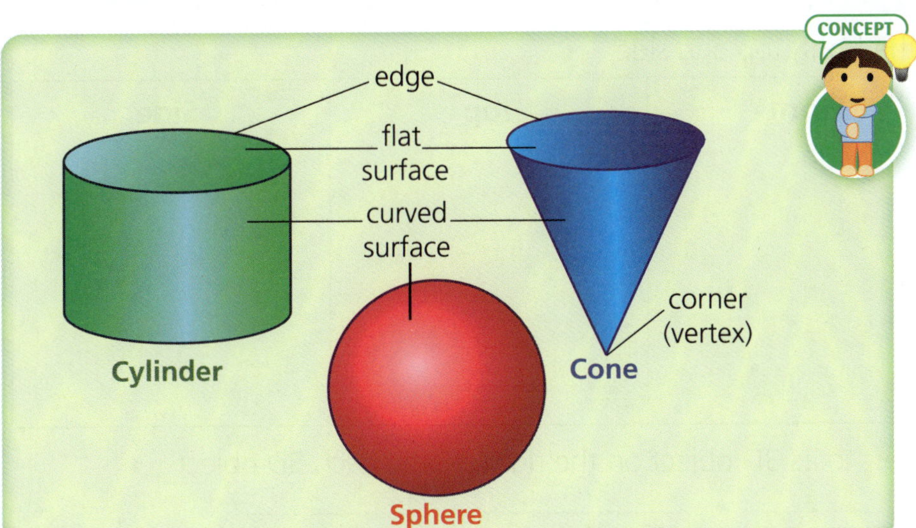

Finish these drawings.

cylinder

cone

sphere

1 Use the pictures above to complete this table.

Shape	Number of surfaces	Number of corners	Number of edges
cylinder			
cone			
sphere			

2 What are some things that look like cylinders? List as many as you can.

3 What are some things that look like cones?

4 What are some things that look like spheres?

5 Write the name of each 3D object under its picture.

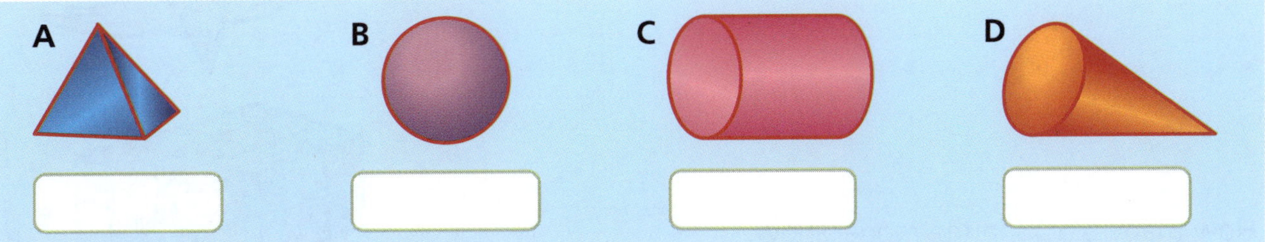

When we cut each 3D object parallel to its base, which of these have:

a uniform cross-sections (always the same)?

b cross-sections that are the same shape but different sizes?

4:15 Views of 3D objects

Can you name the shapes made by each view in Question 2?

1 Draw the table and chair from the front, top and side.

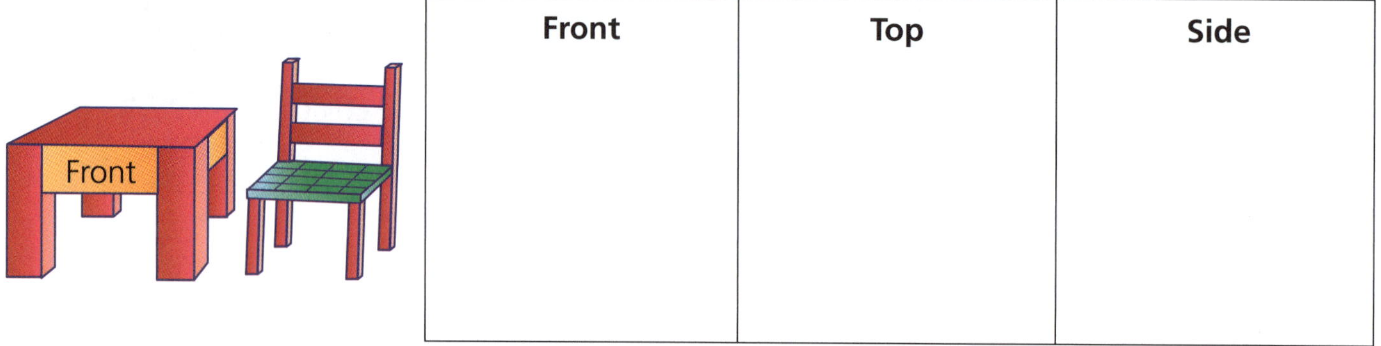

2 Join each set of pictures on the left to its 3D object on the right. Name each 3D object.

Top view	Front view	Side view	3D object	Name

3 Use blocks to make models of these prisms. Write down the number of blocks used in each model.

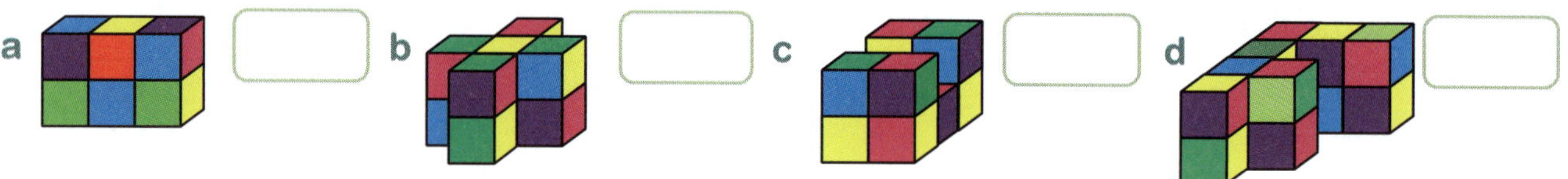

4 Use blocks to make the model in the picture. Study the model and:

ACTIVITY

a draw it from the top

b draw it from the side.

How many blocks in the model show:

c 3 faces?

d 2 faces?

e 1 face?

f 4 faces?

side

front

4:16 Compass directions

The first letters of North, East, West and South make the word NEWS.

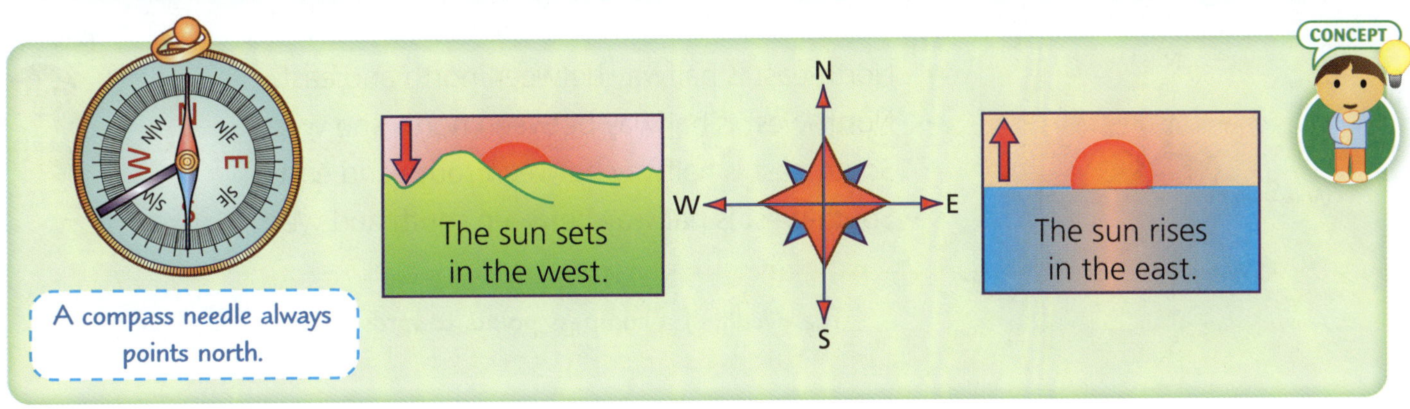

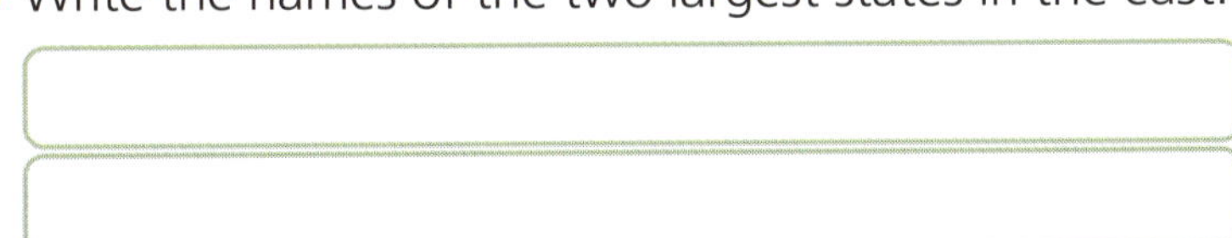

1 Write **north**, **south**, **east** and **west** around the map.

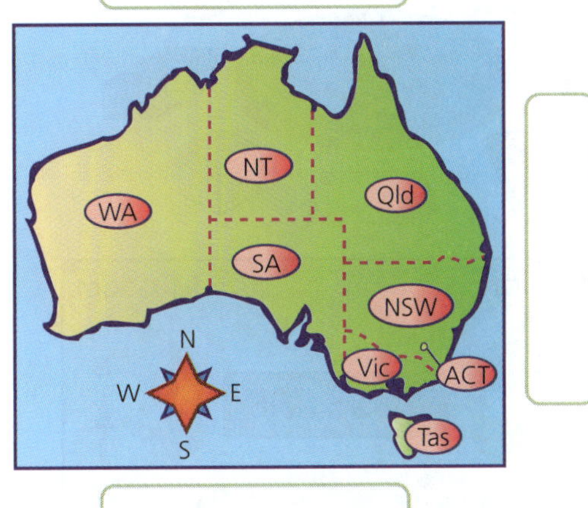

2 Write the full name for:

a WA

b NT

c SA

3 Write the names of the two largest states in the east.

4 Which landmark is:

a north of Bart's Cave?

b west of Queen Hill?

c south of Black Rock?

d west of Red Cove?

e south of Jake's Grave?

f east of Bart's Cave?

g north of Queen Hill?

5 Use the map in Question 4 to answer these questions.

a The treasure is buried east of Land's End and south of Queen Hill. Mark this spot on the map with an **X**.

b Our ship sank north of Land's End and west of Jake's Grave. Mark this spot on the map with an **S**.

c The captain broke his leg south of Bart's Cave and east of Land's End. Mark this spot on the map with a **C**.

 • *AUSTRALIAN SIGNPOST MATHS 4* • ISBN 9780655708780

4:17 Compass directions

We turn the compass until the arrow is pointing to N (north).

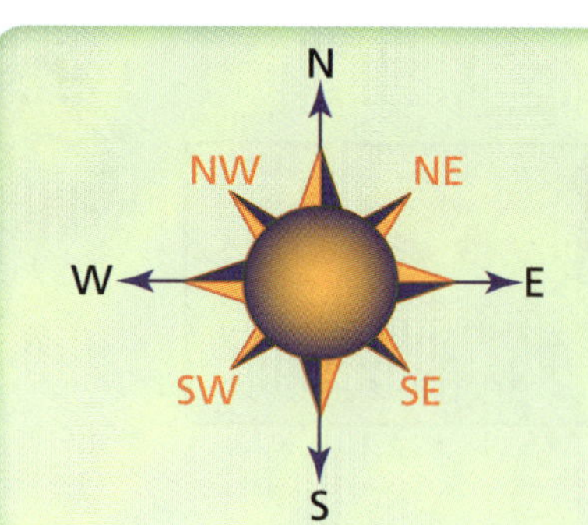

- North-east is halfway between north and east.
- North-west is halfway between north and west.
- South-east is halfway between south and east.
- South-west is halfway between south and west.

The needle of a compass points towards north.

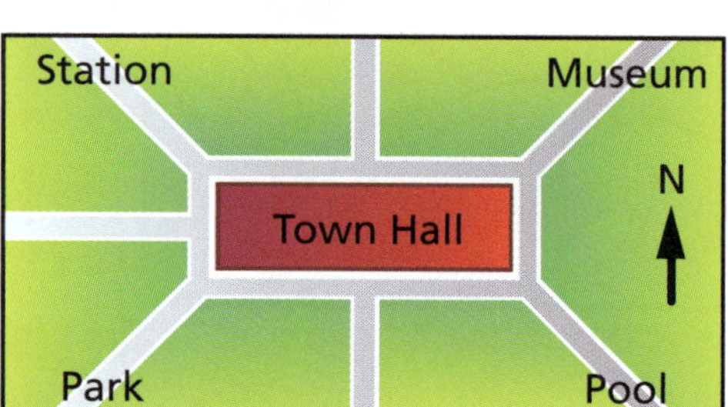

1 Around this compass, find which 3D object is:

a east

b west

c south

d north

e north-east

f south-west

g south-east

h north-west

Station | Museum | Town Hall | N | Park | Pool

2 On the map above, what place is:

a north-east of Town Hall?

b south-east of Town Hall?

c south-west of Town Hall?

d north-west of Town Hall?

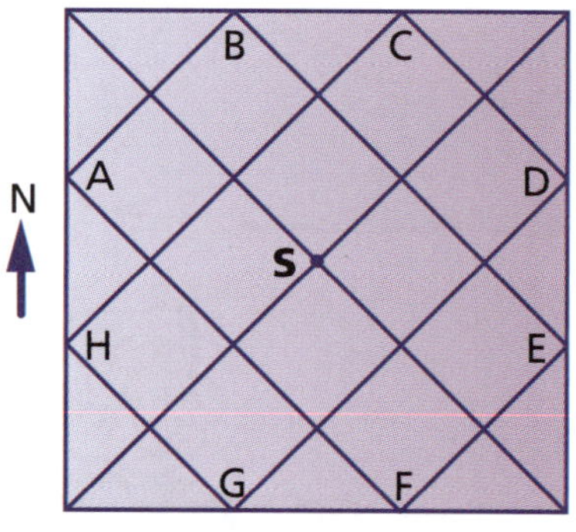

North, East, West, South = NEWS

3 Starting at **S**, where do you finish, if you travel:

a 2 units north-west, then 1 unit south-west?

b 1 unit south-east, then 2 units south-west?

c 2 units north-east, then 1 unit south-east?

d 1 unit south-west, then 2 units north-west?

e 2 units north-west, then 1 unit south-west, then 3 units south-east, then 3 units north-east?

4:18 Describing position

We usually give the column name first. 'Left, top row' is 'pear'.

	left	right
top row	pear	carrot
middle row	apple	strawberry
bottom row	cherries	banana

1 Name the fruit or vegetable in the box that is:

a left, bottom ____ **b** right, top ____
c left, middle ____ **d** right, bottom ____
e left, top ____ **f** right, middle ____

Write down the position of the:

g apple ____ **h** strawberry ____
i cherries ____ **j** pear ____
k carrot ____ **l** banana ____

2 These are desks in a classroom.
Name the person in:

a column one, red row ____
b column three, blue row ____
c column one, blue row ____
d column four, red row ____
e 2, blue ____ **f** 3, red ____ **g** 1, green ____ **h** 4, green ____

blue	Tom	Sophie	Rex	Peter
red	Ruby	Kate	Ethan	Chris
green	Georgia	Rocco	Ben	Oscar
	1	2	3	4

3 Write down the column number and row letter for the:

a rectangle ____
b square ____
c hexagon ____
d triangle ____
e circle ____
f prism ____
g pyramid ____
h cone ____
i net ____
j pentagon ____
k rhombus ____
l trapezium ____

D					
C					
B					
A					
	1	2	3	4	5

m right angle ____ **n** parallel lines ____

4:19 Using position in maps

One grid reference could contain a part of both states.

1 What town can be found in:

a column 2, 5th row?

b column 6, 2nd row?

c column 4, 5th row?

d column 2, 1st row?

e column 2, 3rd row?

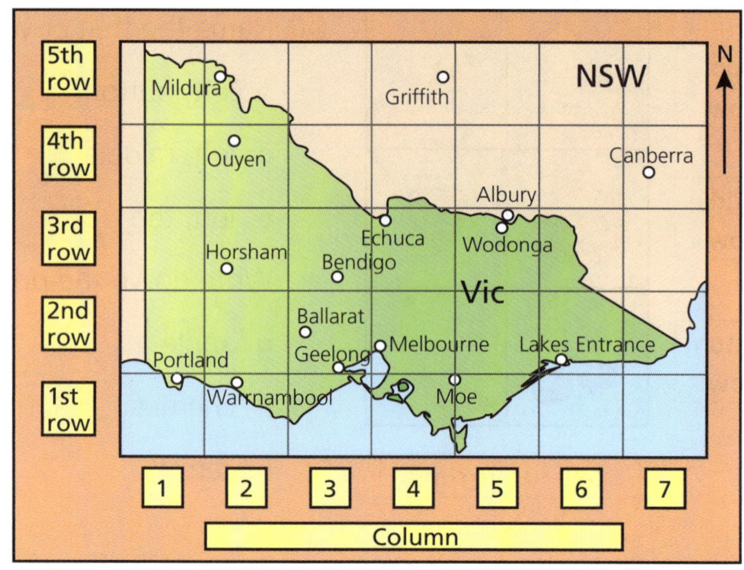

2 Using the map in Question 1, give the position of the box where you find:

a Melbourne

b Echuca

c Geelong

d Ballarat

e Portland

f Wodonga

g Bendigo

h Ouyen

i Which boxes show part of Moe?

j Which town is west of Wodonga and north of Melbourne?

k Which town is east of Echuca and in New South Wales?

l Which town is west of Griffith but in Victoria?

3 On the grid to the right draw:

a a rectangle in C2

b an oval in A3

c a square in A1

d a triangle in C3

e a rhombus in B2

f an octagon in B1

g a trapezium in A2

h a parallelogram in B3

i a pentagon in C1

	A	B	C
3			
2			
1			

Visualising shapes

Use a ruler and a pencil to show how each shape can be cut.

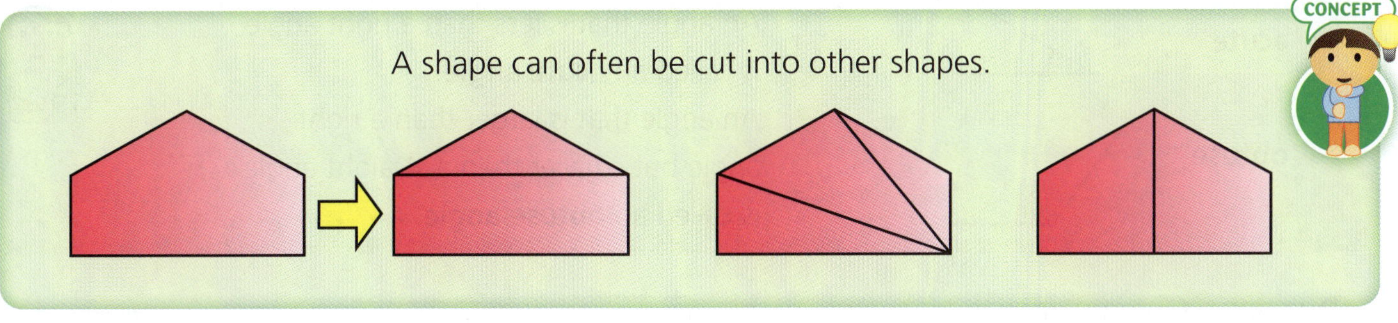

1 Show how the shape could be cut into:

2 triangles

a square and a rectangle

a triangle and a rectangle

5 squares

2 Draw lines only from the vertices (corners) to make 3 triangles.

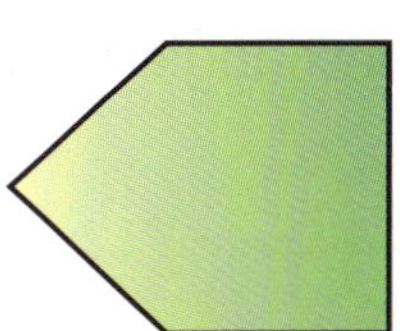

3 Show how the shape could be cut into:

4 triangles and a square

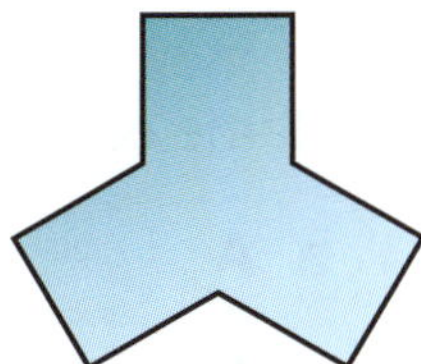

a triangle and 3 squares

3 rectangles and a triangle

4 On square grid paper, copy three of the shapes above that have line symmetry.

ACTIVITY

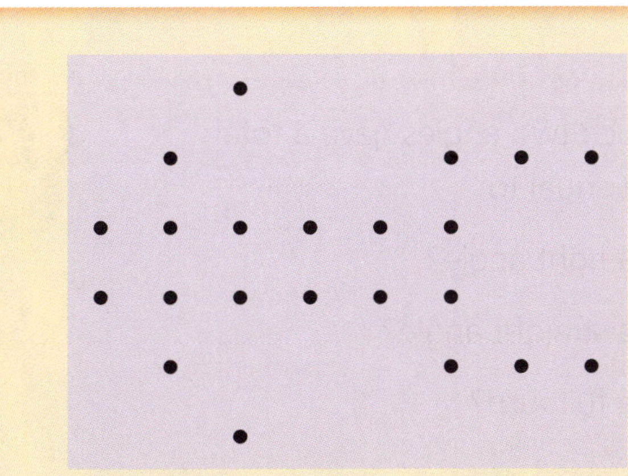

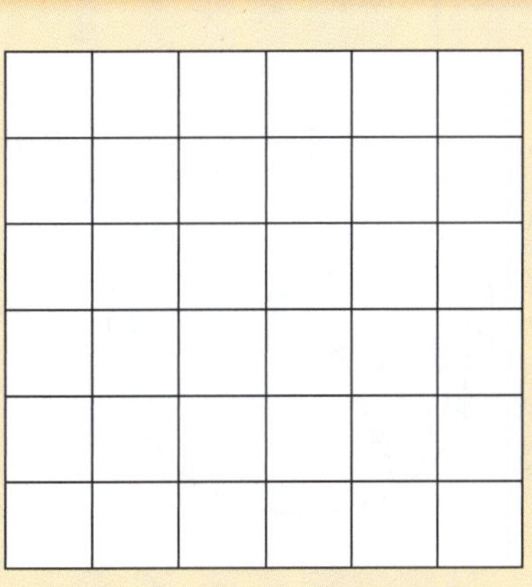

- Use the grid to draw a symmetrical pattern using large dots like the picture on the left.

See *Extra Support 3* (Tangrams) and *Extra Support 4* (Flip, slide and turn).

4:21 Acute and obtuse angles

right angle

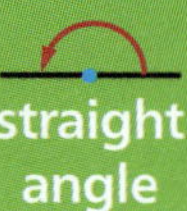
straight angle

full turn

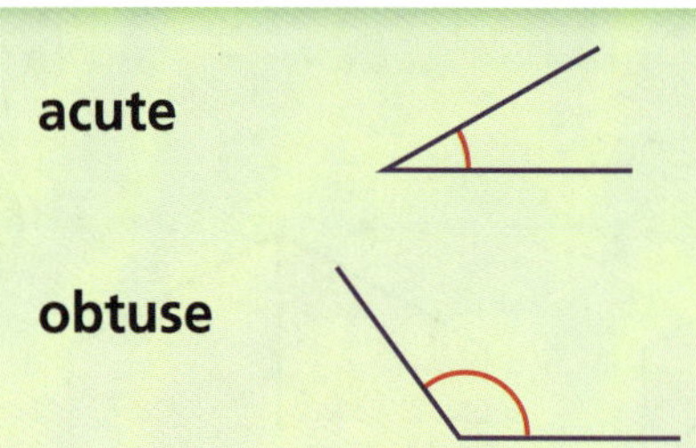

- An angle that is less than a right angle is called an **acute angle**.
- An angle that is larger than a right angle but smaller than a straight angle is called an **obtuse angle**.

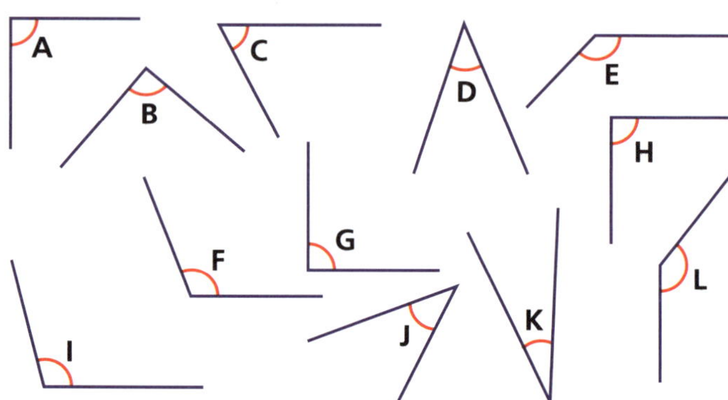

1. Which of these angles are:
   a right angles?
   b acute angles?
   c obtuse angles?

2. Place in order from smallest angle to largest angle:
   a **A**, **C** and **D**
   b **D**, **E** and **G**
   c **F**, **J** and **H**
   d **B**, **K** and **L**
   e **C**, **G** and **K**
   f **G**, **F** and **L**

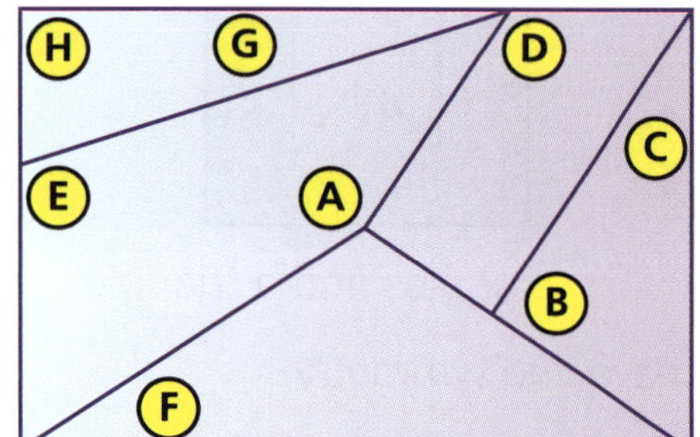

3. Name each angle as acute, right or obtuse.
   a **A**
   b **B**
   c **C**
   d **D**
   e **E**
   f **F**
   g **G**
   h **H**

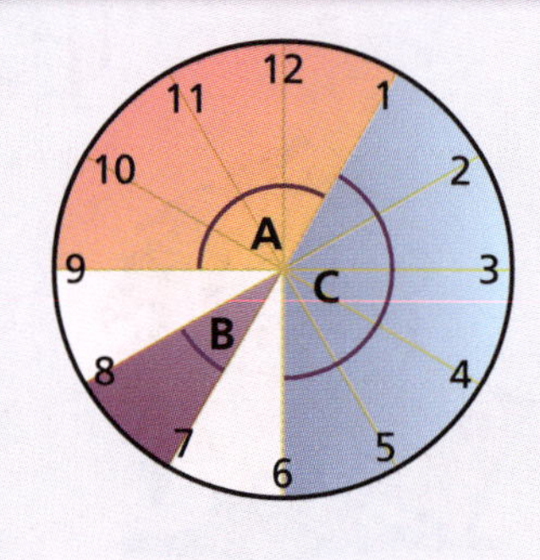

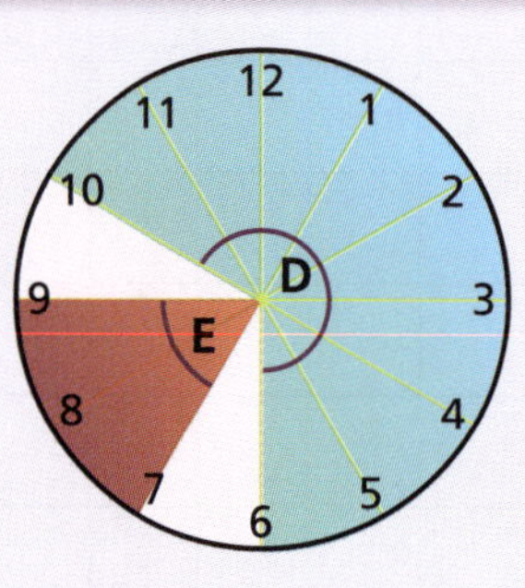

4. Which two angles have a total size equal to:
   a a right angle?
   b a straight angle?
   c a full turn?

Angles of any size

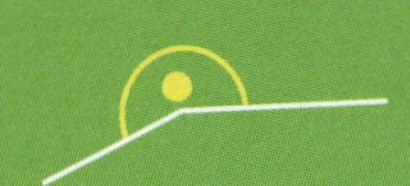
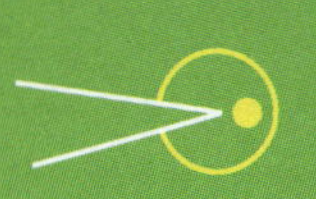

Picture						
Type	acute	right	obtuse	straight	reflex	revolution
Size	less than a right angle	a square corner	between right and straight	like a straight line	between straight and full turn	a full turn

1 Name each type of angle.

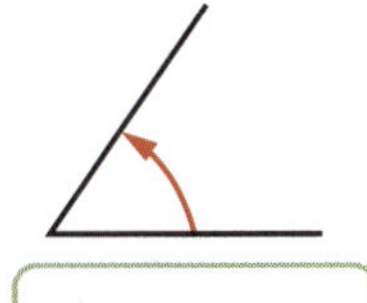

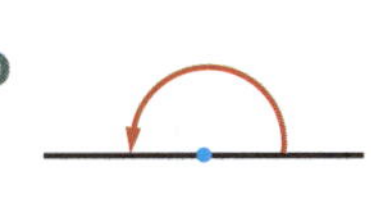
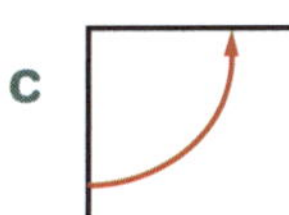

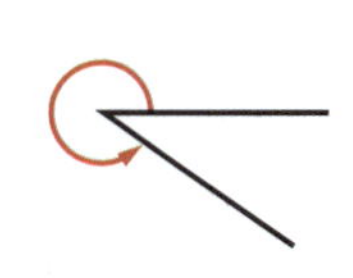
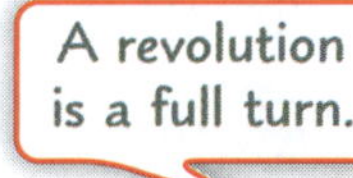

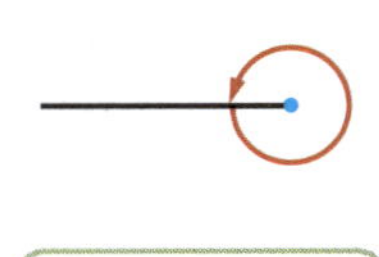
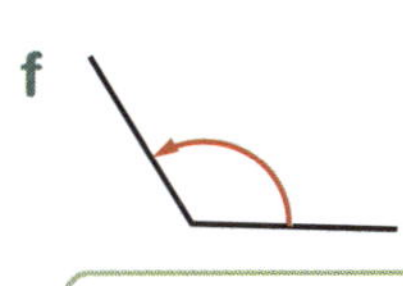
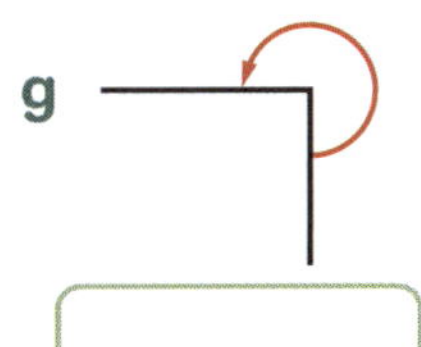
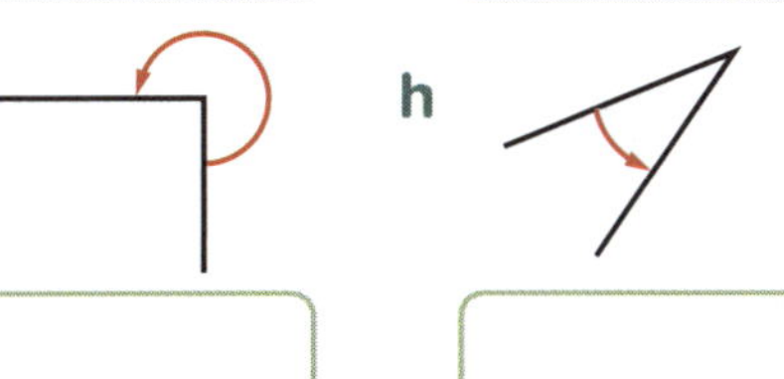

a

b

c

d

e

f

g

h

2 In each circle write Ⓐ for acute angle, Ⓞ for obtuse angle or Ⓡ for reflex angle.

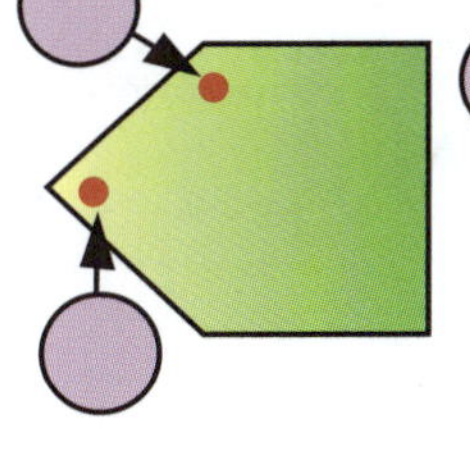
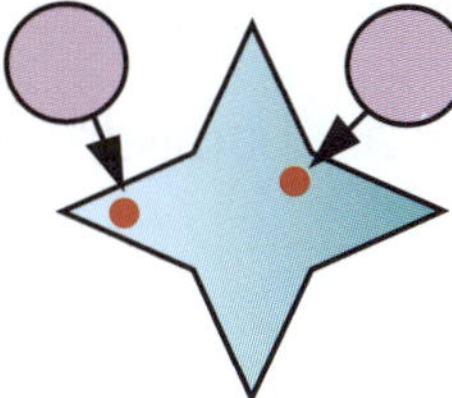
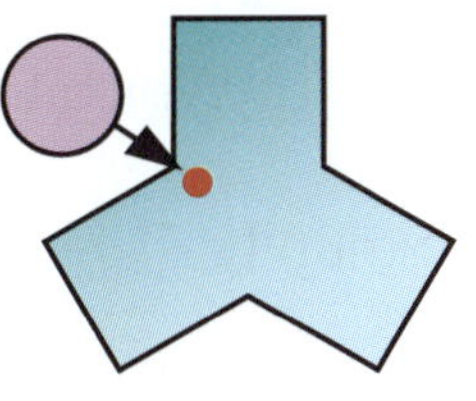
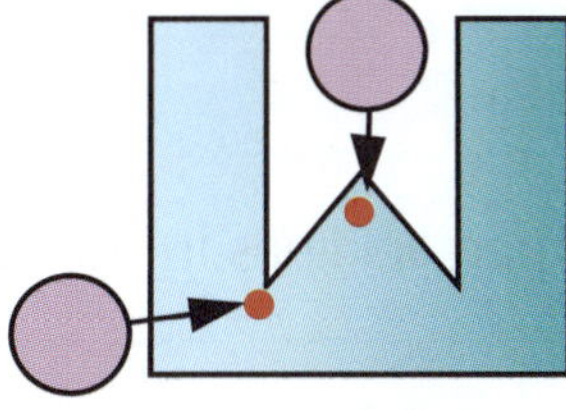
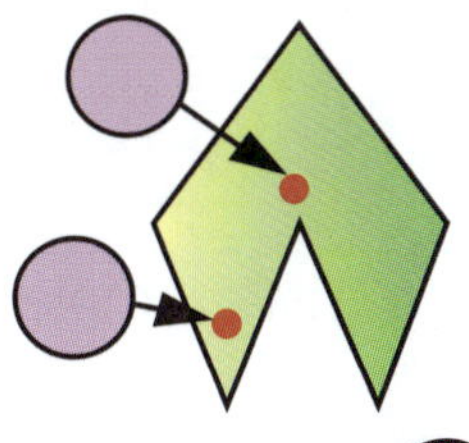
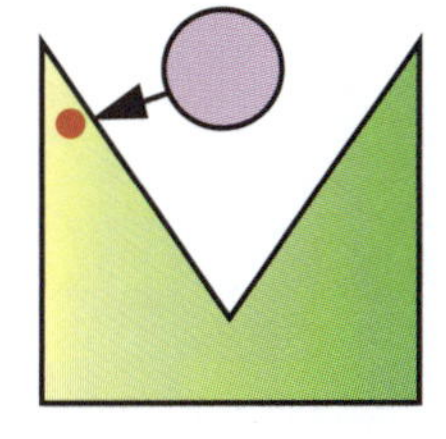
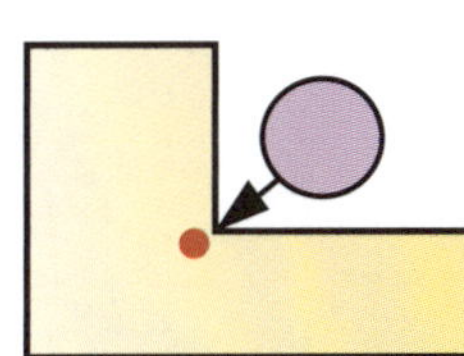
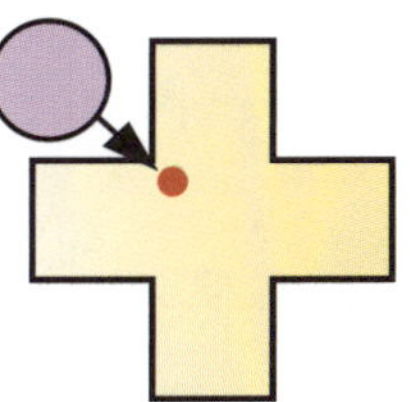
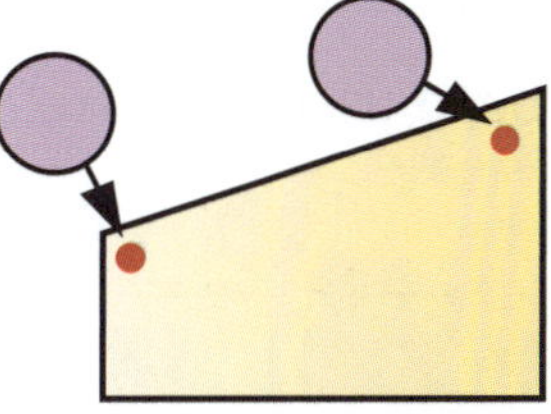
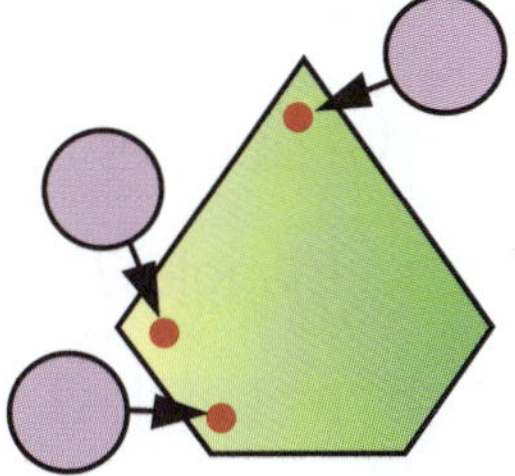

 • *AUSTRALIAN SIGNPOST MATHS 4* • ISBN 9780655708780

4:23 Horizontal and vertical

Without measuring, it is hard to know if a shape is regular.

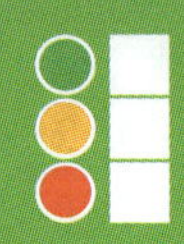

CONCEPT

Surfaces that go straight up and down are **vertical**.

Surfaces that go straight across are called **horizontal**.

1. Naomi and Luke were building a birdcage.
   - Some pipes had to be horizontal, and others vertical. To test these they used a spirit level.

   - When the bubble is in the middle of the glass tube, the spirit level is horizontal (or vertical).

   Which pipes in this cage are:

   a horizontal? ______

   b vertical? ______ c sloping? ______

2. a Why would triangles be used in the cage? ______

   b Which three pipes are parallel to **H**? ______

   c Which three are parallel to **J**? ______

   d Which three are parallel to **A**? ______

   e List examples of parallel lines in our community. ______

3. Which pipes have been used to make:

   a triangles? ______ ______ ______ ______

   b rectangles? ______ ______ ______ ______ ______ ______

4. a Are any of the shapes used in the birdcage regular? ______

   b List the pipes that are perpendicular to pipe **G**. ______

ACTIVITY

- Write down the way you would test a surface to see if it is:
  - horizontal ______
  - vertical ______

  Test as many surfaces as you can.

Tessellations

Will squares of different size tessellate?

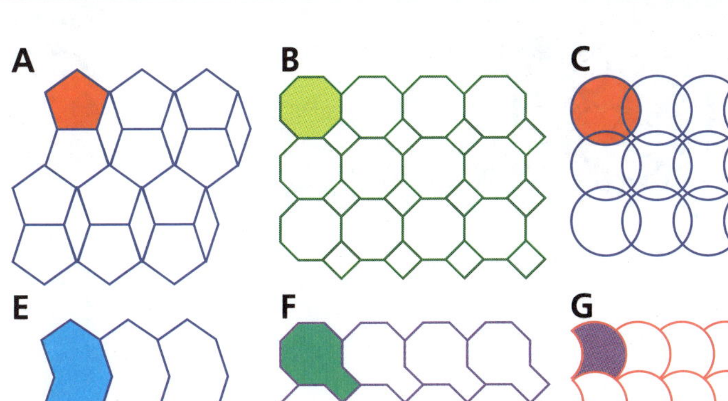

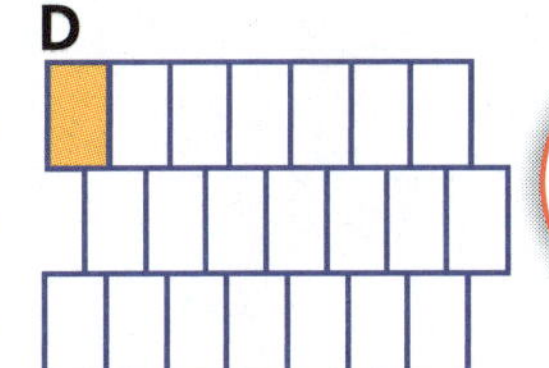

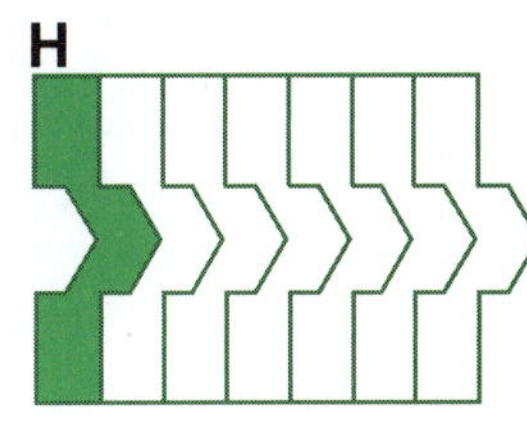

1 **a** In which pictures above does the coloured shape tessellate?

b In **A**, **B** and **C**, colour any gaps or overlaps black.

Identical shapes tessellate if they fit together without gaps or overlaps.

2 Peter wanted to tile his parents' bathroom. He used dot paper to draw the two tile patterns below.

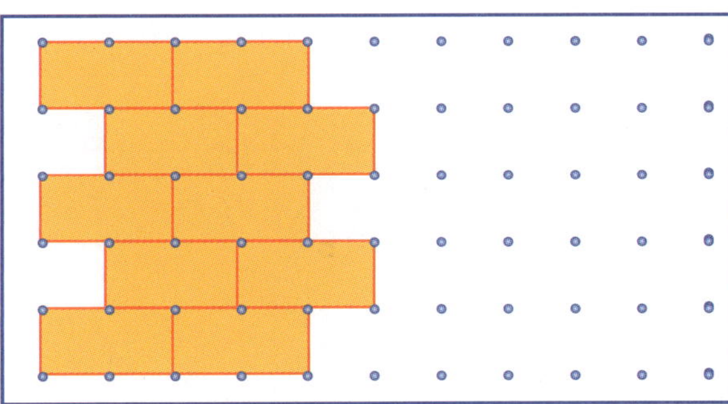

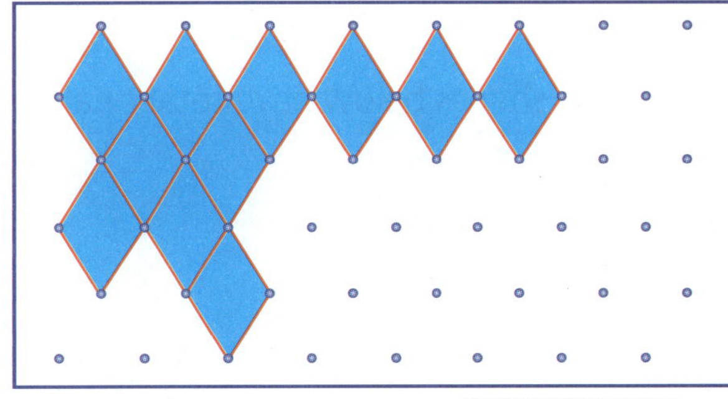

a Draw ten more tiles on each pattern.

b Do the tiles tessellate?

- Alan used this pattern to draw a tessellating bird.
- Complete the tessellation by drawing more birds. Dots have been drawn to help you.
- Use computer drawing tools to create a tessellating design by copying, pasting and rotating regular shapes.

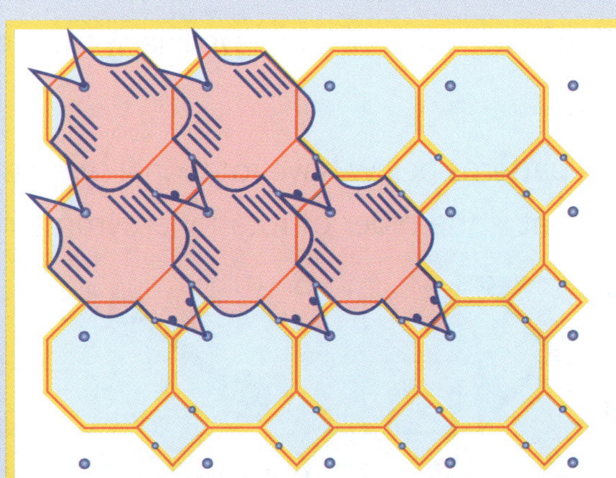

See *Extra Support 3* (Tangrams) and *Extra Support 4* (Flip, slide and turn).

 • *AUSTRALIAN SIGNPOST MATHS 4* • ISBN 9780655708780

4:25 Rotational symmetry

As the flower turns, the picture is repeated.

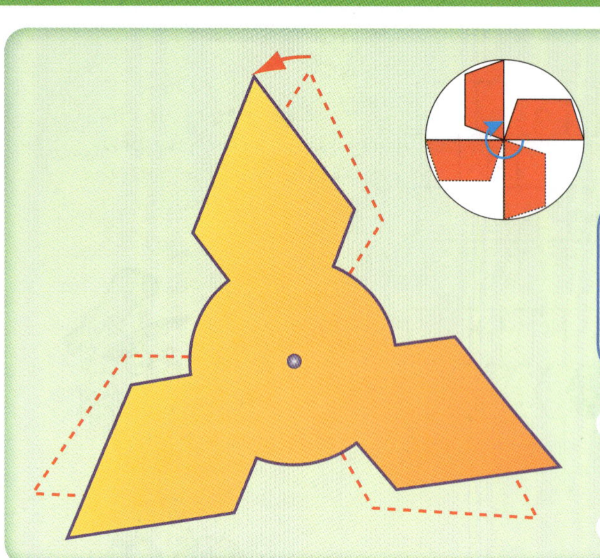

A shape is said to have rotational symmetry if a tracing of the shape matches it after the tracing is rotated part of a full turn around the centre

- If it is rotated about its centre, this shape will match its original position 3 times in one revolution.
- This shape has rotational symmetry of **order 3**.

1 Shape **A** Shape **B**

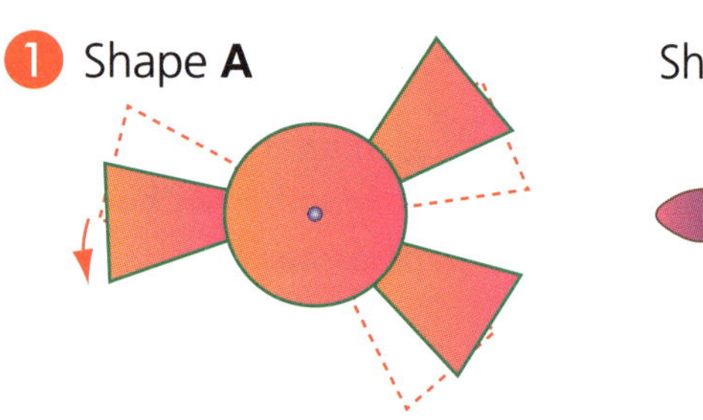
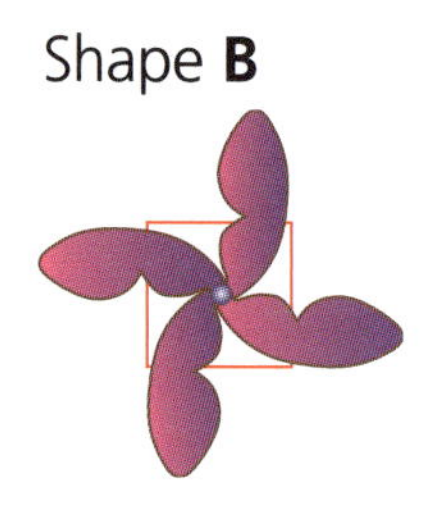

a Does shape **A** have line symmetry? ____
Does it have rotational symmetry? ____

b Does shape **B** have line symmetry? ____
Does it have rotational symmetry? ____

2 Which of the shapes below have rotational symmetry? ____

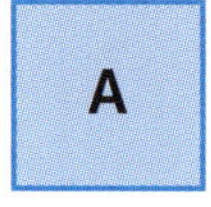

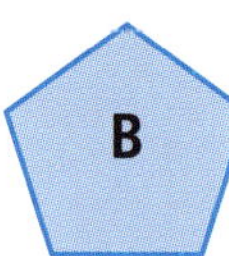

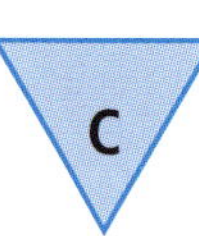

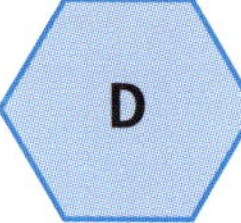

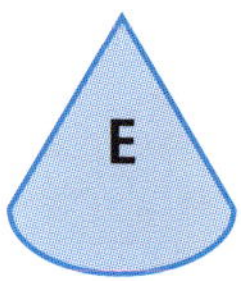

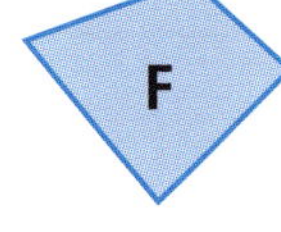

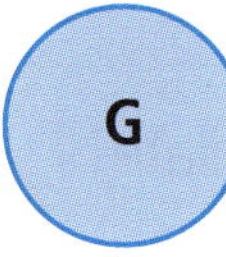

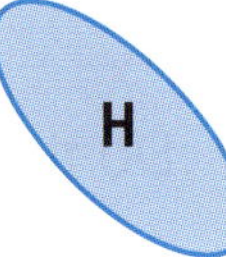

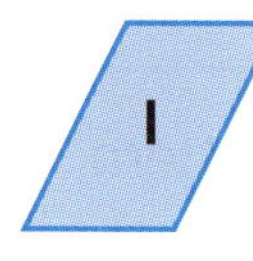

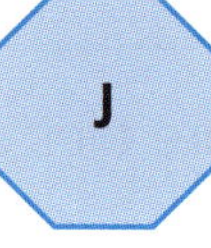

3 Which of the shapes above have line symmetry? ____

4 Do the patterns below have rotational symmetry (**Yes** or **No**)?
If so, what is the order of rotational symmetry? (It must be greater than 1.)

a 

b 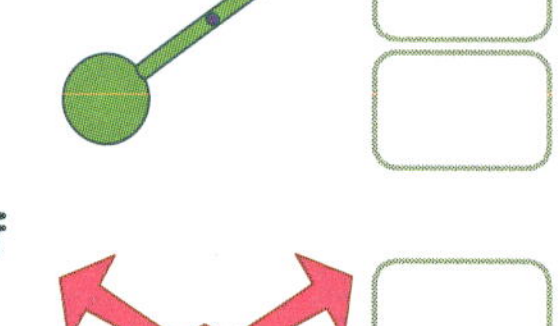

c 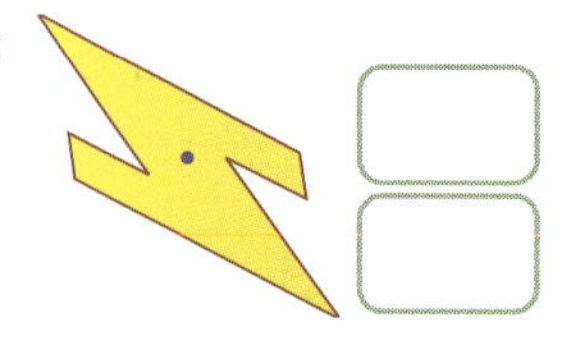

d 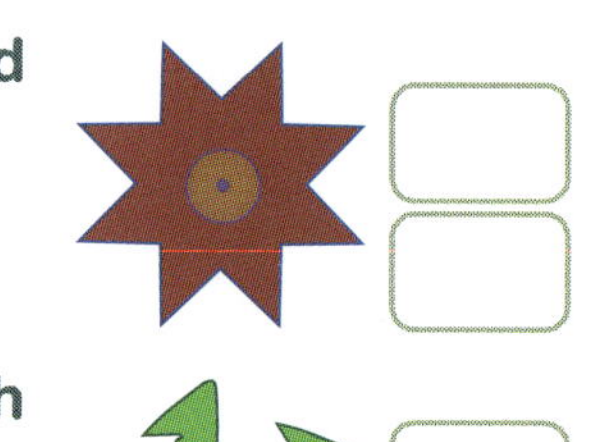

e  

f 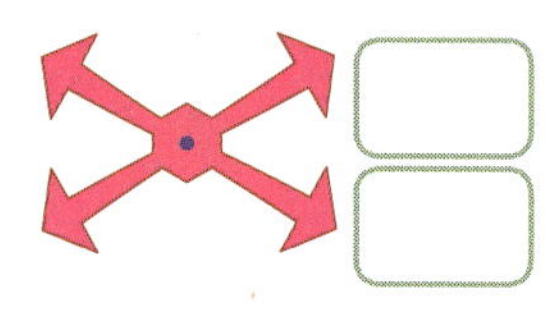

g 

h 

 • *AUSTRALIAN SIGNPOST MATHS 4* • ISBN 9780655708780

Spreadsheets

- We say the column, then the row.
- B14 and C14 have been joined (merged).

CONCEPT

- Susan and Alan were tested on the × 4 and × 5 tables.
- The answers to the × 4 tables are in Column B.
- Discuss the test results of Susan and Alan.

Spreadsheet?

	A	B	C	D	E	F	G	H
	× 4 and × 5 tables facts							
1	× 4 tables				× 5 tables			
2	1	4			1	5		
3	2	8			2	10		
4	3	12			3	15		
5	4	16			4	20		
6	5	20			5	25		
7	6	24			6	30		
8	7	28			7	35		
9	8	32			8	40		
10	9	26			9	45		
11	10	40			10	50		
12	11	44			11	55		
13	12	48			12	60		
14		Test results				Test results		
15	Susan	8	11		Susan	10	12	
16	Alan	7	10		Alan	12	12	

Title

- This cell is called C15.
- This cell is called F13.

1 Put a tick in:

a C2 **b** A14 **c** D7 **d** G10 **e** H3

2 What number is in:

a B8 ☐ **b** F4 ☐ **c** C16 ☐ **d** F15 ☐ **e** A9 ☐

3 **a** Write K in D14. **b** Write L in H2. **c** Write M in C7.

	A	B	C	D	E	F
1	**Pets kept**					
2	**Birds**	5				
3	**Mice**	6				
4	**Turtles**	1				
5						
6	**Athletics**					
7	**Name**	Amy	Holly	Sam	Yong	Luke
8	**Attendance**	4	5	3	7	6

4 **a** How many birds were kept as pets? ☐

b What was the total number of pets? ☐

c Who attended athletics most? ☐

d What are the coordinates of the cell that has been highlighted in red? ☐

e What are the coordinates of 'Pets kept'? ☐

Drawing tables

This table has 6 different categories. One is 'small blue' button.

1. Use the picture to fill in the two-way table.

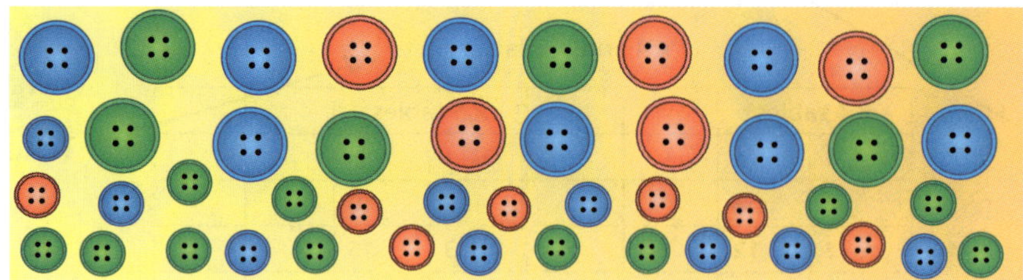

Buttons			
	Red	Blue	Green
Large			
Small			

2. Use the table above to fill in this simpler table.

Buttons		
Red	Blue	Green

3. Use the table above to fill in this simpler table.

Buttons	
Large	
Small	

4. Show the data from Question 2 on a graph.

5. Fill in this table using data about your family and friends.

Name	Age	Male or female
Me		

6. Use the dice to complete the table.

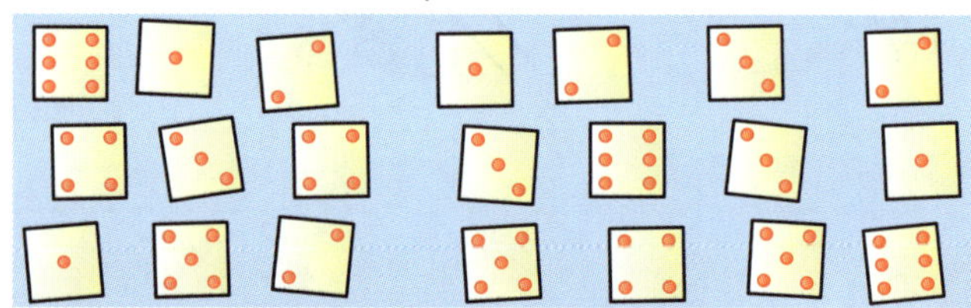

Number of times thrown					
1	2	3	4	5	6

Graphing the weather

ACTIVITY

- For the next month record the weather like this.
- At the end of the month cut up the calendar. Glue the pieces to make a graph like this.
- Use the graph to describe the month's weather.

Chance

'Even chance' means that an outcome is as likely to happen as not to happen.

1 Without looking, Min must choose one card.

a Is she more likely to choose red or black?

b Is she certain to choose an ace?

c Is there an even chance to choose red?

d The chance of choosing black is 1 out of ____.

e The chance of choosing red is 2 out of ____.

2 List all possible outcomes when this spinner is spun.

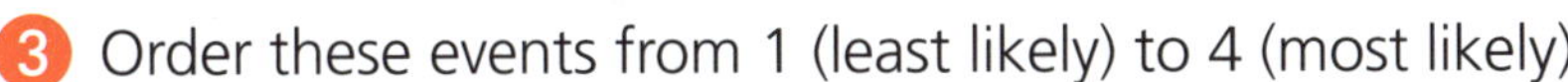

a Which colour is it most likely to land on?

b Which colour is it least likely to land on?

c Which colour has an even chance of occurring?

d What is the chance of spinning pink?

e The chance of landing on red is ____ out of 8.

f The chance of landing on blue is ____ out of 8.

g The chance of landing on yellow is ____ out of 8.

There is also an even chance that red will not be spun

3 Order these events from 1 (least likely) to 4 (most likely).

- The principal will visit our classroom tomorrow.
- It will be sunny tomorrow.
- Our class will use books tomorrow.
- The next person to visit our room will be female.

4 Write three things that might happen tomorrow.

Order each event from 1 (least likely) to 3 (most likely).

Heads or tails?

head

tail

Toss a coin 50 times and keep a tally of the number of heads and tails.

How many heads are most likely to occur in 50 tosses, 15, 25 or 35?

Chance

If all outcomes are just as likely to happen, we say they have an 'equal chance' of happening.

1 Write these events in order from least likely to most likely.

least likely **most likely**

A The principal will come to school on Monday with no shoes on.

B If I throw a normal dice I will get a 4.

C If I drop a glass onto a rock it will break.

D If I toss a coin it will be a head.

E Our next teacher will be from Mars.

2

Rachel **Alan** **Alf** **Mia** **Emma** **Aria**

To decide who works together **two counters** at a time are taken from the jar.

Numbers 1 to 6

Who will work together if the numbers chosen are:

a 3 and 5? ______ **b** 2 and 4? ______

c 1 and 6? ______

d Does each number have the same chance of being chosen? ______

In a random selection, each number has the same chance of being chosen. You could carry out this experiment in your classroom.

3 Choose a label to answer each question.
In Question 2, what is the chance that:

a the numbers 6 and 7 are picked? ______

b the numbers 1 and 2 are picked? ______

c two numbers less than 10 are picked? ______

d when Alf is chosen, he will be working with a girl? ______

e at least one of the pairs will be two girls? ______

impossible | **not likely** | **even chance** | **very likely** | **certain**

 • *AUSTRALIAN SIGNPOST MATHS 4* • ISBN 9780655708773

Using graphs

Column graphs need a title, categories and a scale.

1 Rhonda graphed the number of calls made each day last week by her family.

a How many calls were made on Monday?

b On what day was the greatest number of calls made?

c On what day was the least number made?

d What is the difference between the number of calls made on Saturday and the number made on Thursday?

e What was the total number of calls made for the week?

f Why do you think more calls were made on Sunday and Saturday?

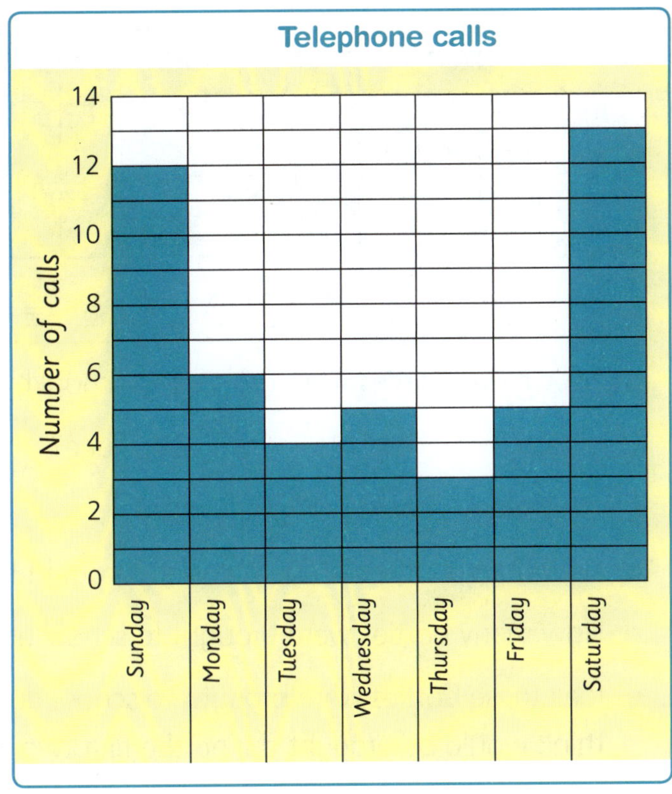

2 Rhonda kept this tally of calls made by her children. Use the tally to draw the graph.

Name	Number of calls
Alana	𝍸 𝍸 ||||
Rachel	𝍸 𝍸
Naomi	||||
Luke	𝍸 𝍸 ||
Heather	|||

Calls made

Alana								
Rachel								
Naomi								
Luke								
Heather								

0 2 4 6 8 10 12 14 16

Number of calls

When columns are drawn across, it is called a bar graph.

INVESTIGATION

3 Trees were planted in a row. A rabbit sat in each space. How many rabbits would there be between:

a 3 trees?

b 7 trees?

c 10 trees?

Draw a picture.

5:05 Reading graphs

One unit on the scale stands for 2 bottles.

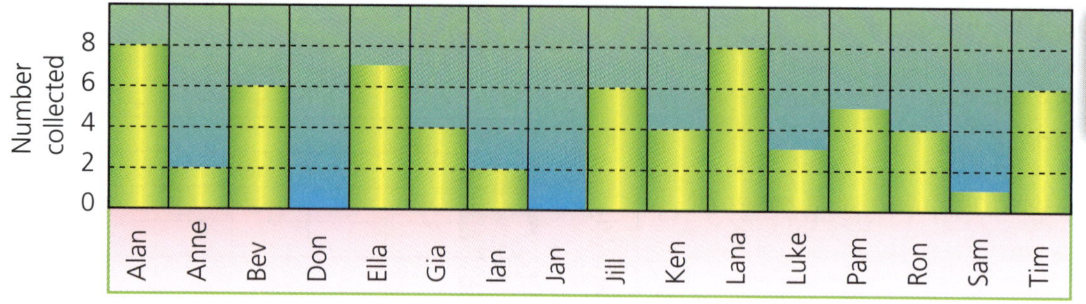

On the graph '3' is between two lines.

a How many bottles were brought to school by:

i Alan? ______ ii Luke? ______ iii Jan? ______

b How many people brought bottles? ______

c How many bottles altogether were brought by Alan, Anne and Bev? ______

d How many bottles were brought to school altogether? ______

e If all these bottles were brought to school during the first week, how many bottles do you think would be brought during the first two weeks? How did you get your answer?

______

2

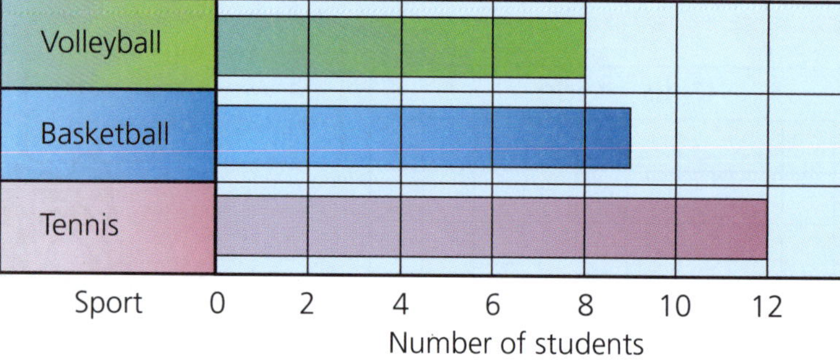

a Which was the most popular sport? ______

b How many students made a choice? ______

c How many sports were chosen? ______

d What is the title of this graph? ______

Tally marks

Tally marks used in South America and Asia also have five lines.
With a partner, create your own five-line tally marks.

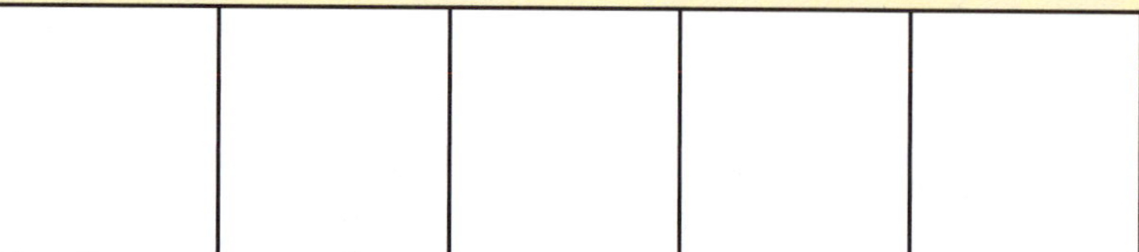

Discuss: When would tally marks be useful?

The only difference between a column graph and a bar graph is that the bar graph is horizontal.

	1	2	3	4	5
South America					
Asia	一	丅	下	止	正

5:06 Ordering events

'Fifty-fifty' is another way of saying 'even chance'.

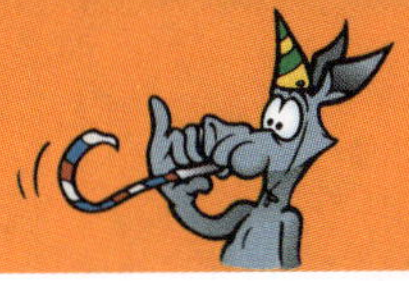

1 Choose the label you think best for each part below.

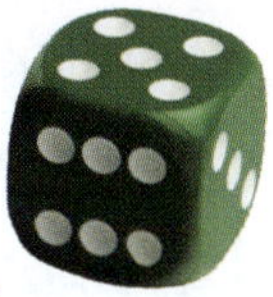

impossible **unlikely** **even chance** **very likely** **certain**

a My first throw of the dice will be a one.

b I will throw a zero on a dice.

c When I throw a dice the number will be greater than one.

In this jar are 3 red and 3 yellow marbles. Blindfolded, I draw one out.

Which label from above is best for each of these statements?

d I will draw out a coloured marble.

e I will draw out a blue marble.

f I will draw out a yellow marble.

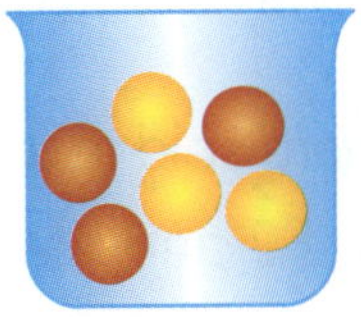

2 Ms Adams placed two red and two blue counters in a hat. She had two more red and two more blue counters. Which two counters must she put into the hat so that she would be:

a more likely to draw out a red than a blue counter?

b more likely to draw out a blue than a red counter?

c equally likely to draw out a blue or a red counter?

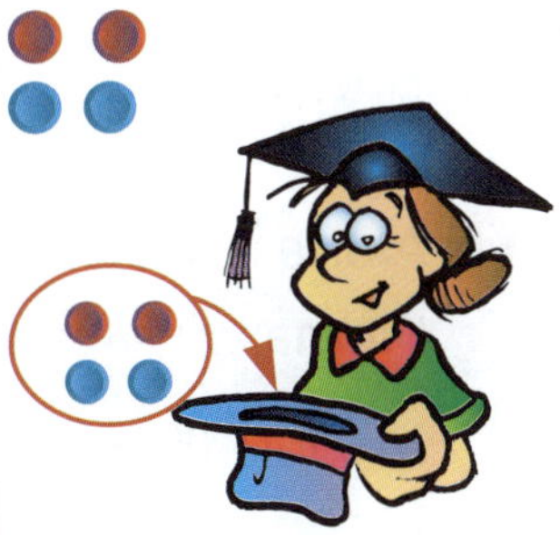

3 A B C D E F

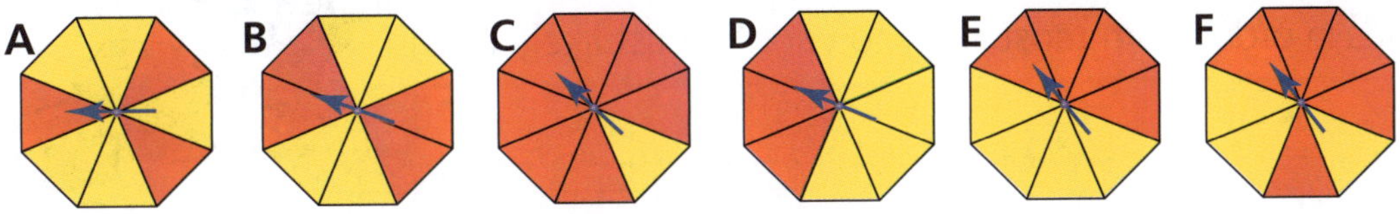

The spinners above stop on either red or yellow.

a Which spinners are equally likely to stop on red as on yellow?

b Which spinners are more likely to stop on red than on yellow?

c Which spinners are more likely to stop on yellow than on red?

4 Here is the head and tail of an old Australian penny.

a If I toss a coin in the air, would a head be more likely to show than a tail?

b If two coins are tossed, what outcomes could result?

5 heads have been tossed in a row. What is likely to happen if I toss the coin again? Discuss.

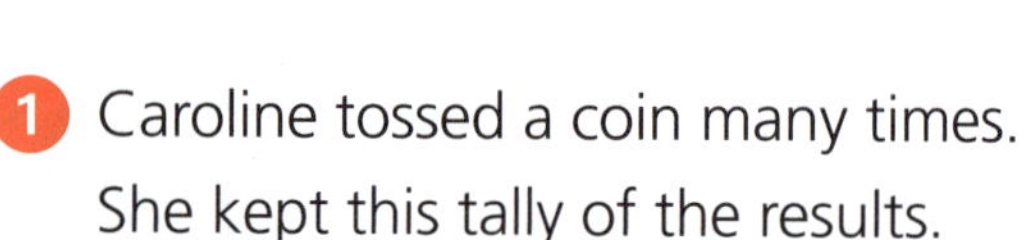

5:07 Chance used in games

Is it best to start at a corner when playing *Noughts and Crosses?*

1 Caroline tossed a coin many times. She kept this tally of the results.

Tossing a coin		
Tossed	Tally	Total
Heads	𝍸 ||||	
Tails	𝍸 𝍸 |	

a How many times did she toss the coin?

b What fraction of the time did she toss:

i a head? ii a tail?

2 When playing cricket, we toss a coin to see who will bat first. How would you describe the chance that our team will win the toss?

3 100 tickets were sold in a raffle. John bought 70 of the tickets, Peta bought 25, Jeremy bought 2 and Alan bought none.

Choose a label that describes the chance that the winner will be:

a John b Peta

c Alan d Jeremy

e none of the four people mentioned

impossible	even chance
very unlikely	likely
unlikely	certain

4 A dice is rolled. **Jack** wins if an odd number is rolled. **Emma** wins if a 6 is rolled and **Luke** wins if a 2 or 4 is rolled.

a Write their names in order from most likely to win, to least likely to win.

b Which person has an even chance of winning?

What's my age?

FUN SPOT

- Ask friends to write the month in which they were born. (1 for January, 2 for February, 3 for March, etc.)
- Tell them to multiply this number by 5, then add 2, then multiply by 20, then add their age in years, then subtract 40.
- Ask the person their answer.

Solution

- The last two digits of the answer give you the age. The other digits give you the month of birth. For example, 714 means the person is 14 and was born in July (the 7th month).

Tally marks

Why do we use tally marks?

Tally the colours

- Start on any white square.
- Throw a dice and move that many spaces clockwise.
- Each time, record the colour you land on as a tally mark.
- Throw the dice 50 times.

ACTIVITY

Colour	Tally	Total
White		
Blue		
Red		
Green		
Yellow		
Orange		

Green	Red	Blue	White
Yellow			Orange
Red			Yellow
White	Blue	Red	Green

Use squared paper to graph your results.

1 Eric asked 300 people to name their favourite sport. He made this tally of their answers.

Sport	Tally	Total
Tennis	卌 卌 卌 卌 卌 卌 卌 卌 卌	
Athletics	卌 卌 卌 卌 卌 卌 卌	
Swimming	卌 卌 卌 卌 卌 卌 卌 卌 |||	
Hockey	卌 卌 卌 卌 卌 |||	
Basketball	卌 卌 卌 卌 卌 卌 卌 |||	
Cricket	卌 卌 卌 卌 卌 卌 卌 卌 ||	
Football	卌 卌 卌 卌 卌 卌 卌 卌 卌		
Other	卌 卌 卌 卌 ||||	

a Complete the **Total** column.

b What was the most popular sport? ______

c How many more people chose swimming than athletics? ______

d Altogether, how many chose athletics and tennis? ______

e Name two sports which might have been included in *Other*. ______

INVESTIGATION

- Ask 50 people to name their favourite sport.
- Keep a tally, like the one above, of their answers.
- Before you begin, estimate how many out of 50 will choose each sport.

 • *AUSTRALIAN SIGNPOST MATHS 4* • ISBN 9780655708773

5:09 Collecting information

A prediction is your best guess.

INVESTIGATION

You are to measure the hand length of 12 boys and 12 girls, in centimetres (to the nearest cm).

Compare your results with the results of others.

1 Who will you measure?

2 How will you measure hand length?

I will use

3 Make some predictions.

Who will have the longest hand, a boy or a girl?

Who will have the shortest hand, a boy or a girl?

4 Measure a few hands before you decide which measurements you will use in the left column.

5 Use tallies to record your results below.

Hand lengths of boys and girls

Measurement in centimetres	Boys' tally	Total	Girls' tally	Total
cm				
cm				
cm				
cm				
cm				
cm				
cm				
cm				
cm				

6 **Results**

The longest hand belonged to a ______. The shortest hand belonged to a ______.

7 Make a strip of paper that has the same length as:

a the shortest male hand
b the shortest female hand
c the longest male hand
d the longest female hand

8 **Your comments**

5:10 Constructing spinners

I wonder which spinner would give more red outcomes.

Aim: To compare the chances of spinning red on different spinners.

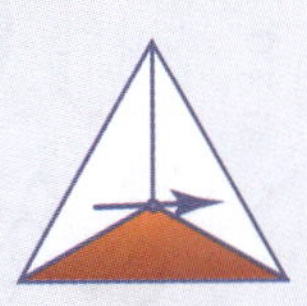
A

B

C

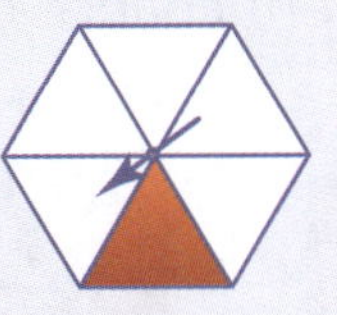
D

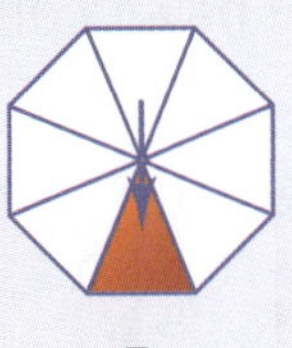
E

1 Experiment

- Find or make spinners like these.
- One student will spin each spinner 20 times while another student records the tally of red outcomes in the table below.

a Which spinner do you think will have most red spins? ☐

b Which spinner do you think will have least red spins? ☐

c Carry out the experiments.

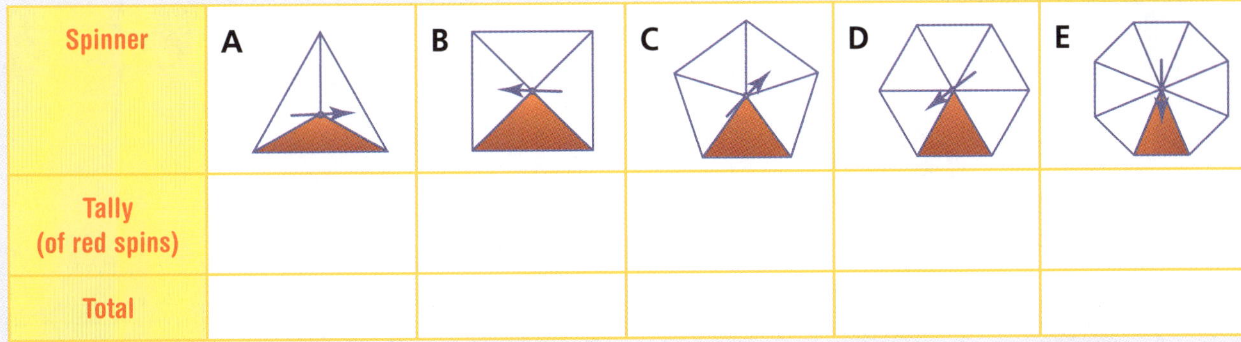

Spinner	A	B	C	D	E
Tally (of red spins)					
Total					

d Which spinner had most red spins? ☐

e Which spinner had least red spins? ☐

From your results, on which spinner is red:

f most likely to be spun? ☐ **g** least likely to be spun? ☐

h If we combined the results of many students, would we have a better idea of the answers to parts **f** and **g**? ☐ Why or why not?

____

____

i Put **A** to **E** in order, from most likely to spin red to least likely to spin red.

____

 • *AUSTRALIAN SIGNPOST MATHS 4* • ISBN 9780655708773

5:11 Unequal outcomes

An 'even' or 'fifty-fifty' chance means the outcome is as likely to happen as not happen.

CONCEPT

- Each side of these squares has the same chance of being spun.
- The two colours usually have a different chance of being spun.

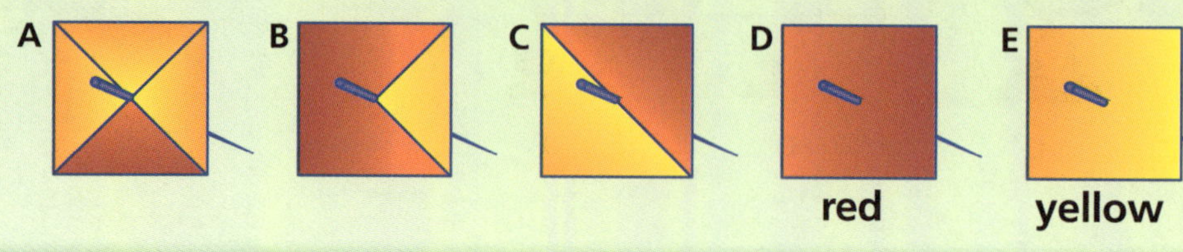

1. For which of the spinners above is the chance of spinning red:

   a impossible? ______ b certain? ______ c an even chance? ______

   d unlikely? ______ e likely? ______

2. Put the spinners above in order, from least likely to most likely of spinning red. Discuss your answer. ______

3. Put the spinners in order, from least likely to most likely of spinning red.

   a 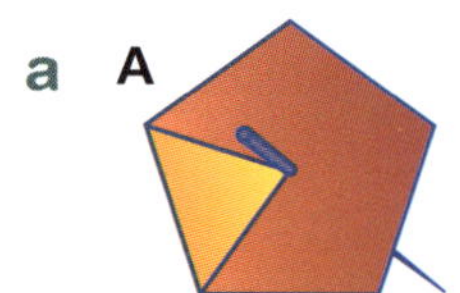 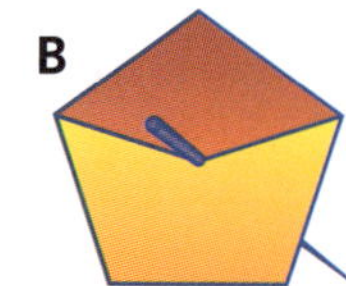  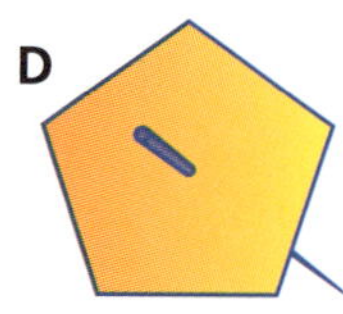 

______

   b 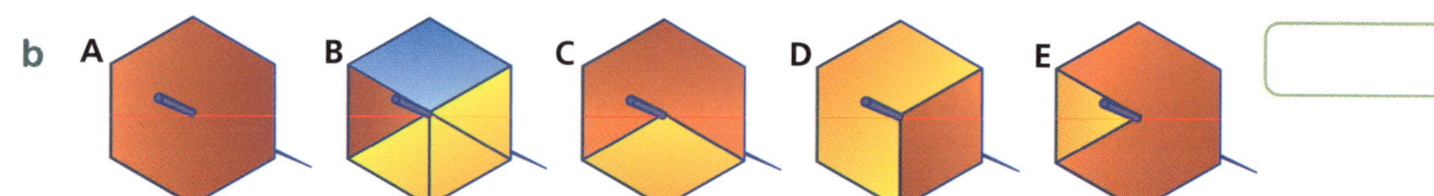

______

   c 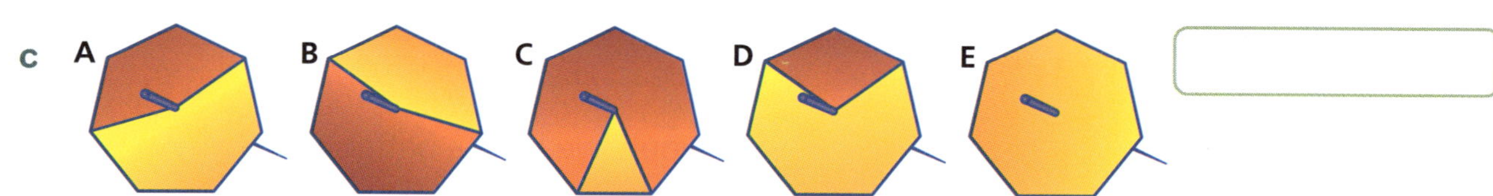

______

INVESTIGATION

4. Put the numbers 1 to 6 on the faces of a matchbox.
   Are the faces equally likely to land face up when the box is tossed? ______
   Carry out this experiment 50 times, keeping a tally of the results.
   What did you discover? ______

Tally					
1	2	3	4	5	6

 • *AUSTRALIAN SIGNPOST MATHS 4* • ISBN 9780655708773

5:12 Surveys

Each person could be given a form to fill in, or you could record each response yourself.

- **Surveys** are used to discover information, to give us a general view of a situation or to check predictions.
- If everyone is surveyed from the group we wish to study, we have carried out a **census**.
- We can use a spreadsheet to graph the data we collect.
- These graphs were made by a spreadsheet to show ***When my classmates go to bed***.

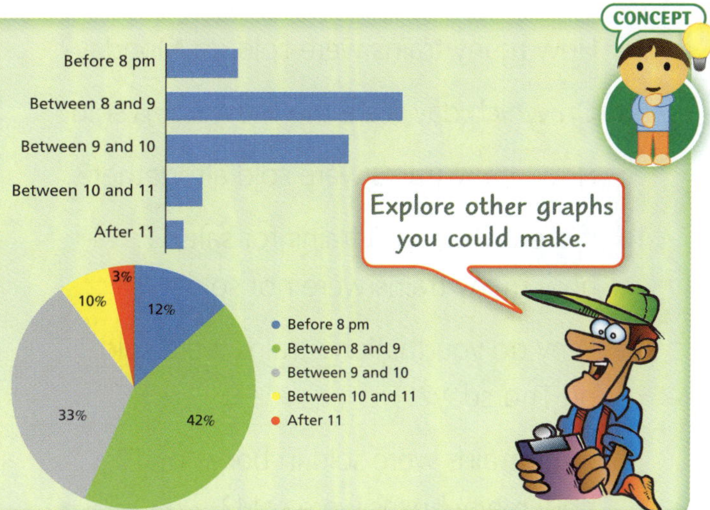

1 Abbie conducted a survey of the students in her class. This, of course included herself. Her topic was: ***How many children are in your family***? Complete the **Number** column below.

Abbie's survey — Children in families

Tick the box next to the number of children in your family.

- ☐ 1 child
- ☐ 2 children
- ☐ 3 children
- ☐ 4 children
- ☐ 5 children
- ☐ 6 children
- ☐ more than 6

Abbie's survey — Children in families

Category	Tally	Number
1 child	卌 |	
2 children	卌 卌	
3 children	卌 ||	
4 children	|||	
5 children	||	
6 children		
more than 6	|	

Enter this data into a spreadsheet. Use this to create a horizontal column graph.

2 Conduct this survey in your class and use the results to complete the table.

Children in families

Tick the box next to the number of children in your family.

- ☐ 1 child
- ☐ 2 children
- ☐ 3 children
- ☐ 4 children
- ☐ 5 children
- ☐ 6 children
- ☐ more than 6

Children in families

Category	Tally	Number
1 child		
2 children		
3 children		
4 children		
5 children		
6 children		
more than 6		

 • *AUSTRALIAN SIGNPOST MATHS 4* • ISBN 9780655708773

5:13 Graphing data

How much does each picture stand for?

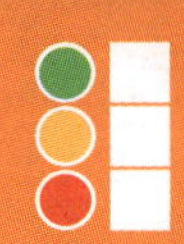

1 a How many trains were sold on Monday?

b On which day were the most trains sold?

c How many trains were sold altogether?

d If there were 200 trains for sale, how many trains were not sold?

e Why do you think no trains were sold on Thursday?

f If the trains were sold in boxes of 10, how many boxes were sold?

Toy trains sold	(train) = 10 toy trains
Monday	(train) (train) (train)
Tuesday	(train) (train) (train) (train)
Wednesday	(train)
Thursday	
Friday	(train) (train)

2 Katie surveyed students at her school to find out how they travelled to school. She recorded her results (to the nearest 10).

Bus	30
Walk	60
Car	70
Bike	40

a Which option was most common?

b How many students use a bus or car?

c Approximately how many students did she survey?

d Should Katie expect the same results every day?

e Complete the picture graph to display her results.

f Why is it useful to make (person) = 10 students? Discuss.

Key: (person) = 10 students	
Bus	
Walk	
Car	
Bike	

INVESTIGATION

3 Eva rolled two dice 25 times and found each total. She used a column graph to record her results.

a Carry out this activity and record your results.

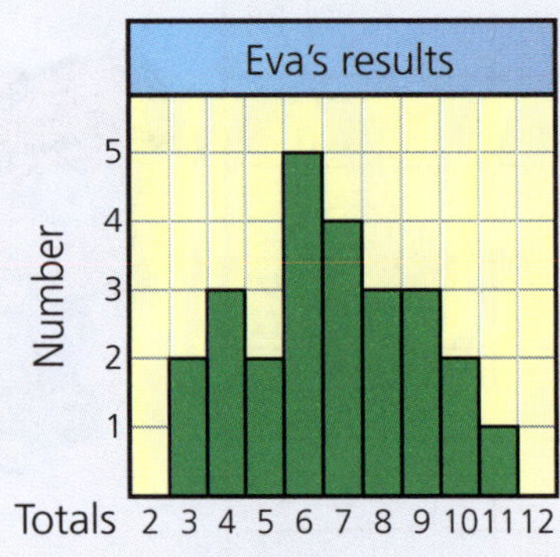

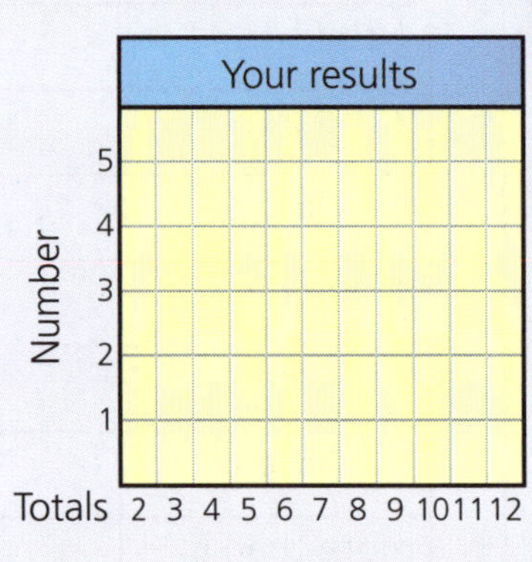

b Compare your results with Eva's results. Discuss the shape of these graphs.

Chance experiments

I will not return the counter.

1 **We begin with 4 green counters and 3 red counters. We will choose 3 counters.**

One counter will be taken at random as each choice is made, and it is not replaced.

Use *likely*, *equally likely/unlikely* or *unlikely* to describe the chance of choosing a **red counter** each time.

a 1st choice: Chance of choosing a red counter is ______.

b 2nd choice: Chance of choosing a red counter if a green counter was chosen first is ______.

c 3rd choice: Chance of choosing a red counter if two green counters have already been chosen is ______.

Conclusion: In this experiment, the first choice affects the chances in the second and third choices. When tossing a coin, this is not the case.

d If the counter is replaced after each choice, would the chance of choosing a red counter on the second choice be the same as it was for the first choice? ______

2 Put the same number of red and green counters in a container. One counter will be drawn out and then replaced.

a How many red counters would you expect to get in 10 turns? ______

b Give a reason for your answer. ______

c Carry out this experiment. The number of red counters chosen = ______. Discuss.

d Carry out this experiment a second time. Were your results the same?

3

- Take a counter at random from a bag containing 5 red counters, 3 blue counters and 1 yellow counter. Record a tally mark for that colour.
- Return the counter to the bag.
- Repeat the experiment 50 times.

Choosing a counter

	Tally	
Red		
Blue		
Yellow		

4 Write **equally likely** (**E**) or **not equally likely** (**N**) in each case.

a It will land on 1, 2 or 3. ______

b The drawing pin will land face up or face down. ______

c The next child born will be a girl or a boy. ______

 • *AUSTRALIAN SIGNPOST MATHS 4* • ISBN 9780655708773

5:15 Carry out your own survey

Choose your question carefully.

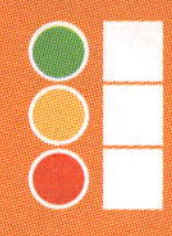

INVESTIGATION

Step 1: Choose a topic you are interested in for your survey.

Topic:

Step 2: Write a question to ask people about your topic.

Question:

Step 3: Decide how you will collect and record the answers (data).

Step 4: Predict what the data will show.

I think

Step 5: Represent your result using tables and graphs. (You could use technology to do this.)

Step 6: Reflect and write what you have learnt from your data.

I found

Step 7: Share your results.

Reflection: Was using a survey useful ? What did you do well and what could you do better next time? What other topics could you research using a survey?

5:16 Chance experiments

A head was tossed more than twice as much.

1 Matt tossed a coin 10 times and made this graph.

Heads	(coin)	(coin)	(coin)	(coin)	(coin)	(coin)	(coin)
Tails	(coin)	(coin)	(coin)				

a Which outcome occurred more often?

b Do these results mean that heads is more likely to be tossed than tails?

Why or why not?

2 a If you tossed a coin 10 times, how many heads would you predict?

b Toss a coin 10 times. Colour a circle after each toss.

Heads	○	○	○	○	○	○	○	○	○	○
Tails	○	○	○	○	○	○	○	○	○	○

c Do you think heads or tails is more likely, or are they equally likely?

d If many students combined their results would we have a better idea of whether heads and tails are equally likely?

e Why or why not?

3 a If we toss two coins we could toss **2 heads**, **2 tails** or **1 head and 1 tail**. Which of these do you think is most likely?

b Toss two coins 50 times and make a tally of the results.

c Which outcome occurred most often?

d Did this agree with your prediction?

e Compare your results with others in the class.

f What do you think is the likelihood of the three results occurring? Report your findings here.

Tally		
2 heads	1 head 1 tail	2 tails

Addition and subtraction facts

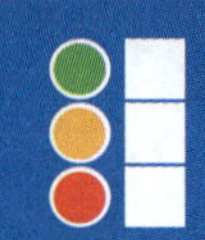

CONCEPT

Make sure you know your addition and subtraction facts.

Once you learn your addition tables, use them for subtraction.

- If 6 + 7 = 13, then 13 – 6 = 7 and 13 – 7 = 6.
- If 8 + 9 = 17, then 17 – 8 = 9 and 17 – 9 = 8.

1 Join each question to the correct answer using a ruler and pencil. You could practise your tables facts by rubbing out your answers and doing them again.

a +

Question		Answer
2 + 6		1
4 + 6		7
0 + 1		8
5 + 7		9
5 + 6		10
0 + 7		11
4 + 5		12
7 + 10		15
8 + 7		17
10 + 10		18
9 + 9		20
Speed:		

b +

Question		Answer
2 + 3		4
4 + 3		5
2 + 2		7
5 + 4		9
8 + 5		8
8 + 0		10
7 + 5		11
1 + 9		12
10 + 5		13
6 + 5		15
10 + 9		19
Speed:		

c +

Question		Answer
3 + 6		6
2 + 8		7
4 + 2		8
5 + 2		9
4 + 7		10
3 + 5		11
9 + 6		12
6 + 6		13
8 + 8		14
7 + 6		15
10 + 4		16
Speed:		

d +

Question		Answer
3 + 4		5
6 + 2		6
4 + 5		7
3 + 2		8
2 + 4		9
8 + 4		10
4 + 9		11
5 + 5		12
4 + 7		13
7 + 8		14
5 + 9		15
Speed:		

e –

Question		Answer
8 – 6		1
10 – 4		0
1 – 0		2
12 – 5		4
11 – 6		6
7 – 7		5
9 – 5		7
17 – 7		8
15 – 7		10
11 – 8		9
18 – 9		3
Speed:		

f –

Question		Answer
5 – 2		2
7 – 3		3
4 – 2		4
9 – 4		5
13 – 5		0
8 – 8		1
12 – 5		6
10 – 9		7
15 – 5		8
11 – 5		10
19 – 10		9
Speed:		

g –

Question		Answer
6 – 4		0
5 – 2		1
10 – 9		2
7 – 7		3
9 – 3		4
7 – 3		5
10 – 3		6
14 – 5		7
9 – 4		8
18 – 8		9
10 – 2		10
Speed:		

h –

Question		Answer
6 – 5		0
9 – 9		1
6 – 3		2
8 – 6		3
8 – 4		4
16 – 9		5
9 – 4		6
16 – 7		7
17 – 7		8
10 – 4		9
17 – 9		10
Speed:		

See 2:05 (Addition, no trading); 2:06 (Addition and subtraction, no trading); 2:07 and 2:08 (Addition to 99 with trading).

Building to the next 10

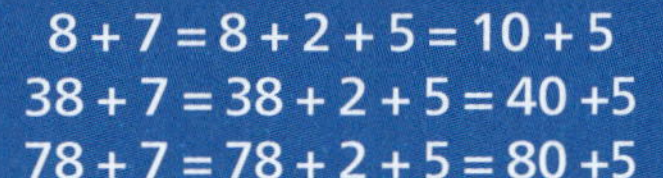

- When adding a single-digit number to a 2-digit number, build to the **next 10** and then add the part of the single-digit number that you have not used.

$28 + 8 = 28 + 2 + 6$
$= 30 + 6$
$= 36$

Build to the next 10 to find the answer.

1
a 7 + 5 = 7 + 3 + ☐
= ☐
b 8 + 4 = ☐
c 19 + 7 = ☐
d 18 + 9 = ☐
e 17 + 4 = ☐
f 19 + 8 = ☐
g 17 + 5 = ☐
h 18 + 3 = ☐
i 19 + 5 = ☐
j 17 + 6 = ☐
k 18 + 8 = ☐
l 19 + 6 = ☐
m 19 + 9 = ☐
n 18 + 5 = ☐
o 19 + 4= ☐

2
a 29 + 5 = 29 + 1 + ☐
= ☐
b 29 + 3 = ☐
c 27 + 4 = ☐
d 28 + 7 = ☐
e 21+ 5 = ☐
f 28 + 2 = ☐
g 29 + 4 = ☐
h 37 + 6 = ☐
i 39 + 5 = ☐
j 38 + 5 = ☐
k 37 + 4 = ☐
l 39 + 6 = ☐
m 38 + 4 = ☐
n 39 + 3 = ☐
o 37 + 5 = ☐

3
a 48 + 4 = 48 + 2 + ☐
= ☐
b 47 + 5 = ☐
c 49 + 6 = ☐
d 47 + 6 = ☐
e 48 + 5 = ☐
f 47 + 4 = ☐
g 49 + 4 = ☐
h 57 + 4 = ☐
i 59 + 3 = ☐
j 58 + 3 = ☐
k 57 + 5 = ☐
l 59 + 4 = ☐
m 58 + 4 = ☐
n 57 + 6 = ☐
o 58 + 5 = ☐

See 2:09 (Jump strategy, +); 2:35 (Mental strategies, + and –).

Tangrams

7-piece tangrams were invented in China 4000 years ago.

1

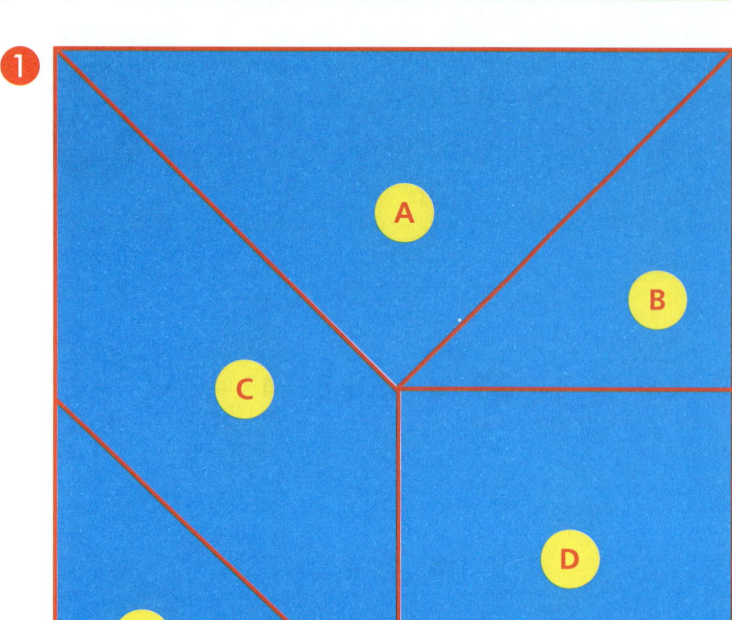

a Trace this tangram onto paper, cut it into 5 pieces and label them **A** to **E**.

b Without looking at this page, arrange your 5 pieces to make a square.

c Use your 5 pieces to make these pictures.

d Make patterns of your own.

e Paste your best pattern onto cardboard or coloured paper.

2

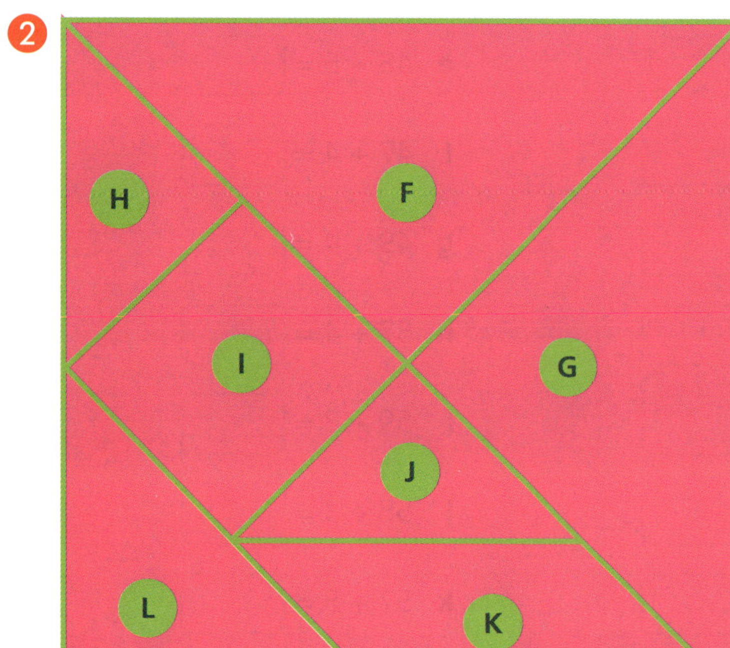

a Trace this tangram onto paper, cut it into 7 pieces and label them **F** to **L**.

b Without looking at this page, arrange your 7 pieces to make a square.

c Use your 7 pieces to make these pictures.

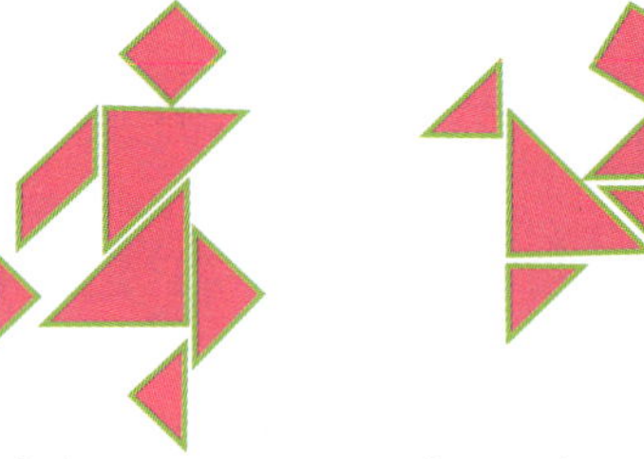

d Make a square using pieces **F** and **G**.

e Using pieces **H**, **I** and **J**, make these shapes:

e Use the seven pieces to make these pictures

f Copy two of the pictures here.

See 4:01 (Flip, slide, turn); 4:11 and 4:20 (Visualising shapes); 4:24 (Tessellating designs); 4:25 (Tessellations).

 • *AUSTRALIAN SIGNPOST MATHS 4* • ISBN 9780655708780

Flip, slide, turn

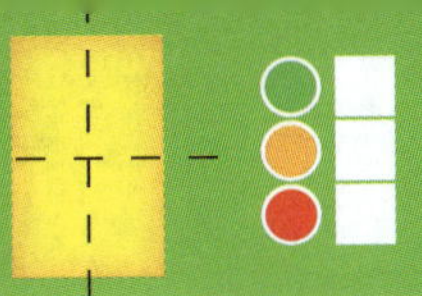

A shape has **symmetry** if one side is the reflection of the other.

CONCEPT

There are 3 ways to repeat a shape:

A flip the shape (reflect it)
B slide the shape (translate it)
C turn the shape (rotate it).

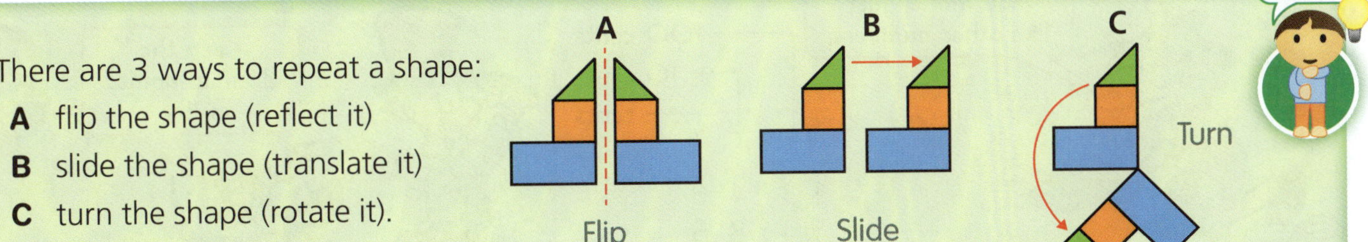

1 Is the coloured shape made by a **flip** (reflection), **slide** (translation) or **turn** (rotation)?

a

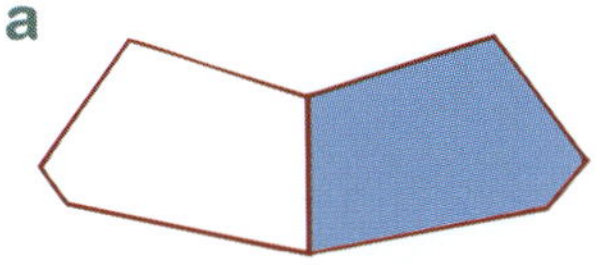

b

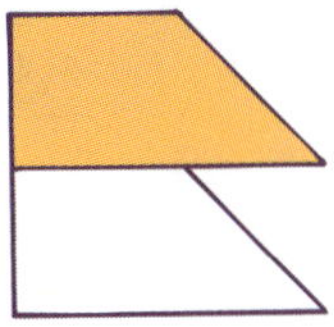

c

d

e

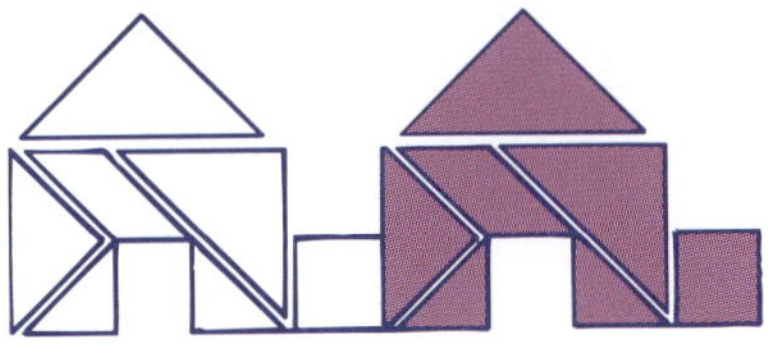

f

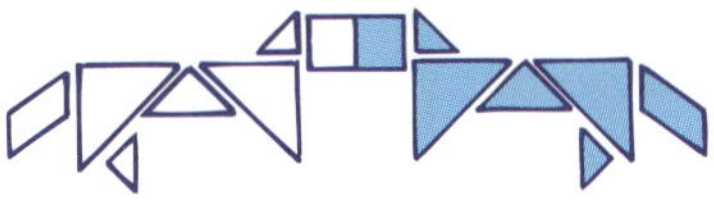

g

h

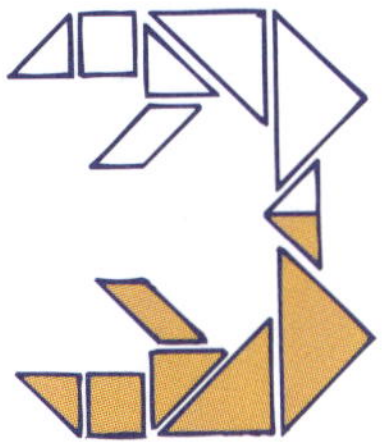

i

j

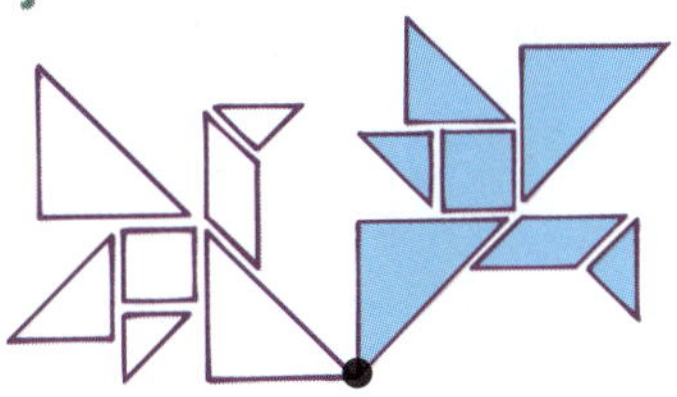

k Discuss which of these shapes are symmetrical.

2 Draw all lines of symmetry. Is the coloured shape made by a flip, a slide or a turn?

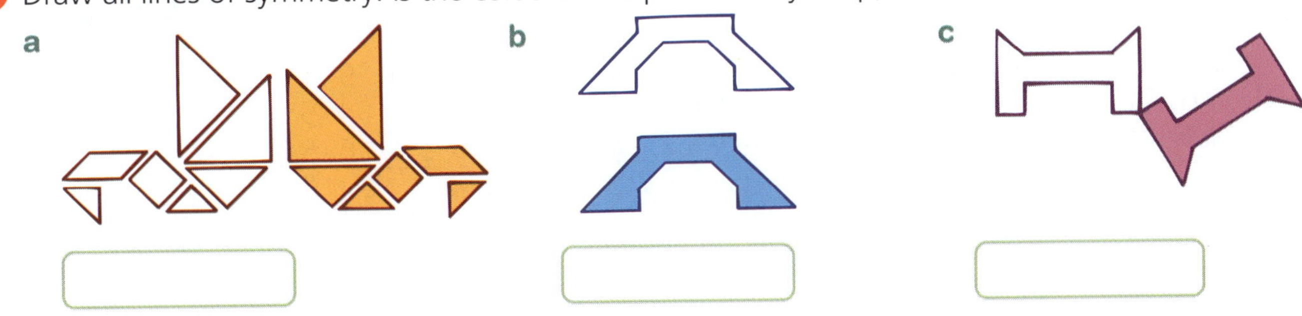

See 4:01 (Flip, slide, turn); 4:11 and 4:20 (Visualising shapes); 4:24 (Tessellating designs); 4:25 (Tessellations).

Addition of money

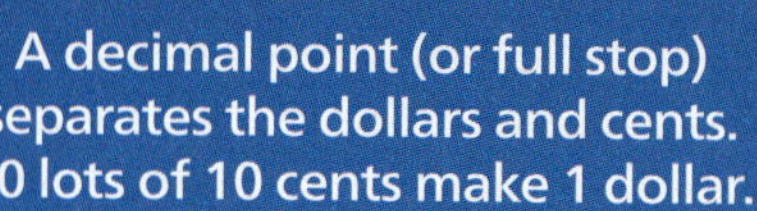

1

a $0.41 + $0.37	**b** $0.64 + $0.88	**c** $1.26 + $3.47	**d** $2.24 + $3.07	**e** $3.75 + $2.94
f $4.69 + $3.56	**g** $2.63 + $2.07	**h** $5.83 + $2.68	**i** $4.96 + $1.47	**j** $2.79 + $4.32
k $2.41 + $3.67	**l** $4.06 + $2.91	**m** $3.77 + $1.63	**n** $1.92 + $4.37	**o** $5.16 + $1.98

2 Write each as an algorithm or use a mental strategy to find your answer.

a $1.56 + $2.23 ______ **b** $4.01 + $1.76 ______

c $3.51 + $2.17 ______ **d** $5.03 + $3.65 ______

e $2.37 + $4.12 ______ **f** $6.45 + $2.03 ______

3 Find the total if I bought:

a a cake for $5.50 and a drink for $4.05. ______

b a dessert for $4.95 and a drink for $3.25. ______

c a sandwich for $7.30 and a drink for $1.55. ______

d a biscuit for $3.75 and a drink for $4.95. ______

4

a $2.21 + $0.85 + $1.82	**b** $1.61 + $3.17 + $4.05	**c** $4.68 + $1.83 + $2.86	**d** $5.91 + $1.45 + $1.65

See 2:23 and 2:24 (Addition to 999); 2:25 (Writing algorithms).

Addition to 9999

Th means thousands.
H means hundreds.

T means tens.
U means ones.

CONCEPT

Rebecca had 1559 stamps. Jake had 756. How many stamps altogether?

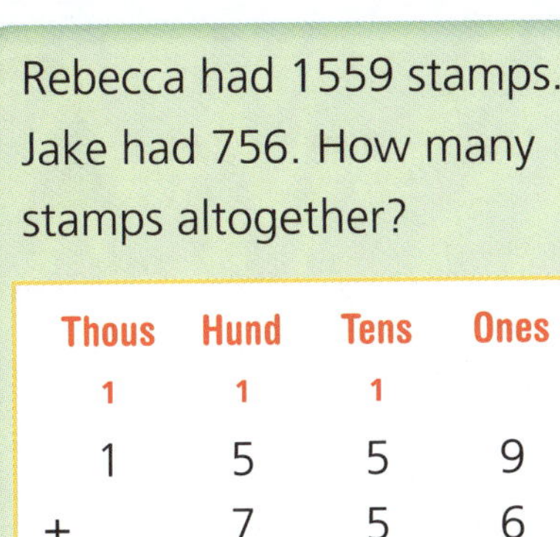

	Thous	Hund	Tens	Ones
	1	1	1	
	1	5	5	9
+		7	5	6
	2	3	1	5

2315 stamps altogether.

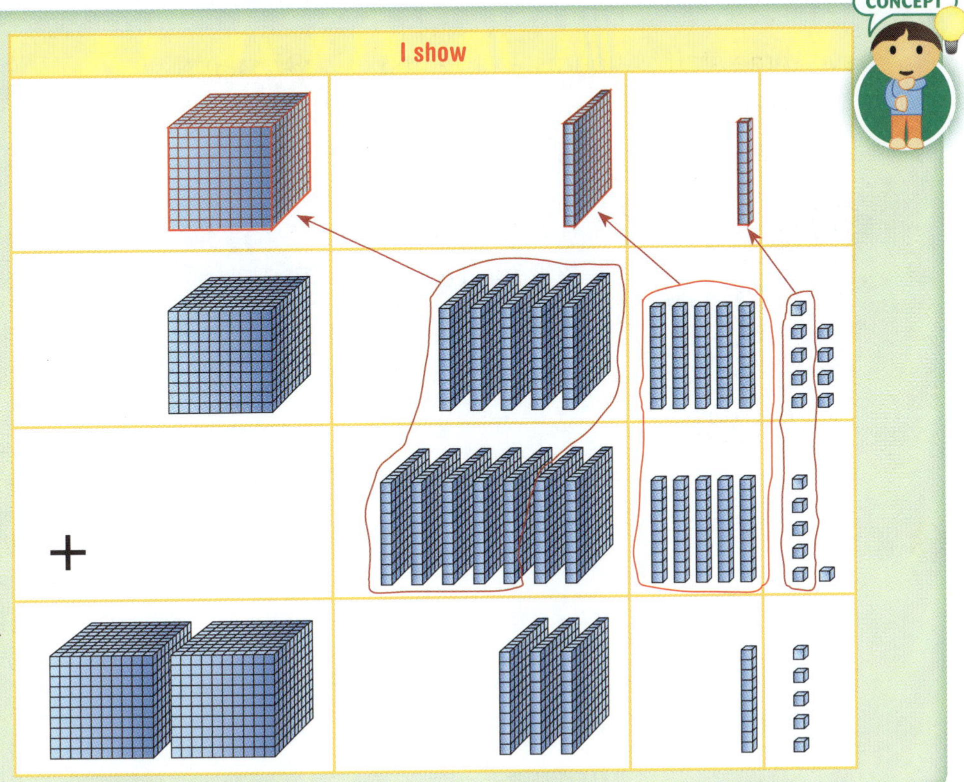

1

a	3416 + 2052
b	8104 + 871
c	6318 + 1270
d	392 + 3406
e	35 + 7932
f	3418 + 2906
g	7950 + 650
h	6087 + 1164
i	946 + 2627
j	6492 + 1748

(Column headings for a–e: Th H T U)

2

a	5071 + 2124
b	3831 + 1054
c	2516 + 1827
d	3195 + 5730
e	7041 + 978
f	4692 + 2813
g	7472 + 1809
h	479 + 3860
i	1793 + 5824
j	6097 + 1835

3

a	\$7542 + \$1607
b	\$6549 + \$1742
c	\$3581 + \$4328
d	\$2591 + \$3706
e	\$7059 + \$2371

See 2:23 and 2:24 (Addition to 999); 2:25 (Writing algorithms).

Extra Support 7 Addition to 9999

13 hundreds
= 1 thousand + 3 hundreds

CONCEPT

I have three stamp albums. In the first is 3087 stamps, in the second 1872 stamps and in the third 4378. How many stamps do I have altogether?

How many stamps?

3087 + 1872 + 4378 = ☐

Answer

I have 9337 stamps.

	Thous	Hund	Tens	Ones
	1	2	1	
	3	0	8	7
	1	8	7	2
+	4	3	7	8
	9	3	3	7

1

a

	Th	H	T	U
	1	8	3	5
		4	0	8
+	5	3	1	8

b

	Th	H	T	U
		9	9	9
	4	2	5	6
+	1	6	8	0

c

	Th	H	T	U
	8	4	1	8
		6	4	7
+		7	5	3

d

	Th	H	T	U
	3	8	4	2
		7	0	6
+	2	9	3	4

2

a

```
    3 8 6
  2 5 1 4
    9 7 7
+     2 7
```

b

```
    1 8 3
    9 6 4
  1 8 6 3
+ 2 0 9 8
```

c

```
  5 1 4 2
    8 6 3
    7 4 4
+ 1 0 8 8
```

d

```
  2 0 9 9
  1 8 4 7
  1 9 3 5
+ 1 2 0 7
```

3

a

```
 $61.29
 $13.91
+$10.94
```

b

```
 $28.18
 $14.63
+$ 9.72
```

c

```
 $ 8.47
 $60.08
+$21.55
```

d

```
 $28.47
 $29.66
+$28.67
```

4 Estimate then calculate. (E = estimate, A = answer)

a Residents were phoned at 3187 homes in Bendigo, 1394 in Ballarat and 914 in Geelong. How many residents were phoned? E = ☐ A = ☐

b A bookshop kept 3096 books in room A, 2515 in room B and 2845 in room C. How many books were in the three rooms? E = ☐ A = ☐

c Sandy spent $3245 renovating her laundry, $2188 on landscaping and $2840 on furniture. How much did she spend? E = ☐ A = ☐

See 2:23 and 2:24 (Addition to 999); 2:25 (Writing algorithms).

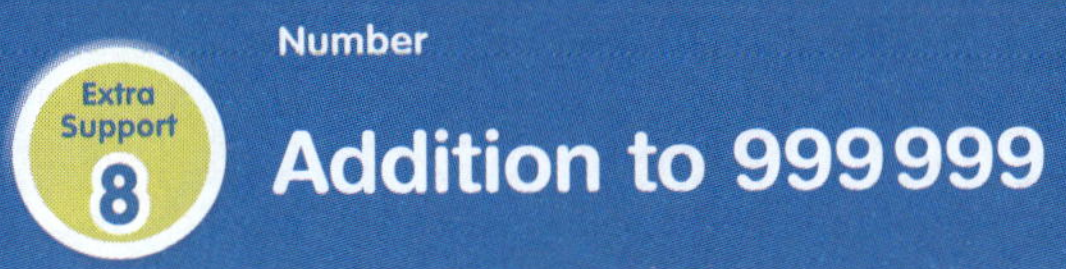

Addition to 999 999

Check answers by rounding to 100 000s.

400 000
+ 400 000

At the last count Jock's two sheep stations had 374 295 and 439 015 sheep. How many sheep did he have altogether?

```
 1 1   1 1
 3 7 4 2 9 5
+4 3 9 0 1 5
 8 1 3 3 1 0
```

374 thousands
295 ones
374 295

Altogether Jock had 813 310 sheep.

1

a) 42 300 + 19 200

b) 35 321 + 11 800

c) 56 684 + 9066

d) 18 957 + 61 846

e) 175 800 + 94 250

f) 405 312 + 6918

g) 125 094 + 609 887

h) 354 500 + 267 600

2

a) 35 256 + 9184 + 4215

b) 8645 + 26 314 + 83 021

c) 43 400 + 48 915 + 8335

d) 75 340 + 10 659 + 10 936

e) 340 000 + 75 900 + 471 550

f) 87 366 + 135 344 + 218 900

g) 9560 + 28 537 + 696 315

h) 650 000 + 97 000 + 165 000

3

a) 386 915 + 9084 + 16 121 + 103 514

b) 55 950 + 4831 + 130 090 + 7346

c) 246 176 + 164 308 + 127 351 + 263 867

Use rounding to check your answers.

4

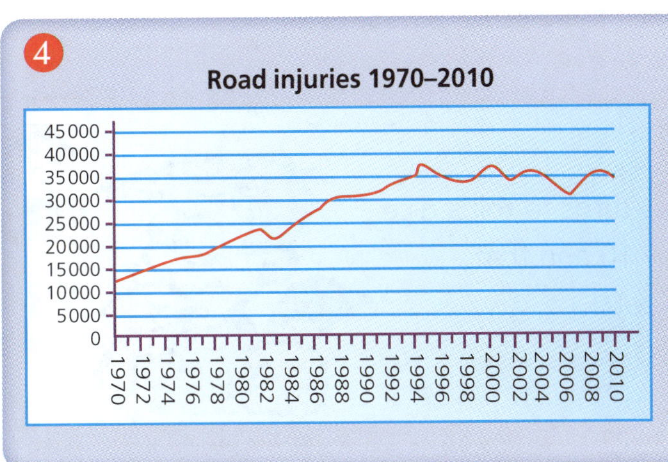

- This graph shows the number of road injuries in each year. (It could be drawn as a line of dots.)
- Find an approximation for the total number of injuries that occurred from:

a) 1971 to 1980 ______

b) 1991 to 2000 ______

c) 2001 to 2010 ______

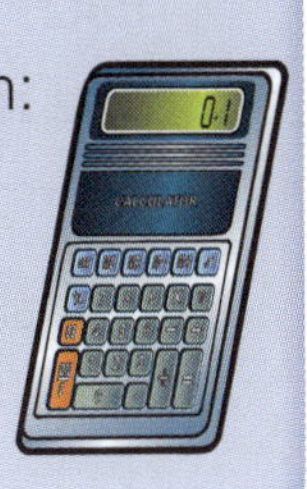

See 2:23 and 2:24 (Addition to 999); 2:25 (Writing algorithms).

Extra Support 9

Number

Subtraction of money

Trade 2 five-cent coins for 10 cents.
Trade $1 for 10 ten-cent coins.

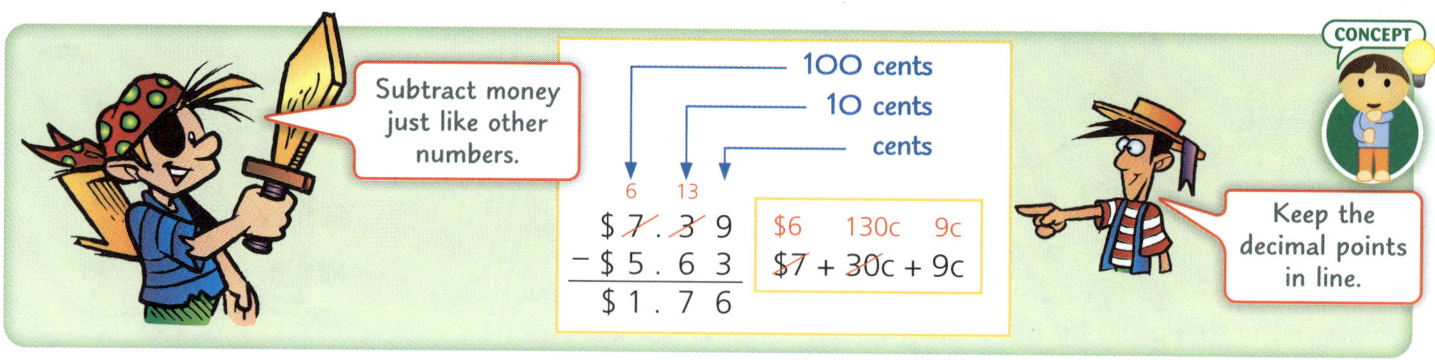

1

a $6.52 − $1.30

b $8.79 − $3.62

c $9.85 − $3.51

d $7.82 − $5.43

e $6.24 − $2.07

f $4.47 − $2.63

g $5.38 − $2.61

h $7.50 − $1.42

i $3.54 − $0.20

j $7.55 − $3.47

k $8.57 − $6.87

l $9.57 − $6.99

m $6.50 − $2.61

n $7.90 − $2.45

o $3.52 − $1.48

2 Write each as an algorithm or use a mental strategy to find your answer.

a $3.35 – $1.24

b $8.98 – $4.00

c $8.56 – $3.21

d $4.54 – $4.49

e $7.00 – $1.50

f $3.50 – $1.99

3 I started with $8.50. What is my change if I buy:

a a book for $7.45?

b an icy pole for $2.30?

c a drink for $3.05?

d a keyring for $7.30?

e a pen for $4.95

f marbles for $3.55?

FUN SPOT

First to $5

- Each player begins the game with $10 and takes turns to roll a dice.
- The number shown on each dice is multiplied by 10 and that number of cents is subtracted from the player's total.
- The game continues until one player reaches $5.

See 2:32 and 2:33 (Subtraction with trading to 999); 2:34 (Subtraction with 2 trades to 999).

Subtraction with trading to 9999

1 thousand can be traded for 10 hundreds.

CONCEPT

2216 people started in a *Town To Surf* race, but 865 people dropped out before the finish. How many people finished the race?

- We can show 2216 with place-value blocks.
- Trade 1 hundred for 10 tens.
- Trade 1 thousand for 10 hundreds.
- Now we can subtract 865 by taking away 8 hundreds, 6 tens and 5 ones.

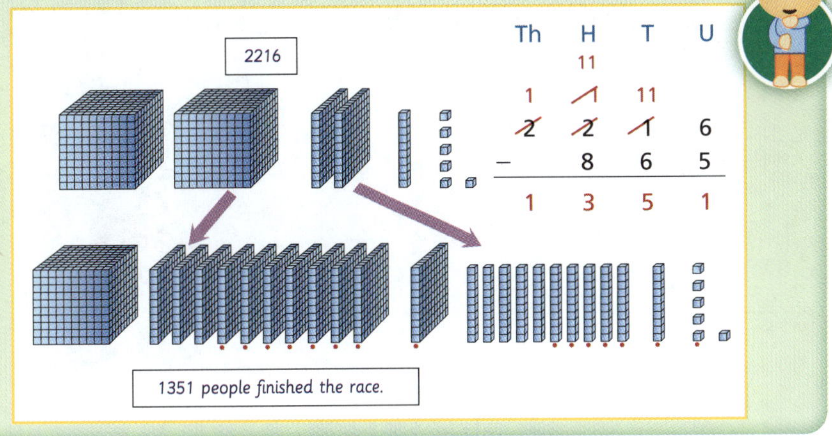

1

a) 5695 − 1342 =

b) 7850 − 750 =

c) 6925 − 1505 =

d) 8046 − 46 =

e) 9388 − 3175 =

f) 6450 − 380 =

g) 2392 − 1950 =

h) 7500 − 2180 =

i) 6432 − 129 =

j) 5299 − 3475 =

2

a) 4381 − 1605 =

b) 2186 − 993 =

c) 4506 − 3800 =

d) 7860 − 870 =

e) 9945 − 6877 =

f) 2315 − 1946 =

g) 6105 − 3827 =

h) 9031 − 7429 =

i) 7637 − 888 =

j) 5455 − 1966 =

3

a) Stephanie used her phone 9690 times last year. If 7815 were related to her business, how many were not business calls?

b) 3495 calls were on her mobile phone. How many were not on her mobile phone?

c) During June her business received $8475 and paid out $4816. How much money did her business make in June?

4 Tran bought 8095 bricks to pave part of his backyard. He used only 7186 bricks. How many were not used?

See 2:32 and 2:33 (Subtraction with trading to 999); 2:34 (Subtraction with 2 trades to 999).

 • *AUSTRALIAN SIGNPOST MATHS 4* • ISBN 9780655708780

Four-digit subtraction from 1000s

1 thousand can be traded for 10 hundreds.

CONCEPT

We received 6000 books from the printers. We have sold 3721. How many do we have left?

	Th	H	T	U
		9	9	
	5	~~10~~	~~10~~	10
	~~6~~	~~0~~	~~0~~	~~0~~
−	3	7	2	1
	2	2	7	9

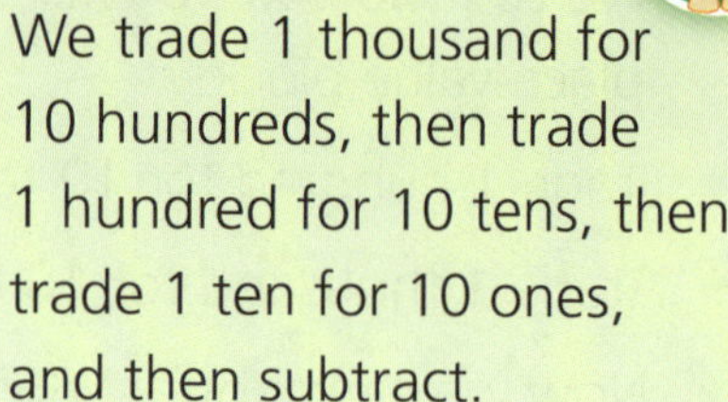

We trade 1 thousand for 10 hundreds, then trade 1 hundred for 10 tens, then trade 1 ten for 10 ones, and then subtract.

2279 books are left.

1

a 1000 − 436

b 2000 − 301

c 1000 − 897

d 3000 − 725

e 7000 − 1832

f 4000 − 2860

g 5000 − 3900

h 9000 − 4427

2

a 8000 − 3450

b 6000 − 2988

c 2000 − 1225

d 7000 − 5355

e 7000 − 4186

f 4000 − 2695

g 9000 − 8972

h 8000 − 1367

3

a The longest river in the world is the Nile in North Africa (6690 km). Australia's longest river system is the Murray–Darling which is 3370 km. How much shorter is this than the Nile?

b How much deeper is the Indian Ocean (7125 m at the Java Trench) than the Arctic Ocean (5450 m at the Eurasia Basin)?

c Mount Everest, the highest mountain on Earth, has an altitude of 8850 m. We needed to use a supply of oxygen as we climbed the last 5192 m of our ascent to the top. At what altitude did we begin to use oxygen?

d Tom McSeveny was born on 24 March 1916. How old was he on 24 March 2004?

e Chip Travers was born on 27 March 1913. How old was he on 27 March 2004?

● Use estimation to check your answers.

See 2:32 and 2:33 (Subtraction with trading to 999); 2:34 (Subtraction with 2 trades to 999).

 • *AUSTRALIAN SIGNPOST MATHS 4* • ISBN 9780655708780

Subtraction to 999 999

100 thousand can be traded for 10 ten-thousands.

HTh means hundred thousands.
TTh means ten thousands.

986 270 people left a country during a war, and 146 523 did not return. How many returned?

HTh	TTh	Th	H	T	U
		15			
	7	~~5~~	12	6	10
9	~~8~~	~~6~~	~~2~~	~~7~~	~~0~~
− 1	4	6	5	2	3
8	3	9	7	4	7

CONCEPT

¹2 means 12.

Another setting out:

```
  9 ⁷8̸ ¹⁵6̸ ¹2 ⁶7̸ ¹0
− 1  4   6   5  2   3
  8  3   9   7  4   7
```

839 747 returned.

1

a 56 340 − 9160

b 87 115 − 33 485

c 64 009 − 21 333

d 32 457 − 8098

e 96 000 − 81 000

f 89 693 − 65 355

g 65 250 − 9346

h 22 760 − 897

2

a 193 583 − 27 638

b 345 350 − 18 181

c 560 499 − 20 716

d 783 615 − 9999

e 620 650 − 136 177

f 750 000 − 385 000

g 684 326 − 232 895

Ask: Does the answer make sense?

3

a Mr Rich wanted to buy a house advertised for sale at $895 000. He offered $819 900 and the offer was accepted. How much less than the advertised price did he pay?

b Mr Rich earned $555 360 last year but had to pay $257 285 in tax. How much did he have left?

c The house Mr Rich bought was on 120 hectares of land. 45 000 m² of the land was covered with trees. How many square metres were not covered by trees? (1 ha = 10 000 m²)

d On this land, Mr Rich grew apple trees. This year he produced 112 000 apples. He sold 85 000 apples. How many were not sold?

e In February 2012 there were 842 300 part-time workers in Victoria. If 626 800 of the workers were in Melbourne, how many were outside of Melbourne?

See 2:32 and 2:33 (Subtraction with trading to 999); 2:34 (Subtraction with 2 trades to 999).

Comparing decimal measurements

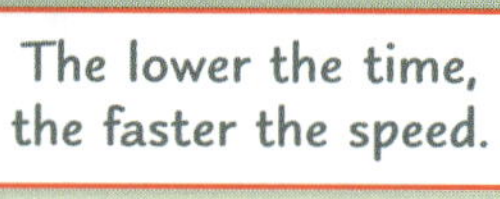

15·45 **s** means …

15 and forty-five hundredths **seconds**.

9·31 **s** means …

9 and thirty-one hundredths **seconds**.

1 Yes or No?

a The fastest time for a race is the smallest time. ☐

b 31·14 s is faster than 31·65 s. ☐

c 9·65 s is slower than 8·1 s. ☐

2 Match these race times to the number line to show their order.

21·43 s | 21·38 s | 21·8 s | 21·65 s | 22·36 s | 22·6 s | 22·48 s

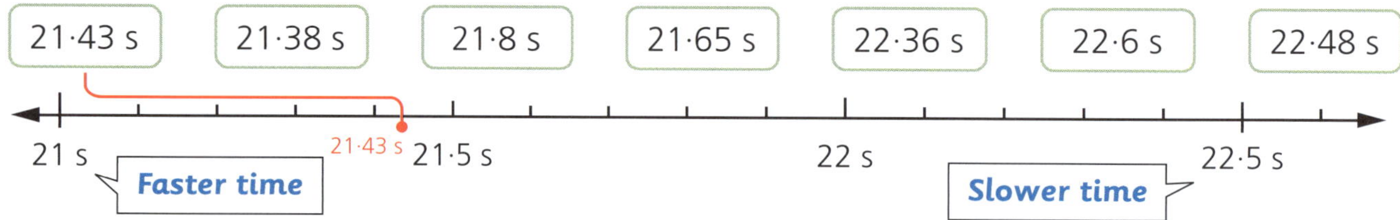

3 Circle the faster time (smallest decimal) in each pair.

a	b	c	d
4·75 s 4·70 s	31·46 s 30·40 s	39·74 s 40·06 s	59·60 s 59·50 s

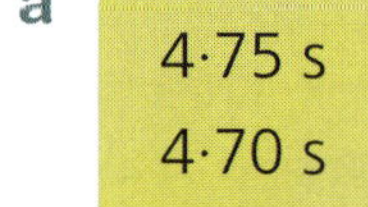

e	f	g	h
29·56 s 29·83 s	19·14 s 26·99 s	36·43 s 27·86 s	19·63 s 19·62 s

A stopwatch allows accurate measurement of time intervals.

4 These are the fastest times run over 100 metres in world competition up to 2023.

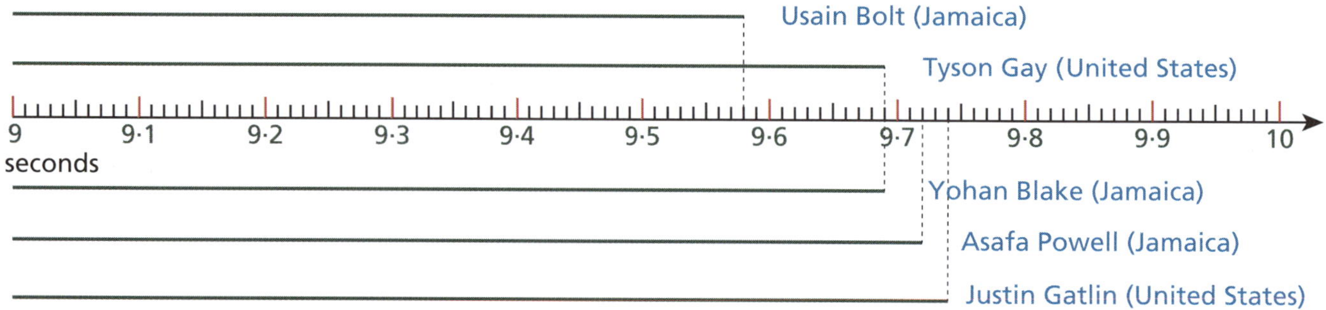

Use the number line above to write the time in seconds (using 2 decimal points) run by:

a Usain Bolt ☐ b Tyson Gay ☐ c Yohan Blake ☐

d Asafa Powell ☐ e Justin Gatlin ☐

See 3:30 (The passage of time).

 • ISBN 9780655708780

Answers

1:01

1 a
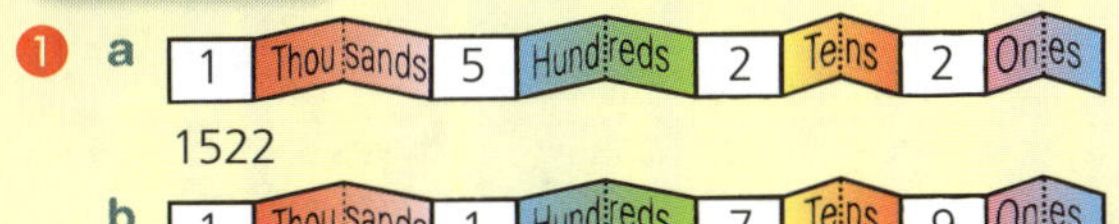

1522

b 1 Thousands 1 Hundreds 7 Tens 9 Ones
1179

2 a 3 b 4 c 4 d 3
e 4 f 3 g 2 h 4

3 a 1040 b 7018 c 5179 d 9007
e 2634 f 2600 g 8568 h 4030

4 a four thousand and twenty-three
b nine thousand and thirty
c seven thousand, five hundred
d two thousand, nine hundred and one

1:02

1 a 10 b 10 c 10 d 100
e 100 f 1000

2 a A b D c F d H

3 a E b A, B c E, F d A, B
e 10

1:03

1 a 3700 b 4200 c 1400 d 9300
e 6500 f 6700 g 9000 h 5900

2 a 32 000 b 83 000 c 11 000 d 57 000
e 23 000 f 52 000 g 47 000 h 69 000

3 a 50 000 b 80 000 c 30 000 d 90 000
e 90 000 f 30 000 g 70 000 h 70 000

4 a 52 967, 52 849, 52 621, 53 297, 53 346 will be circled.
b 79 621, 81 119, 75 000, 83 713, 76 014 will be circled.

5 a true b false c false d true
e true

6 2 Thousands 3 Hundreds 1 Tens 8 Ones

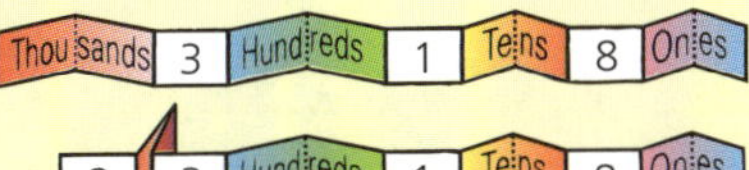

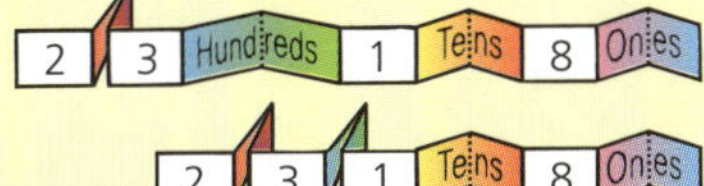

1:04

1 a $\frac{1}{12}$ b $\frac{2}{3}$ c $\frac{2}{6}$ d $\frac{3}{12}$ e $\frac{7}{12}$
f $\frac{5}{12}$ g $\frac{3}{6}$ h $\frac{11}{12}$

2 a $\frac{11}{12}$ b $\frac{1}{3}$ c $\frac{4}{6}$ d $\frac{9}{12}$ e $\frac{5}{12}$
f $\frac{7}{12}$ g $\frac{3}{6}$ h $\frac{1}{12}$

3 a b c d
e f g h

4 a $\frac{5}{6}$ b $\frac{3}{12}$ c $\frac{5}{12}$ d $\frac{11}{12}$ e $\frac{2}{6}$ f $\frac{9}{12}$

5 a $\frac{1}{6}$ b $\frac{9}{12}$ c $\frac{7}{12}$ d $\frac{1}{12}$ e $\frac{4}{6}$ f $\frac{3}{12}$

1:05

1 a $\frac{1}{2}$ b $\frac{1}{4}$ c $\frac{1}{4}$ d $\frac{1}{4}$ e $\frac{1}{2}$ f $\frac{1}{8}$

2 a b c
d e f
g h

3 a true b false c true d true e false f true

4 a $\frac{1}{2}$ b $\frac{1}{5}$ c $\frac{1}{10}$ d $\frac{1}{5}$
e $\frac{1}{2}$ f $\frac{3}{5}$ g $\frac{7}{10}$ h $\frac{3}{10}$

1:06

1 a $\frac{5}{4}$ b $\frac{4}{3}$ c $\frac{7}{6}$ d $\frac{3}{2}$ e $\frac{7}{4}$ f $\frac{11}{8}$

2 a $1\frac{3}{4}$ b $2\frac{2}{3}$ c $2\frac{1}{6}$ d $2\frac{1}{2}$ e $3\frac{3}{4}$ f $2\frac{3}{5}$

3 0, $\frac{1}{4}$, $\frac{2}{4}$, $\frac{3}{4}$, $\frac{4}{4}$, $\frac{5}{4}$, $\frac{6}{4}$, $\frac{7}{4}$, $\frac{8}{4}$ (continues below)
0, $\frac{1}{4}$, $\frac{2}{4}$, $\frac{3}{4}$, 1, $1\frac{1}{4}$, $1\frac{2}{4}$, $1\frac{3}{4}$, 2

$\frac{9}{4}$, $\frac{10}{4}$, $\frac{11}{4}$, $\frac{12}{4}$, $\frac{13}{4}$, $\frac{14}{4}$, $\frac{15}{4}$, $\frac{16}{4}$, $\frac{17}{4}$
$2\frac{1}{4}$, $2\frac{2}{4}$, $2\frac{3}{4}$, 3, $3\frac{1}{4}$, $3\frac{2}{4}$, $3\frac{3}{4}$, 4, $4\frac{1}{4}$

4 a $\frac{3}{2}$ b $\frac{11}{5}$ c $\frac{14}{4}$ d $\frac{9}{5}$
e $\frac{11}{4}$ f $\frac{13}{4}$ g $\frac{14}{3}$ h $\frac{21}{8}$

5 a $1\frac{3}{4}$ b $1\frac{4}{5}$ c $2\frac{3}{4}$ d $2\frac{1}{5}$
e $1\frac{3}{5}$ f $3\frac{1}{4}$ g $2\frac{4}{5}$ h $4\frac{1}{4}$

1:07

1 a $2\frac{1}{2}$
b $3\frac{1}{2}$, $\frac{7}{2}$, 7 halves
c $4\frac{1}{2}$, $\frac{9}{2}$, 9 halves
d $1\frac{1}{4}$, $\frac{5}{4}$, 5 quarters
e $2\frac{3}{4}$, $\frac{11}{4}$, 11 quarters
f $3\frac{3}{4}$, $\frac{15}{4}$, 15 quarters
g $2\frac{2}{3}$, $\frac{8}{3}$, 8 thirds
h $1\frac{2}{6}$, $\frac{8}{6}$, 8 sixths
i $2\frac{1}{5}$, $\frac{11}{5}$, 11 fifths

2 a 3, $3\frac{1}{3}$, $3\frac{2}{3}$ b five-thirds, six-thirds or 3

3 a 1 b $1\frac{1}{2}$ c 2 d $2\frac{1}{2}$

4 a $1\frac{2}{5}$ b $2\frac{1}{2}$ c $2\frac{3}{5}$ d $2\frac{1}{4}$
e $1\frac{5}{8}$ f $2\frac{2}{5}$ g $7\frac{1}{2}$ h $3\frac{2}{5}$

5 a $\frac{6}{5}$ b $\frac{11}{2}$ c $\frac{17}{5}$ d $\frac{19}{3}$
e $\frac{11}{8}$ f $\frac{17}{6}$ g $\frac{24}{5}$ h $\frac{17}{10}$

1:08

1 a 49 734 b 68 392 c 56 438 d 32 584

2

	T Thous	Thous	Hunds	Tens	Ones
a	2	6	3	2	4
b	3	5	1	6	2
c	8	2	9	7	0

3 a 34 528 b 67 934 c 58 462
d 92 748 e 82 359 f 48 673

4 Answers will vary, e.g. recording the population of towns.

1:09

1 a 49 768 b 37 281 c 84 971 d 345 022

2 a 26 301 b 69 309 c 692 997

3 a 28 747 b 50 378 c 839 625 d 417 713

4 a 526 493 b 895 651

5 a 8 thousands (8000) b 1 thousand (1000)
c 6 hundred thousands (600 000) d 8 tens (80)
e 9 hundreds (900) f 4 hundred thousands (400 000)

1:10

1 a $\frac{2}{2}$ or 1, $\frac{3}{2}$ or $1\frac{1}{2}$. Rule: Add $\frac{1}{2}$

b $\frac{3}{4}$, $\frac{4}{4}$ or 1. Rule: Add $\frac{1}{4}$

c $\frac{2}{3}$, $1\frac{2}{3}$, 2, $2\frac{1}{3}$, $2\frac{2}{3}$, $3\frac{1}{3}$. Rule: Add $\frac{1}{3}$

d $\frac{1}{8}$, $\frac{2}{8}$ or $\frac{1}{4}$, $\frac{3}{8}$, $\frac{4}{8}$ or $\frac{2}{4}$ or $\frac{1}{2}$, $\frac{5}{8}$, $\frac{6}{8}$ or $\frac{3}{4}$, $\frac{7}{8}$.
Rule: Subtract $\frac{1}{8}$

e $\frac{2}{5}$, $\frac{5}{5}$ or 1, $\frac{7}{5}$ or $1\frac{2}{5}$, $\frac{8}{5}$ or $1\frac{3}{5}$, $\frac{9}{5}$ or $1\frac{4}{5}$, $\frac{10}{5}$ or $1\frac{5}{5}$ or 2.
Rule: Add $\frac{1}{5}$

f $\frac{1}{6}$, $\frac{2}{6}$ or $\frac{1}{3}$, $\frac{3}{6}$ or $\frac{1}{2}$, $\frac{4}{6}$ or $\frac{2}{3}$, $\frac{5}{6}$, $\frac{6}{6}$ or 1, $1\frac{1}{6}$.
Rule: Subtract $\frac{1}{6}$

1:11

1 a $\frac{2}{10}$ b $\frac{2}{5}$ c $\frac{8}{10}$ d $\frac{3}{5}$
e $\frac{1}{2}$ f $\frac{4}{10}$ g $\frac{5}{10}$ h 1

2 a $\frac{1}{10}$ b $\frac{1}{2}$ c $\frac{3}{5}$ d $\frac{4}{5}$

3
0, $\frac{1}{4}$, $\frac{2}{4}$, $\frac{3}{4}$, 1 or $\frac{4}{4}$

0, $\frac{1}{8}$, $\frac{2}{8}$, $\frac{3}{8}$, $\frac{4}{8}$, $\frac{5}{8}$, $\frac{6}{8}$, $\frac{7}{8}$, 1 or $\frac{8}{8}$

4 a $\frac{2}{8}$ b $\frac{2}{4}$ or $\frac{1}{2}$ c $\frac{1}{2}$ or $\frac{4}{8}$ d $\frac{2}{4}$ or $\frac{4}{8}$
e $\frac{3}{4}$ f $\frac{6}{8}$ g $\frac{1}{4}$ h $\frac{2}{2}$ or $\frac{4}{4}$ (or 1)

5 a true b true c false d yes e yes

1:12

1 a $\frac{1}{2}$ or $\frac{4}{8}$ b $\frac{1}{2}$ or $\frac{2}{4}$ c $\frac{3}{4}$
d 1 or $\frac{2}{2}$ or $\frac{8}{8}$ e $\frac{2}{2}$ or $\frac{4}{4}$ or $\frac{8}{8}$ f $\frac{2}{4}$ or $\frac{4}{8}$

2 a $\frac{1}{3}$ b $\frac{2}{3}$ c 1 or $\frac{2}{2}$ or $\frac{3}{3}$
d 1 or $\frac{2}{2}$ or $\frac{6}{6}$ e $\frac{2}{6}$ f $\frac{4}{6}$

3 a T b T c T d F e T f T

4 a T b T c T d F e F f T

5 a $\frac{4}{3}$, $\frac{5}{3}$, $\frac{6}{3}$, $\frac{7}{3}$ or $1\frac{1}{3}$, $1\frac{2}{3}$, 2, $2\frac{1}{3}$

b $\frac{4}{4}$, $\frac{5}{4}$, $\frac{6}{4}$, $\frac{7}{4}$, $\frac{8}{4}$ or 1, $1\frac{1}{4}$, $1\frac{2}{4}$, (or $1\frac{1}{2}$), $1\frac{3}{4}$, 2

c $\frac{4}{6}$, $\frac{5}{6}$, $\frac{6}{6}$, $\frac{7}{6}$, $\frac{8}{6}$, $\frac{9}{6}$ or $\frac{4}{6}$, $\frac{5}{6}$, 1, $1\frac{1}{6}$, $1\frac{2}{6}$, $1\frac{3}{6}$, (or $1\frac{1}{2}$)

d $\frac{4}{8}$, $\frac{5}{8}$, $\frac{6}{8}$, $\frac{7}{8}$, $\frac{8}{8}$, $\frac{9}{8}$, $\frac{10}{8}$
or $\frac{4}{8}$, $\frac{5}{8}$, $\frac{6}{8}$, $\frac{7}{8}$, 1, $1\frac{1}{8}$, $1\frac{2}{8}$ (or $1\frac{1}{4}$)

6 three-quarters, four-quarters, five-quarters, six-quarters

1:13

1 a 26 000 000 b 310 000 000

2 a 82 483 000 b 19 642 000 c 6 372 840
d 85 945 000

3

	Ten millions	Millions	Hundred thousands	Ten thousands	Thousands	Hundreds	Tens	Ones
a		7	3	0	2	4	2	4
b	7	1	6	5	0	8	9	5
c	5	5	6	5	0	0	0	0
d			8	6	9	0	0	0

1:14

1 a 5 000 000 b 3 000 000 c 11 000 000
d 22 000 000 e 9 000 000 f 14 000 000

2 a 9 264 000 b 12 648 000 c 42 256 000
d 7 888 000 e 13 706 000 f 67 436 000

3 a 12 563 852 will be circled. 12 099 762 will be underlined.
b 8 730 132 will be circled. 8 373 964 will be underlined.
c 36 832 000 will be circled. 35 932 000 will be underlined.
d 10 102 533 will be circled. 9 476 350 will be underlined.
e 12 261 032 will be circled. 9 643 850 will be underlined.
f 23 618 864 will be circled. 23 609 320 will be underlined.

4 a 3 millions (or 3 000 000) b 0 hundred thousands
c 20 millions (or 20 000 000) d 60 thousands (or 60 000)
e 5 millions (or 5 000 000) f 50 thousand (or 50 000)

Activity: Answers will vary, e.g. a house, a shop, a large business.

 AUSTRALIAN SIGNPOST MATHS 4 • ISBN 9780655708780

1:15

1. a $\frac{10}{100}$ b $\frac{16}{100}$ c $\frac{32}{100}$ d $\frac{48}{100}$
   e $\frac{57}{100}$ f $\frac{69}{100}$ g $\frac{83}{100}$ h $\frac{91}{100}$
2. a 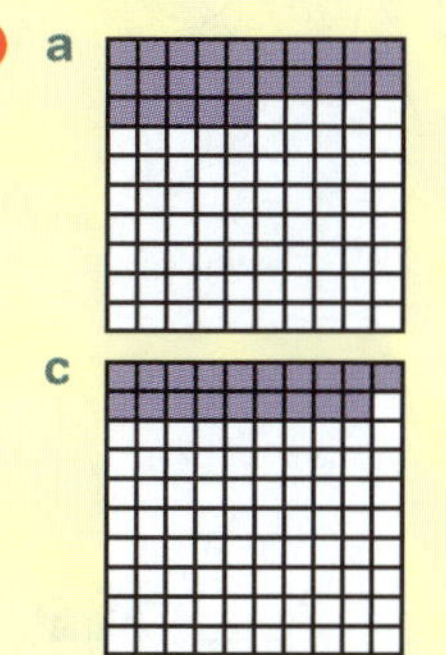 b 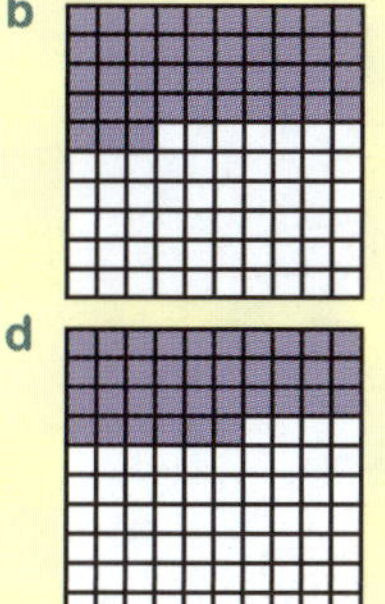
   c d
3. Estimates will vary. $\frac{30}{100}$ has been covered.
   Pictures will vary.

1:16

1. 100
2. a 16 out of 100 $\frac{16}{100}$ 0·16
   b 27 out of 100 $\frac{27}{100}$ 0·27
   c 18 out of 100 $\frac{18}{100}$ 0·18
   d 45 out of 100 $\frac{45}{100}$ 0·45
3. 0·39
4. a 0·36, $\frac{36}{100}$ b 0·79, $\frac{79}{100}$ c 0·57, $\frac{57}{100}$
   d 0·85, $\frac{85}{100}$ e 0·27, $\frac{27}{100}$ f 0·18, $\frac{18}{100}$
   g 0·62, $\frac{62}{100}$ h 0·44, $\frac{44}{100}$

1:17

1. a 0·7 b 0·5 c 0·6 d 0·1 e 0·8 f 0·9
   g 0·2 h 0·4 i 1·1 j 1·3 k 1·9 l 1·8
2. a 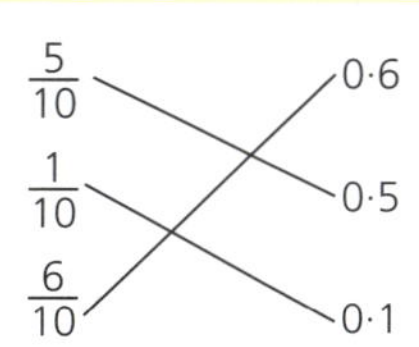

   b 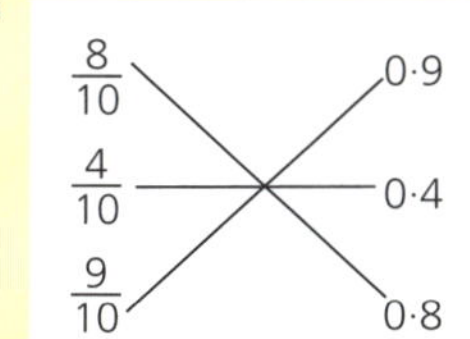

   c 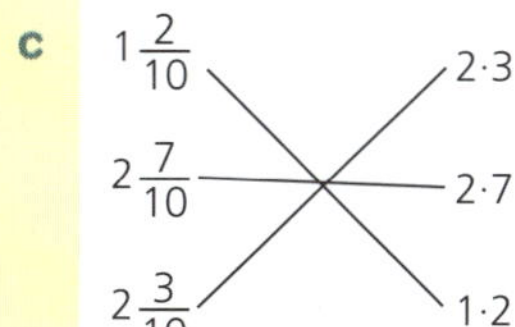

3. a 0·9 b 0·7 c 0·6 d 0·2 e 0·8 f 0·3
   g 0·5 h 1·0 or 1 i 0·1 j 0·8 k 0·5 l 1·9
   m 1·3 n 1·0
4. 0 $\frac{1}{10}$ $\frac{2}{10}$ $\frac{3}{10}$ $\frac{4}{10}$ $\frac{5}{10}$ $\frac{6}{10}$ $\frac{7}{10}$ $\frac{8}{10}$ $\frac{9}{10}$ 1
   0 0·1 0·2 0·3 0·4 0·5 0·6 0·7 0·8 0·9 1·0

5. a 0·7 b 0·25 c 0·5 d 0·15

1:18

1. A 0·34 B 0·50 C 0·30
   D 0·06 E 0·03
2. a C b A c A d D e B
   f B g C h B i B j A
3. a C b A c B d A e B
4. a 0·28 b 0·85 c 0·49 d 0·37
5. 1·4 1·5 1·6 1·7 1·8 1·9 2 2·1 2·2 2·3 2·4 2·5 2·6 2·7
6. a 0·3 b 0·7 c 0·37 d
   0·61 e 0·5 f 0·9
   g 0·3 h 0·2 i 1·21 j 2.23 k 2·4 l 2·2

1:19

1. Each decimal will be modelled by placing tens blocks (rods) and ones blocks (units) on top of a hundreds block.
   a 0·3 b 0·06 c 0·09 d 0·5 e 0·9
   f 0·02 g 0·4 h 0·1 i 0·05 j 0·7
2. 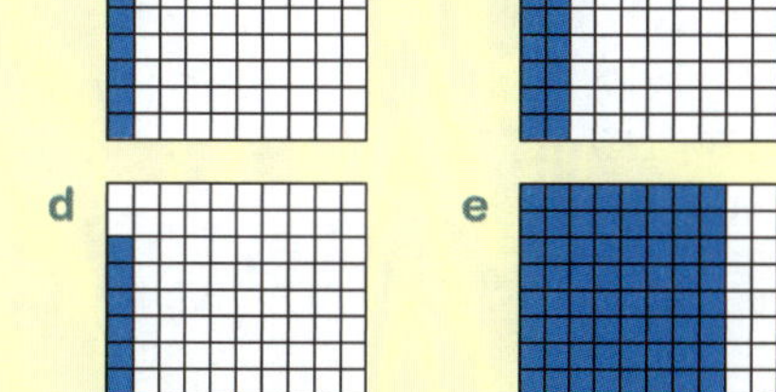
   d e
3. a 5 rods b 3 units c 4 rods and 7 units
   d 3 rods e 7 rods f 2 units
   g 6 units h 4 rods i 5 rods and 2 units
   j 8 rods and 9 units k 7 rods and 2 units
   l 6 rods and 7 units m 9 rods and 9 units

1:20

1. a 1·48 b 1·46 c 1·62 d 1·59 e 1·61
2.

	Units		Tenths	Hundredths
a	2	·	5	9
b	6	·	7	3
c	9	·	4	1
d	5	·	2	6
e	8	·	4	8
f	7	·	1	3
g	6	·	7	9

3. a 2 hundredths b 4 tenths c 3 units (or 3 ones)
   d 8 hundredths e 1 unit (or 1 one) f 5 tenths
   g 2 units (or 2 ones) h 2 hundredths
   i 6 tenths i 1 hundredth
   j 8 rods and 9 units k 7 rods and 2 units
   l 6 rods and 7 units m 9 rods and 9 units

 • AUSTRALIAN SIGNPOST MATHS 4 • ISBN 9780655708780

1:21

Header: No

1. a 19·75 b 40·91 c 67·82 d 30·06
   e 52·14 f 27·43
2. a 8 tenths and 6 hundredths b 0 tenths and 9 hundredths
   c 6 tenths and 0 hundredths
3. a 629·37 b 463·09 c 731·6 d 957·42
   e 5·6 f 10·3 g 2·8 h 7·9
4. a 6 tens b 9 units (or ones) c 8 hundreds
   d 4 tenths e 2 hundredths f 3 tenths
   g 1 ten h 5 tens i 8 tenths
   j 9 hundredths k 6 tenths l 5 hundredths

2:01

1. a 5, 6, 7, 8, 9, 10, 11
   b 10, 12, 14, 16, 18, 20, 22
   c 15, 18, 21, 24, 27, 30, 33
   d 20, 24, 28, 32, 36, 40, 44
   e 25, 30, 35, 40, 45, 50, 55
   f 30, 36, 42, 48, 54, 60, 66
   g 35, 42, 49, 56, 63, 70, 77
   h 40, 48, 56, 64, 72, 80, 88
   i 45, 54, 63, 72, 81, 90, 99
   j 50, 60, 70, 80, 90, 100, 110
2. a 12, 13 b 24, 26 c 36, 39 d 48, 52
   e 60, 65 f 72, 78 g 84, 91 h 96, 104
   i 108, 117 j 120, 130
3. a The last digits 2, 4, 6, 8 and 0 repeat.
   b The last digits 0, 4, 8, 2 and 6 repeat.
   c The last digits 5 and 0 repeat.
   d The last digits 0, 6, 2, 8 and 4 repeat.
   e The last digits 0, 8, 6, 4 and 2 repeat.
   f The last digit decreases by 1 for each term, i.e. 5, 4, 3, 2, 1, 0, 9. (Once it reaches 0 it goes back to 9.)
   g The last digit is always 0.
4. Answers will vary.

2:02

1.

×	0	1	2	3	4	5	6	7	8	9	10
1	0	1	2	3	4	5	6	7	8	9	10
2	0	2	4	6	8	10	12	14	16	18	20
3	0	3	6	9	12	15	18	21	24	27	30
5	0	5	10	15	20	25	30	35	40	45	50
10	0	10	20	30	40	50	60	70	80	90	100

2. a ×2: 0, 14, 8, 18, 10, 4, 16, 6, 20, 12 (inner: 0, 7, 4, 9, 5, 2, 8, 3, 10, 6)
   b ×5: 45, 35, 25, 10, 50, 15, 30, 5, 40, 20 (inner: 9, 7, 5, 2, 10, 3, 6, 1, 8, 4)
   c ×3: 3, 6, 15, 30, 21, 12, 27, 18, 24, 9 (inner: 1, 2, 5, 10, 7, 4, 9, 6, 8, 3)
3. a 4 b 30 c 70 d 10 e 12 f 8 g 60 h 14

2:03

1. a 2, 4 b 14, 28 c 20, 40 d 16, 32
2. a 24 b 28 c 16 d 36 e 32
3.

×	0	1	2	3	4	5	6	7	8	9	10
2	0	2	4	6	8	10	12	14	16	18	20
4	0	4	8	12	16	20	24	28	32	36	40

4. a 3 × 4 = 12 b 5 × 4 = 20 c 10 × 4 = 40 d 11 × 4 = 44
5. a ×2: 2, 8, 0, 12, 18, 4, 14, 10, 6, 16 (inner: 1, 4, 0, 6, 9, 2, 7, 5, 3, 8)
   b

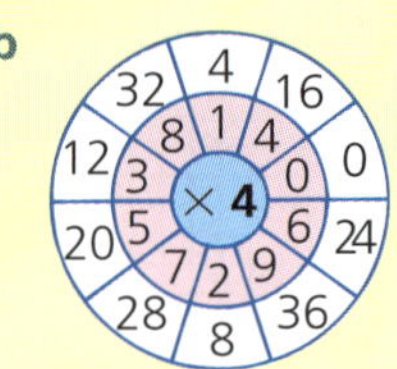

2:04

a ×4

0 × 4	4
1 × 4	12
2 × 4	0
3 × 4	20
4 × 4	8
5 × 4	16
6 × 4	36
7 × 4	24
8 × 4	40
9 × 4	28
10 × 4	32

b ×4

3 × 4	0
0 × 4	12
5 × 4	4
1 × 4	28
7 × 4	20
2 × 4	32
8 × 4	40
4 × 4	8
6 × 4	36
10 × 4	24
9 × 4	16

c ×

6 × 10	0
3 × 1	10
4 × 0	2
5 × 2	3
2 × 1	60
7 × 2	12
4 × 10	10
6 × 2	80
10 × 1	14
9 × 2	40
8 × 10	18

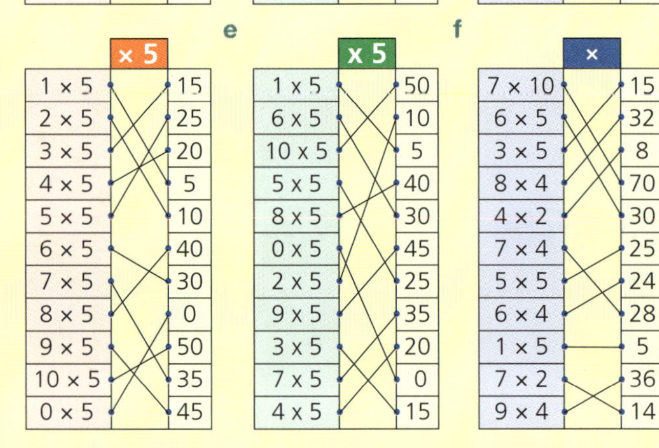

2:05

Header: 9 tens and 5 ones

1. a 98 b 93 c 97 d 38 e $69 f $38 g $88 h $78
2. a 69 b 75 c 76 d 69 e 76 f 78 g 69 h 88
   i $87 j $88 k $77 l $99

2:06

Concept box: 1 ten and 3 ones

1. a 23 b 35 c 32 d 37 e 1 f 26 g 33 h 10
   i $4 j $30 k $67 l $44
2. a 88 candles b 69 lollies
3. a $6779 b 27
4. a 47 – 35 = 12 b 56 – 34 = 22 c 74 – 61 = 13

2:07

1. a 41 b 90 c 73 d 84 e 43 f 82 g 90 h 95 i 92 j 90 k 51 l 84
2. a $71 b $62 c $66 d $62
3. a 61 b 84 c 55

2:08

1. a 94 b 90 c 97 d 74 e 99 f 86 g 85 h 92 i $93 j $71 k $76 l $71
2. a 30 emus b 83 kiwis c 54 metres d 40 birds

2:09

Header: 68, 78, 38, 48, 69, 79

1. a 55 b 83 c 84 d 84 e 84 f 83
2. a 58 b 71 c 87 d 81 e 82 f 76

2:10

Header: 32, 22, 62, 52, 21, 11

1. a 57 b 13

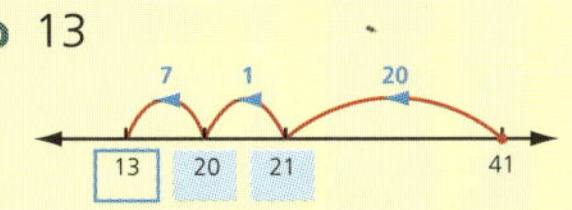

c 27 d 44 e 17 f 57

2. a 35 b 27 c 26 d 39 e 36 f 16

2:11

1. a 8 b 16 c 24 d 32 e 40 f 48 g 56 h 64 i 72 j 40, 80 k 4, 8 l 8, 16 m 12, 24 n 24, 48 o 20, 40
2. a 24 b 48 c 40 d 32 e 56 f 64 g 8 h 72 i 16 j 0 k 80 l 88
3.

×	0	1	2	3	4	5	6	7	8	9	10
8	0	8	16	24	32	40	48	56	64	72	80

×	5	3	7	4	2	9	10	1	8	6	0
2	10	6	14	8	4	18	20	2	16	12	0
4	20	12	28	16	8	36	40	4	32	24	0
8	40	24	56	32	16	72	80	8	64	48	0
3	15	9	21	12	6	27	30	3	24	18	0

2:12

a

× 8	
0 × 8	16
1 × 8	24
2 × 8	0
3 × 8	48
4 × 8	8
5 × 8	32
6 × 8	56
7 × 8	80
8 × 8	40
9 × 8	64
10 × 8	72

b

× 8	
3 × 8	0
0 × 8	24
5 × 8	56
1 × 8	64
7 × 8	32
2 × 8	8
8 × 8	40
4 × 8	80
6 × 8	16
10 × 8	72
9 × 8	48

c

×	
10 × 6	72
3 × 4	40
9 × 8	30
5 × 6	60
5 × 8	16
7 × 8	12
4 × 4	64
8 × 4	24
8 × 8	56
3 × 8	48
6 × 8	32

d

× 5	
1 × 5	10
2 × 5	20
3 × 5	5
4 × 5	35
5 × 5	0
6 × 5	15
7 × 5	30
8 × 5	25
9 × 5	50
10 × 5	40
0 × 5	45

e

× 5	
1 × 3	24
6 × 3	30
10 x 3	0
5 × 3	3
8 × 3	18
0 × 3	15
2 × 3	27
9 × 3	21
3 × 3	12
7 × 3	6
4 × 3	9

f

×	
7 × 4	24
6 × 4	28
3 × 4	32
8 × 4	16
4 × 4	32
8 × 4	20
5 × 4	12
6 × 4	36
1 × 4	28
7 × 4	4
9 × 4	24

2:13

1. a 62 b 74 c 81 d 103 e 73 f 76 g 96 h 82 i 84
2. a 76 b 79 c 92 d 82 e $91 f $80

Investigation: Adding 3 odd numbers gives an <u>odd</u> number.

2:14

1 a 61 + 88 = 149,149 b 94 + 53 = 147,147

2 a 118 b 138 c 157 d 106 e 159 f 128 g 155 h 127 i 129

3 Estimates for Question 1

a 60 + 90 = 150 b 90 + 50 =140

Estimates for Question 2

a 60 + 60 = 120 b 90 + 50 = 140

c 90 + 70 = 160 d 60 + 40 = 100

e 70 + 90 = 160 f 40 + 90 = 130

g 90 + 60 = 150 h 60 + 60 = 120

i 70 + 60 = 130

2:15

1 a 49 b 64 c 83 d 91 e 51 f 37

2 a 77 b 45 c 87 d 91

2:16

1 a 6 b 12 c 18 d 24 e 30 f 36 g 42 h 48 i 54 j 30, 60 k 3, 6 l 6, 12 m 9, 18 n 18, 36 o 15, 30

2 a 18 b 36 c 30 d 24 e 42 f 48 g 6 h 54 i 12 j 0 k 60 l 66

3

×	0	1	2	3	4	5	6	7	8	9	10
3	0	3	6	9	12	15	18	21	24	27	30
6	0	6	12	18	24	30	36	42	48	54	60

×	5	3	7	4	2	9	10	1	8	6	0
3	15	9	21	12	6	27	30	3	24	18	0
6	30	18	42	24	12	54	60	6	48	36	0

2:17

a

× 3	
0 × 3	6
1 × 3	9
2 × 3	0
3 × 3	18
4 × 3	3
5 × 3	12
6 × 3	21
7 × 3	30
8 × 3	15
9 × 3	24
10 × 3	27

b

× 3	
3 × 3	0
0 × 3	9
5 × 3	21
1 × 3	24
7 × 3	12
2 × 3	3
8 × 3	15
4 × 3	30
6 × 3	6
10 × 3	27
9 × 3	18

c

×	
8 × 5	27
7 × 2	80
9 × 3	56
7 × 8	40
8 × 10	0
6 × 1	14
4 × 0	24
9 × 5	35
8 × 3	6
7 × 5	72
9 × 8	45

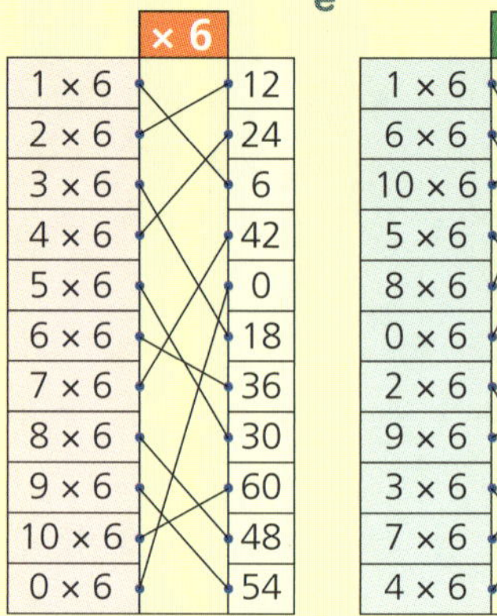

d

× 6	
1 × 6	12
2 × 6	24
3 × 6	6
4 × 6	42
5 × 6	0
6 × 6	18
7 × 6	36
8 × 6	30
9 × 6	60
10 × 6	48
0 × 6	54

e

× 6	
1 × 6	48
6 × 6	60
10 × 6	0
5 × 6	6
8 × 6	36
0 × 6	30
2 × 6	54
9 × 6	42
3 × 6	24
7 × 6	12
4 × 6	18

f

×	
7 × 3	42
7 × 6	21
6 × 3	36
6 × 6	24
8 × 3	48
8 × 6	15
5 × 3	18
5 × 6	12
9 × 3	54
9 × 6	27
4 × 3	30

2:18

1 a 26 b 36 c 37 d 44 e 19 f 18 g 73 h 47 i 38 j 18

2 a 26 b $45

2:19

1 a

Tens	Ones
4	10
~~5~~	~~0~~

b

Tens	Ones
6	10
~~7~~	~~0~~

c

Tens	Ones
3	10
~~4~~	~~0~~

d

Tens	Ones
8	10
~~9~~	~~0~~

2 a 52 b 46 c 83 d 24 e 9 f 35 g 18 h 7 i 16 j 31 k $14 l $13 m $45 n $48

3 $62

2:20

1 a 6 b 7 c 8 d 7 e 18 f 16 g 19 h 15 i 16 j 19 k 38 l 44 m 28 n 29 o 19 p 55 q $26 r $18 s $37

2:21

1 a 9 b 18 c 27 d 36 e 45 f 54 g 63 h 72 i 81 j 90, 9

2 a 90 b 81 c 72 d 63 e 54 f 45 g 36 h 27 i 18 j 9

3 a 45 b 81 c 63 d 72 e 36 f 9 g 27 h 54 i 18

3

×	0	1	2	3	4	5	6	7	8	9	10
3	0	3	6	9	12	15	18	21	24	27	30
9	0	9	18	27	36	45	54	63	72	81	90

×	5	3	7	4	2	9	10	1	8	6	0
3	15	9	21	12	6	27	30	3	24	18	0
9	45	27	63	36	18	81	90	9	72	54	0

2:22

a

	× 9	
0 × 9		18
1 × 9		27
2 × 9		0
3 × 9		54
4 × 9		9
5 × 9		36
6 × 9		63
7 × 9		90
8 × 9		45
9 × 9		72
10 × 9		81

b

	× 9	
3 × 9		0
0 × 9		27
5 × 9		63
1 × 9		72
7 × 9		36
2 × 9		9
8 × 9		45
4 × 9		90
6 × 9		18
10 × 9		81
9 × 9		54

c

	×	
8 × 4		27
7 × 5		72
9 × 3		56
7 × 8		32
8 × 9		16
6 × 9		35
4 × 4		24
9 × 5		63
8 × 3		54
7 × 9		48
6 × 8		45

d

	× 9	
6 × 9		9
1 × 9		90
3 × 9		54
10 × 9		18
5 × 9		0
7 × 9		27
2 × 9		63
8 × 9		45
4 × 9		81
9 × 9		72
0 × 9		36

e

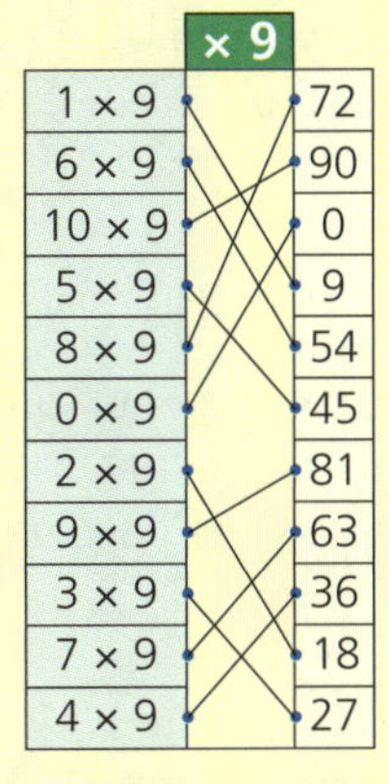

	× 9	
1 × 9		72
6 × 9		90
10 × 9		0
5 × 9		9
8 × 9		54
0 × 9		45
2 × 9		81
9 × 9		63
3 × 9		36
7 × 9		18
4 × 9		27

f

	×	
7 × 2		42
7 × 6		14
6 × 3		30
6 × 5		8
8 × 1		72
8 × 9		20
5 × 4		18
5 × 10		36
9 × 0		54
9 × 6		0
4 × 9		50

2:23

1 a 154 b 117 c 108 d 283 e 790
f 388 g 516 h 510 i 428 j 331
k 514 l 733

2 a 60 + 90 = 150 b 70 + 50 = 120 c 30 + 80 = 110
d 260 + 30 = 290 e 80 + 700 = 780 f 400 + 20 = 420
g 400 + 80 = 480 h 400 + 90 = 490 i 90 + 300 = 390
j 200 + 100 = 300 k 400 + 100 = 500 l 500 + 300 = 800

2:24

1 a 328 b 601 c 815 d 713 e 561
f 456 g 342 h 463 i 570 j 293

2 a 365 b 605 c 628 d 779 e 414
f 819 f 819

2:25

Header: 800

1 a 334 b 662 c 361 d 432 e 615
f 531 g 792 h 657 i 727 j 762
k 321 l 731 m 805 n 640 o 962

2 a 432 minutes b 374 people c 377 bags d 921 m²

2:26

1 a 8 b 13 c 14 d 24 e 1 f 125
g 96 h 30 i 10

2 a Add 2 b Add 4 c Subtract 2
d Multiply by 2 e Divide by 3 f Multiply by 5
g Subtract 1 h Add 7 i Divide by 2

3 a 7, 14, 21 b 21, 16, 11 c 4, 16, 64
d 44, 22, 11 e 34, 45, 56 f 38, 29, 20
g 12, 24, 48 h 9, 3, 1

4 a 4, 8, 12, 16, … Add 4 b 5, 9, 13, 17, … Add 4

2:27

1 a 40, 35, 30, 25 b 137, 147, 157, 167
c 995, 1095, 1195, 1295 d 1696, 2696, 3696, 4696

2 a 77 b 99 c 400 d 88
e 1543 f 500 g $3\frac{1}{2}$ h 2

3 a 40, 100, 120 b 499, 509, 529 c 2, $2\frac{1}{2}$ d 40, 56

4 a

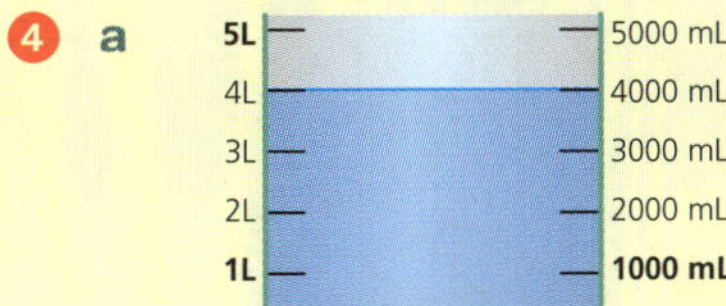

Volume of water = 4 L or 4000 mL.

b

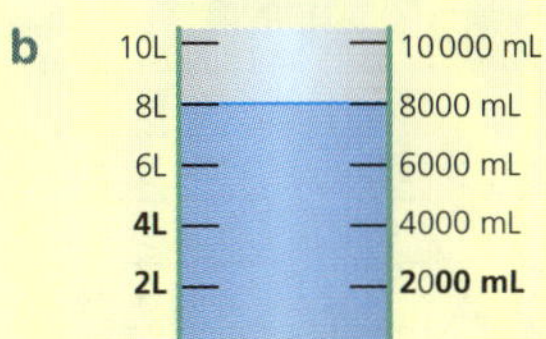

Volume of water = 8 L or 8000 mL.

5 a 4 kg, 5 kg b 4000 g, 5000 g
c 8 km, 9 km d 8000 m, 9000 m
e 8 kg, 10 kg f 8000 g, 10 000 g or 10 kg

2:28

1 a 21 b 21 c 28 d 28 e 35
f 35 g 42 h 42 i 56 j 56
k 63 l 49

2 a 0 b 0 c 7 d 7 e 14
f 14 g 21 h 21 i 40 j 72
k 48 l 64

3 a 28 b 42 c 56 d 49 e 70
f 63 g 42 h 63

×	0	1	2	3	4	5	6	7	8	9	10
4	0	4	8	12	16	20	24	28	32	36	40
2	0	2	4	6	8	10	12	14	16	18	20
5	0	5	10	15	20	25	30	35	40	45	50
8	0	8	16	24	32	40	48	56	64	72	60
1	0	1	2	3	4	5	6	7	8	9	10
6	0	6	12	18	24	30	36	42	48	54	60
3	0	3	6	9	12	15	18	21	24	27	30
0	0	0	0	0	0	0	0	0	0	0	0
9	0	9	18	27	36	45	54	63	72	81	90
10	0	10	20	30	40	50	60	70	80	90	100
7	0	7	14	21	28	35	42	49	56	63	70

4

×	0	1	2	3	4	5	6	7	8	9	10
7	0	7	14	21	28	35	42	49	56	63	70

×	5	3	7	4	2	9	10	1	8	6	0
7	35	21	49	28	14	63	70	7	56	42	0

2:29

a

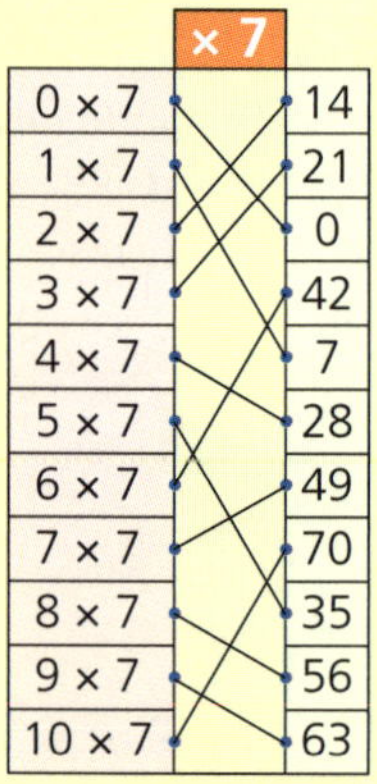

× 7	
0 × 7	14
1 × 7	21
2 × 7	0
3 × 7	42
4 × 7	7
5 × 7	28
6 × 7	49
7 × 7	70
8 × 7	35
9 × 7	56
10 × 7	63

b

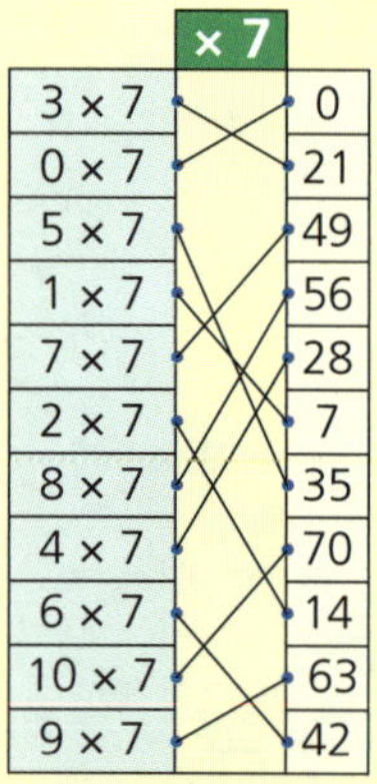

× 7	
3 × 7	0
0 × 7	21
5 × 7	49
1 × 7	56
7 × 7	28
2 × 7	7
8 × 7	35
4 × 7	70
6 × 7	14
10 × 7	63
9 × 7	42

c

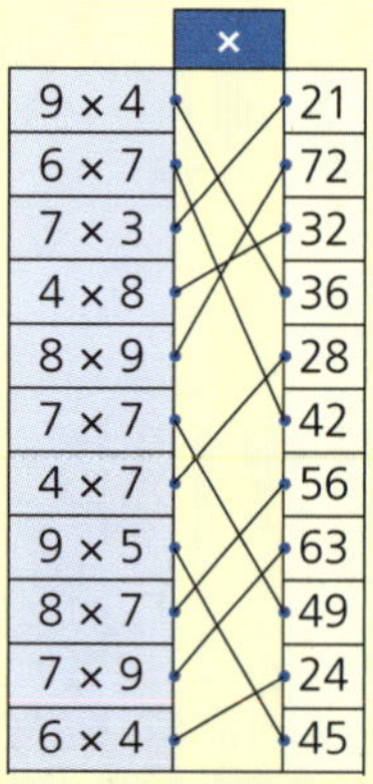

×	
9 × 4	21
6 × 7	72
7 × 3	32
4 × 8	36
8 × 9	28
7 × 7	42
4 × 7	56
9 × 5	63
8 × 7	49
7 × 9	24
6 × 4	45

d

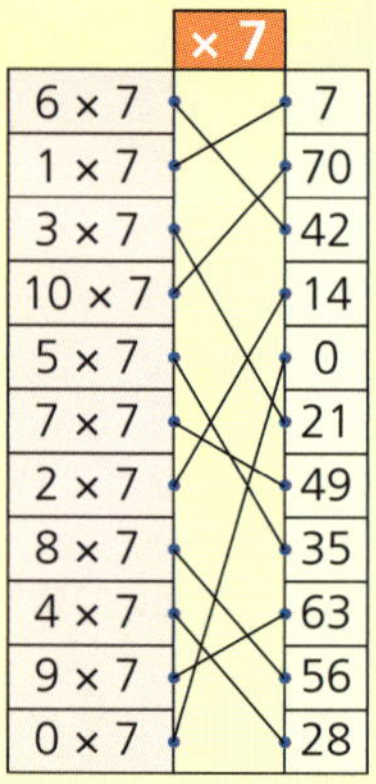

× 7	
6 × 7	7
1 × 7	70
3 × 7	42
10 × 7	14
5 × 7	0
7 × 7	21
2 × 7	49
8 × 7	35
4 × 7	63
9 × 7	56
0 × 7	28

e

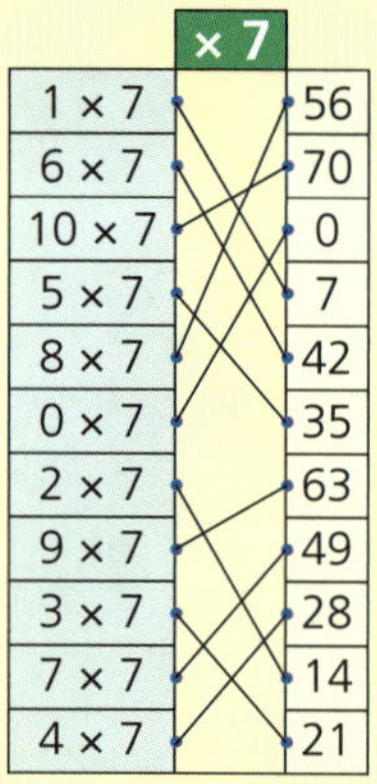

× 7	
1 × 7	56
6 × 7	70
10 × 7	0
5 × 7	7
8 × 7	42
0 × 7	35
2 × 7	63
9 × 7	49
3 × 7	28
7 × 7	14
4 × 7	21

f

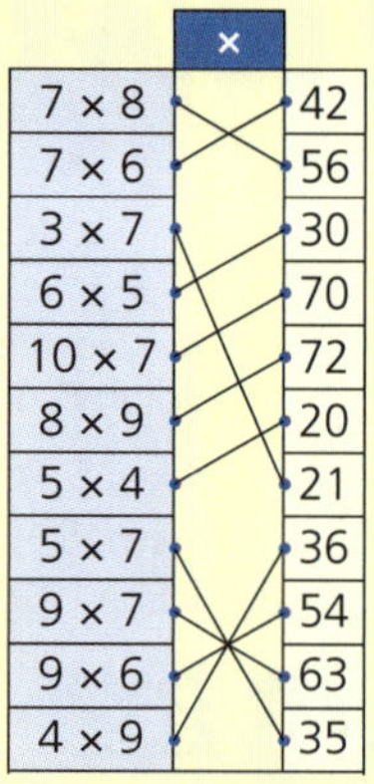

×	
7 × 8	42
7 × 6	56
3 × 7	30
6 × 5	70
10 × 7	72
8 × 9	20
5 × 4	21
5 × 7	36
9 × 7	54
9 × 6	63
4 × 9	35

2:30

1 a

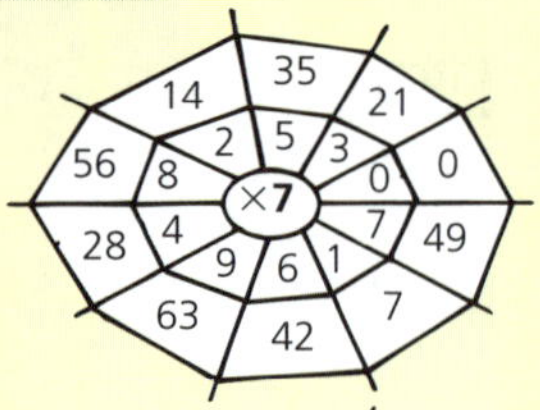

×7	
5	35
3	21
0	0
7	49
1	7
6	42
9	63
4	28
8	56
2	14

b

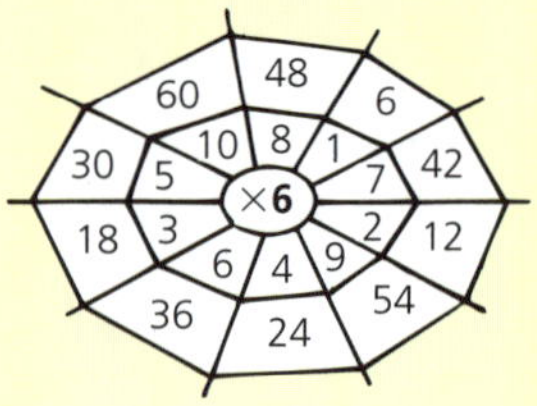

×6	
8	48
1	6
7	42
2	12
9	54
4	24
6	36
3	18
5	30
10	60

c

×9	
7	63
10	90
0	0
6	54
3	27
9	81
4	36
5	45
1	9
8	72

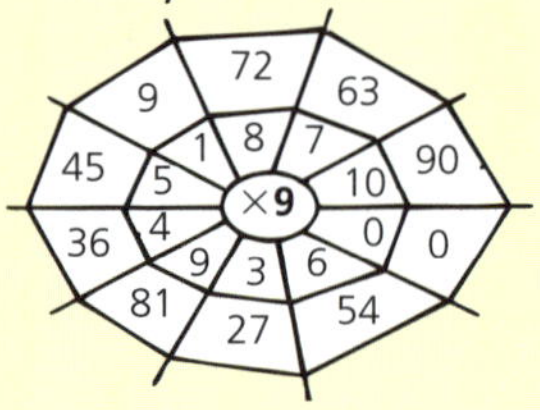

2 a 28 b 28 c 45 d 90 e 90 f 27
g 54 h 54 i 36 j 72 k 63 l 81
m 27 n 49 o 72 p 63 q 45 r 36

3 a 12 b 30 c 18 d 12 e 30 f 18
g 6 h 24

4 a 42 b 0 c 21 d 45 e 36 f 48

5

×	5	3	7	4	2	9	10	1	8	6	0
3	15	9	21	12	6	27	30	3	24	18	0
9	45	27	63	36	18	81	90	9	72	54	0

2:31

1 a 2 hundreds 4 tens 5 ones
b 6 hundreds 4 tens 5 ones
c 131 d 733 e 533 f 331
g 674 h 934 i 682 j 743
k 362 l 129 m 123 n 443
o 178 p 429 q 70 r 205

2:32

1 a 528 b 315 c 229 d 421 e 264
f 108 g 836 h 908 i 711 j 315
k 248 l 628 m 727 n 55 o 105
p 608 q 6 r 734 s 16

 • *AUSTRALIAN SIGNPOST MATHS 4* • ISBN 9780655708780

2:33

1 a 464 b 255 c 194 d 691 e 376
f 255 g 594 h 40 i 311 j 291
k 312 l 638 m 625 n 80 o 193
p 206 q 434 r 491

2:34

1 a 258 b 179 c 34 d 646 e 274
f 63 g 489 h 589 i 138 j 177
k 659 l 567 m 29 n 99 o 87
p 28 q 457 r 417 s 228

2:35

1 a 81 b 90 c 1200
2 a 269 b 709 c 239
3 a 544 b 795 c 852
4 a 401 b 386 c 652
5 a 539 b 897 c 977
d 985 e 788 f 878
6 a 294 b 456 c 416

+50 +2 +4
238 288 290 294

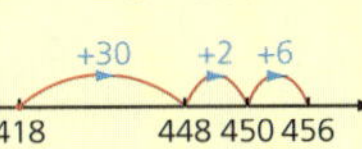

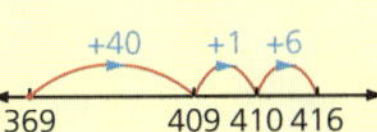

7 a 711 b 908 c 823
8 Strategies will vary.
a 399 b 99 c 431
d 84 e 1700 f 583

2:36

1 a 289 b 522 c 635 d 423 e 780 f 372
g 641 h 682 i 526
2 a 808 b 208 c 911 d 515 e 815 f 511
g 917 h 807 i 728
3 a 734 b 212 c 569 d 326 e 685 f 178
g 445 h 538 i 333
4 a 724 b 121 c 608 d 536 e 174 f 813
g 512 h 236 i 844

2:37

1 a 73 b 162 c 839 d 545 e 398
f 107 g 294 h 47
2 a 66 b 101 c 126 d 32
3 a 113 points b 419 albums c 253 books

2:38

1 a 63 b 252 c 829 d 231 e 215
f 63 g 79 h 307 i 254 j 329
k 551 l 344
2 a $703 b $826 c $144 d $676

2:39

1 a 3 b 2 c 4
2 a 3 groups, 15 ÷ 5 = 3 b 6 groups, 30 ÷ 5 = 6
c 5 groups, 15 ÷ 3 = 5 d 6 groups, 36 ÷ 6 = 6
e 10 groups, 30 ÷ 3 = 10 f 9 groups, 36 ÷ 4 = 9
g 6 groups, 24 ÷ 4 = 6 h 8 groups, 48 ÷ 6 = 8
i 4 groups, 36 ÷ 9 = 4 j 3 groups, 24 ÷ 8 = 3
k 6 groups, 48 ÷ 8 = 6
3 a 7, 42 ÷ 6 = 7 b 7, 35 ÷ 5 = 7
c 8, 32 ÷ 4 = 8

2:40

1 a 6 b 2 c 9 d 1
2 a 6 b 3 c 12 d 8 e 4 f 2
3 a 3 b 3 c 18 d 5 e 4 f 2
4 a 20 ÷ 4 = 5, 5 b 16 ÷ 8 = 2, 2
c 20 ÷ 2 = 10, 10

2:41

Header: 4, 8
1 a 4, 2 b 10, 2 c 9, 3
2 a 12, 4 b 16, 8 c 28, 4 d 27, 3 e 30, 5 f 15, 3
3 a 3, 4 b 8, 5 c 10, 9 d 6, 10 e 7, 8 f 5, 9
4 a 2, 2 b 6, 6 c 7, 7 d 6, 6 e 10, 10 f 3, 3
5 a 10 b 8 c 7
6 $34. Answers will vary.

2:42

1 a 24 ÷ 3 = 8, 24 ÷ 8 = 3 b 36 ÷ 4 = 9, 36 ÷ 9 = 4
c 30 ÷ 6 = 5, 30 ÷ 5 = 6
2 a 2 b 2 c 7 d 5 e 3 f 2
g 2 h 5 i 2
3 a 8 b 7 c 6 d 8 e 1 f 9
g 6 h 7 i 4 j 9 k 9 l 5
4 a

18	÷ 2	=	9
	÷ 3	=	6
	÷ 6	=	3
	÷ 9	=	2

b

24	÷ 3	=	8
	÷ 4	=	6
	÷ 6	=	4
	÷ 8	=	3

c

30	÷ 3	=	10
	÷ 5	=	6
	÷ 6	=	5
	÷ 10	=	3

2:43

1 83, 109, 111, 125, 127, and 3005 will be coloured red.
100, 118, 120, 130, and 6112 will be blue.
2 These numbers cannot be arranged in pairs.
3 38, 66, 50, 74, 14, 92, 36, 100, 482, 764,
3106, 988, and 24 000 will be circled.
75, 87, 29, 53, 41, 35, 2221, and 3825 will be underlined.

4 **a** 78 **b** 65 **c** 94 **d** 99

5 **a** 20,18,184, 28, 48, 162, 32, 112, 188
even + even = even
b 2, 0, 28, 12, 66, 356, 18, 190, 598
even – even = even

2:44

1 **a** 14, 14, 100, 100, 34, 160, 88, 108,110
odd + odd = even
b 6, 6, 6, 10, 14, 2, 22, 58, 12
odd – odd = even
c 24, 48, 8, 32, 40, 36, 24, 40, 16
even × even = even
d 24, 1, 40, 10, 6, 5, 3, 3, 6

2

Number types	+	–	×	÷
Even and Even	even	even	even	odd or even
Odd and Odd	even	even	odd	odd
Odd and Even	odd	odd	even	

3 There will be crosses next to:
6248 + 396 = 6645, 6107 ÷ 31 = 196
283 × 654 = 28 353, 7319 + 2997 = 10 313
173 × 881 = 152 416, 366 × 47 = 17 201
2817 – 199 = 2617 and 68 019 + 79 = 862

2:45

1 **a** 5 **b** 4 **c** 2 **d** 9 **e** 7
f 1 **g** 4 **h** 6 **i** 8 **j** 9
k 6 **l** 5 **m** 8 **n** 4 **o** 2
p 9 **q** 3 **r** 6 **s** 5 **t** 9
u 5 **v** 5 **w** 8 **x** 7

2 **a** 4 **b** 1 **c** 3 **d** 3 **e** 2
f 3 **g** 8 **h** 3 **i** 5 **j** 4
k 6 **l** 3 **m** 8 **n** 8 **o** 3

3 2 → 6, 3, 18, 2, 20, 5, 50, 10, 80, 10 → 2

2:46

1

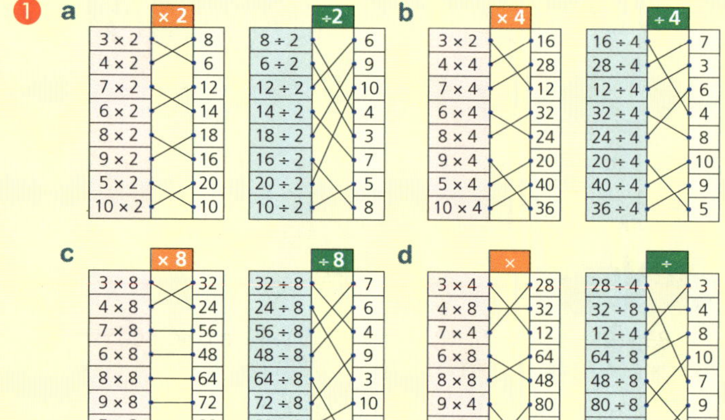

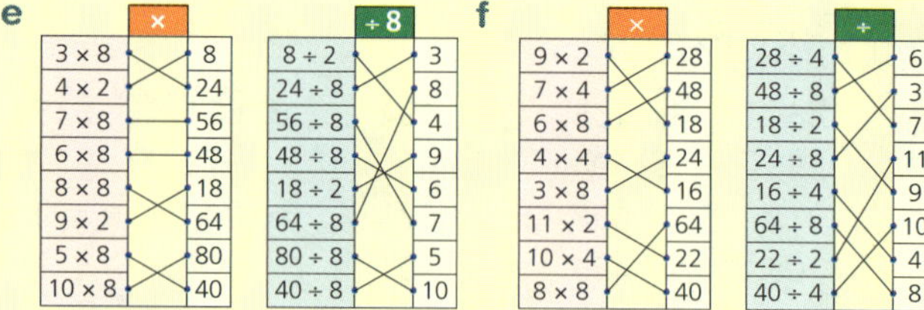

2:47

1 **a** 9 **b** 7 **c** 4 **d** 8 **e** 8 **f** 6
2 **a** 72 **b** 48 **c** 96 **d** 84 **e** 123
3 **a** 80 **b** 70 **c** 90 **d** 900 **e** 700 **f** 1000
4 **a** 56 **b** 96 **c** 90 **d** 168 **e** 195 **f** 231
5 **a** 160 **b** 210 **c** 320 **d** 420 **e** 180 **f** 280
6 **a** 1400 **b** 1600 **c** 3500 **d** 1800 **e** 5400 **f** 7200
7 **a** 16 **b** 37 **c** 40 **d** 20 **e** 101 **f** 30

2:48

1 about 40 2 6 × 7 = 42 and 7 × 6 = 42
3 42 ÷ 6 = 7 and 42 ÷ 7 = 6 4 8 (children) 5 18
6 **a** 200, 100, 50, 25, $12\frac{1}{2}$ **b** 80, 40, 20, 10, 5
c 128, 64, 32, 16, 8, 4, 2, 1, $\frac{1}{2}$, $\frac{1}{4}$
d 6, 12, 24, 48, 96, 192 **e** 18, 36, 72, 144, 288, 576
7 **a** 48, 96, 192 **b** 36, 72, 144
c 126, 252, 504
8 9 ways (5 using one layer and 4 using two)
9 **a** 414 (For **9a** and **b** you should have made an
b 213 estimate and shown working.)
Investigation: True

2:49

Header: 9

1

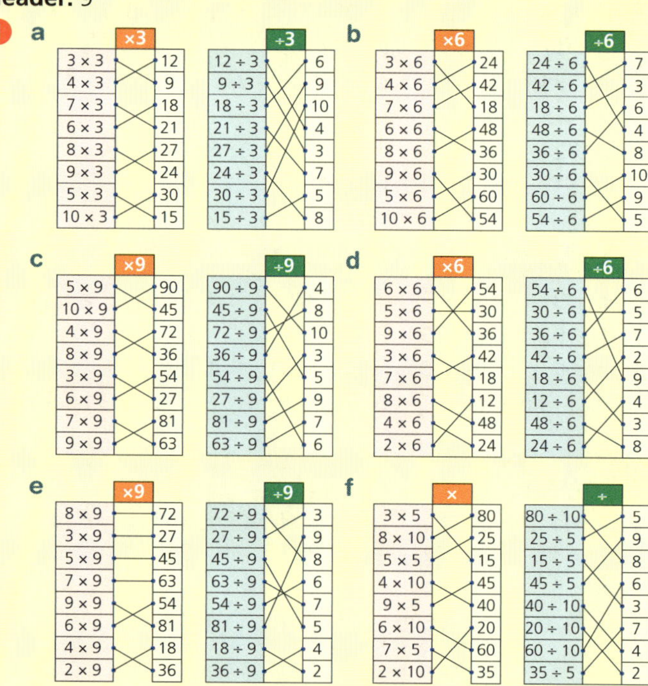

2:50

1 a 10, 6 b 5, 8 c 6, 9 d 9, 8
e 7, 6 f 4, 9

2 a 6 b 3 c 5 d 2 e 6
f 8 g 1 h 6 i 7 j 8
k 4 l 9

3 a 8 b 5 c 5 d 4 e 10
f 6 g 5 h 10 i 3 j 8
k 8 l 6 m 9 n 10 o 7
p 6 q 9 r 8 s 9 t 9
u 9 v 6 w 2 x 6

2:51

Header: 4 coins: 20c, 20c, 20c, 10c or 50c, 10c, 5c, 5c, and 5 coins: 20c, 20c, 20c, 5c, 5c or 20c, 20c, 10c, 10c, 10c

1 a $50, $5, $2 b $50, $1, 50c
c $20, $2, $1 d $50, $10, 20c, 10c
e $100, $50, $20, $10, $5, $2, $1, 50c, 10c
f $50, $20, $20, $5, $1, 50c, 20c, 20c, 5c
g $100, $20, $10, $2, $1, 50c, 20c, 10c
h $100, $50, $10, $5, 50c, 20c, 5c
i $50, $10, $5, 20c, 10c, 5c
j $100, $50, $2, $1, 20c, 10c, 5c
k $100, $100, $50, $20, $5, 20c, 20c
l $100, $100, $10, $2, 50c, 20c, 10c
m $100, $5, $2, 20c, 5c

2 Answers will vary.

2:52

1 a 85c b $0.85 c $1.50 d $6.90
e $3.25 f $9.45 g $8.90 h $4.50
i $7.45 j $5.05 k $0.60 l $8.75
m $7.15 n $4.90 o $0.40 p $8.75
q $3.55 r $8.05

2 a $11.75 b $19.80 c $60 d $17.20

3

	Total	Total rounded	Count on to give change	Change
a	$11.66	$11.65	5c $11.70 30c $12 $8 $20 $30	$38.35
b	$20.33	$20.35	5c $20.40 60c $21 $9 $30 $20	$29.65
c	$21.59	$21.60	40c $22 $8 $30 $20	$28.40
d	$10.02	$10.00	$10	$10.00
e	$2.77	$2.75	25c $3 $7 $10 $10	$17.25
f	$30.51	$30.50	50c $31 $9 $40 $60	$69.50
g	$53.68	$53.70	30c $54 $6 $60 $40	$46.30

2:53

1 a 50c, $1, $2, $20, $20 = $43.50
b 10c, 20c, 50c, $1, $2, $5 = $8.80
c 10c, 20c, $1, $20, $20 = $41.30
d $2, $5, $20, $20, $50 = $97
e $36.50 … $37 … $39 … $40 … $50
10c 50c $2 $1 $10
= $13.60
f $67.40 … $67.50 … $68 … $70 … $90 … $100
20c 10c 50c $2 $20 $10
= $32.80

2 Answers may vary.
a 50c, $1, $2, $10; change = $13.50
b 20c, 10c, 50c, $20, $20; change = $40.80
c 20c, 50c, $1, $20, $10; change = $31.70

3 Answers will vary.
a 5c, $2, $1, $5 b 5c, 50c, 50c, $2, $5
c 5c, $1, $1, $1, $2, $2, $1

2:54

1 a 560 b 910 c 330 d 6200
e 29 170 f 441 880 g 7800 h 1500
i 4800 j 91 300 k 405 400 l 750 000
m 79 000 n 98 000 o 80 000
p 300 000 q 5 835 000 r 60 000 000

2 a 302 500 b 914 500 c 700 000
d 1 974 200 e 7 500 000 f 4 056 500
g 19 500 000 h 60 300 000 i 74 000 000

3 a 2 884 820 b 28 848 200 c 288 482 000

2:55

Header: 10

1 a 66 b 20 c 83 d 670
e 8537 f 2200 g 78 h 480
i 414 j 333 k 536 l 500
m 19 n 31 o 80 p 300
q 104 r 700

2 a 1100 b 622 c 356
d 600 000 e 2917 f 84188
g 710 000 h 9000 i 5054

3 a 9 520 000 b 952 000 c 95 200

2:56

1 a 21 b 45 c 35 d 126
e 145 f 39

2 a 68 b 162 c 167 d 37
e 56 f 108

3 a 16 b 52 c 68 d 126
e 25 f 27 g 26 h 27
i 25

2:57

Header: True

1 a 7 b 9 c 5 d 0
e 10 f 20 g 15 h 9

2 a 2 b 4 c 7 d 3
e 9 f 0 g 4 h 5
i 0 j 6 k 5 l 2
m 11 n 10 o 29

3 a 2 b 5 c 9 d 3
e 5 f 9

4 a 887 + 100 – 4 = 983 b 416 + 50 – 1 = 465
c 1076 + 100 – 3 = 1173 d 476 + 90 – 1 = 565

5 a 3 b 7 c 6 d 9
e 5 f 3 g 10 h 5
i 8 j 6 k 7 l 7
m 16 n 12 o 40 p 8
q 6 r 3

6 a 2 b 10 c 5 d 2
e 4 f 6 g 4 h 5
i 3

2:58

1 a 83 b 54 c 693 d 116
e 472 f 123, 664, 464

2 a 24 b 27 c 227 d 77
e 266 f 218, 403, 269

2:59

1 a 61 b 72 c 93 d 392
e 284 f 685

2 a 356 – 100 = 256, 256 – 20 = 236, 236 – 7 = 229
b 562 – 100 = 462, 462 – 30 = 432, 432 – 4 = 428
c 472 – 100 = 372, 372 – 40 = 332, 332 – 5 = 327

3 a We add 5 to both. 56 – 30 = 26
b We add 3 to both. 65 – 40 = 25
c We add 2 to both. 73 – 40 = 33
d We subtract 2 from both. 379 – 200 = 179
e We add 3 to both. 565 – 400 = 165
f We subtract 4 from both. 464 – 300 = 164
g We add 4 to both numbers. 535 – 500 = 35
h We subtract 4 from both. 667 – 400 = 267

4 a (– 2 and + 2), 21 + 40 = 61
b (+ 1 and – 1), 70 + 31 = 101
c (+ 2 and – 2), 60 + 41 = 101
d (+ 2 and – 2), 160 + 23 = 183
e (– 2 and + 2), 243 + 40 = 283
f (+ 1 and – 1), 460 + 33 = 493
g (– 4 and + 4), 343 + 100 = 443
h (– 5 and + 5), 455 + 200 = 655

3:01

Header: 25 minutes to the next hour

1 a 5 to 2 b 25 to 6 c 10 past 10
d 20 to 5 e 20 past 12
f 15 past 11 (or quarter past 11) g 15 to 7 (or quarter to 7)
h 25 past 2 i 10 to 8 j 5 past 3

2 a b c

d e

3 a 10 past 8 b a quarter past 7 (or 15 past 7)
c 5 to 12 d 20 past 6
e a quarter to 8 (or 15 to 8)
f 10 to 3 g 25 past 3 h 20 to 3 i 9 o'clock

4 a 20 past 1 b 5 past 4 c 20 to 4
d a quarter to 5 (or 15 to 5)
e a quarter past 6 (or 15 past 6) f half past 7 (or 30 past 7)
g 10 past 10 h 25 to 11 i 2 o'clock

3:02

1 a 11:16, 16 past 11 b 7:24, 24 past 7
c 4:32, 28 to 5 d 5:08, 8 past 5
e 3:47, 13 to 4 f 12:32, 28 to 1
g 9:29, 29 past 9 h 6:53, 7 to 7
i 10:04, 4 past 10 j 8:58, 2 to 9
k 18 to 3 l 2 to 5
m 19 past 9 n 9 past 7
o 22 to 12

2 a 3:17 b 2:48 c 7:29 d 9:04 e 11:42
f 4:40 g 12:25 h 5:21 i 6:56

3 a 4:18 b 9:46 c 7:37 d 10:59
e 8:21 f 6:03

3:03

Header: 26 minutes

1 a 26 past 7 b 6 to 7 c 19 past 12 d 2 past 10
e 18 to 12

2 a 27 past 6 b 16 past 7 c 10 past 8 d 4 past 12
e 26 past 4

3 43 min, 35 min, 15 min, 1:46, 2:00

4 2 hours and 17 minutes 5 8:38, 8:58

3:04

1 14 cm, 142 mm

2 a 7 mm b 67 mm c 29 mm d 54 mm
e 22 mm f 60 mm g 32 mm h 64 mm

3 Answers will vary.

3:05

1 a 45 mm b 52 mm c 29 mm d 73 mm
e 82 mm f 16 mm

2 a 19 mm b 47 mm c 61 mm d 36 mm
e 55 mm f 72 mm g 28 mm h 93 mm

3 a 2 cm 5 mm b 6 cm 8 mm c 5 cm 1 mm
d 9 cm 2 mm e 4 cm 3 mm f 8 cm 7 mm

3:06

1 a 36 mm b 22 mm c 17 mm d 59 mm e 48 mm
2 a 38 mm b 63 mm c 19 mm d 75 mm e 58 mm
f 41 mm
3 a 32 mm b 81 mm c 19 mm d 53 mm e 74 mm
f 28 mm g 46 mm h 95 mm i 55 mm j 37 mm
k 100 mm l 1000 mm
4 a 3 cm 8 mm b 1 cm 9 mm c 4 cm 7 mm
d 8 cm 2 mm e 5 cm 1 mm f 2 cm 5 mm
g 6 cm 4 mm h 9 cm 3 mm i 7 cm 6 mm
5 a 12 cm or 120 mm b 14 cm or 140 mm
c 12 cm or 120 mm

3:07

1 A = 15 cm², B = 9 cm², C = 24 cm², D = 12 cm²
E = 2 cm², F = 22 cm² 2 E, B, D, A, F, C

3:08

1 a 4 cm² b 18 cm² c 20 cm² d 9 cm² e 15 cm²
f 10 cm² 2 a 12 cm² b 16 cm² c 24 cm²

3:09

1 a 6 cm² b 10 cm² c 12 cm² d 14 cm² e 8 cm²
2 a A = 15 cm², P = 16 cm b A = 18 cm², P = 18 cm
c A = 8 cm², P = 12 cm d A = 24 cm², P = 22 cm

3:10

1 The boiling point of water • • is cool to warm weather.
35°C to 45°C • • is cold weather.
25°C to 35°C • • is 100°C
15°C to 25°C • • is 0°C
5°C to 15°C • • is very hot weather.
The freezing point of water • • is warm to hot weather.

2 a 10°C b 90°C c 5°C d 40°C
e 80°C f 15°C g 45°C h 95°C
3 a b, e, h b a, c, f c d, g

3:11

1 a 25°C b 0°C c 18°C d 58°C
e 86°C f 37°C g 41°C h 73°C
2 a 40°C b 28°C c 36°C d 14°C
e 8°C f 33°C g 27°C h 15°C
3 a 2°C b 40°C c 26°C d 70°C
e 96°C f 9°C g 100°C h 37°C
i 67°C j 17°C

3:12

1 a mL b mL c L d L e mL f mL
2 a mL b L c mL d mL e L
f L g mL h L
3 a 1 L b 4 L c 2 L d 6 L e 5 L
f 7 L g 9 L h 3 L

3:13

1 Answers will vary. 2 Answers will vary.
3 a mL b L c mL d mL e L f mL
4 a 2000 mL b 7000 mL c 3000 mL d 5000 mL
e 8000 mL f 4000 mL g 6500 mL h 9500 mL
i 3500 mL j 8500 mL k 2500 mL l 3500 mL
m 7500 mL n 8300 mL o 5250 mL p 7250 mL
5 a 1 L b 7 L c 5 L d 3 L
e 6 L f 4 L g 2 L h 8 L
6 a 400 mL b 200 mL c 700 mL d 900 mL

3:14

1 a 1500 mL b 1250 mL c 1750 mL d 1600 mL
2 a 1300 mL b 1490 mL c 1875 mL d 1625 mL
e 1750 mL f 2500 mL
3 a 1 L 600 mL b 1 L 900 mL c 1 L 350 mL
d 1 L 250 mL e 1 L 425 mL f 2 L 750 mL
4 a L b mL c mL d mL e mL
f L g mL h mL
5 a 2 L b 1·5 L c 2·5 L d 0·5 L

3:15

1 a 60 g b 1 kg c 350 g d 700 g e 500 g
f 3 kg g 9 kg h 900 g i 16 kg
2 a g b g c kg d g e g
3 a 1000 b 3000 c 5000 d 9000
4 a 1 b 4 c 6 d 8

3:16

1 a 100 g b 600 g c 1 kg d 500 g e 3 kg
f 300 g g 10 kg h 956 g i 875 g
2 a 3 kg b 7 kg c 2 kg d 5 kg e 9 kg
f 4 kg

3 a 2000 g b 1200 g c 3000 g d 1600 g
e 5000 g f 1450 g g 1980 g h 1500 g
i 7000 g

4 a 500 g b 750 g c 250 g d 1500 g
e 1750 g f 1250 g g 2500 g h 3500 g

5 C, A, B, D

3:17

Concept: 20 past 7, 7:20, 22 past 1 or 1:22, 14 to 6 or 5:46, 23 to 11 or 10:37

1 a 10 past 11, 11:10 b 20 to 12, 11:40
c 18 past 12, 12:18 d 27 to 5, 4:33
e 22 to 4, 3:38 f 7 to 8, 7:53

3:18

1 a b c d e

2 a 10 to 10 b 19 past 4
c a quarter to 8 (or 15 to 8) d 28 past 8 e 5 to 3

3 a 9, the time is 9 to 7 b 22, the time is 22 to 5
c 17, the time is 17 to 1 d 3, the time is 3 to 9
e 11, the time is 11 to 2

4 a 49 b 42 c 2 d 21 e 11
f 7 g 3 h 5 i 2

5 a 3, 1 b 1095 c 36 d 2 e 5
f 156 g 4

6 4:02, 4:10

3:19

1 a 5:14 pm b 3:32 am c 7:23 pm d 4:43 am
e 10:09 pm

2 a after midday b before midday c before midday
d before midday e after midday

3 15 hours (15 h), 15 hours 11 minutes (15 h 11 min)

4 a 2 h 30 min b 1 h 40 min c 4 h
d 7 h e 8h 30 min f 7 h 45 min

5 7 days 5 hours, 20 h, 5 h 30 min

3:20

Header: The perimeter of the blue rectangle is about 84 cm.

1 a 256 cm b 316 cm c 540 cm d 781 cm
e 495 cm f 179 cm g 863 cm h 628 cm

2 a 1 m 19 cm b 8 m 53 cm c 5 m 82 cm
d 6 m 97 cm e 9 m 35 cm f 3 m 74 cm

3 a 2 cm 7 mm b 3 cm 6 mm c 5 cm 1 mm
d 1 cm 9 mm e 4 cm 2 mm f 8 cm 5 mm

4 a 54 mm b 69 mm c 11 mm d 87 mm
e 43 mm f 26 mm g 450 mm h 1040 mm
i 3000 mm

5 a m b cm c m d mm
e cm f m g mm h mm

3:21

Header: 7 mm

1 a 16 mm b 24 mm c 32 mm d 8 mm
e 16 mm f 8 mm

2 a 36 mm b 32 mm c 69 mm d 64 mm
e 8 mm f 48 mm g 53 mm

3 a 40 mm b 4 mm c 11 mm
d 61 mm e 32 mm f 33 mm
g 24 mm h 28 mm i 16 mm

3:22

1 a 2 cm, 22 mm b 4 cm, 37 mm c 2 cm, 17 mm
d 3 cm, 33 mm e 1 cm, 8 mm f 5 cm, 46 mm
g 0 cm, 3 mm. h A measurement of 0 cm means that the length is closer to 0 than to the next highest division on the scale.

2 a 8 kg b 15 kg c 1 kg d 11 kg
e 3 kg f 12 kg

3:23

1

Millimetres	cm and mm	Rounded to the nearest cm
39 mm	3 cm 9 mm	4 cm
63 mm	6 cm 3 mm	6 cm
56 mm	5 cm 6 mm	6 cm
72 mm	7 cm 2 mm	7 cm
81 mm	8 cm 1 mm	8 cm
45 mm	4 cm 5 mm	5 cm
94 mm	9 cm 4 mm	9 cm
26 mm	2 cm 6 mm	3 cm

2 Answers will vary.

3 a 35 mm b 29 mm c 46 mm
d 13 mm e 62 mm f 38 mm
g 81 mm h 56 mm

4 a 140 mm b 95 mm c 130 mm

3:24

Answers will vary.

3:25

1 a 2 m^2 b 6 cm^2 c 5 m^2 d 12 cm^2 e 10 m^2
f 15 cm^2

2 a cm^2 b m^2 c cm^2 d m^2 e cm^2
f m^2 g m^2 h cm^2 i cm^2

3:26

1 7 2 29 days 3 9

4 a Paris b Istanbul c Dubai d Rome

5 a 4 b 3 c 2 d 2

6 a London b Paris c Istanbul d Dubai

7 1 day 8 hours 30 minutes

8 Answers will vary.

3:27

1 a 6:10 b 8:45 c 11:40 d 7:50 e 10:05 f 1:15

2 a Richmond b Christmas Ck c Black Hill d Ironbark e Mulga f Wandong

3 a 8:10 b 1:40 c 3:15 d 12:05 e 2:30 f 10:45

4 a 12:00 or noon b 8:15 c 11:10 d 12:45 e 5:40 f 9:35

5 a Black Hill b Mulga c Richmond d Wandong e Carbor f Mt Gordon

6

6am 7am 8am 9am 10am 11am 12noon 1pm

Ironbark, Christmas Ck, Mt Gordon, Richmond, Wandong, Carbor, Black Hill, Mulga

3:28

1 a Friday b 3rd c 25th d four e five f Tuesday g 29 h 28

2 a 2nd b 6th c 26th d 14th

3 a Thursday b Friday c Saturday d Monday

4 a 5th and 6th b 12th and 13th c 19th and 20th d 2nd, 9th, 16th and 23rd

3:29

1 a January b October c May d September

2 a 30 b 31 c 31 d 31

3 a 5th b 1st

4 a 19th September b 25th September

5 a Friday b Friday c Saturday d Friday e Thursday f Thursday

6 a 1 week 6 days b 6 weeks c 11 weeks 5 days d 23 weeks 5 days

7 a 14 weeks 4 days b 11 weeks

3:30

1 A 23 past 7, 7:23 B 4 past 11, 11:04 C 27 to 2, 1:33 D 20 to 5, 4:40

a yes b A c A and B d C and D

2 a 3 h 41 min b 2 h 29 min c 3 h 7 min d 9 h 17 min

3 a 2 h 45 min b 2 h 56 min c 2 h 16 min d 6h 48 min

3:31

1 a 1 kg b 450 g c 3 kg d 1 kg 560 g e 2 kg 125 g

2 a 3000 g b 5000 g c 9000 g d 7000 g e 4000 g f 6000 g

3 a 1 kg b 8 kg c 2 kg d 4 kg e 6 kg f 5 kg

4 a 0·1 kg b 0·3 kg c 0·9 kg d 0·5 g e 0·7 g f 1·4 kg

5 a 500 g b 200 g c 800 g d 600 kg

6 a 1 kg 500 g b 4 kg 250 g c 3 kg 500 g d 2 kg 250 g

3:32

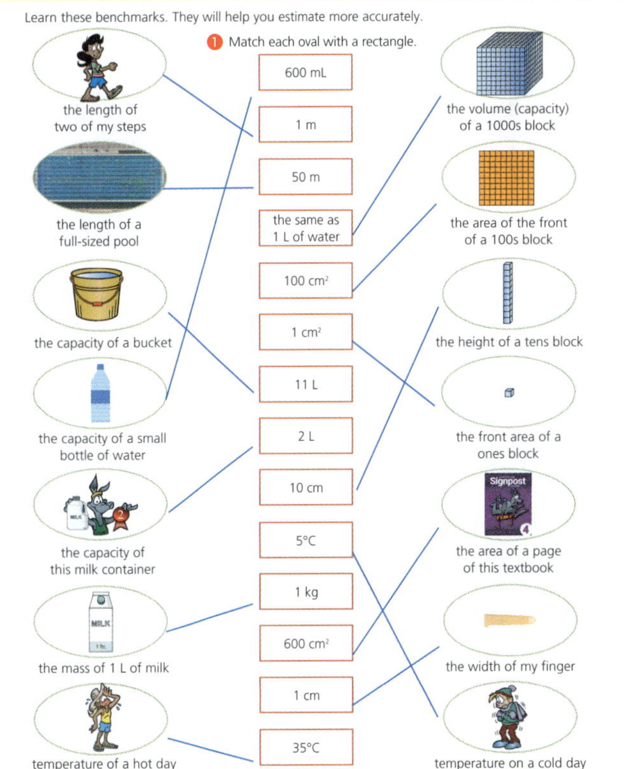

3:33

1 a 14 cm² b 13 cm² c 12 cm² d 9 cm² e 11 cm² f 10·5 cm² g 8 cm² h 7·5 cm²

2 a 8 cm² b 8 cm² c 4·5 cm² d 4 cm²

3:34

1 a 5600 mm b 5 m 600 mm

2 a 3520 mm b 3 m 520 mm

3 a 1650 mm b 3345 mm

4 a true b true c true d false

3:35

1 a 3 km b 7 km c 6 km

2 a 5 km b 10 km c 9 km

3 a 5100 m b 1400 m

 • AUSTRALIAN SIGNPOST MATHS 4 • ISBN 9780655708780

3:36

1 18 m, House width is about 15 m.
The length of the truck is about 9 m.

2 20°C (20 degrees Celsius) 3 725 mL

4 1450 g (or 1 kg 450 g) 5 **a** 7:22 pm **b** 1 h 50 min

6 7 days 7 **a** 2 kg 500 g (or 2·5 kg) **b** 3 kg 365 g

8 1545 mm (1 m 545 mm)

9 **a** 16 (laps) **b** 1050 m (21 laps)

3:37

Concept: 10 and 8, 11 and 9

1 **a** 100 and 97, 101 and 98, 102 and 99 2 8
b 1000 and 998, 1001 and 999

3 **a** 4150 (mL) **b** 4 L 150 mL **c** 4170 g (or 4 kg 170 g)

4 7 h 20 min

5 **a** 603 m **b** 750 m **c** 503 m

6 2000 cm^2

7 **a** 175 cm **b** 155 cm 8 1000 cm^2

4:01

1 **a** C, E, F, I, J **b** B, E, G **c** A, D, H 2 E

3 **a** 1 **b** 2 **c** 1 **d** 0 **e** 1
f 1 **g** 0 **h** 0 **i** 1

4:02

1 **a** yes **b** no **c** no

2 **a** C and E **b** B, D and E **c** B and E
d 4, 4 **e** 3, 3 **f** yes

3 **a** A and D **b** B **c** C **d** yes

4 Answers may vary. Diagrams may look like this:

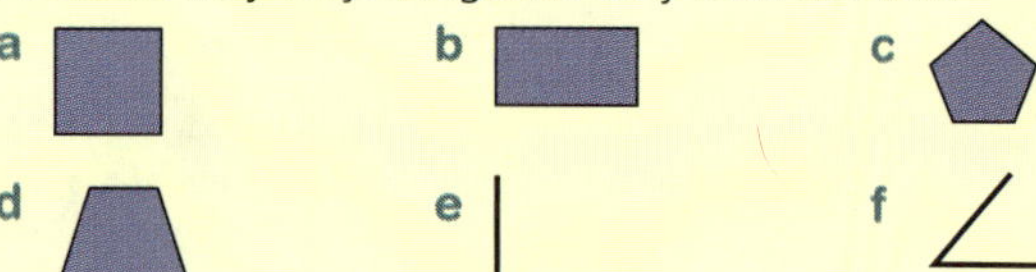

5 **a** B **b** C **c** A **d** A

4:03

1

My angle (Right angle)	Smaller	The same	Larger
	E, C, G, I	A, F, D	B, H

2 **a** A **b** C **c** E **d** G

3

My angle	Smaller	The same	Larger
	C, E	G, I	A, B, D, F, H

4 **a**

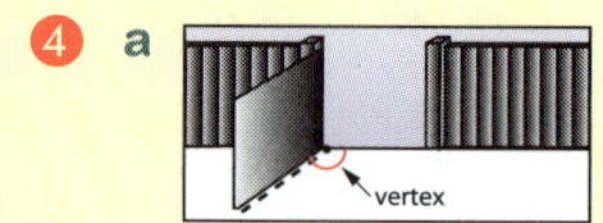

b

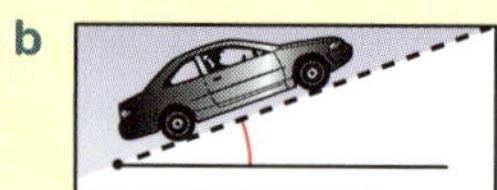

c

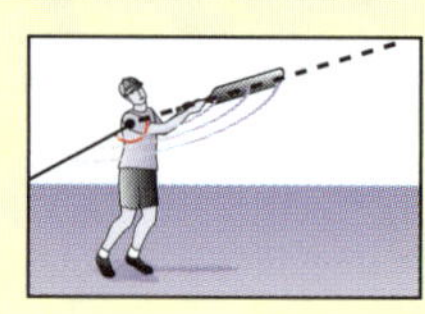

Activity: Answers will vary.

4:04

Header: yes

1 **a** The prisms will be coloured red, the cylinders blue and the pyramids green.

2 **a** A, B, D, E **b** C, F
c A, D, E. The prisms will be coloured red.
d C. The cylinder will be coloured blue. **e** D

3 **a** A **b** D (or B) **c** E (or A) **d** B

Investigation: Answers will vary, e.g. a box.

4:05

Concept: pyramid, prism

1 **a** D, E, G, H **b** A, B, C, F **c** D, F
d A, E (also D, F) **e** C, G **f** B

2 **a** pyramid (square pyramid)
b prism (rectangular prism)
c pyramid (triangular pyramid)
d prism (square prism)
e prism (triangular prism)

4:06

1 **a** A (prism) **b** B (pyramid) **c** A (prism) **d** B (pyramid)

2 **a** prism **b** pyramid **c** prism

4:07

1

	Name of the object	Number of faces	Number of corners	Number of edges
A	triangular prism	5	6	9
B	triangular pyramid	4	4	6
C	cube	6	8	12
D	square pyramid	5	5	8
E	rectangular prism	6	8	12
F	pentagonal pyramid	6	6	10

2 Answers may vary.

 • *AUSTRALIAN SIGNPOST MATHS 4* • ISBN 9780655708780

4:08

Header: 1, 3, 2

1 a A b C c C d A e D

2 a b c Answers will vary.

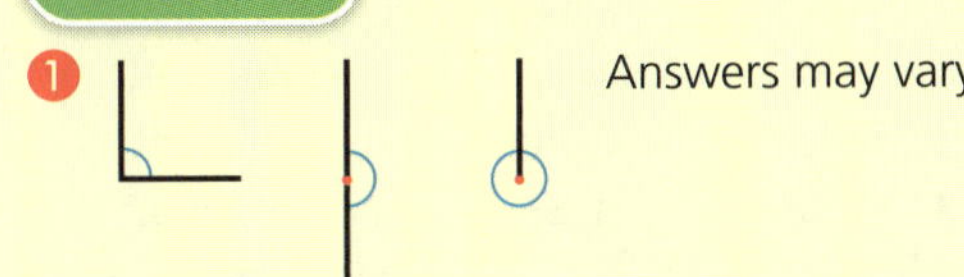

3 A right angle is a quarter of a full turn. It is a square angle.

4 D, C, A, B

Activity: Answers may vary.

4:09

1 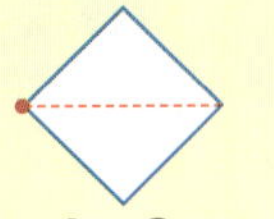 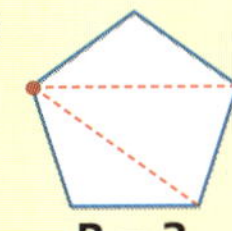 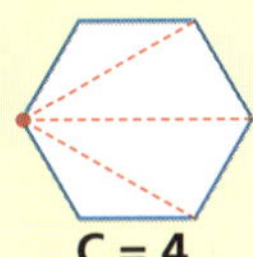 Answers may vary.

2 a a half turn clockwise b a quarter turn clockwise
c two quarter turns anticlockwise

3 a 4 b 4 c 2

4 a 3 b 12

Activity: Answers may vary.

4:10

1 A A = 2 B B = 3 C C = 4

D D = 6

The number of triangles is 2 less than the number of sides.

2

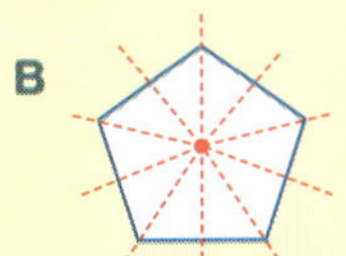

A 4, 4 B 5, 5

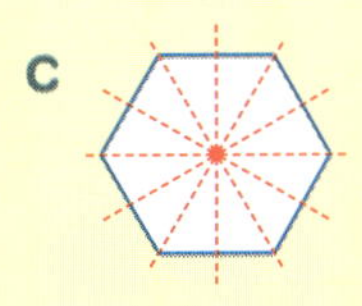

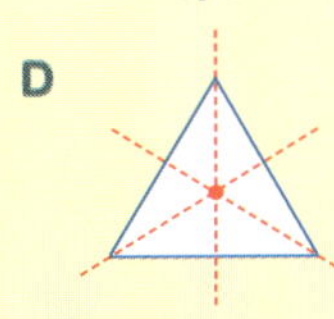

C 6, 6 D 3, 3

3

Regular shape	Number of sides	Number of angles	Number of lines of symmetry
square	4	4	4
pentagon	5	5	5
hexagon	6	6	6
triangle	3	3	3

4:11

1 a

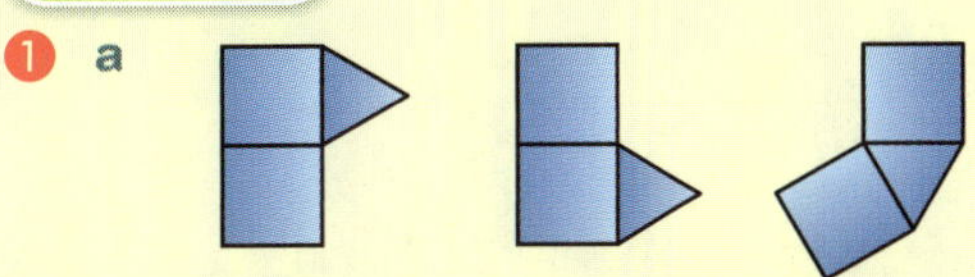

b 2

2 a 1

b

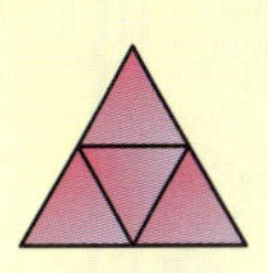

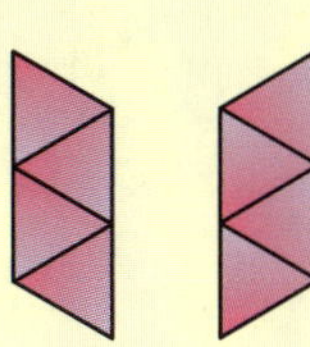

3 The complete set of tetrominoes is:

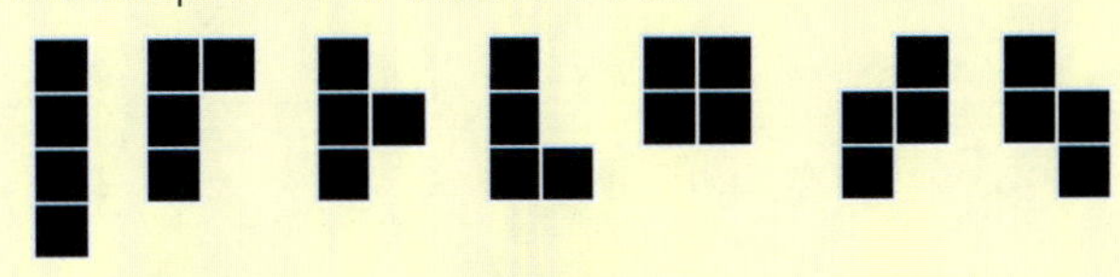

a

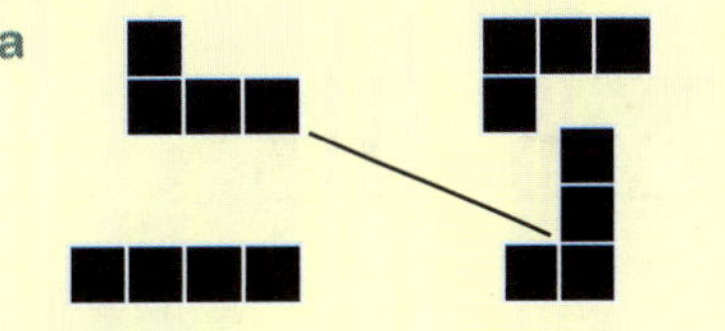

b 7

4:12

1 a Warn St b March St or Munn St c Joseph St
d Meg St e school f hospital
g police station h traffic lights

2 a school b police c hospital

3 The intersection of March St and Munn St.

4 a 2 km by road b 9 km by road

Activity: Answers may vary.

4:13

Answers will vary.

4:14

Header: A face has straight edges but the base of a cone has a curved edge.
A cylinder, cone and sphere will be drawn.

1

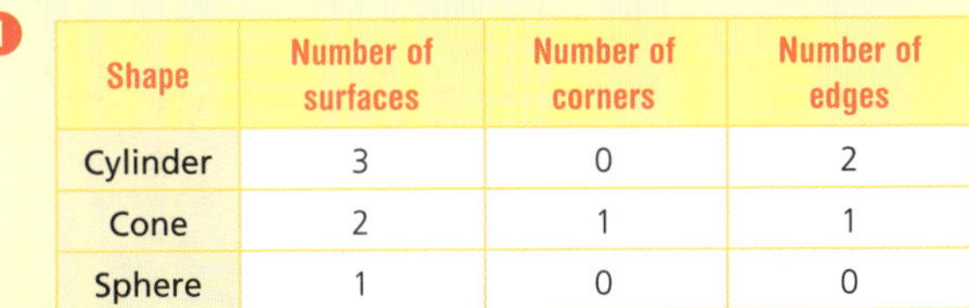

Shape	Number of surfaces	Number of corners	Number of edges
Cylinder	3	0	2
Cone	2	1	1
Sphere	1	0	0

2–4 Answers will vary.

5 A 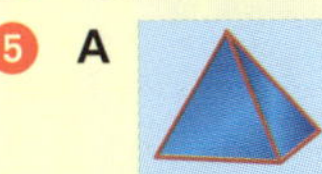 pyramid B 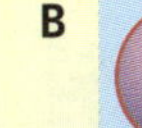  sphere C 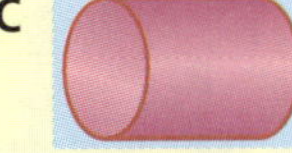 cylinder

D 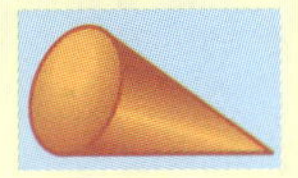 cone

a C
b A, D (also B, but B has no base)

4:15

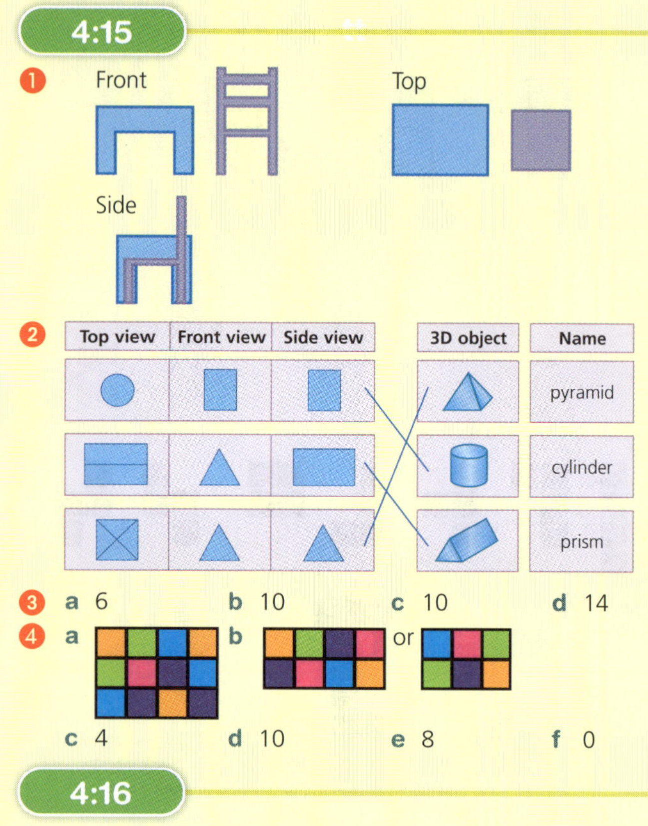

1

2

3 a 6 b 10 c 10 d 14

4 a b or

c 4 d 10 e 8 f 0

4:16

1

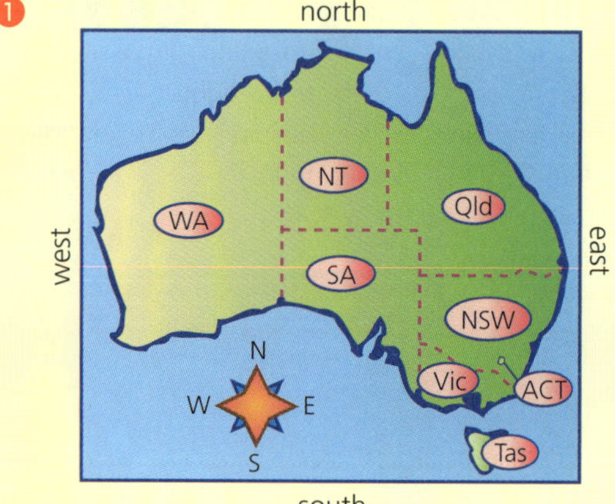

2 a Western Australia b Northern Territory
c South Australia

3 Queensland and New South Wales

4 a Jake's Grave b Bart's Cave c Queen Hill
d Land's End e Bart's Cave f Queen Hill
g Black Rock

5

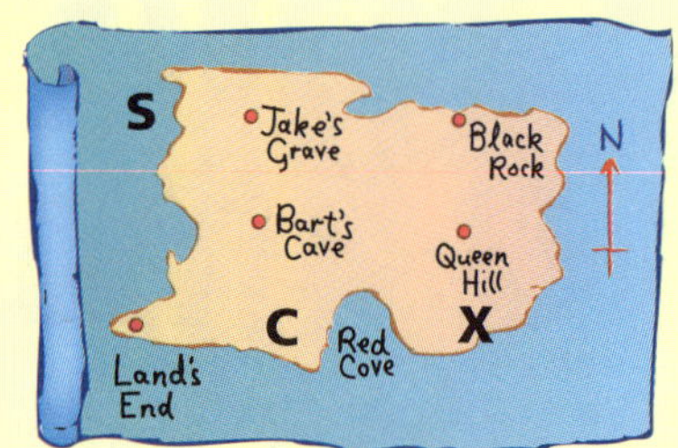

4:17

1 a prism (rectangular) b pyramid (triangular)
c prism (triangular) d pyramid (square or rectangular)
e sphere f cone g cube h cylinder

2 a museum b pool c park d station

3 a A b G c D d A e D

4:18

1 a cherries b carrot c apple
d banana e pear f strawberry
g left, middle h right, middle i left, bottom
j left, top k right, top l right, bottom

2 a Ruby b Rex c Tom d Chris
e Sophie f Ethan g Georgia h Oscar

3 a 2, A b 4, C c 2, B d 2, D e 1, B
f 1, A g 5, A h 1, C i 5, D j 5, C
k 3, B l 5, B m 3, A n 4, A

4:19

1 a Mildura b Lakes Entrance c Griffith
d Warrnambool e Horsham

2 a column 4, 2nd row b column 4, 3rd row
c column 3, 2nd row d column 3, 2nd row
e column 1, 1st row f column 5, 3rd row
g column 3, 3rd row h column 2, 4th row
i column 4, 1st row and column 5, 1st row
j Echuca k Albury l Mildura

3

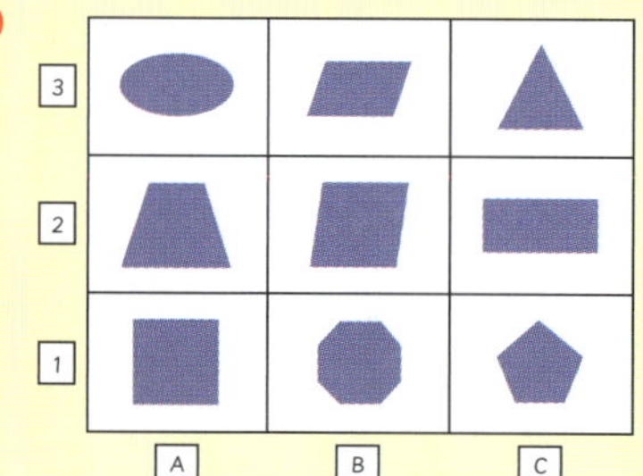

4:20

Answers will vary.

1

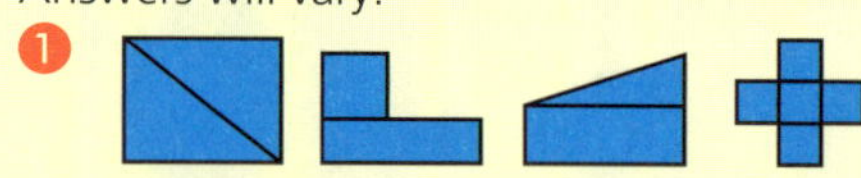

2

3

4 Any 3 of the shapes except the 2nd and 3rd shape in Question 1 will be copied.

Activity: Answers will vary.

 • *AUSTRALIAN SIGNPOST MATHS 4* • ISBN 9780655708780

4:21

1. **a** A, B, G, H **b** C, D, J, K **c** E, F, I, L
2. **a** D, C, A **b** D, G, E **c** J, H, F **d** K, B, L **e** K, C, G **f** G, F, L
3. **a** obtuse **b** right **c** acute **d** obtuse **e** obtuse **f** acute **g** acute **h** right
4. **a** B and E **b** B and C, or A and E **c** A and D

4:22

1. **a** acute **b** straight **c** right **d** reflex **e** revolution **f** obtuse **g** reflex **h** acute
2.

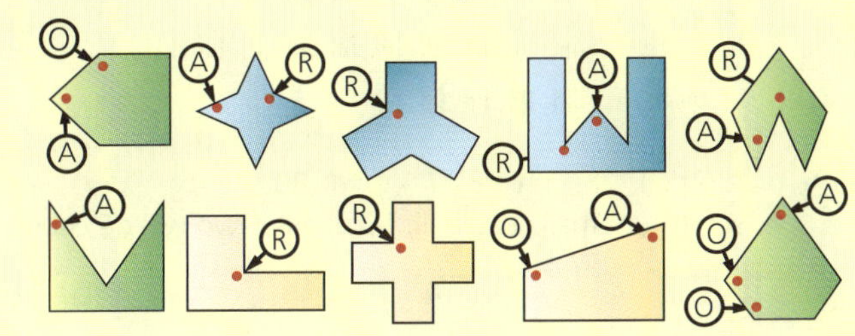

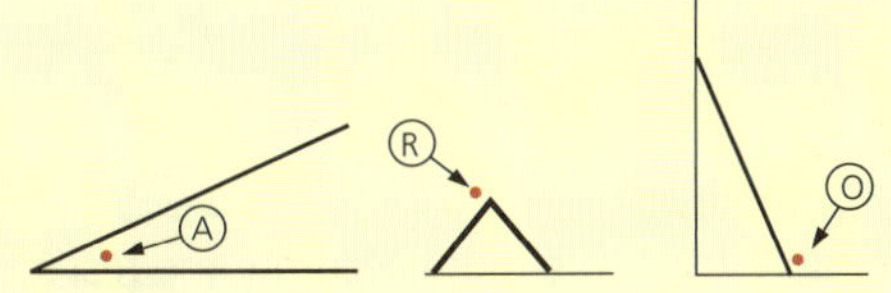

4:23

1. **a** E, F, G, N, A, J, L, P **b** H, O, D, M **c** B, C, K, I
2. **a** Triangles are used to make rigid shapes in the structure, making it strong. **b** O, D, M **c** P, N, F **d** L, E, G
   e Answers will vary, e.g. rows of bricks, train lines.
3. **a** ABI IKP KLC CJB
   b AHGO FHPM DEML DNOJ AJLP EFGN
4. **a** It is hard to be sure without measuring the sides. Yes, if the base or a side is a square, or if any of the triangles have all sides equal; no, if otherwise. **b** H, O, F and N

Activity: Answers may vary, e.g. use a spirit level, see if a marble starts to roll on it, hang a mass on a string next to it.

4:24

Header: Sometimes, for example if a whole number of smaller squares fit along the side of the larger square.

1. **a** D, E, F, G, H
   b

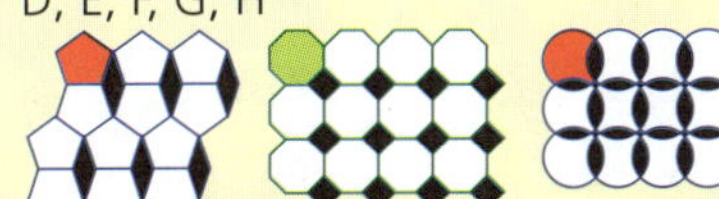

2. **a** Answers may vary.

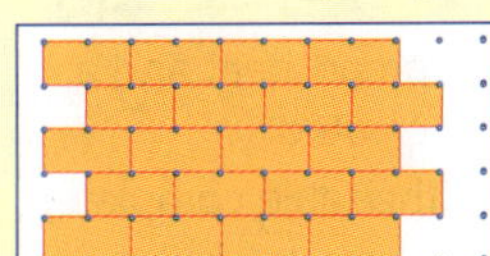

Ten more tiles will be drawn on each. **b** yes

4:25

1. **a** yes, no **b** no, yes
2. A, B, C, D, G, H, I, J
3. A, B, C, D, E, G, H, J
4. **a** yes, 4 **b** no **c** yes, 2 **d** yes, 8 **e** yes, 6 **f** yes, 2 **g** yes, 3 **h** no

4:26

1 & 3

× 4 and × 5 tables facts

O	A	B	C	D	E	F	G	H
1	× 4 tables				× 5 tables			
2	1	4	✓		1	5		L
3	2	8			2	10		✓
4	3	12			3	15		
5	4	16			4	20		
6	5	20			5	25		
7	6	24	M	✓	6	30		
8	7	28			7	35		
9	8	32			8	40		
10	9	26			9	45	✓	
11	10	40			10	50		
12	11	44			11	55		
13	12	48			12	60		
14	✓	Test results		K		Test results		
15	Susan	8	11		Susan	10	12	
16	Alan	7	10		Alan	12	12	

2. **a** 28 **b** 15 **c** 10 **d** 10 **e** 8
4. **a** 5 **b** 12 **c** Yong **d** F5 **e** A1

5:01

1.

Buttons	Red	Blue	Green
Large	5	8	6
Small	7	9	11

2.

Buttons		
Red	Blue	Green
12	17	17

3.

Buttons	
Large	19
Small	27

4. Graphs may vary.

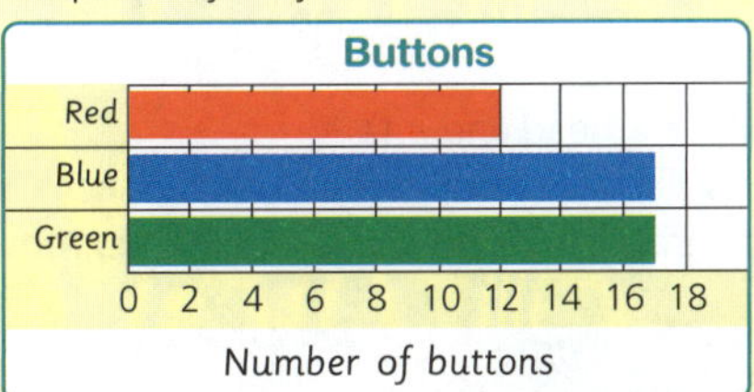

5. Answers will vary.
6.

Number of times thrown					
⚀	⚁	⚂	⚃	⚄	⚅
4	4	4	3	3	3

5:02

1. **a** red **b** yes **c** no **d** 3 **e** 3
2. red, yellow, blue
   a red **b** yellow **c** red **d** zero **e** 4
   f 3 **g** 1
3. Answers will vary.
4. Answers will vary.

Activity: 25

5:03

1. E A B D C
2. **a** Alf and Emma **b** Alan and Mia
   c Rachel and Aria **d** yes
3. **a** impossible **b** not likely **c** certain
   d very likely **e** certain

5:04

1. **a** 6 **b** Saturday **c** Thursday
   d 10 **e** 48 **f** Everyone was at home.
2.

3. **a** 2 **b** 6 **c** 9

5:05

1. **a** i 8 i 3 iii 0
   b 14 **c** 16 **d** 66
   e Answers will vary. You could double the number from the first week.
2. **a** tennis **b** 29 **c** 3 **d** Sport chosen by class 4R

5:06

1. **a** unlikely **b** impossible **c** very likely
   d certain **e** impossible **f** even chance
2. **a** two red **b** two blue **c** a blue and a red
3. **a** B and E **b** C and F **c** A and D
4. **a** no
   b 2 heads, 2 tails or a head and a tails.

Investigation: If I toss the coin again there is an equal chance of heads or tails. The earlier tosses do not affect the next toss.

5:07

1. **a** 20 **b** i $\frac{9}{20}$ ii $\frac{11}{20}$
2. even chance
3. **a** likely **b** unlikely **c** impossible
   d very unlikely **e** very unlikely
4. **a** Jack, Luke, Emma (Emma has 5 ways of rolling a 6, Luke has 4 ways of rolling a 2 or a 4.) **b** Jack

5:08

1. **a**

Sport	Tally	Total
Tennis	𝍸 𝍸 𝍸 𝍸 𝍸 𝍸 𝍸 𝍸 𝍸	45
Athletics	𝍸 𝍸 𝍸 𝍸 𝍸 𝍸 𝍸	35
Swimming	𝍸 𝍸 𝍸 𝍸 𝍸 𝍸 𝍸 𝍸 III	43
Hockey	𝍸 𝍸 𝍸 𝍸 𝍸 III	28
Basketball	𝍸 𝍸 𝍸 𝍸 𝍸 𝍸 𝍸 III	38
Cricket	𝍸 𝍸 𝍸 𝍸 𝍸 𝍸 𝍸 𝍸 II	42
Football	𝍸 𝍸 𝍸 𝍸 𝍸 𝍸 𝍸 𝍸 𝍸 I	46
Other	𝍸 𝍸 𝍸 𝍸 IIII	24

   b football **c** 8 **d** 80
   e squash, netball, baseball, T-ball etc. (Two will be chosen.)

5:09

Answers will vary.

5:10

1. **a–g** Answers will vary.
   h Yes, the more trials, the more accurate the result.
   i A, B, C, D, E

5:11

1. **a** E **b** D **c** C **d** A **e** B
2. E, A, C, B, D
3. **a** D, C, B, A, E **b** B, D, C, E, A **c** E, D, A, B, C
4. Answers will vary.

5:12

1. **Abbie's survey**

Children in families

Category	Tally	Number
1 child	𝍸 I	6
2 children	𝍸 𝍸	10
3 children	𝍸 II	7
4 children	III	3
5 children	II	2
6 children		0
more than 6	I	1

This data should be entered into a spreadsheet and a horizontal column graph should be created.

2. A survey should be conducted and the table completed.

 • AUSTRALIAN SIGNPOST MATHS 4 • ISBN 9780655708780

5:13

1. **a** 30 **b** Tuesday **c** 100 **d** 100
   e Answers will vary. The shop may have been closed on Thursday. **f** 10
2. **a** car **b** 100 **c** Approximately 200 students **d** no
   e

Key: 🧍 = 10 students	
Bus	🧍🧍🧍
Walk	🧍🧍🧍🧍🧍🧍
Car	🧍🧍🧍🧍🧍🧍🧍
Bike	🧍🧍🧍🧍

   f Answers will vary. It is quicker to draw and count the number of students.
3. Answers will vary.

5:14

1. **a** unlikely **b** even chance **c** likely **d** yes
2. **a** 5
   b There is a 1 in 2 chance of choosing a red each time.
   c–d Answers will vary.
3. Answers will vary.
4. **a** equally likely **b** not equally likely **c** equally likely

5:15

Answers will vary.

5:16

1. **a** heads
   b No, the results will vary each time the experiment is completed. There is an even chance that heads or tails will be tossed.
2. **a** 5 **b** Answers will vary.
   c equally likely **d** yes
   e The more often an experiment is completed, the more accurate the results.
3. **a** 1 head and 1 tail **b–e** Answers will vary.
   f 2 heads and 2 tails have the same chance of occurring. 1 head and 1 tail is likely to occur twice as often as 2 heads or 2 tails.

ES 1

1. **a**

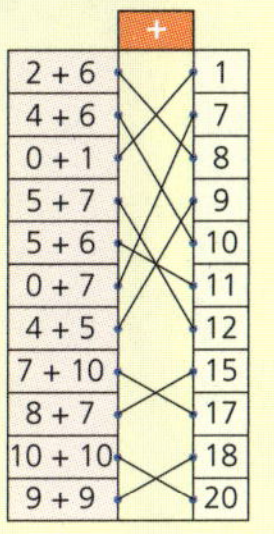

b

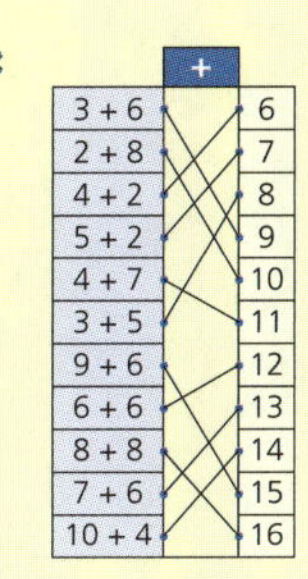

c

+	
3 + 6	6
2 + 8	7
4 + 2	8
5 + 2	9
4 + 7	10
3 + 5	11
9 + 6	12
6 + 6	13
8 + 8	14
7 + 6	15
10 + 4	16

d

+	
3 + 4	5
6 + 2	6
4 + 5	7
3 + 2	8
2 + 4	9
8 + 4	10
4 + 9	11
5 + 5	12
4 + 7	13
7 + 8	14
5 + 9	15

e

−	
8 − 6	1
10 − 4	0
1 − 0	2
12 − 5	4
11 − 6	6
7 − 7	5
9 − 5	7
17 − 7	8
15 − 7	10
11 − 8	9
18 − 9	3

f

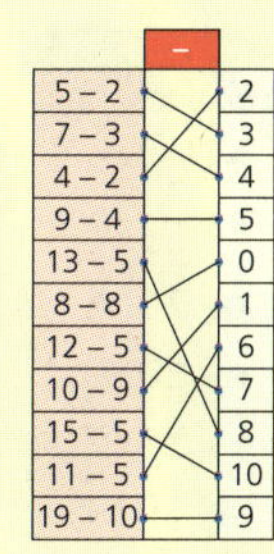

g

−	
6 − 4	0
5 − 2	1
10 − 9	2
7 − 7	3
9 − 3	4
7 − 3	5
10 − 3	6
14 − 5	7
9 − 4	8
18 − 8	9
10 − 2	10

h

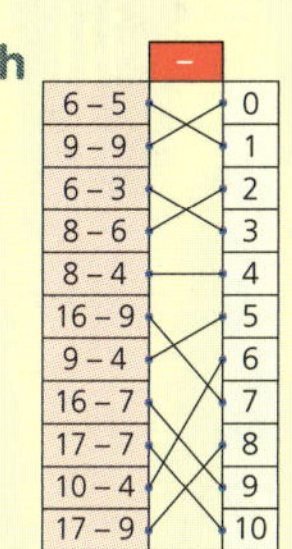

ES 2

1. **a** 7 + 5 = 7 + 3 + 2 = 12 **b** 12 **c** 26 **d** 27
   e 21 **f** 27 **g** 22 **h** 21 **i** 24 **j** 23
   k 26 **l** 25 **m** 28 **n** 23 **o** 23
2. **a** 29 + 5 = 29 + 1 + 4 = 34 **b** 32 **c** 31 **d** 35
   e 36 **f** 30 **g** 33 **h** 43 **i** 44 **j** 43
   k 41 **l** 45 **m** 42 **n** 42 **o** 42
3. **a** 48 + 4 = 48 + 2 + 2 = 52 **b** 52 **c** 55 **d** 53
   e 53 **f** 51 **g** 53 **h** 61 **i** 62 **j** 61
   k 62 **l** 63 **m** 62 **n** 63 **o** 63

ES 3

1–2 Trace and cut activity.

ES 4

1. **a** flip **b** slide **c** flip **d** turn **e** slide
   f flip **g** turn **h** flip **i** slide **j** turn
   k a, c, f and h are symmetrical (and g has rotational symmetry).
2. **a**

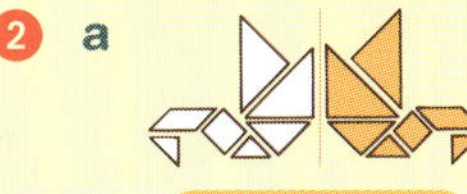
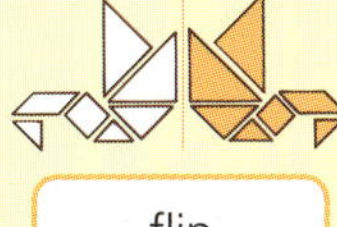

flip

b

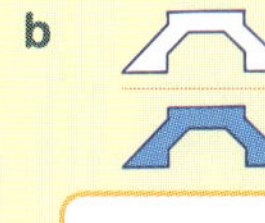

slide

c

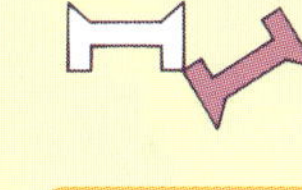

turn

ES 5

1. **a** $0.78 **b** $1.52 **c** $4.73
   d $5.31 **e** $6.69 **f** $8.25
   g $4.70 **h** $8.51 **i** $6.43
   j $7.11 **k** $6.08 **l** $6.97
   m $5.40 **n** $6.29 **o** $7.14
2. **a** $3.79 **b** $5.77 **c** $5.68
   d $8.68 **e** $6.49 **f** $8.48
3. **a** $9.55 **b** $8.20 **c** $8.85 **d** $8.70
4. **a** $4.88 **b** $8.83 **c** $9.37 **d** $9.01

ES 6

1. a 5468 b 8975 c 7588 d 3798 e 7967
   f 6324 g 8600 h 7251 i 3573 j 8240
2. a 7195 b 4885 c 4343 d 8925
   e 8019 f 7505 g 9281 h 4339
   i 7617 j 7932
3. a $9149 b $8291 c $7909
   d $6297 e $9430

ES 7

1. a 7561 b 6935 c 9818 d 7482
2. a 3904 b 5108 c 7837 d 7088
3. a $86.14 b $52.53 c $90.10 d $86.80
4. a your estimate, 5495 b your estimate, 8456
   c your estimate, $8273

ES 8

1. a 61 500 b 47 121 c 65 750 d 80 803
   e 270 050 f 412 230 g 734 981 h 622 100
2. a 48 655 b 117 980 c 100 650 d 96 935
   e 887450 f 441 610 g 734 412 h 912 000
3. a 515 634 b 198 217 c 801 702
4. Answers will vary.
   a about 175 000 b about 350 000 c about 350 000

ES 9

1. a $5.22 b $5.17 c $6.34
   d $2.39 e $4.17 f $1.84
   g $2.77 h $6.08 i $3.34
   j $4.08 k $1.70 l $2.58
   m $3.89 n $5.45 o $2.04
2. a $2.11 b $4.98 c $5.35
   d $0.05 e $5.50 f $1.51
3. a $1.05 b $6.20 c $5.45
   d $1.20 e $3.55 f $4.95

ES 10

1. a 4353 b 7100 c 5420 d 8000 e 6213
   f 6070 g 442 h 5320 i 6303 j 1824
2. a 2776 b 1193 c 706 d 6990 e 3068
   f 369 g 2278 h 1602 i 6749 j 3489
3. a 1875 b 6195 c $3659
4. 909

ES 11

1. a 564 b 1699 c 103 d 2275
   e 5168 f 1140 g 1100 h 4573
2. a 4550 b 3012 c 775 d 1645
   e 2814 f 1305 g 28 h 6633
3. a 3320 km b 1675 m c 3658 m
   d 88 years old e 91 years old

ES 12

1. a 47 180 b 53 630 c 42 676 d 24 359
   e 15 000 f 24 338 g 55 904 h 21 863
2. a 165 945 b 327 169 c 539 783 d 773616
   e 484 473 f 365 000 g 451 431
3. a $75 100 b $298 075 c 75 000 m²
   d 27 000 apples e 215 500

ES 13

1. a yes b yes c yes
2.

3. a 4.70 s b 30.40 s c 39.74 s d 59.50 s
   e 29.56 s f 19.14 s g 27.86 s h 19.62 s
4. a 9.58 s b 9.69 s c 9.69 s d 9.72 s
   e 9.74 s